The
FBI
Nobody
Knows

FRED J. COOK

The
FBI
Nobody
Knows

THE MACMILLAN COMPANY

NEW YORK

Fourth Printing, 1964
The Macmillan Company, New York.
Collier-Macmillan Canada, Ltd., Toronto, Ontario.
Library of Congress catalog card number: 64–19995
Printed in the United States of America

Acknowledgment is gratefully made to the following copyright holders for
permission to reprint previously published material:

The Estate of Bessie (White) Bloom, Waban, Massachusetts, for an excerpt
from *Harry D. White—Loyal American,* by Nathan I. White.

Farrar, Straus & Co., Inc., for excerpts from *Room 3603,* by H. Montgomery
Hyde, copyright © by H. Montgomery Hyde, 1962.

Harper & Row, Publishers, Incorporated, for an excerpt from an article by
Howard McClellan in *Harper's Magazine,* January, 1936, copyright © 1935,
by Harper & Row, Publishers, Incorporated, reprinted from *Harper's Maga-
zine* by Special Permission; and for an excerpt from an article by William
Seagle in *Harper's Magazine,* November, 1934, copyright © 1934 by Harper
& Row, Publishers, Incorporated.

McGraw-Hill Book Company, for excerpts from *Tragedy in Dedham,* by
Francis Russell, copyright © 1962, by Francis Russell.

William Morrow & Company, Inc., for excerpts from *The Federal Bureau
of Investigation,* by Max Lowenthal, copyright © 1950, by Max Lowenthal.

The Nation, for excerpts from "Hoover and the Red Scare," by Jack Levine,
copyright © The Nation, October 20, 1962.

The New Yorker, for excerpts from "The Director," by Jack Alexander,
from *The New Yorker* of September 25, October 2, and October 9, 1937,
copyright © 1937, The New Yorker Magazine, Inc.

The Viking Press, Inc., for excerpts from *Harlan Fiske Stone: Pillar of the
Law,* by Alpheus Thomas Mason. Copyright © 1956 by Alpheus Thomas
Mason. Reprinted by permission of the Viking Press, Inc.

Contents

The
FBI
Nobody
Knows

1 An Agent Talks

The young man was of medium height, compactly and solidly built. He had close-cropped dark hair, bright dark eyes, and that thoroughly clean-cut, all-American-boy look that one almost automatically associates with a Special Agent of the Federal Bureau of Investigation. But he was no ordinary agent. He was, indeed, virtually unique—that rarity of rarities, a former agent who was willing to talk about the FBI nobody knows.

Jack Levine was his name. A qualified lawyer, he had gone through the FBI training school and had spent nearly a year as an agent in the Detroit office. It was an experience that had been virtually the reverse of his expectations. He had been lured at the outset by the FBI's public image, by the lofty ideal it projected of honest, dedicated law enforcement and unselfish public service. He had been revolted by the reality—by his discovery that the FBI was in fact a ruthless autocracy reflecting the whims and beliefs of the one man who dominated every facet of its existence. It was an autocracy that ruled and dictated the private lives of agents; an autocracy that was superior to and above the law it was supposed to serve; an autocracy so powerful, so unchallengeable, that it intimidated, if at times it did not actually terrify, even senators and congressmen.

Such, in essence, on intimate acquaintance, had become the conclusions of Jack Levine. Sitting with him in a small Greenwich Village restaurant one sunny day in late September, 1962, I asked if he could give me an overall, capsule impression of his feelings toward the FBI. He thought carefully for a moment.

"I guess the closest I can come to it," he said at last, slowly, "is to say that I have come out of it with a mixture of love, fear, and hate."

1

He explained that he still had a great fondness for the organization itself. He admired and respected the many fine fellow agents whom he had met during his tour of service. They were, he felt, an exceptional group of high-class men, and he felt proud of the fact that he had belonged, that he had been one of them. He retained, too, a devotion to the ideal of the FBI, a faith in the possible reality of the image that had lured him into its service. Compounded of such strands was his enduring love.

But the fear and hate lived with him, too. He had seen closehand, from the inside, evidences of the FBI's unchecked and unbridled power. He recognized that the FBI could—and did—tap any telephone it wished at will; he felt certain that his own phone had been tapped, and this made him uncomfortable and resentful, though he had learned to live with it. He had seen the scowl of the FBI close the doors to jobs he had been promised. He had seen other agents, even former agents, practically flee his presence, reacting as though he had the plague, fearful to be seen associating with him lest such contact bring down on their heads wrath and retribution, the wrath and retribution of the one man who matters—J. Edgar Hoover, the Director of the FBI, the man who in the minds of overwhelming millions of Americans wears a glowing and unblemished halo.

It was this widespread and illogical hero worship, this myth of the superman which democratic Americans so unthinkingly embraced, that most disturbed young Jack Levine.

"I have," he said, "the greatest respect for the FBI itself—at least, for the kind of organization it could become—but I hate the things, even giving him full credit for his great work in the past, that Hoover is now doing to it."

He had already spelled out the reasons for his disenchantment, he had already described the flaws in the FBI as he saw them, in lengthy statements to Hoover's titular superiors in the Department of Justice. In magazine articles and radio interviews, he was soon to turn a brief spotlight on the issue of the role and power of the FBI in American democracy. He had hoped, as he frankly said, that by speaking out he might encourage others to speak. This was a hope that was to prove largely illusory; and yet, significantly, not completely so. Even in a hostile public climate, even in his David-and-Goliath role, which encouraged spectatorship rather than participation, Jack Levine was not entirely deserted. He gained some support. He was corroborated, in part, by the fact that his charges in the end stood largely unanswered by effective refutation. Since this is so, it becomes a matter of some public moment to take a closer look at the detailed story of Jack Levine.

■ 1 ■

The disillusionment began early. Jack Levine was one of forty-one special agents in the FBI's New Agents Class No. 2, 1960. They began their training in mid-September. Almost from the outset of the three-months program, Levine later reported, the men were "heavily indoctrinated with radical right-wing propaganda." He added: "This propaganda is taken by the men as the truth or 'inside story' by reason of the fact that instruction is given by FBI officials, who by virtue of their positions are assumed to be in possession of all the facts. I am convinced that this indoctrination is more than the personal opinion or expression of individual Bureau officials. I believe it to be the off-the-record position of the Bureau." [1]

Levine had good reason for this belief, for in early October he raised the point specifically with the class counselor and adviser. Of special significance in the light of what was to follow was his reply to Levine's question. "He stated," Levine wrote, "that any comments made by a Bureau official in our training class were in accordance with Bureau thinking or policy and that it would be naïve to think otherwise."

This official ratification of what common sense suggests must be the case becomes especially important in view of Levine's enumeration of repeated instances of radical right-wing indoctrination. On one occasion a Bureau official, in deriding the suggestion that a National Crime Commission be established to ride herd on big-league crime, commented, according to Levine, that "this proposal was the product of Harvard and Yale pseudo-intellects who are presumptuous enough to think that they know more about crime and law enforcement than the Director. He further stated that these people would be putting their energies to better use if they did something about the Communists that they have teaching at those schools. He also stated that 'they have more Communists in Harvard Yard than you can shake a stick at.' "

On another occasion "a Bureau official commented that it was very fortunate that Adlai Stevenson did not receive the Democratic nomination for the Presidency. He stated that if Stevenson was ever elected President, the Bureau's security problems would be staggering because his close advisers and supporters were Communists, Communist sympathizers, and pseudo-intellectual radicals. This official further commented on how easily 'eggheads' like Stevenson have been duped by the Communists."

Clearly, the Communists were everywhere, plotting to undo the good work of the Bureau. In a training class in November, a Bureau official on the Civil Rights desk solemnly informed the new agents that the National Association for the Advancement of Colored People was a Communist-front group. In another class, a Bureau official tarred a number of liberal organizations with the Communist-front label—organizations like the NAACP and the American Civil Liberties Union, which, he said, had frequently tried to embarrass and discredit the Bureau. On still another occasion the chief of the Bureau's Research Section, in discussing press and public relations work, added a further dimension to the picture of horrendous Communist conspiracy and dominance. Many of the country's leading newspapers, he said, were infested with Communists and Communist sympathizers. Levine wrote: "He mentioned among others the *Washington Post,* the *New York Post,* the *Denver Post,* and the *St. Louis Post-Dispatch.* He stated that these papers were enemies of the Bureau and frequently attack the Director and the Bureau because of our security program. He stated that these papers were doing a great disservice to the country and the Director by aiding the Communist cause."

One may note in passing how, in this peculiar police-mind ideology, the cause of the Director and the cause of the country inevitably were equated as one cause. Any liberal sentiment, any dissent, any criticism of the Bureau or its Director, automatically became the work of Communists or traitors. This attitude applied not just to civil liberties organizations and newspapers, but even to the Supreme Court of the United States. The Bureau's attitude toward the Court, made clear in repeated critical utterances, would have exalted the spirits of the John Birch Society's Robert Welch.

On one occasion in September, 1960, a Bureau official commented to the class "on the growing sentiment for the impeachment of Chief Justice Earl Warren and several other members of the United States Supreme Court." According to Levine: "He stated that the Director is very much in sympathy with this movement and that the Director feels that this country would be a lot better off without Communist sympathizers on the Court."

This was not an isolated Robert Welch–type utterance. Repeatedly, in training classes from late September through December, 1960, "derogatory and obscene remarks were frequently made attacking the motives and integrity of the Supreme Court," Levine wrote. On one occasion a Bureau official interrupted a lecturer to report to the class that a man freed by a court decision had just been arrested for raping another woman. He "commented that this illustrates the stupidity of the Supreme Court and that they ought to be impeached."

The effect of such constantly reiterated doctrines was noticeable. None of the new agents had any doubt that statements like these reflected "the attitude of the Director and the Bureau." Most had "rather conservative views to begin with." They were impressed by the image and prestige of the FBI and instinctively looked up to the instructors the FBI had assigned to them. They naturally assumed that the instructors would not utter such extreme and critical sentiments without substantial supporting evidence. And so, though a few remained skeptical, a great number were "easily led to accept this type of indoctrination without question."

■ 2 ■

To Jack Levine, New York–bred and a reader of what he now discovered was that infinitely suspect journal the *New York Post,* the right-wing indoctrination of agents went hand-in-glove with another distasteful aspect of the FBI—the dictatorial rule of its remote god,

J. Edgar Hoover. New agents quickly learned that throughout the Bureau the slightest Hoover whim was the first law of the universe. They came to know the abject, almost slavish terror inspired not only by an actual frown from the great man but even by the prospect of a possible frown. From the outset, in addition to their technical training in such matters as taking fingerprints and gathering evidence, the new agents received almost constant instruction on the likes and dislikes of the master of their destinies, and on the steps to be taken properly to placate this austere and august power.

During the first week of training, Levine later reported, "new agents are required to purchase and read *Masters of Deceit* by J. Edgar Hoover and *The FBI Story* by Don Whitehead." They were required to submit book reports on these volumes. This, of course, might be considered legitimate intellectual training, except for what followed. In the latter part of November, the class adviser informed the trainees that "the Director had consented to autograph the hard-cover editions of either of these books for those who wished to purchase them as personal mementos or as gifts for friends or relatives." He then passed around a list for agents to sign who wished to purchase the books.

Levine didn't sign, and the next day he was approached by both FBI counselors for the class. They informed him that he was the only new agent who had not ordered at least one of the Director's books.

"I told them," Levine recalls, "that the literary quality of these books was such that I did not care to insult the intelligence of my friends and family by sending them copies."

This, definitely, was not the proper attitude for a good, new, little FBI man who hoped to get ahead. The counselors were shocked, but Levine informed them that he had already read both books and was thoroughly acquainted with the Communist menace. The counselors were still worried. They pointed out to him, Levine says, that the purchase list would "receive the Director's personal attention and that he would want to know the names of those agents who did not purchase any." Levine, however, had exceptional resistance to this hard sell; he just wouldn't buy.

On more personal levels the new agents were being reminded constantly that they must tailor their conduct to conform to the standards of Hoover, their boss. The first assistant to one of Hoover's Assistant Directors interrupted one lecture on Bureau personnel policies to point out that a married agent in the previous 1960 training class had just been fired because he had been seen by a Bureau official in a Washington nightclub without his wife. The agent, it developed, had accompanied two fellow agents and their dates to the club, but this was no mitigation. Such conduct, it was explained, "was incompatible with the Director's moral standards," and so the case was cited to the new agents as "a good illustration of how much emphasis the Bureau places on the personal conduct of its agents."

The entire training period was pockmarked, according to Levine, either with the recitation of other horrendous examples of misconduct or with direct incidents that drove home to the new agents how circumspect they must be to avoid unwittingly giving mortal offense. One example cited to them, Levine recalled, was the fate of an Assistant Director who was forced to resign in December, 1960. The two supervisors under him were severely disciplined. Their offense: they had had the bad judgment to hire a filing clerk with pimples on his face.

In Levine's own class, a couple of innocent peccadillos, if one can call them even that, almost ballooned into mountains of offense demanding dismissal. In November one of Levine's fellow trainees, Special Agent James Sturgis, was severely criticized by the class counselors for buying a copy of *Playboy* Magazine. The two class counselors warned Sturgis that if the Bureau's officials ever learned of this dereliction he would be fired "because the Director looks upon those who read such magazines as moral degenerates." During the latter part of this same month, the counselors searched the quarters of Levine and Special Agent John McDowell. They found a half-empty bottle of Cutty Sark Scotch Whisky. Possession of such inebriating liquor, McDowell and Levine were informed, was a major and unforgivable sin. The discovery, they were told, instilled great doubts in the minds of the counselors about whether they were qualified to be FBI agents, and it was repeatedly suggested to Levine that perhaps he would like to resign. Levine refused. And, since he was a bright lad, though a bit obdurate and intractable, he survived to the end of the training period.

The approach of graduation day introduced a new element of frenzy into the training class. During the latter part of November, with training soon to end, one new agent took the rostrum and suggested to the class that its individual members should send letters to the Director thanking him for his trust and confidence in them and stressing the benefits they had derived from the training program. The agent who made this proposal, when questioned about it later, said that the class counselors had told him to make the suggestion to the class. The counselors were then questioned by several of the trainees. "They stated," Levine subsequently wrote, "that if the Director does not receive adulatory letters from the agents he takes this as an indication of apathy towards the Bureau and a sign of disloyalty and lack of dedication. They further stated that it is difficult to receive promotions and grade raises in the Bureau without sending a great number of letters to the Director. Assistant Director John Malone, in his after-dinner speech at our graduation dinner, dwelt at great length on the importance of sending congratulatory and adulatory letters to the Director on the occasion of his birthday, on the anniversary of his assuming the Directorship, and on the occasion of his Appropriations message to the Congress."

All such instructions in the art of making the proper obeisances paled in Levine's mind, however, beside the elaborate arrangements that were made for the presentation of the graduating class to Hoover himself. This, the culminating act of the three-months training program, consisted of the simple matter of an introduction and a handshake. But this introduction, this handshake, constituted an event of such supreme importance that elaborate preparations for its flawless stage-management began to be made weeks in advance. That far ahead of H-Day, the class counselors examined the new agents and advised those with crew cuts or short haircuts to let their hair grow. This was necessary "because the Director considers short haircuts a sign of immaturity."

As the dread day came near, the class went into an eight-hour rehearsal designed to guarantee that no untoward event should mar their approach to the imperial handshake. A Bureau official thoroughly familiar with the physical layout of the Director's office lectured the class for an hour, using maps and sketches as visual aids. Such a thorough briefing was necessary, it was explained, because in the past there had been tragic incidents in which new agents had walked in or out of undesignated doors, stumbled into desks, or tripped over door saddles. These awkward misadventures had happened "all in the presence of the Director," and when they had, "those new agents did not graduate from the training program."

The hour's briefing on the physical layout of the Director's office was followed by an hour's briefing on the personal appearance that the new agents must present on the day of the great event. They were advised that they must not smoke before their meeting with the Director "because of his dislike for the smell of tobacco." They must wear dark suits, with a folded handkerchief in their breast pocket. They must wear white shirts with French cuffs. Their ties must match the Director's preference in ties, and their socks must conform to his conservative taste in socks.

These sartorial instructions given, the agents were then lined up in the order of descending height and given twenty minutes' instruction in the art of handshaking. They were advised that they must carry an extra handkerchief with them, and they must pat their palms on the handkerchief before entering the Director's office. This procedure was especially important, they were warned, because "the Director distrusts persons with moist palms, as he considers this to be an indication of weak character." In the past, before the handkerchief-patting trick was devised, they were told, "several new agents were fired for shaking hands with the Director with moist palms."

Now followed a long rehearsal. One counselor took position, impersonating Hoover. The class patted handkerchiefs, filed in, approached, shook his hand. The other class adviser stood behind them, observing each man's performance under stress. Over and over again, the scene was rehearsed. After each rehearsal, the two class counselors gave a critique of each man's performance, and then the men were put through their paces again. They patted handkerchiefs, approached, shook hands, until finally, after as many retakes as Hollywood lavishes on the crucial scene of a multimillion-dollar movie, they were adjudged letter-perfect for their imminent ordeal.

The following morning the class assembled, and each man's attire underwent the closest scrutiny. One Special Agent was sent out to buy a new pair of socks, since those he wore, though conservative by most standards, were adjudged too loud to suit the Director's discriminating taste. When the agent and his new socks had rejoined the ranks, the class was rehearsed several more times in the appropriate approach and handshake procedure. At last, deemed ready to meet its first fierce test, the class was conducted to the fifth floor of the Justice Department and to the inner sanctum of J. Edgar Hoover.

The approach to the Director's office lay through an adjoining office. There the new agents, after a last-minute palm-pat, gulped and entered the presence. One by one they filed up to the Director, introduced themselves, and shook his hand. Then they turned and retreated through Hoover's main reception room. All went like clockwork except for one unfortunate agent who, understandably nervous, stammered, "Pleased to meet your acquaintance," when introducing himself. The class counselors anticipated the worst—that his resignation might be requested on the spot—but, fortunately for the blunderer, this was a day when a benign mood prevailed, and he was forgiven his cardinal offense, escaping with only severe reprimands from Bureau officials.

Such was Jack Levine's initiation into the service of the FBI. In the report that he later filed with Assistant Attorney General Herbert J. Miller, Jr., he wrote:

> I am fully aware that the above incident may appear to be like a burlesque comedy of a kindergarten class. The incidents have not been exaggerated. If anything they have been understated. This was not a kindergarten class, this group was mainly composed of law school graduates over the age of 25 years who were shortly to become fully qualified law enforcement officers of the Federal Government. Nor was this an occasion for humor by the Bureau officials who nervously spent many hours in preparing us for this meeting. The stark terror and apprehension with which these Bureau officials acted towards this event served to clearly demonstrate and illuminate the fear which the Director and the Bureau engender in their subordinates and is the key to an understanding of the Bureau.

■   3   ■

Why do mature, self-respecting, and generally high-class men permit themselves to be treated like children? Why do they accept this kind of tyrant's rule that dictates everything from the color of their socks to the length of their haircuts?

The answers, as Jack Levine gives them, explain much that otherwise seems inexplicable. Quite early in the training program, it becomes clear to most agents (indeed, they are usually frankly told by their instructors) that the FBI harbors a split personality. There is the Bureau—the central office staff dominated by Hoover and jitterly responsive to his slightest nod—and there are the field divisions, fifty-five of them strategically scattered throughout the nation. The Bureau's ideological brainwashing, its virtually old-maidish prejudices about whether a man smokes or reads *Playboy* or how he parts his hair, are annoying foibles that agents have to put up with while in training or close to Washington under the direct scowl of the Man. But once they are out in the field, they are told, they will find many things are different.

"And this," says Jack Levine, "is largely true. If you get a good field office, with a good SAC (Special Agent in Charge) and a good supervisor—and there are lots of them—it can be pretty nice. Also there is this great camaraderie that develops among the agents; they're rather high-class fellows, and they have this tremendous pride in just being themselves, being FBI agents. Out in the field, if you have this kind of setup and if you can just take it and not worry about the implications of certain things you see and do, it's a pretty good life, and that's why a lot of good guys stick with it."

This "good life" rests, however, on an essentially queasy and unstable foundation—the success of the field offices in their *sub rosa* internecine war with the Bureau; the kind of covert success that can be achieved only by the tricky process of hoodwinking Washington and that, even at the best, can never be achieved completely.

Frequently, during the training program, the new agents in Levine's class were apprised of these basic facts of bureaucratic life. During breaks in the lectures, when no Bureau officials were around, the two counselors would admonish the class "that the Bureau officials are our enemies and that we must never cooperate with them while we are here or in the field offices. They explained that the greatest danger to a SAC, a supervisor, or one's fellow agents is an agent who is naïve about the relationship of the Bureau's agents to the Bureau.

"They further explained," Levine wrote in his report to Miller, "that the Bureau and its field offices have lived in a state of adultery with each other since the Bureau's inception and that they have long since become entirely divorced. They stated that the Bureau does not know what goes on in the field offices, and if they ever found out it would only cause trouble.

"They frequently stated that there is nothing more dangerous in the eyes of the Bureau's agents than a naïve agent who gets his SAC, his supervisor, or his fellow agents in trouble by cooperating with the Bureau in any situation where there is a possibility of Bureau discipline. They explained that Bureau discipline is never an individual matter, and if anyone from a field office gets in trouble, everyone suffers. They stated that all Bureau agents receive this off-the-record indoctrination from those that are experienced in Bureau affairs."

In Levine's view, "the authoritarian, overdemanding, perfectionist policies of the Director" had created a situation in which agents were humiliated and punished for trivia. And so, inevitably, in concentrating on evasive and protective measures, the field offices became more concerned at times with avoiding censure than in taking action —and accepting the risks that go with action. Indicative of the emphasis placed on self-preservation was the speed with which the latest horror stories traveled on the Bureau grapevine, passing in a matter of days from Boston to Honolulu, from Butte to San Juan.

When Levine arrived in the Detroit office, he found it still quaking from the trauma of its latest upheaval. In 1959, he was told, a conscientious agent from Detroit had gone to Washington to take the periodic two-week refresher course prescribed for all agents. While there, the agent happened to mention that the field offices were engaged in falsifying Bureau time sheets and locator cards. Bureau investigators instantly swooped down on Detroit; by the time they were done, the Detroit SAC and several of his supervisors had been demoted and transferred. And, crowning irony, the overly conscientious agent who had caused all the trouble had been fired.

In February, 1961, another Detroit agent returned from a similar in-training program in Washington, bringing with him a matching incident. During the annual inspection, a clerk at the SOG (Seat of Government) had confided to the Inspection Division that sometimes he did not have enough work to keep him occupied. The Assistant

Director in charge of the clerk's division was forced to resign, and several supervisors were subjected to severe disciplinary action.

Such contretemps helped to keep FBI field offices in a perpetual stew of apprehension, but the effect on morale was relatively mild compared to the damage wrought by the affair of Special Agent Nelson H. (Skip) Gibbons. Gibbons had been a New York State Trooper for five years before joining the Bureau in 1955. His feat in breaking one espionage case had made him virtually a living FBI legend, and the story of his excellent detective work, far above and beyond the call of duty, had been cited repeatedly to new classes of trainees as a prime example of FBI initiative and dedication.

Gibbons had been stationed in the Detroit field office when a woman crossing the border from Canada aroused the suspicions of an Immigration guard. The woman appeared to be an American citizen. She had been born more than 20 years before in a small town that was then on the outskirts of Detroit. But the suspicions of the Immigration guard were aroused when he discovered in questioning her that she did not appear to be aware that the town no longer existed; it had long since been incorporated into the city of Detroit. The suspicious guard, having no real basis for action, let the woman go, but he made careful note of the license number of her car, her name, and her stated destination. Then he notified the FBI.

Gibbons' superiors in the Detroit office were not inclined at first to attach much significance to the report. But Gibbons, after questioning the Immigration guard, decided that there was something peculiar about the conduct of a woman who did not know her native town had vanished. On his own time he investigated, and bit by bit he built the evidence that led to the arrest of the woman spy. It developed that she had indeed been born in the town she had mentioned, but as an infant she had been taken back to Russia. She had been reared there, and the Soviet Secret Service, sensing that her American citizenship offered an ideal opportunity, had trained her carefully for her espionage role. But it had overlooked the fact that the town of her birth had since been swallowed up by the mushrooming metropolis of Detroit, an oversight that might never have mattered except for the diligence of Skip Gibbons.

One might expect that the hero of such a spy tale would have been immune to picayune faultfinding by the FBI bureaucracy, but the sequel of what happened to Skip Gibbons would seem to indicate that in this, as in other bureaucracies, the nonessential often outweighs and outranks the essential. In the fall of 1960, Gibbons took a physical examination. An ex-boxer and football player, he passed on all counts. The Air Force doctor who performed the examination noted that he was of medically proper weight. But when Gibbons received his examination form back from the Detroit office to sign, signifying that he had read its contents and approved its recommendations, the doctor's comments on his weight had been deleted and he was instructed to lose five pounds. Hoover and the Bureau, as it happened, were just then in an exceedingly weight-conscious phase.

Gibbons, annoyed and rebelling against the Bureau's casual overriding of medical authority, refused to sign the form. He was threatened with a charge of insubordination. Reacting to the threat, he consulted his lawyer. For this "indiscretion" he was given an "unsatisfactory" performance rating as to judgment and was transferred to Mobile, Alabama. His transfer papers, which he managed to see, contained the notation that in three months he was to be uprooted again and shipped to Oklahoma City, a post that has acquired the reputation within the Bureau of acting as a special purgatory for agents who have fallen from grace. When he reported for duty in Oklahoma City, Gibbons later charged, the SAC greeted him with "I'm going to give you an ulcer."

From this point on, the relations of Gibbons and the Bureau steadily deteriorated. On one occasion Gibbons went to Washington and tried to see Hoover. He had three weeks' time at his disposal, but unfortunately, according to the Bureau, Hoover was tied up for every minute of those three weeks and could not possibly see him. Charges were piled upon charges against Skip Gibbons. At one stretch, he was suspended without pay for seven out of nine weeks. Within the space of six months he received five disciplinary transfers in what appeared to be a calculated campaign of harassment designed to force his resignation. Obviously, in Gibbons' case, the catching of a Soviet spy counted for far less, when weighed in the balance, than five pounds of flesh and the sanctity of a Bureau decree.[2]

The effect of such incidents has been to place a premium on the avoidance of trouble and responsibility. When a man knows that he may be severely disciplined or even driven from the service for the slightest minor misstep, he tends to avoid taking any step at all that could possibly put him in harm's way. This elementary fact of life in the FBI was impressed graphically on Jack Levine only a few months after he went to work in the Detroit office.

In July, 1961, he was riding in a Bureau car with three other agents when a bank robbery alarm came over the radio. The bank was only a short distance away in the direction that the car was traveling. To Levine's amazement, the agent who was driving, instead of speeding to the scene, whipped the car around and trod down hard on the accelerator to go as fast as possible in the opposite direction. Levine, in his new agent's innocence, protested that they should rush to the bank, but his companions explained that this would be a ridiculous and risky course of action.

Several years ago, they said, an agent in another field office had sped to the scene of a bank robbery and had had the misfortune to be the first to arrive. Automatically, in such circumstances, the FBI agent first on the scene assumes charge of the case and responsibility for it. In this instance, the second and third agents to reach the scene, in trying to lift some fingerprints, had unfortunately smudged them so badly that the FBI laboratory was unable to identify them. The agents who had bungled the job were disciplined with proper severity, but—and this was the point—the first agent on the scene, himself innocent of any dereliction, had been disciplined with equal severity because he was theoretically in charge of the case and therefore responsible.

The moral, Levine's fellow agents pointed out, was obvious. There wasn't, they said, an experienced agent in the Bureau who, if he could help it, would risk his record by indiscreetly appearing first on the scene of a bank robbery. The attitude, Levine later wrote, was simply this: "The possibility of making a mistake and suffering the disastrous consequences which flow from this is not worth the gamble of success in apprehending a bank robber. The Bureau would expect the bank robber to be caught and would not consider this much of an accomplishment." It was a case, as the agents saw it, of all risk and no gain.

■ 4 ■

One of the most galling aspects of FBI life, Jack Levine found, was the system of compulsory and unnecessary overtime. Each year when J. Edgar Hoover goes before the House Appropriations Committee, he stresses the enormous number of hours of overtime that the dedicated men of his Bureau have donated to the law and the service of the American people. The presentation always makes it appear as if individual agents, by noble disregard of the time clock and unselfish devotion to duty, have actually saved the taxpayers millions of dollars and made unnecessary the hiring of additional and costly personnel. The truth, Levine quickly found, was virtually the opposite of this propagandistic pretense.

By Public Law 763, passed in 1954, Congress provided for minimal overtime payments for agencies like the FBI in which employees had duties that, by their very nature, defied regular work scheduling. At that time the Bureau's statistics indicated that, in 1953, its agents had worked one hour and twelve minutes a day in overtime, and this figure became the basis for overtime pay in the Bureau. But it did not become the standard for actual overtime.

The propagandistic uses Hoover made of the overtime issue distorted it and divorced it from all context with reality, for it is obvious that, if 1 hour and 12 minutes of "voluntary overtime" expresses noble dedication, 2 hours and 24 minutes denote double noble dedication. It is obvious that if 1 hour and 12 minutes of "voluntary overtime" can be pictured as "saving" the taxpayers impressive millions, double that amount of overtime can be pictured as "saving" double the number of millions.

So began the spiral of ever mounting overtime, for only a small portion of which agents actually get paid. Overtime became an end in itself and a gauge of merit. The agent who put in more hours of overtime was presumed to be the more dedicated; the field office that had the highest overtime rating was presumed to be the hardest-working, the most energetic and efficient. Conversely, the field office, the SAC's, the supervisors, the agents who were low in overtime ratings, were in effect flaunting a demerit. They were practically begging for trouble, for reprimands, for transfers, for demotions.

"The whole system," Jack Levine says, "now puts a premium on inefficiency. The object is not to see how quickly and thoroughly and efficiently you can do your work, but how long you can drag it out in order to build up your own and your office's overtime rating."

Regular working hours in the Bureau are from 8:15 A.M. to 5 P.M., but agents are now expected to work, on an average, some three hours of overtime a day. There are, of course, times when an office is engaged in a major investigation; then the services of every agent are needed, and virtually round-the-clock work becomes the order of the day. Few agents, Jack Levine found, begrudge this kind of hard, dedicated labor. Indeed, most of them are happiest at such times, interested and excited in their work, proud to be doing the kind of tough job they were trained for. But every day is not a day of crisis. Inevitably, long stretches occur when only routine, minor cases are handled—cases that are neither particularly difficult nor particularly demanding of time and effort. Then the agents are not happy, for it is not enough for them just to do their work and do it well. That overtime average must still be maintained.

"During this mad scramble for more and more overtime," Jack Levine subsequently wrote in his report to the Justice Department, "the basic reason for overtime has been overlooked, i.e., only when there is work to do. At present I don't believe that anyone in the Bureau knows how much of the Agents' working time is constructive and how much is spent in time-killing pursuits. . . . I have found from my own personal experience and from discussions with many Bureau Agents that unless there is a 'hot' case working in an office, the Bureau's work-load in most offices can be thoroughly and effectively handled in a fraction of the time now spent in enforced idleness."

Levine himself found it difficult to maintain a high overtime average. He was not a born boondoggler, and though he padded his time as much as he felt in all conscience he could, he wasn't adept enough at the process to avoid trouble. On May 18, 1961, he received a memorandum from his SAC, a copy of which he thoughtfully preserved. The memorandum pointed out that his overtime average for the previous five months had been low. Average office overtime had ranged from a low of 2 hours and 45 minutes a day to a high of 3 hours and 5 minutes, whereas Levine's overtime showed a low of 1 hour and 58 minutes a day and a not much more satisfactory high of 2 hours and 37 minutes.

"You are one of eleven agents whose overtime has been consistently below the office average during the past five months," the memorandum read. "It is apparent that you have not performed your share of overtime during the above period.

"Please submit a memorandum reflecting your explanation for your low overtime, and indicating your intentions with respect to overtime in the future."

This, clearly, was the reverse of the business attitude that, for the sake of efficiency, tries to hold overtime down. Here overtime had been elevated to the status of an independent virtue, valued for its own sake, divorced from all consideration of cause or need.

Inevitably, in the human desire to avoid disapproving scowls from superiors, a great number of agents calmly put in for time they don't work and then devote themselves to private, time-killing enterprises. Even in training class, Levine later recalled, a Bureau official had related an incident involving an agent in the New York office. This gentleman, it seemed, had devoted more than eight hours a day to his private law practice while employed as a Special Agent, and he had kept this up for five years before he was finally found out. The Bureau official, Levine wrote, "was at a loss to explain how this could happen." Actually, as Levine later discovered, "outside jobs are not uncommon" among Bureau personnel.

"Unfortunately," he wrote, "not all of the Agents spend their time as constructively. . . . Many of the Agents spend their working hours in bars, in movies, in sunbathing, in playing golf, in mowing their lawns, in shopping and at ball games. The poignant aspect of the overtime program is that the majority of Agents do not enjoy this type of existence. . . . Unfortunately, there is a growing minority among the Bureau's Agents who just lie back and enjoy their life after acknowledging that they are powerless to oppose the forces which set Bureau policy."

Common sense suggests that the best agents would be the ones most irked by such a phony overtime program and that only the most slothful and unprincipled would be happy with it. This, according to

Levine, is indeed the case. The honest and dedicated agent, rebelling against the program, is helpless, for the Bureau's overtime fetish, like its weight fetish and all its other fetishes, is sacrosanct. Its discipline falls with harsh and merciless hand on all dissidents. And there is no court of appeal.

Levine recalled that in May, 1961, a Special Agent received a disciplinary transfer to a southern office "for his opposition to the Bureau's fraudulent overtime program." The transfer worked a special hardship on the agent. He and his family had been residents of the city where he worked for more than ten years. His wife had a thriving real-estate business there. The agent estimated, according to Levine, that this enforced uprooting of himself and his family would cost him some $25,000, but he had no recourse. He departed for his southern assignment, and a few days later an agent from the same southern office to which he had been assigned arrived in the northern city to take his place.

When agents can be autocratically shuttled across the nation to the purgatory of Oklahoma City or the isolation of Alaska as punishment for the slightest failure to worship every Bureau ukase as Holy Writ, they have no alternative but to yield in the best yes-man fashion or to resign. Even this last hard choice is in reality no choice at all, for resignation from the Bureau can be unbelievably hazardous. Indeed, it is a well-established fact of Bureau life "that the Director takes all resignations as a personal affront and that an Agent who resigns under any circumstances will rarely, if ever, receive a favorable recommendation from the Bureau."

Typical, according to Levine, was the case of a Special Agent of the New York office, who in 1961 was transferred and placed on probation because he had had the temerity to obtain a job offer from the United States Treasury Department. After receiving a firm commitment for the Treasury job, he submitted his resignation to the Bureau. What happened next is instructive. Levine wrote:

> Treasury sent his fingerprint card over to the Bureau's Identification Division, and when it was discovered that the prints were those of a Bureau employee, the Bureau was notified. A few days later, this Agent was informed by the Treasury Department that the job he was to fill was no longer available. The Bureau returned this Agent's letter of

resignation together with his disciplinary transfer. The Treasury Department official who hired this Agent told him that the Bureau had contacted a high official in the Department in Washington and that this official had instructed the regional office to withdraw the position.

The Bureau's policies and attitudes toward resignations are well known to all the Bureau's Agents and they have resulted in the lowest personnel turnover ever achieved by an employer in government or in private industry. The turnover among the Bureau's Agents, past and present, averages about three-tenths of one percent. The average turnover rate for all Federal employees is about 1.5 percent and in manufacturing industries, 4 percent.

It is a source of outrage and indignation when the Director goes before Congress each year for the Bureau's Appropriation and attributes the low turnover to the high morale and dedication of the Agents. In truth and in fact the Bureau's Agents are bitter, frustrated, frightened men who are helpless victims of the Bureau's policy of economic coercion.

■ 5 ■

Aside from such dictatorial aspects of the Bureau's rule, there were deep-seated elements of prejudice and at times a disregard for individual rights in the sacred cause of investigation. Jack Levine quickly discovered that he, as a Jew, was a distinct novelty in the FBI. Wherever he went, circulating among other agents, his very presence caused discussion because none of them could recall ever having encountered an active Jewish agent in the Bureau previously. The same was true of Negroes. There were a couple who served as receptionists in the Director's office; some were used as chauffeurs or in strictly menial capacities. But of full-time, full-fledged Special Agents there appeared to be virtually none.

It might be argued, of course, that Jews are not attracted to FBI work as certain other groups are, or that great numbers of Negroes, as a result of inferior educational opportunities, could not meet the Bureau's high standards. Nevertheless, it seemed odd that these two elements—religious and racial—representing large segments of the American population, should be virtually without representation in the FBI.

In June, 1961, Levine was assigned to make a background investigation on a man who had applied for a position as a labor specialist with the Peace Corps. A former neighbor of the applicant advised Levine that the man was a Communist. How did he know? Levine asked. It was simple, the former neighbor said; the applicant was Jewish, and he suspected all Jews of being either Communists or having strong inclinations toward Communism. The neighbor added that he had seen books about Communism in the man's home and that the man had even received Negro guests. When Levine asked the informant if he would sign a statement about the applicant's alleged "Communist" affiliations, the neighbor declined. Levine returned to his office and wrote out in exact detail just what the neighbor had said.

Great was the consternation. The report normally would have been forwarded to the Bureau and to the Peace Corps as the prospective employing agency. But his Relief Supervisor informed Levine that the report could not possibly be forwarded in its present form. It was Bureau policy, he said, not to permit any anti-Negro or anti-Semitic references to be made in a report. He referred Levine to a section of the Bureau's *Manual of Instructions,* but after studying this Levine pointed out that it applied only to remarks made by agents, not to evidence, not to statements made by potential witnesses whom the agents interviewed.

The Supervisor wouldn't yield the point. He said he had discussed the matter with the Squad Supervisor and with the SAC himself. They all agreed that the statements made by Levine's witness could not be reported. The question, the Supervisor said, had come up before, and he suggested that Levine defer to his judgment and keep them all out of trouble. In the end, Levine's report was altered. All anti-Semitic remarks by the suspicious neighbor were eliminated, and references to Walter Reuther and the labor movement were substituted as the basis for the neighbor's belief in the applicant's "Communist" affiliations. Apparently there was no rule in the FBI against altering a witness's statement to display an anti-Reuther and antilabor bias.

On the Negro issue, about which the Bureau was as sensitive as it was about any public display of anti-Semitism, its private attitude was even more obvious. A great number of the Bureau's agents, Levine found, were recruited from the South, and their bitter prejudice was clear in almost every thought and deed. To them a Negro was always "a nigger."

This personal attitude inevitably colored their actions, as a number of incidents indicated. In late October, 1960, during the training period, a Bureau official, Special Agent Thomas Westphal, was lecturing the class about techniques of interviewing and the necessity of establishing rapport with a prospective witness. Always shake hands, he advised. A new Special Agent asked whether it would be necessary for him to shake hands with "niggers." Westphal replied that it was the Bureau's policy to shake hands with everyone, no matter how distasteful it might be. During a recess period following the lecture, a number of the new agents discussed this mandate, and the agent remarked that he didn't care what the Bureau's policy was, he wasn't going to shake hands with "any goddamn niggers." Several of the other agents heartily agreed with him.

Far more appalling to Levine was an incident that occurred in November when another Bureau official, a Special Agent, was delivering a "first aid" lecture at the FBI Academy Building in Quantico, Virginia. He described the mouth-to-mouth method of resuscitation and explained that this was currently thought to be the most effective. Then he added that the back-pressure, arm method could be used in the event anyone came across a "nigger" lying in the street.

Throughout his tour of duty with the FBI, Levine encountered constant expressions of anti-Negro sentiment among its agents. References to the "fact" that the NAACP was a Communist-front organization were constant; it was a virtual article of faith. In May or June, 1961, a group of agents emerging from the Federal Building in Detroit began to complain that the building was being overrun with "niggers" since the Kennedy Administration had taken office. One agent remarked that it was a good thing the Bureau wasn't under Civil Service because, if it were, the "niggers" would be getting into the Bureau, too. Another opined that this was one of the reasons the Director had fought so strenuously and so successfully to keep the Bureau outside the Civil Service system.

Such scuttlebutt, while not conclusive in itself, was indicative, Levine felt, of a pervasive attitude that infested the Bureau and could not help affecting its actions. This was especially true since the FBI was the principal reliance of the Federal Government in guarding civil rights in the South. With such prevalent anti-Negro attitudes in the Bureau, what kind of dedication could one expect the FBI to bring to its civil rights task? The answer seemed obvious to anyone who was familiar with the long sequence of bombings, murders, and lynchings that had gone virtually unpunished in the South.

Some of the underlying reasons for the FBI's inertia in the South, in addition to the anti-Negro prejudice of its southern agents, were brought into focus for Levine in 1961, when a Special Agent who had been previously assigned to a southern city came to the Detroit office. During a lunch break, Levine later reported, the agent explained that the whitewashing of civil rights cases in the South stemmed in large part from the unremitting pressure of the Bureau for ever higher conviction statistics.

A near-perfect conviction record has been for years a principal publicity, propaganda fetish of Hoover's. He likes to advertise the virtual infallibility of the FBI, contending (sometimes on the basis of dubious records) that his agency maintains a conviction record that approximates 98 percent. Such contentions build the public image of the FBI as an agency of almost superhuman perfection and foster the widespread and dangerous belief that, if the FBI brings a charge, it has the goods—the accused must be guilty.

No doubt this public faith helps the FBI's conviction record, and Hoover strives his mightiest for ever more perfect conviction ratios. Improving on near-perfection takes a lot of doing, and the FBI needs all the help it can get. It gets a tremendous amount—a point that has never been sufficiently appreciated by the public—from local police who often develop the leads, even much of the positive evidence, on which the FBI may later base an arrest and conviction. Since this is a fact of life, the Special Agent stated, according to Levine: "The SAC's were instructing the agents to go easy on the local police because of the need for their cooperation in other Bureau matters. This agent further stated that the Bureau has been successful in not antagonizing the local police because they know the agents will take it easy on them when writing up their reports. This agent pointed out that under the current Civil Rights laws the offenders are tried by local juries and that both the agents and the police officers realize that if enough of a loophole is left the juries will find it and acquit them."

■ 6 ■

The pressure for convictions and the awesome reputation of the FBI both combine at times to foster actions that are carried out with scant regard for individual or human rights. The right of the individual to privacy, his right to be secure in his home and his person unless the law can show adequate reason for intruding upon him— this philosophy, the basis of the Bill of Rights, in the view of many the most precious contribution the American system has made to Western civilization—is regularly flouted in the FBI's preoccupation with obtaining convictions at whatever cost. Wiretapping, for instance, has been repeatedly held by the federal courts to be illegal, and the evidence so obtained has been banned. Yet the FBI admittedly wiretaps. It contends that it does so only in security, in espionage, cases in which the welfare of the nation conceivably may be at stake, but "security" obviously is an elastic term that can be stretched to cover a wide swath of suspicion. Does the FBI, in fact, limit its electronic eavesdropping only to bona fide spy-security cases in which the eavesdropping is partially legitimized by approving orders from the central Bureau or the Attorney General? Jack Levine contends it does not.

"In each of the FBI field offices," he stated in his report to the Justice Department, "there are carefully concealed rooms in which the wiretaps are monitored. Access to these Sutech (Technical Surveillance) Rooms is limited to the SAC, ASAC, and those Agents in each field office who are assigned to the monitoring. The information received from wiretaps is credited to 'informants' which are designated by symbols and numbers. These informant records are kept in top-security files in the field offices. . . . It is a matter of common knowledge among the Bureau's Agents that much of the wiretapping done by the field offices is not reported to the Bureau. This is the result of the pressure for convictions. A still greater number of taps are not reported by the Bureau to the Attorney General or to the Congress."

Expanding on this statement in a subsequent interview over radio station WBAI in New York, Levine pointed out that the FBI, with its power and prestige, has little difficulty in establishing a close liaison with telephone companies throughout the nation. This simplifies its task of electronic eavesdropping, since the easiest, most foolproof way to tap a telephone is to "bridge" a pair right in the telephone exchange into which subscribers' lines feed. If the tapping is done in this way, even the most suspicious or the most concerned telephone user could never prove it, for an expert could check his line until Doomsday without discovering a thing, as there would be no actual, physical tap of the line anywhere near the premises. Hence a cozy relation between telephone officials and the FBI—a fact of life that may almost be taken for granted—eliminates all possibility of detection and, in Levine's words, lets the FBI "use the company's trunk lines with the cooperation of the company officials."

The FBI, Levine said, "recognizes that much of this sort of dirty law enforcement and security work is illegal, but they feel that without it they'll be hampered in getting the information they need." This is, of course, the crux of everything. In a really important case, in which the approval of Bureau headquarters in Washington could be obtained, a formal application to tap would be made through channels, and the illegal act would be performed with as great an appearance of legitimacy as the orders of authority could give it. But, said Levine, "in many instances, the agents in charge of the various field offices feel that it would be better to go ahead and tap a phone, let's say, without clearing it through FBI headquarters because of the concern which they have for building up their conviction statistics and getting valuable information. There are many cases in which illegal activity is going on in the Bureau field offices in which it is not cleared."

Levine said he had been "interested in finding out from the agents in the office where I was working whether all the taps that were going on in the Detroit office had been approved either by the FBI's headquarters in Washington or the Justice Department. And I found out from talking to the agents who monitored the taps that many of these cases are not approved and are not known by Bureau officials or by any one in the Justice Department."

A similar invasion of privacy is sometimes practiced on a person's mail. The FBI and the Post Office Department, brethren in the federal stable, usually work closely together. "This is not widely known," Levine said in his radio interview. "Neither the Post Office Department nor the FBI likes to advertise the fact that this is going on. But in incoming mail, particularly, it's easy for the FBI, through contacts that they have at the local post offices, to keep a close watch on this. They *generally* will not open mail unless it's a case that they're very, very concerned with. In the ordinary criminal security case, it's very doubtful whether the FBI would actually open someone's mail. But if the case was important enough and the information was reliable enough, they'd do it and will."

To wiretapping and mail surveillance, the FBI adds what is known in the Bureau as a "bag job." This is nothing less than the entering of a person's home in his absence without a search warrant, in direct violation of the Fourth Amendment to the Constitution. "This is very often resorted to," Levine said, "although it's generally unknown that the FBI engages in this kind of practice." Bag jobs were, he said, "done every day in the Bureau."

Evidence obtained in such illegal fashion cannot be used, of course, in a court trial unless it can in some way be legitimized. It can be utilized, however, for investigative leads, and information so gained can be used to pressure confessions. It is obvious, too, though Levine emphasized that he had never heard of the FBI's fabricating a case, that secret knowledge so gained is easily subject to abuse and could conceivably enable an agent, if he were unscrupulous enough and if the pressure for a conviction were strong enough, to build a chain of evidence to fit the needs of his case.

Levine had never worked a bag job, he said, but he told how it is done: "My roommate was working on a big tire theft case out in Detroit, and he and another agent were assigned to pick someone's lock and search this person's premises for evidence of participation in the crime. Here's the way a bag job works. You, the agents, are instructed—and this is given in our FBI training course in Washington—on these so-called jobs that you are on your own. In other words, you're working inside a bag; this is how they get the name. If you're found trying to break into an apartment or a building by the local police, let's say, who sometimes are unaware that the FBI is going to be there on that particular night, and if you're arrested and there's any publicity on this, then you're on your own and the FBI, you know, will deny that you had any authority to do that."

Knowledge of such techniques and intimate acquaintance with the inner mechanics of the FBI brought Jack Levine to conclusions that conflict starkly with the agency's public image. "I don't know whether the FBI has ever deliberately fixed a case," he said in his radio interview, "but I will say this: There's almost an obsession in the FBI with conviction statistics and with trying to—well, I think they have a very strong prosecutive personality, let us say. Generally I would say the FBI does not attempt, on an equal basis, to find evidence of innocence as it does evidence of guilt, and I think that this type of mentality or attitude can lead, or might or could conceivably lead, to some . . . in some investigations to innocent people being convicted of crimes or of lack of loyalty."

Under such circumstances, Levine decided that a long career in the FBI was not for him. He knew, too, that if he was going to quit he must quit soon; for among his fellow agents he saw many who would like to get out but were trapped by the long years they had spent in the Bureau and the family responsibilities they had acquired. Determined not to become such a victim, Levine wrote out a brief letter of resignation, stating his intention of returning to New York and resuming the practice of law. The resignation was accepted without prejudice, a significant point, on August 4, 1961. Jack Levine, in effect, had obtained his honorable discharge.

■ 7 ■

Once out of the FBI, Levine decided to see whether something could be done to eliminate the flaws he had observed. While an agent in the ranks, he had not been able to criticize openly; for, as he had well known, the slightest criticism, the slightest deviation from Bureau protocol, would have brought swift retribution. But, he reasoned a bit naïvely, once out he could talk. It might be that Hoover himself was not aware of the true situation in his vast organization; it might be that Hoover, if his eyes could be opened, would be willing to change. Assigning himself this eye-opening task, Levine went to Washington and tried to see the Director. He tried several times, but Hoover was never at home to an agent who had just quit the FBI.

Levine then began to talk to other government officials. He discussed big-time crime with some of the investigators in Robert Kennedy's Organized Crime Section, which was supposed to be mounting a hard crackdown on the bigwigs of the underworld. The section was quite impressed by some of the things Levine told it; it felt that a knowledgeable FBI man might be of considerable assistance to it; and Levine was interviewed and offered a job. For the briefest of brief spells, everything appeared to be fine. Then, suddenly, the door to the Crime Section closed; the job that had been available there just didn't exist any more. Trying to determine what had happened, Levine finally got an appointment with Assistant Attorney General Herbert J. Miller, Jr., in the Criminal Division of the Department of Justice. Miller gave him to understand that the FBI was miffed, to use a mild word, that he had left it and had then talked to other agencies in the Justice Department; therefore it had been decided that it was impossible to hire him "because of the estranged relations that might result."

Levine then discussed with Miller his experiences in the FBI and, at the latter's request, submitted a 38-page report detailing his criticisms. Subsequently he underwent hours-long questioning by Miller. All the information so obtained, Levine was given to understand, was passed up the chain of command to Deputy Attorney General Byron (Whizzer) White, now a Supreme Court Justice, and to Attorney General Robert Kennedy himself.

But a hollow silence greeted it.

Levine continued poking around Washington. He discussed the FBI's shadowboxing in the civil rights field in the South with the Commission on Civil Rights; he made contact with White House aides and discussed with them Hoover's fixation with the internal Communist menace. Everybody was willing to talk and listen, but it soon became obvious that nobody was going to *do* anything. Levine now began to appreciate the true extent of the Hoover muscle about which he had heard so much. It was a muscle that intimidated virtually all of official Washington. You could hear it talked about, you could hear it discussed for years, and you would never really appreciate it unless you saw it working, firsthand.

Attorney General Kennedy was, of course, on paper, the superior of J. Edgar Hoover, since the FBI, technically, is only one subsidiary bureau within the Department of Justice. But it is a bureau that has achieved a curious independence of, even a superiority to, the entire department of which it is a part. Back in the FBI training class, a Bureau official had stated flatly that the FBI considers itself an independent agency, accountable to no one except the Director. The class had been discussing the possibility of the creation of a National Crime Commission, a proposal much favored at the time both by the President and his brother the Attorney General. An agent asked the Bureau official what would happen if the Kennedys did establish such a commission. The Bureau would not cooperate, the official said bluntly. But, he was asked, wouldn't it be compelled to cooperate since it was a part of the Department of Justice? Technically, this was true, the Bureau official conceded, but he added that "the Bureau takes its instructions from the Director and not from the Justice Department." The Bureau, he maintained, was "not subject to the policies of the Department," and the Director had made up his mind "from the bitter experiences of the Roosevelt and Truman Administrations, when the Justice and State Departments were infiltrated with Communists, that the Bureau must be free of the control of any department or executive in Government so that the Bureau can fulfill its responsibilities." Now, in Washington, Jack Levine was seeing the reality firsthand. Hoover had flatly opposed a National Crime Commission; and even though the President and the Attorney General had wanted it, the idea now was dead. Obviously, the Director of the FBI was a potentate dealing on at least equal terms with his superior, the Attorney General, and with his superior's brother, the President of the United States.

What was the source of this amazing power? Levine concluded, as many others had before him, that a major portion derived from the FBI Director's close relationship with the Southern Democratic–

Conservative Republican coalition that, for approximately a quarter
of a century, has controlled the legislative machinery of Congress.
"Hoover's closest friends in Washington seem to be from the right-
wing and Southern reactionary conservative bloc, and he's very
closely allied with these people and these elements," Levine reported
in his WBAI interview.

This solidarity with those who control the committee machinery
of Congress has endowed Hoover with enormous power in building
his immunity from the control of the executive branch that he ostensibly serves. It means that any move against Hoover would touch
off a political war in which the administration would have to be
prepared to jeopardize its entire program in Congress. This is an
awesome and daunting prospect, but even so it is not the ultimate
prospect. Political support in Congress is only one of the high trumps
in the pat hand that Hoover holds.

Equally important is the unblemished image of himself that
Hoover, by more than a quarter of a century of assiduous press
agentry, has made a basic faith of America. In the minds of the overwhelming majority of Americans he is truly the one and only superman, the infallible executive, the indispensable public servant. So
deep-rooted has this image become that the slightest criticism of
Hoover or the FBI is almost instantaneously equated with treason.
As a result, the FBI Director's position has become unique, the only
one, not excepting the Presidency itself, that is unassailable in American public life. After repeated visits to "the Hill," Levine reported,
"I found nobody could afford to take any action or in any way
criticize Mr. Hoover, or the FBI . . . because it would be political
suicide for them to do so."

At this point, practically "in desperation," as he said, Levine
turned to the press. He talked to James Reston and Anthony Lewis
of *The New York Times;* to J. Russell Wiggins, editor of the *Washington Post;* to reporters of the *New York Post,* the Associated Press,
the *Chicago Sun-Times,* the *Louisville Courier-Journal.* Everywhere,
in the press as on "the Hill," he found the same fear and timidity.
Hoover's superman posture had made him such an unquestioned folk
hero that the press, like the politicians, felt it would be cutting its own
throat to utter the faintest whisper of criticism. It would do so only

if and when an impossible condition was fulfilled; only if and when it had some official, documented report on which to peg its disclosures.

"If an impartial investigation was conducted," Levine said in his radio interview, "I'm sure all these facts [the charges he had been discussing] can be verified and probably many other things as well. But these . . . these members of the press . . . in view of the FBI's strong image, they felt that to do a news article that would be critical of the FBI would certainly raise a tremendous furor, and unless they had . . . you know . . . documentary evidence . . . absolute proof . . . they'd find it very difficult to back up." Hoover and the FBI had become "sacrosanct" in the popular imagination, and this had introduced, Levine found, "an element of intimidation" into the picture, since "criticizing Mr. Hoover has become almost tantamount to . . . to being a traitor." Newspapermen and newspaper publishers naturally wanted to avoid "this stigma."

Power with the public and power in Congress—dual power that overwhelmed and intimidated—these were the two prime sources of Hoover's immunity. In themselves, it would seem, they would be enough to explain all, but they did not stand alone. There was still a third element, a secret weapon of intimidation that most effectively reinforced Hoover's twin pillars of power. This consisted of the enormous secret investigative resources of the FBI, its freedom to probe into any man's background and uncover the things that he might wish to remain hidden. Levine found that "many people are afraid . . . individual reporters and newspapermen are afraid of recriminations by Mr. Hoover in terms of investigations being conducted into their past life."

He cited the case of Jack Anderson, an aide to Washington columnist Drew Pearson. Some ten years previously, Anderson and Pearson had printed a column that aroused Hoover's ire. Anderson, Levine said, "soon found that the FBI was conducting an investigation into his personal background." He went down to FBI headquarters and demanded to know the reason. The FBI "emphatically denied that they were conducting any investigation" of Anderson. But Anderson was still not satisfied. Shortly afterward, said Levine, "he had been able to obtain through a friend of his in the FBI a copy of his file, and he actually saw with his own eyes the fact that the FBI had done an extensive investigation into his personal life. And this is something which apparently the FBI is not above doing."

Such personal checkups, Levine said, "are widely known or suspected by a great number of people in Washington," and they added to "the intimidating factors." At this point, the WBAI interviewer asked a pertinent question:

"Do you suppose that, if we broadcast this program, we'll be investigated?"

Levine laughed.

"Well," he said, "that's a pretty difficult question to answer. I really don't know. I think that . . . it's a thought that certainly should be considered, and I mean that seriously."

The event was to prove the vision of the question and the soundness of the answer.

■ 8 ■

The hopelessness of Jack Levine's efforts to interest anyone in Washington in reforming the FBI is best illustrated by an incident that occurred in the spring of 1962. On a visit to the capital earlier in the year, Levine had called on a former agent who headed the Ex-FBI Agents Association in Washington. This association of former agents in good standing, though it is little known to the public, constitutes an important cog in Hoover's massive power structure. It supports Hoover and the Bureau down the line, and in turn its members may rely on the good will and favor of the Bureau. This return bounty, as agents privately acknowledge, can be a potent factor in a man's life and career. It can open doors of advancement. In inestimable ways, long after a man has left the Bureau, the good will of the FBI can be a help; its scowl, a decided hindrance.

Levine's first meeting with the head of the Washington group of former agents had been friendly enough, but a second chance encounter near the steps of the Capitol brought a startlingly different reaction. The Washington agent regarded Levine with anger and terror.

"What do you mean by coming to see me?" he cried. "Don't you know they'll follow you, watch you? Suppose they ever saw you calling on me. It might mean my job, and I've got a family to support."

He wheeled and fled Levine's presence as fast as his legs could take him. Obviously, Levine concluded, awe of Hoover, fear of Hoover's power, blanketed Washington—and, indeed, much of the nation.

Turned down on every front, Jack Levine finally walked into the New York office of *The Nation* in September, 1962. He had an article he wanted published, debunking the myth of the internal Communist menace that, ever since the end of World War II, had been J. Edgar Hoover's principal stock-in-trade. Levine talked to Carey McWilliams, editor of *The Nation,* and in him found an editor who was not afraid. His article, published by *The Nation* in October, 1962,[3] broke through the sound barrier for Levine and brought the story he had been trying to tell to public attention. *The New York Times* noted Levine's disclosures. Wire services carried accounts to other newspapers. The extremely long and detailed WBAI radio interview followed.

What did Jack Levine say that produced such a furor?

In his article he made these statements: FBI sources showed that Communist Party membership had declined from a peak of about 80,000 to a mere 8,500. Of these 8,500 "Communists," 1,500 were FBI informants, an average of one informant for every 5.7 legitimate Party members. As a result of paying this small army of informants, the FBI had become the Communist Party's largest financial angel.

Levine traced the rise and fall of Communism within the United States. He pointed out that the idealistic and altruistic who had been lured into Communist ranks in pursuit of some Utopian dream during the harsh days of the depression of the 1930's had been to a great extent disillusioned by the ruthless Stalin purges and the callous Soviet-Nazi Pact. The first Berlin crisis, the Cold War, Korea, the bloody suppression of the Hungarian revolt, completed the job of disillusionment. And the Communist Party, numerically never a very great force in American public life, suffered an attrition that left it practically gasping at the point of extinction.

As this process took place, the FBI enjoyed a veritable Red-hunting field day. In hordes, a mixture of disillusioned idealists and rats deserting the sinking ship descended upon the FBI, offering help and information. The agency welcomed them, paid them, kept them undercover in the party, and used them to develop more informants. Levine wrote:

> The original defectors, after carefully determining the sympathies of their former Comrades, encouraged them to also become informants for the Bureau. For those remaining in the Party who could not be cajoled by appeals to patriotism and reason, the Bureau utilized other methods of persuasion. Fear of criminal prosecution under the various internal security laws has been an important factor in making some Communists see the error of their ways. There was also the possibility of publicly embarrassing and humiliating recalcitrant Communists by leaking their names to the House Committee on Un-American Activities. Those obdurate enough to survive these pressures can sometimes be forced into a more amenable disposition by means of economic duress. Even Communists have to eat and pay the rent. For those who are not self-employed or working for other Communists, a phone call from the FBI to an employer can result in chronic unemployment for a Party member from whom the FBI wants information. Tactics such as these over a prolonged period of time can break down the resistance of even the most dedicated and hard core Communists.

As the Communist Party's legitimate membership waned and the number of FBI informants within its ranks grew, a situation developed, Levine wrote, in which the FBI practically threatened to become the dominant force in the Communist Party. He put it this way:

> By 1960 the end of the Communist Party U.S.A. as a viable organization already was in sight. In a highly confidential memorandum to all Bureau Offices, Hoover announced that the development of additional Communist Party informants, except at the highest policy making levels, would serve no useful purpose. This momentous decision was motivated by a number of factors.
> First of all, the Bureau had discovered that they had at last reached the point of diminishing returns. Much of the information being developed by informants was in many instances being duplicated by other informants. Secondly, because of their desire to protect the identity of their informants, informants were not told by the Bureau who other in-

formants were. Consequently, informants began informing on informants with increasing regularity. Thirdly, the vast sums of money being expended for the payment of informants was constituting a severe drain on FBI appropriations. It was also a source of some anguish to the Bureau that they had become the largest single contributor of financial aid to Communist Party activities through their dues-paying FBI contingent.

The Bureau's penetration of the Party now extends from the lowest echelons, where the concentration of informants is highest, right up to and including the officers of the National Committee. To add to the woes of the Party, one FBI informant was recently assigned by the National Committee to act as a security officer for the purpose of weeding out FBI informants. In order to further demoralize the Party, he had been given instructions by the Bureau to "frame" loyal Party members and to give "security clearances" to FBI informants for higher positions in the Party apparatus. . . . In the forthcoming years, as the total membership continues to decline and the percentage of informants increases, it is anticipated that the day will soon arrive when FBI informants, who are rising rapidly to the top, will capture complete control of the Party.

The Supervisor in charge of the Communist Party desk at FBI headquarters in Washington, during a briefing of Agent personnel on recent developments in the Party, summed up the current situation as well as anyone when he said: "The Communist Party U.S.A. has long ago become a paper tiger. The hard core members have been reduced in size to a manageable bunch of harmless crackpots. We here at the Bureau are starting to feel sorry for them."

The FBI, Levine wrote, had documented "all current members of the Communist Party." There wasn't a Communist in the entire nation unknown to it. Its up-to-date list of Party members was being used for prosecutions of the Party hierarchy, working from the top down into its lower echelons, and it was also kept in reserve for an awesome, potential operation labeled significantly, "Operation Dragnet."

Levine explained that, should United States–Soviet relations ever deteriorate to the point where armed conflict seemed imminent, the FBI was prepared to put "Operation Dragnet" into action, rounding up and sending off to concentration camps every offender whose name was on its list. Levine wrote that "the Bureau estimates each and every potential saboteur in the United States can be located and arrested within a matter of hours."

This, Levine declared, was the reality, the truth—but a reality, a truth, that had been withheld from the American public, even from the White House. During his visits to Washington, he said in his subsequent radio interview, he had talked to members of the White House staff and had been astonished to find how little they knew about the thorough manner in which the FBI had penetrated the ranks of the Communist Party, how completely it had reduced the Party to "a paper tiger." It was after this discussion, Levine said, that Hoover had been called to the White House for a conference, and it was after this conference that he had issued a decidedly uncharacteristic statement warning that right-wing extremism and irresponsible charges could have a very divisive effect on the country.

This awakening to the menace from the right, if such it was, came "too little and too late," Levine wrote, to undo the brainwashing of approximately a decade and a half—a time during which millions of Americans had been led to search for Communists under every bed; a period in which, in accents of growing frenzy, every setback on the complicated world stage had been ascribed to the insidious influence of the serpent and to treason in high places. It had been an era noted for its almost unremitting barrage of McCarthyite emotionalism. And in this time of spiritual sickness, few voices had been more earnestly devoted to rabble-rousing than J. Edgar Hoover's. Levine gave a brief sampling, typical of his phraseology:

"We must continue to stiffen our national backbone in dealing with Communists and their dupes, sympathizers, and apologists."

"The Communist Party in this country has attempted to infiltrate and subvert every segment of our society."

"If we relax our guard for one moment, we court national disaster."

"The Communist threat from without must not blind us to the Communist threat from within. The latter is reaching into the very heart of America through its espionage agents and a cunning, defiant, and lawless Communist Party which is fanatically dedicated to the Marxist cause of world enslavement and destruction of the foundations of our Republic."

Repeatedly, in his best-selling *Masters of Deceit* and other effusions, Hoover had taken the position that the waning membership rolls of the Communist Party were no cause for jubilation, for as the party weakened it became more insidious—and, anyway, each avowed member must be multiplied by ten to account for secret allies, sympathizers, and dupes.

The obvious struggle to build and nourish an ever greater menace, when in reality the FBI had the "paper tiger" in chains, seems paradoxical. Why, if the FBI had been so successful in penetrating the Party, wouldn't Hoover proclaim his agency's feat as its greatest victory? Perhaps because to do so would be like killing the goose that laid the golden egg. Levine wrote:

> It is the belief of many in the Bureau that the suppression of the FBI's successes in dealing with the Communists is largely attributable to policy decisions made by Hoover based on the theory that support for the Bureau's activities in this highly sensitive sphere (which borders on investigating people's political beliefs) can best be obtained by continually stirring up the American public and by playing on their fears of an extensive Communist conspiracy existing here. It is also felt that Hoover's exaggerated estimate of the "threat from within" is due in part to the personal stature and the autocratic power he has gained from his image as the Nation's No. 1 protector against Communism. If the danger to be reckoned with from the internal Communist subversion was thought to have receded, it would eventually lead to a decline in such stature and power.

And that, of course, is a positively nightmarish thought.

■ 9 ■

How reliable was this version of the FBI as rendered by Jack Levine?

Levine was 28 years old, a graduate of New York University Law School, clean-cut, moderate, and sensible in his speech. There was about him no suggestion of the wild-eyed fanatic. Yet it was possible that he could be drawing a distorted picture. Was he? Or did his portrayal hit closer to the eye of truth than any that had been given previously?

These are vital questions, and it is difficult for any outsider to be positive. Yet Levine's story did provide certain checkpoints. In addition, as controversy developed about it, confirmatory data came to light and, equally significant, the official rebuttals degenerated into vituperation but never once met the test of contesting facts. It is important from the standpoint of credibility to see just how well Levine's story stood up, just how the counterattack, such as it was, developed.

The first reaction of the FBI and the Justice Department to the publication of Levine's article in *The Nation* was silence. Though the issue was on the newsstands on Monday, October 15, 1962, *The New York Times* on Thursday was unable to get any official comment from anyone. It was on that same evening that Levine's two-and-a-half-hour prerecorded interview was to go on the air. Advance text was available, but again the FBI and the Justice Department would not comment.

The radio station, before going ahead with the broadcast, had spent several days attempting to determine whether anyone in official capacity had any refutation of Levine's charges. It discovered that quite a number of persons had nasty things to say about Levine. Obviously, he was a most disliked man. But when it came to discussing his charges, point by point, no one seemed eager to undertake the task. The best that WBAI could present by way of official rebuttal was a telephone interview with Jack Rosenthal, assistant director of public information at the Justice Department, in which he declared that "the FBI informed me he [Levine] was fired."

Q. You state the FBI informed you? That's official?

A. That's correct.

Q. That he was fired for cause?

A. Yes.

This was not true, and the FBI subsequently confirmed that Levine had resigned. As for the rest, Rosenthal contended that Levine's charges to Miller had been reviewed "and I think that ought to answer your question." Presumably, the mere fact of review and inaction was to be accepted as judgment. Unwilling to concede this, WBAI reached Herbert J. Miller, Jr., at his home in Potomac, Md., but Miller refused to comment either about Levine or about Levine's charges. The pattern that was being set was one of reticence that amounted almost, in a negative way, to confirmation.

Not until almost a month later was there really an answering thunderclap. It came in the form of a November 10, 1962, letter to the *Washington Post* from Clyde Tolson, Associate Director of the FBI and one of the officials closest to Hoover. Tolson made much of the fact that Levine had tried to rejoin the FBI within a month of his resignation and had been rejected "because his former record was substandard." As a result of this rejection, Tolson contended, Levine had begun a spite campaign against the FBI.

It was true, as Levine had told Miller during his questioning in January, that he had tried to get back into the FBI, but he had explained that he had hoped to get a post in the training division where, he thought, many of the flaws in the organization might be most easily corrected. Certainly, it had been naïve for Levine to suppose that, once he had resigned, he would ever be reinstated, much less given a more responsible position in the training division. The FBI does not work that way, and he should have known it. Even if one grants that his later campaign against the FBI was waged in retaliation for jobs lost, doors closed to him, this does not necessarily mean that the items of which he spoke from personal knowledge were untrue. Nor does it necessarily mean, as Tolson argued, that he "launched a campaign of vilification against Mr. Hoover and the FBI" or that "in pursuing his vindictive course, he had utterly disregarded the security of the Nation."

The closed, authoritarian mind that equates any criticism of itself with damage to the security of the nation seems to unveil itself in this unconscious self-revelation by Tolson. Levine certainly had criticized the FBI in the strongest terms, but unless this in itself is to be judged a mortal crime, it is difficult to discern how he had "utterly disregarded the security of the Nation."

Actually, after a month's deliberation, Tolson did not contest Levine, fact for fact. Perhaps the closest he came was in contending that Levine had painted "an entirely false picture of the personnel policies of the FBI" because "more than 40 percent of our Special Agents have served for 10 or more years, and 30 percent have at least 20 years' service." These figures, Tolson argued, "speak for themselves."

Assistant Attorney General Miller finally had found his voice. Tolson reported that Miller, when questioned by a radio station "last week," had stated that Levine's allegations "were found to be baseless." The FBI Associate Director concluded: "Unfortunately, the irresponsible and unsubstantiated charges made by this former employee have received far greater circulation than Mr. Miller's factual appraisal of them."

Possibly the reason that they had was that neither the FBI nor the Justice Department was meeting issues with facts, but was relying on a generalized judgment that had to be accepted or rejected on faith. This was the process of authoritarianism as distinguished from the processes of democratic debate, and it did not satisfy station WBAI. Seeking a judgment that would not fall into the "it's so because we say it's so" category, the station on November 29 indulged in a panel discussion, seeking to reach some conclusion on the validity of Levine's charges. The panelists were distinguished lawyers and authors long interested in the field of civil rights—Ephraim London, Osmond K. Fraenkel, and William Kunstler. London, speaking first, seemed to express a general sentiment when he said:

"I am impressed . . . because there has been so little said by the FBI or the Department of Justice to contradict these statements."

Officialdom had contended, he continued, that Levine had "exaggerated"; it did not flatly deny all. This, to London, was important. As a lawyer given to weighing evidence, he felt official statements were "significant in what they did not deny, what they did not contradict." He cited as a vivid example the responses of the FBI and the Justice Department to Levine's charge that the FBI had one informant for every 5.7 Communist Party members. In telegrams and correspondence, the most WBAI had been able to educe in reply was the charge that Levine's charge was an "exaggeration."

"The mere fact that they say it is an exaggeration," London said, "would indicate to me that there are a number of FBI informants in the Communist Party, who form a substantial phalanx or an important part of the Party. Mr. Levine spoke, among other things, of a memorandum received from Hoover in which he indicated in 1960 that there were diminishing returns from this program of the FBI because so many people working for the FBI had infiltrated the Party. This was not denied by the FBI or by the Department of Justice, and I am inclined to accept it as being true."

Anyone who takes the trouble to examine the newspaper files of recent years must be inclined to accept it, too. As long ago as May 23, 1950, for example, Attorney General J. Howard McGrath declared in a Washington speech that the FBI knew "every Communist in the United States" and that none was employed by the Federal Government.[4] McGrath, of course, was replying to the wild-swinging treason charges of Senator Joseph R. McCarthy. The emotional impact of spy hunts and treason accusations was such that the man who made them was believed and the man who denied them was thought to be merely defending himself and the Truman Administration. But McGrath was, after all, the Attorney General; he was Hoover's titular superior. Could it be that he knew whereof he spoke?

Piecemeal disclosures over the years have added to the impression that the FBI's informants within the Communist Party must be exceptionally numerous; for, even with the best of planning, presumably, the FBI and the Justice Department have not been able to avoid some moments of red-faced embarrassment when their informants, from the witness stand, have accused each other of being Communists. The news stories dealing with such crossed-wire incidents usually have rated only a few obscure paragraphs in the nation's press, but they have been reported with a frequency sufficient to suggest that the informants, just as Jack Levine wrote, are getting in each other's way.

On March 24, 1950, for example, Matthew Cvetic, an FBI informer, testified before the House Un-American Activities Committee. He identified R. J. Hardin, of Large, Pennsylvania, as a Party organizer for Cambria County, Pennsylvania. The testimony turned Hardin's neighbors against him. Stones were hurled through his windows; he was "roughed up" personally; he was fired from his miner's job; he was evicted by his landlord. Hardin, then working and living in Johnstown, had to leave town. Subsequently he appeared as a government witness before the Subversive Activities Control Board in its investigation of the Civil Rights Congress. Only then was it disclosed that he had been, just like his accuser, Cvetic, an undercover informant for the FBI.

In St. Louis, in 1954, at a trial of five Communist Party leaders, Joseph Schoemehl, 71, another FBI undercover operative, testified that he knew the Reverend Obadiah Jones, a previous witness. But he hadn't known, he said, right up to the time of the trial, that the Reverend Jones was also working for the FBI.

"I presume you reported on his activities?" the defense asked Schoemehl in cross-examination.

"That is the truth," the witness said.[5]

More recently, on June 6, 1962, FBI informants collided head-on in a Cleveland case. Mrs. Julia Brown testified before the House Un-American Activities Committee that Melvin F. Hardin, Jr., 29, a guard at the county workhouse, was a member of the Communist Party. So, too, she said, was Hardin's wife. This seemed like a horrendous state of affairs until Hardin took all sensation out of the disclosure by revealing that he, too, was working for the FBI. He had joined the Party, he said, at the FBI's specific request; he had been reporting to the FBI regularly for eight years, and his wife had been an informant for the Bureau ever since 1958. The FBI confirmed his story, too.[6]

When informants become so plentiful that they cannot be disentangled before they take the House Un-American Activities Committee witness stand and begin accusing each other, it would seem that Jack Levine gave the correct impression, whatever might be the precise arithmetic of the matter, when he wrote that the Communist Party stood in danger of a virtual FBI take-over.

About some of the other charges made by Levine there appears to be even less doubt. The one that had drawn Tolson's hottest fire—the criticism of the Bureau's personnel policies and the bad morale stemming from its compulsory overtime system—is probably the least debatable of all. As long ago as July 1, 1953, the *Washington Post* had commented editorially on this aspect of the Bureau's administration. It had received and published a number of letters from agents who "resent bitterly being required to work 10 hours a day [the average then] for eight hours' pay." It had received numerous phone calls from others. The *Post* added:

> In his testimony before the House Appropriations Subcommittee in April, Mr. Hoover spoke of the nearly three million hours of overtime put in by his subordinates, of the 5,679 days of annual leave they forfeited, of the average 2 hours and 4 minutes of "voluntary" uncompensated overtime worked by each agent each day during August, 1952, as though these reflected great credit on the bureau. They suggest, to some degree at least, poor administration.
>
> The complainants are not malcontents. They share the pride felt by Mr. Hoover and by most Americans in the prestige and the accomplishments of the elite corps they serve. But they don't like to be coerced into "voluntary" overtime—under threat of losing their jobs or their chances of advancement—merely to pile up a glamorous paper record. We think their grievance is a real one and deserves consideration—as a matter of simple justice and for the sake of FBI morale.

In the nearly ten years that had passed since that editorial was written, all that had happened was that the hours of compulsory-voluntary overtime had grown to more than three hours a day.

If further confirmation is needed regarding Bureau personnel policies, it may be found in the case of Special Agent William W. Turner. He was one of those 40 percenters of whom Clyde Tolson was so proud; he had been in the FBI more than ten years. But in 1960 he was transferred to Oklahoma City, where he quickly ran afoul of the SAC.

The transfer ostensibly had been made because the SAC needed a technically trained agent to serve as a relief supervisor for a headquarters city. Turner, who had had four years' experience as a relief supervisor and had a working knowledge of French, usually had drawn large-city assignments; but on his transfer to Oklahoma he was assigned to a rural district, covering four sprawling counties. Understandably, he was unhappy.

His indignation increased when he discovered that another agent, who had qualifications similar to his and who had been serving with him in the Seattle office, actually had sought the Oklahoma City job but had been shipped to Chicago. Thinking that possibly some clerical error had been made in drafting the assignment papers, Turner applied for a transfer. His SAC gave him an unsatisfactory performance rating; Turner protested; and the fat was in the fire.

Turner, who in the previous year had received three personal letters of commendation from Hoover, now received a severe letter of censure from him. He was placed on indefinite probation, and he was not to be used, Hoover wrote, in any supervisory capacity. With his career at stake, Turner demanded an investigation. The FBI granted his request. But when he made charges against his SAC, he was judged guilty of making unfounded allegations and was suspended for thirty days.

The angry FBI agent then compounded all past offenses by writing letters of protest to Senator Estes Kefauver (Democrat of Tennessee); Senator Jacob K. Javits (Republican of New York); and Representative Emanuel Celler (Democrat of New York), chairman of the House Judiciary Committee. Having no other immediate recourse, Turner wanted a Congressional hearing both for himself and Skip Gibbons. In asking it, he pointed out that their two cases were not unusual, and he charged that morale in the FBI was at an all-time low. In his letter to Celler, he wrote: "The threat of economic sanction weighs heavily on any Agent questioning the fairness of disciplinary action taken against him. It is indeed frustrating to work under conditions where every action (or lack of action) is predicated upon the potentiality of embarrassment to the Bureau. Most Agents would prefer to lock horns with organized crime, but are saddled with wresting minor violations from local authorities for the purposes of statistics-gathering."

That did it. Hoover, charging that Turner had made inaccurate and unfounded allegations in his letters to the senators and to Celler, promptly fired him.

Since Turner was a veteran, he was protected by the Veterans' Preference Act of 1944; once dismissed, he had the right to appeal to the Civil Service Commission and the courts. With Edward Bennett Williams as his attorney, he began a fight for reinstatement that, at this writing, still goes on.

After Jack Levine blew the whistle, Station KPFA in Berkeley, California (both WBAI and KPFA are operated by the Pacifica Foundation), got in touch with Turner and interviewed him over the radio. Even though Turner was in a quite different position from Levine, not irrevocably outside the Bureau but actually fighting for reinstatement in it, he confirmed many of Levine's disclosures.

On the religious and racial issue: In five different FBI offices, in more than ten years of service, and in periodic retraining classes in Washington, where he met agents from all over the nation, he had never encountered—except for Jack Levine—an agent who was either a Negro or a Jew.

On the right-wing bias of the FBI: "I was more or less apolitical. . . . Now there is no question about the fact that the Bureau . . . would be right-wing . . . oh, patriotism, this kind of thing being a very predominant issue . . . I feel that it's been carried to extremes by the Bureau, that sometimes individual rights get trod on. . . . I find that a lot of times this treading on individuals and individual rights merely serves the purposes, selfish purposes, of individuals rather than the ends of patriotism."

On Hoover: "Yes, he does have some very firm convictions, and they permeate the Bureau. There's no deviation from them at all." Hoover, he added, was "very inflexible . . . and I think he has a tendency to consider the act rather than the actor. If you read his books, this strain does run through them. There is no question about it."

On Hoover's power: "I had a member of Congress tell me he'd like to help, but there really wasn't much he could do, that Hoover was more powerful than the President and long ago had been awarded sweeping powers which, right now, there isn't a thing they could do about."[7]

■ 10 ■

The members of Congress who could not help William Turner have not been so powerless, or so disinclined to action, where FBI Director J. Edgar Hoover has been concerned. In 1958 they moved with feverish alacrity when Cyrus Eaton, Cleveland industrialist and billionaire, presumed to utter some stinging criticisms of Hoover and the FBI.

Eaton had gone before Mike Wallace's television seeing-eye on Sunday evening, May 4, 1958, and had uttered some thoughts that made an idolatrous nation gasp. Speaking of the FBI, he said:

"I think it's had a tremendous buildup. It has enjoyed wonderful propaganda and sold itself in a marvelous way. But I always worry when I see a nation feel that it is coming to greatness through the activities of its policemen. And the FBI is just one of scores of agencies in the United States engaged in investigating, in snooping, in informing, in creeping up on people. This has gone to an extent that is very alarming."

Eaton's heresy brought Congressional defenders of Hoover trumpeting to the fore. The House Un-American Activities Committee announced it was going to subpoena Eaton. Eaton dared and defied it, and in a private showdown told members of the committee in no uncertain terms precisely what he thought of their activities. This bold defiance, coupled with an unexpectedly unfavorable reaction to these activities on the part of the American press and public, evidently impelled some soul-searching second thoughts, for the House committee's "phantom subpoena," as Eaton derisively called it, never was issued. Its projected investigation died.

Abortive though the whole affair was, the attempt to harass Eaton raised vital questions, and for once the American press, not noted on the whole for its fighting liberalism, perceived and asked them. Questions like: Is the House committee trying to prove that Cyrus Eaton was right when he charged we are becoming a police state? And: Where is our vaunted freedom of speech if, the moment a man opens his mouth to express an unorthodox opinion, he is subjected to a Congressional inquisition to explain himself?[8]

The questions were important then and remain important today, for the Eaton incident, stemming directly from Eaton's criticism of Hoover and the FBI, was virtually duplicated by a covert attack on the Pacifica Foundation. This time the offensive was led by the Senate Internal Security Subcommittee, chaired by Senator James O. Eastland, the eminent segregationist from Mississippi.

The Senate group's approach was much more deft than the earlier blundering charge of the House committee against Eaton. Eastland's minions made no mention of the Levine and Turner offenses, but it seemed of some significance that they acted only a little more than a month after the final broadcast in the Levine–Special Agent series. The action took the form of subpoenas against seven officials and directors of the Pacifica Foundation, summoning them to Washington for private hearings before the committee on January 10, 1963.

Unlike the earlier House action in the Eaton case, the Senate committee's move was strictly *sub rosa* and might have remained so, for some time at least, if Pacifica had been willing to hold still for a little quiet dissection. The private abattoir, however, held no charms for the foundation, and it decided at once to take its case to the public. Trevor Thomas, president of the foundation, in a sharp public statement, questioned the authority of the committee and its purposes.

"We do not know what the Senators have in mind," he said, "but respectfully remind them that any legislative pressures to curtail broadcasting are dangerous and unwarranted."

He pointed out that the Pacifica stations do not carry commercials; that they are not "subsidized by government or industry, nor are we endowed by a few." Revenues came from some 30,000 listeners who support the stations, Thomas maintained, and he emphasized:

"Such radio stations exist nowhere else in the world. They could not exist under a Communist or Fascist government, nor under any government which cannot abide freedom or anything but the official position in matters where it counts. Such freedom—or its absence— marks the main difference between governments.

"The only way to preserve this freedom is by practicing it." [9]

This blunt statement of the basic issue struck a responsive chord on both the East and West coasts. Newspapers, in editorials, expressed disapproval of the committee's action. Some citizens' groups took out advertisements backing the Pacifica stations. And, since the stations have listening audiences that are above average in intelligence and articulation, senators from California, New York, and Connecticut began to catch a backfire from their constituents. The result was that the Eastland committee's probe, after two private hearings, quietly expired.

As in the earlier Eaton case, however, the significance lies not in the failure but in the attempt. For those Americans who feel that their

nation's most precious heritage is to be found in the Bill of Rights—
in those guarantees of free speech and belief without which men
shrivel in stature and cease to be free—it seems decidedly disturbing
that, the instant any temerarious critic opens his mouth to disagree
with Hoover or to criticize the FBI he is menaced with the prospect
of being haled to the witness stand and ordered to explain himself.
It is not of great significance that such attempts have failed in the
past. It is of tremendous significance that the attempts have even been
made. Obviously, such oppressive gestures crimp the freedom of
which we boast. They serve to still a great number of voices, to daunt
all but the dauntless.

The chapters that follow tell how we came to this pass; how
J. Edgar Hoover became the Mr. Untouchable; how the FBI itself
became such a sacrosanct institution that the preservation of its image
is today held more important than the Bill of Rights guarantees of
freedom to free men.

■ Notes ■

[1] The Jack Levine material is based on three sources: my interview with
him on Sept. 24, 1962; his report to Herbert J. Miller, Jr., Assistant Attorney
General, Criminal Division, U.S. Department of Justice, Jan. 23, 1962; and
the text of his interview over radio station WBAI in October, 1962. The quotations are from the Miller report and the WBAI interview. In order to avoid
frequent footnotes, I have sometimes indicated the source in the text. When
I use the word "report" and "reported," I refer to Levine's statements to the
Justice Department.

[2] The Gibbons case is mentioned by Levine in his report to Miller, but many
of the details given here have been taken from formal letters of complaint sent
by Special Agent William W. Turner on Apr. 3, 1961, to Sen. Jacob Javits
(R., N.Y.) and on May 21, 1961, to Rep. Emanuel Celler (D., Brooklyn),
chairman of the House Judiciary Committee.

[3] Jack Levine, "Hoover and the Red Scare" (*The Nation*, Oct. 20, 1962).

[4] *New York Times*, May 24, 1950.

[5] Associated Press dispatch in the *New York Herald Tribune*, Mar. 25, 1954.

[6] Associated Press article in the *New York Times*, June 7, 1962; also editorial in the *New York Post*.

[7] William W. Turner. From transcript of KPFA interview in October, 1962.

[8] For a fuller discussion of the Eaton incident, see my account in "The
FBI" (*The Nation*, Oct. 18, 1958).

[9] Trevor Thomas statement issued to the press, Jan. 4, 1963.

2 Strange and Stormy Beginnings

The FBI is indebted for its birth and its present stature to two of the strongest Presidents of the twentieth century. Both were men who believed in stretching executive power to the utmost, in using it almost to the point of abuse. Both were liberals; both were battlers; both showed little aversion to cutting corners in single-minded pursuit of what they were convinced were estimable ends. And so it is perhaps ironic that, in such pursuit, Theodore Roosevelt and Franklin D. Roosevelt should have created and nourished an organization whose reach and power were to awe senators and congressmen and make even Presidents pause.

To Theodore Roosevelt, the FBI owes the fact of its birth. To Franklin Roosevelt, it owes the patronage and support that made it the all-powerful organization it is.

The process of creation and growth makes a fascinating story, for probably no secret investigative agency was ever more aptly born than the FBI. It was created in secrecy, by executive order, in defiance of the will of Congress. And once created, it just grew and grew until, by 1962, it had 14,055 employees and a budget of $130,-700,000—"almost 50 percent of the entire personnel and appropriated funds for the Department of Justice as a whole." [1]

Yet this enormous bureaucracy, with its far-reaching power over the life of the nation, led an autonomous existence, its Director ostensibly functioning at the will and pleasure of the Attorney General, with no provision in law concerning that eventual necessity, the appointment of a successor. Senator Everett M. Dirksen, the mellifluous Republican Minority Leader from Illinois, "discovered" this decidedly odd situation, to use his own term, and reported on July 10,

49

1962, in accents of great surprise, that "strangely enough, the Director of the Federal Bureau of Investigation is not legally required to be appointed by the President, nor is confirmation by the Senate required." [2] To remedy this astonishing state of affairs, Senator Dirksen introduced a bill providing for the first time, fifty-four years after the event, a definite legal procedure for naming the next Director of the FBI. Under Dirksen's bill, both the Director and Associate Director would be appointed by the President for terms of fifteen years, subject to the confirmation of the Senate.

This belated action to regularize the irregular is perhaps, in itself, sufficient comment on the devious manner in which the FBI was born.

■ 1 ■

Theodore Roosevelt was a President who was always riding to the roundup. His tempestuous Administration was marked by an unceasing series of crusades against the forces of evil—the despoilers of public lands in the West, the railroad barons, the great trusts which threatened to obtain a stranglehold on the economy of the nation, the processors of adulterated foods. On every front Roosevelt was at war with the "malefactors of great wealth" and with their kept men in Congress. In this war he was frequently handicapped by the fact that the Department of Justice had no investigative agency of its own. When detectives were needed to gather evidence, the department had to borrow them from the Post Office Department or from the Secret Service of the Treasury Department. The "lending" institutions were not always happy at being called upon to part with some of their best detectives to help out Justice. It was, any way one looks at it, a most inconvenient and inefficient way to conduct great prosecutions.

The result was that Roosevelt's Attorney General, Charles J. Bonaparte (a grandnephew of Emperor Napoleon I), appealed to Congress in 1907 to create a permanent detective force within the Department of Justice. The plea came at an especially sensitive time. In its investigation of western land frauds, the Roosevelt Administration had discovered a truly unsavory mess. Tens of thousands of acres of public land, much of it covered with virgin timber worth millions, had been swindled from the public domain, and all kinds of officials, high and low, had been involved in the looting as partners of unscrupulous land speculators and timber barons. One of the most sensational cases that the administration had developed, with the help of borrowed Secret Service agents, had resulted in the indictment and conviction of a congressman and a senator from Oregon. This prosecution of two of their own was fresh in the minds of members of Congress when Bonaparte made his plea for the creation of a detective force. Congress, understandably, did not take at all favorably to the idea.

Bonaparte returned to the attack when the Sixtieth Congress met in 1908, and the resulting debate over his proposal contained overtones significant in our own day. A major theme that developed was the expressed fear of Congress that "a secret police" would be created, a force so powerful that it might escape all control and turn its investigative energies against even senators and congressmen.

Congressman Walter I. Smith, of Iowa, a veteran member of the House Appropriations Committee, put it this way:

"No general system of spying upon and espionage of the people, such as has prevailed in Russia, in France under the Empire, and at one time in Ireland, should be allowed to grow up." [3]

The press was as incensed as Congress. Some editorialists conjured up the specter of Fouché, Napoleon Bonaparte's slippery police minister, who had intimidated officialdom of the Empire until he gained so many state secrets that he was able to intimidate and eventually double-cross even Napoleon himself. With such horrible precedents in history, said the press, Congress had "no desire" to create "a general detective service"; rather, it had "an utter abhorrence of such a scheme."

This seems to be borne out both by the actions that Congress did and didn't take. It didn't approve Bonaparte's request. On the contrary, it began investigating the use that was being made of the other federal detective forces, and just before it adjourned on May 30, 1908, it passed a law specifically forbidding the Justice Department to borrow any more detectives from Secret Service or other federal agencies. This was, in effect, a complete hamstringing of Justice Department investigations, for, if the department could not have its own detective force and if it could not borrow, nothing could be done. Roosevelt was furious. And when Roosevelt was furious, things happened.

What happened in this case was that on July 1, 1908, a month after Congress had adjourned and gone home, Bonaparte on his own authority quietly established in the Justice Department the very detective force that Congress had refused to authorize. He called it the Bureau of Investigation, the name it was to retain until July 1, 1935, when, by Congressional enactment, it became the Federal Bureau of Investigation.

When the Sixtieth Congress reassembled, it was shaken by righteous outrage at the *fait accompli* that confronted it in spite of its disapproval. Bonaparte, called upon to explain his conduct, blandly turned the responsibility back upon Congress by contending it was all the Congressmen's fault. They had forbidden him to borrow detectives; he had had to have detectives—and so he had no alternative but to create his own force.

Such sophistry did not mollify Congress. It only enraged the legislators further. Both houses started investigations of the federal detective agencies, both of the old, limited ones and of the new, much more general force that Bonaparte had created. The probes were conducted to the accompaniment of a new series of sensational charges and countercharges. Roosevelt, never a man to endure the defensive, charged to the assault with the declaration that Congress, by forbidding Justice to borrow detectives, actually had been aiding and promoting crime. It was the kind of black-and-white accusation that everyone could understand, and so it was devastating. Congress had opposed the detective force; ergo, the congressmen must be personally in league with the black forces of evil. Sensitive to the damage this kind of equation could do to its public image, Congress spent most of the session defending itself and proving meticulously that it just wasn't so. When Congress was not thus preoccupied, it attempted to mount a counterattack of its own by contending that Roosevelt was using the new detectives to compile dossiers on the private lives of his opponents in Congress. Detectives, congressmen charged, were following them, spying on them, and opening their mail.

Roosevelt denied all. Detectives whose duty it was to uphold the law, he said righteously, would never violate it. But then, in almost the next breath, he seemed to confirm the worst charges of his severest critics when he said, "Sometimes through the accidental breaking of such [a mail] package the contents are exposed." With this explanation, he published some of the private correspondence of Senator Benjamin R. Tillman, of South Carolina, one of his principal Congressional foes.

This act, not unnaturally, convinced Congress that its fears had been well founded. In a new wave of indigation and fury, Bonaparte was grilled by hostile committees about the character of his new detective force, its potential dangers, the degree of control he intended to exercise over it. The ensuing debate developed attitudes that still appear to be highly relevant to any discussion of the FBI.

Attorney General Bonaparte conceded that "there are certain inherent dangers of abuse in any system of police and especially in any system of detective police." But, he assured Congress, his new force would never be used for political ends, though admittedly the temptation to do so at times might be strong. This reassurance, consisting solely of one man's avowal, was not very convincing to congressmen who still had the Tillman mail episode fresh in their minds. How, they wanted to know, did Bonaparte intend to supervise his detectives to prevent their abuse of their powers?

Bonaparte, in his annual report of December, 1908, replied that there was just one effective way. "The Attorney General knows, or ought to know, at all times what they are doing," he wrote. Each detective, he said, was required to make a full report every day on his activities. The head of the Bureau summarized these reports, and the Attorney General himself studied these daily summaries. It was, Bonaparte conceded, "a good deal of a bore to read these things all over," but such close surveillance of the detectives' activities was "indispensable to a proper control of a force of this description." If Bonaparte was correct in this assessment of the problem, it is obvious that the FBI long since escaped from the effective control of its superiors.

Congress, even in the simpler era of 1908, was not ready to accept Bonaparte's reasoning that his new detective force could be so easily controlled. Congressman J. Swagar Sherley, of Kentucky, feared that, sooner or later, there would be a tendency "to employ secret service men to dig up the private scandals of men." He foresaw, too, that the infant Bureau of Investigation would not remain always an infant. "All forces have a tendency to grow and . . . the zeal . . . of a good officer frequently carries him beyond the needs of the service," he said.

Bonaparte's suggestion that Congress itself could always investigate any abuse of force and so hold a checkrein on the new bureau did not inspire any great faith in skeptical congressmen. Representative John J. Fitzgerald quite accurately predicted that the time would come when the secret police, either to protect themselves in their own wrongdoing or for the alleged good of their service, would contend that they had to maintain secrecy, even against Congress itself.

In the end, Bonaparte, revealing the typical mental bias of the prosecuting official, became impatient with the whole discussion. The only thing that mattered, he argued, was the catching of criminals; and, for the rest, Congress was sparring at a lot of shadows and agitating itself needlessly. What difference did it make if detectives followed people? "Anybody can shadow me as much as they please," the Attorney General proclaimed boldly. "They can watch my coming in and my going out. I do not care whether there is somebody standing at the corner and watching where I go or where I do not go."

This glib reasoning, so superficially impressive, essentially met basic issues with nothing more convincing than a grandstand, personal flourish. There could be no question that such surveillance, should it be practiced, would curb the freedom of man. Not all men are so spotless in their private lives that they can risk a stand, even for the most exalted of principles, if they know that a powerful agency of government is privy to their most personal secrets. It is obvious, too, that such unrestrained snooping, the gathering of secret and illicit knowledge, poses for the individual the threat of harm in countless ways: It can ruin business deals, it can harass a man in his profession, it can even, in extreme cases, provide the knowledge to fabricate and support a criminal charge.

The Congress of 1908, not as divorced from the principles of our own Revolutionary era as we are today, was fully sensitive to potential dangers. It greeted with applause Congressman Sherley's summation when he said:

> In my reading of history I recall no instance where a government perished because of the absence of a secret-service force, but many there are that perished as a result of the spy system. If Anglo-Saxon civilization stands for anything, it is for a government where the humblest citizen is safeguarded against the secret activities of the executive of the government. . . .
>
> Not in vain did our forefathers read the history of the Magna Charta and of the Bill of Rights. . . . When our Constitution was adopted, the people's restlessness under it and fear of oppression was not removed until there was embodied in it the ten Amendments constituting our American Bill of Rights.
>
> The Fourth Amendment declares: "The right of the people to be secure in their persons, houses, papers, and effects, against unreasonable searches and seizures, shall not be violated. . . . "
>
> The view of government that called it into existence is not lightly to be brushed aside.

Eloquent though the congressman was, cogent as was his reasoning, no mere eloquence, no mere exercise in logic, could undo the *fait accompli*. Roosevelt's charge that Congress had been protecting criminals, the innuendo that some of the congressmen might even be actively in league with the forces of darkness, had registered with the public and placed Congress in a highly untenable position. To abolish the already established Bureau would only lend substance to these charges in the public eye. Congress had no stomach for such an outcome, and so the Bureau, established in defiance of its wishes, remained—with the reluctant acquiescence of Congress—a permanent fixture of the Department of Justice.

■ 2 ■

Having failed to block the creation of the Bureau of Investigation, Congress had no choice but to live with it and try to find tasks for it. At first the Bureau occupied itself with odds and ends of investigations that did not fall within the purview of other agencies—crimes committed on government reservations, bankruptcy and fraud cases, antitrust prosecutions. Gradually Congress broadened the scope of the Bureau's work by assigning it investigations under the interstate commerce clause of the Constitution. A number of laws were passed forbidding the interstate shipment of stolen goods, contraceptives, obscene books, and prizefight films, and the Bureau was entrusted with the task of enforcing these interdictions. This was still not very inspiring headline work. But in 1910 Congress passed the Mann Act, and the Bureau got its first eye-catching national assignment.

Prostitution in that supposedly more innocent era was big business, just as it is today. Records seized in one Chicago case indicated that, in a ten-year period, a syndicate headed by a French couple had imported some 20,000 women and girls into the United States for the purposes of prostitution. In the single twelve-month period before the raid, the ring's books showed an income of $102,000, quite an enormous sum in those days of high-value dollars.[4] The disclosures, in an age that conceived of itself as the heir of Victorian morality, led to an outcry for stern law enforcement action, and the Mann Act, forbidding the transportation of women across state lines for immoral purposes, was the result

The Act opened up an entirely new field of detective endeavor and proved an invaluable windfall for the bureaucracy-building purposes of the new Bureau of Investigation. The Bureau was then headed by Stanley W. Finch, who had been appointed by Bonaparte and had been retained by Attorney General George W. Wickersham when the Administration of President William Howard Taft took office. Finch quickly saw the Mann Act as a golden opportunity to apply to Congress for ever more funds and for ever more agents. The technique he developed, it is interesting to note, is virtually the same technique that J. Edgar Hoover has employed during the long years of his directorship. First, there needs must be a Menace. Next, this must be such a tremendous Menace that the entire nation is convinced it stands at a crossroads, shuddering and trembling in need of succor. And who can save it? Only the Bureau.

Chief Finch was a master at painting the Menace. Listen to his horrifying portrait of the White Slave Traffic:

"Unless a girl was actually confined in a room and guarded, there was no girl, regardless of her station in life, who was altogether safe. . . . There was need that every person be on his guard, because no one could tell when his daughter or his wife or his mother would be selected as a victim." [5]

Naturally, no red-blooded American wanted to see his "daughter or his wife or his mother" in such jeopardy, and so Finch got practically all the money he requested from Congress. Adequately financed and staffed, he began at once to plan a great nationwide crusade against the White Slave Traffic. His detectives worked closely with local police, going from city to city and compiling a census of the inmates of houses of ill fame. When a new face appeared in these houses, especially if it was a new face that had crossed a state line, the Bureau would pounce. It was greatly aided in this final act by the legion of informers it assiduously cultivated. As Finch confided to Congress, "Some madams are . . . very jealous of other madams . . . and they spy on the other madams."

In their defense of virtue and of every man's daughter, wife, and mother, the zealous agents of the Bureau of Investigation were swept swiftly into actions that had hardly been contemplated when the Mann Act was passed. They became the living embodiments of Congressman Sherley's prediction that eager-beaver agents soon would be performing actions going "far beyond the needs of the service." There could be no question from the debates in Congress that the legislators who had voted for the Mann Act had been concerned about just one thing—commercialized vice. But the Act they had passed was not specific. It was, in fact, so loosely drawn that even the practitioners of private pleasure became its targets once they crossed a state boundary.

Among the first men to be caught was Jack Johnson, the world heavyweight champion. Johnson, ironically enough, had fallen in love with a lady engaged in the forbidden pursuit and had persuaded her to abandon her trade and devote her attentions exclusively to him. Unfortunately for Johnson, before they were married they had committed the indiscretion of crossing a state border. This made Johnson, in the eyes of the federal agents, a Mann Act offender, and he was arrested and sentenced to prison.

There was a ripple of public outcry over such instances of injustice. It became obvious that this intrusion by the Bureau into the realm of private morality opened up a Pandora's box of unsavory possibilities. What better way to blackmail a wealthy man, for example, than to lure him across a state border? In 1922, Congressman Ben Johnson, of Bardstown, Kentucky, asked the Bureau Chief whether it wasn't possible that his so-called "victims" were, in many instances, the enticers, the leaders, and whether it wasn't possible that the males arrested by the Bureau were in fact the sheep that had been led.. A rectifying action—the passage of a simple Congressional ban adjuring Bureau agents to keep their noses out of private affairs—was never taken. The courts, on the one hand, had upheld the Bureau in its broad interpretation of its powers under the Mann Act, and naturally no congressman would dare to cast his vote on the side of sin by putting curbs on actions taken in the name of higher morality. Already, it would seem, the Bureau had become an intimidating restraint on Congress, and, because it had, the prosecutions of men for private immoralities—that fixation with the act rather than the actor that Turner noted as such a prime characteristic of Hoover—continued at such unabated pace that it became, for a time, one of the major activities of the Bureau.

Hoover, writing in 1938, contended that, though the intent of Congress had been only to attack business transactions, Congress had actually, by the phraseology of the Act, moved beyond this limited objective and declared war on private immorality as well. This, as Hoover had phrased it in a 1933 article, put the Bureau in the business of attacking "the problem of vice in modern civilization." The vice problem that so greatly preoccupied the Bureau was not primarily the White Slave syndicates but private indiscretions. Hoover himself acknowledged that "the average case concerns usually one man and one woman or two men and two women." [6]

The significance of this intrusion of secret agents into the field of private morality has been ignored by the American press and public. Mann Act charges generally were regarded as a foolish and prudish irritant; but their deeper significance was seldom appreciated. Lost to view was the fact that here, in action, was the confirmation of the fears of Congressman Sherley and the Sixtieth Congress that the

Bureau would be used "to dig up the private scandals of men." Such digging now had been made a legal and legitimate activity of the Bureau, which, in its eager pursuit of its assigned "duty," began the amassing of those private dossiers whose influence no man can estimate.

The intimidating power that such developments placed in the hands of the Bureau and its Director can hardly be overestimated. During the Wilson Administration, the son of a high-ranking Democrat, one of the President's own subordinates, committed the indiscretion of crossing a state line in pursuit of private pleasure and so fell into the snare of detectives. Republican congressmen seized upon the issue, charging federal prosecutors with delaying the trial out of consideration for the highly placed father. The Democrats were thrown on the defensive. If they opposed the actions of the federal agents, they would be put in the untenable position of seeming to condone sin, a stigma no politician could afford at the ballot box. In the end, they had to join their opposition and plump down hard on the side of virtue. As Max Lowenthal later wrote: "It was going to be a long time before any member of the party in power again challenged the Federal detectives' conception of their duty against vice."

The potential leverage that this legalized invasion of the field of man's privacy places in the hands of the Bureau has been illustrated time and again in a number of disturbing but quickly forgotten cases. In Baltimore in 1937, in raids timed to coincide with the late-May running of the Preakness, Hoover himself supervised the attack on ten houses of prostitution. Forty-seven persons were arrested, and Hoover proclaimed in the Baltimore press that his crusade against vice would continue "until Baltimore is completely cleaned up." This thorough purification turned out to be not quite so easy of accomplishment as had at first appeared. Embarrassingly, most of those arrested fell into the category of local businessmen making nocturnal visits and, the timing being what it was, some rather prominent fish wound up in the FBI dragnet. Three were important Hollywood figures, all friends of Hoover, and though "people were being booked and named liberally," according to a former agent, somehow these three names did not find their way into the press.[7] Another significant aspect of the affair was that Hoover's eager beavers seemed to have had little legal basis for acting. The madams who had been catering to the local and visiting VIP's were local figures, and, exasperatingly, no state lines seemed to have gotten themselves improperly crossed. Prosecution in most cases had to be left to local authorities, and certain captious critics began to wonder what right the FBI had had to go raiding in the first place.

The explanation, when it came, raised a number of eyebrows. The FBI, it seemed, had been wiretapping the telephone conversations of a member of the Maryland legislature. The agents had overheard plans being made for the transportation of some ladies of pleasure to smooth the furrowed brows of hard-working lawmakers. As the eaves-droppers had understood it, this soothing process was to have brought balm to the soul of various overburdened federal legislators. Actu-ally, as it developed, the plans had called merely for the entertainment of members of the Maryland legislature in the state capital. Hence, no crossing of state lines, no interstate commerce, no flouting of federal law. The fiasco was one of the events that led a bipartisan Senate committee to comment that preoccupation with vice, as distinguished from crime, might "become a corrupting influence" on federal agents.

Eventually, the FBI's Mann Act activities became muted. A major vice raid on Miami establishments in the winter of 1940, during the height of the tourist season, touched off a backfire of public sentiment. Justice Department lawyers, taking a closer look at what the FBI had wrought, decided that the government had become involved in areas of private conduct that should be none of its business. And so the FBI was informed that prosecutions in the future would be under-taken only in cases where commercialization was a factor. This cut the ground out from under much of the FBI's vice-crusading work; and, though the FBI did not abandon the field of vice investigations, the big, headline raids were things of the past.

Vice, however, has been good to the FBI. The Mann Act had been for it a bureaucratic bonanza. The Bureau had been expanded and built for the first time into a sizable task force; it had been given freedom to probe into wide areas of American life; it had begun, in the sacred cause of morality, to gather gossip and record the damag-ing scandals of men. It was, in a word, on its way, ready for its next Menace. And World War I was handy.

■ 3 ■

The European war that was to end the peace of a century and turn the twentieth century into a period of strife and turmoil brought the Bureau new challenges and led directly to its further great expansion.

When war broke out in August, 1914, the Bureau was still only one among a number of rival federal detective agencies. Under the wing of the Treasury Department nestled the Secret Service and other potent investigative agencies. The War and Navy Departments each had their own military intelligence organizations. And State and Labor maintained additional squads of operatives. No one agency had over-all responsibility for American security, and the result was that German agents, liberally financed by the Kaiser's gold, had a veritable field day.

From the earliest stages of the war, long before America's direct involvement, German operatives embarked on widespread campaigns of sabotage and subversion. They attempted, on the one hand, to marshal American public opinion against the shipment of munitions to the Allies and involvement in the European war; and they took direct steps, on the other hand, to sabotage ships at sea and blow up munitions dumps ashore. Their greatest success was scored in the early morning of July 30, 1916, when two million pounds of dynamite amassed on Black Tom Island in New York harbor went up in one earth-shattering roar. The far-spreading waves of concussion shattered almost every window in Jersey City and dumped plate-glass store fronts throughout Manhattan and Brooklyn in splintered fragments on the sidewalks. Three men and a child were killed, and Black Tom Island's usefulness as a transshipment point for munitions destined for the Allies was destroyed.

A sequel to the Black Tom explosion occurred in January, 1917, when fire and explosion wrecked a shell assembly plant at Kingsland, New Jersey. The factory went up in flames, and shells spewed from its exploding inferno fell in showers on the surrounding area. Fortunately, most of the shells were not equipped with detonating fuses, and so they did not themselves explode and add to the destruction. Nevertheless, the damage was estimated at some seventeen million dollars, and a second important munitions plant had been reduced to ashes. The American people, even before their own direct involvement in the war, had been treated again to war's terrors.

The public reaction was a compound of fear and hate. The space under every bed became suspect as the refuge of German saboteurs, and with America's actual entry into the war, public passions became inflamed to a point where rationality deserted her throne. Suspicion ruled; and, as always when suspicion rules, the spirit of the vigilante stalked abroad in the land.

In this climate the Bureau of Investigation entered on its next great undertaking. During the preintervention years it had handled scattered assignments, but it had not been a major factor either in tracking down German spies or curbing German sabotage. Once America became directly involved in the war, however, the Bureau's enrollment was increased almost overnight from 300 to 400 agents, and it was given much more specific and arduous tasks to perform. A major responsibility was the detection and tracking down of draft dodgers. This was an assignment into which the Bureau threw itself with zeal. It was soon embarked on a course of action that covered it with opprobrium—the dragnet draft raids of 1918.

Assisting the Bureau in its new endeavor was a volunteer, vigilante-type organization that had been formed with its explicit blessing. In March, 1917, with American entry into the war imminent, A. Bruce Bielaski, then Chief of the Bureau, had received a letter from A. M. Briggs, a Chicago advertising executive. Briggs suggested that a volunteer organization of loyal Americans should be formed to help the Bureau in its war work. Public-spirited citizens, he promised, would bear all the expense of this quasi-legal organization. All that was needed was approval from Bielaski and the Justice Department.

Bielaski, wanting all the help he could get and apparently oblivious of the dangers implicit in bequeathing power to such a private force operating beyond the bounds of official control, espoused the plan. So did his boss, Attorney General Thomas W. Gregory. Briggs, fortified by these sanctions, promptly formed the American Protective League, with headquarters in Chicago. The idea caught on like a prairie fire, and within three months the League had nearly 100,000 members. Badges were issued to its volunteers, reading, "American

Protective League, Secret Service Division." These badges were to be worn concealed and were to be displayed only in emergencies, but every detective buff in the land was, it seemed, avid to possess one. The membership of the League swelled rapidly to 250,000, and branches were formed in every major city.

The vigilante potential seems to have disturbed no one except Secretary of the Treasury William Gibbs McAdoo. He protested the League's use of the words "Secret Service" on its badges because, he said, the term led people to believe APLers were really agents of the Secret Service, which caused the Treasury much embarrassment. Furthermore, McAdoo wrote Gregory, he was concerned about the danger implicit in the entire movement. He recalled that a similar voluntary organization, the Sons of Liberty, had been created during the American Revolution and that it had been responsible for abuses and injustices. McAdoo went on to say that he felt that the "Secret Service" division of the American Protective League contained the same potentialities.[8]

The Justice Department, out of consideration for Treasury, agreed to strike the "Secret Service" label from the badges of its volunteer helpers and to substitute the words, "American Protective League, Auxiliary to the U.S. Department of Justice." But with the single-mindedness of the police intellect, which tends to concentrate on the catching of the wrongdoer regardless of the means or the possible damage to broader human rights, it ignored McAdoo's perceptive warning about the larger issues involved and continued to bestow its prestige upon its volunteer superpatriots.

It was a misplaced faith. For whatever good the American Protective League may have accomplished was more than offset by the undoubted violence it did to basic American principles of justice.

There can be little doubt that one of the motive forces behind the League was the desire of many employers to curb the rising demands of labor. Labor leaders protested angrily that the League was being used to intimidate strikers. In its superpatriotic fervor, the League (and other vigilante organizations having even less of a shadow of official status) perpetrated outrages that made a mockery of justice. A sensational case involved Frank H. Little, of Butte, Montana, a member of the executive committee of the International Workers of the World, popularly known as the IWW, one of the most radical labor organizations of its day. Little, a fiery speaker, had been denouncing the one-sidedness of the war effort to miners, calling for "the capitalists" to be put "in the front trenches." On August 1, 1917, six masked men entered Little's rooming house, dragged him out into the night clad only in his underwear, and hanged him from a railroad trestle on the outskirts of Butte. Burton K. Wheeler, who was then a young United States Attorney in Montana, issued a statement branding the lynching of Little "a damnable outrage" and pointing out that Little had committed no crime for which he could have been arrested and prosecuted. But Wheeler's was a lonely voice. The murder of Little, which was never solved, was hailed by the press and public, even by Vice President Thomas R. Marshall, as a great act of patriotism.[9]

In such an atmosphere, the Bureau of Investigation and its vigilantes went to work to help the Army track down "slackers." The springboard for its activities was a letter dated August 5, 1918, from Secretary of War Newton D. Baker to Attorney General Gregory, in which Baker complained that the "known desertion" from the first and second draft calls had totaled 308,489. Just how this figure had been determined, Baker didn't say. If true, draft-dodging presented a major problem, draining from the services manpower equivalent to twenty-five divisions. Bielaski, whose agents and their APL auxiliary had been rounding up evaders on a spot basis, now mapped a massive campaign to corral shirkers in major cities across the nation.

The target date for the great roundup was 7 A.M. September 3, 1918. In New York City, early morning newspapers of that date carried page one warnings that the draft dragnet was about to close and advised all men to have their draft cards with them or, if they were too young or too old, to have proof of their date of birth. A small army of 20,000 to 25,000 men had been marshaled to conduct the drive in New York City, Westchester County, and the cities of northern New Jersey. The agents of the Bureau of Investigation, who were in charge of the action, had been reinforced by APL volunteers, special deputy policemen, deputy marshals, sailors, soldiers, and marines. It was like fighting the Battle of the Marne on the home front.

At the fateful hour, the raiders swung into action. It became instantly obvious that the warnings in the papers either had appeared too late or had been missed by the men most vitally concerned, for there promptly developed scenes of confusion and outrage unprecedented in American history. Men were snatched unceremoniously from every walk of life and herded like startled rabbits into bullpens hastily improvised to contain the ever growing mob. Commuters were seized at ferry slips and railroad terminals. Men were yanked from barbers' chairs with the lather still on their faces. Streetcars were stopped, and males of apparently martial age were unceremoniously carted off. Men dining with their wives or friends in restaurants had their meals interrupted as they were hustled away from their partners. Business offices were invaded and clerks snatched from behind their desks. One flying column of raiders even invaded Bellevue Hospital and examined both staff and patients in their hunt for skulkers. By unmanageable thousands, the suspects poured into police stations for preliminary examinations and then were passed on to the 69th Regiment Armory, which soon became inadequate to hold them all. Other armories and public schools had to be requisitioned, and some of the most suspicious suspects were incarcerated in the Tombs without writ or warrant, the first time that such use had been made of the prison in the long history of New York.[10]

The human cattle who were bullied into the bullpens in this roundup that flouted every civil right were hapless and bewildered men. One victim had been caught at a shoemaker's shop, holding in his hands a pair of his wife's shoes that he had brought for repair; when he joined the herd in the bullpen, he was still carrying them. Youths who had been proudly cultivating their first fuzz now discovered that this made them seem mature enough in the eyes of the raiders to be draft bait; and middle-aged males who had been striving to hide the gray at the temples paid for their innocent deception by being included in the roundup of suspects. One squad of raiders had interrupted the showing of "Yip, Yip, Yaphank" at the Lexington Avenue theater, causing a miniature riot, and as tokens of their achievement had thrust a number of dress-suited men into the bullpens to join the milling throng. More than 1,000 cots were set up in the 69th Regiment Armory to accommodate the overnight guests. Commissary supplies proved inadequate, and for hours hundreds of imprisoned men went without food. Outside the bullpens, clamoring wives and mothers and sisters gathered, waving draft cards to prove the innocence of their men, or lugging family Bibles in which recorded birth dates showed that their sons or brothers were not of draft age. Pandemonium was the order of the day.

One young man, a pretty girl by his side, was found strolling the streets in the Grand Central Terminal area. Halted by a sailor who demanded his draft card, the youth exclaimed: "Good God! We were only married in Plattsburg yesterday, and you don't suppose I thought anything about draft cards?" He was hustled away, his honeymoon was interrupted, and his bride had to get in touch with relatives in Plattsburg for evidence that he was registered for the draft and was no slacker.

Raiders stopped a young married couple. The man was carrying a two-months-old baby in his arms, but this appealing spectacle of parenthood did not move the hearts of the slacker-seekers. The husband was given only enough time to transfer the baby to his wife before he was hustled off to a bullpen.

Even officials fell victims of other officials in this seizure of men by the thousands. A plainclothes policeman, lacking his draft card, was held a prisoner in his own station house until he could get the evidence to clear himself. A similar fate befell an official of the Mount Vernon draft board who had come to the city without his credentials. A doctor in the Medical Reserve Corps, a Salvation Army man in uniform, an attaché of the British Embassy, a Kearny shipyard worker—all these and others were swept up in the dragnet that spared no man.

For some, the detention lasted only a few hours until they could get the draft cards or birth records to establish their innocence. For others, incarceration became a matter of moment. "The plight of the out-of-town men was indeed serious," *The New York Times* reported. "The only thing that they could do was to telegraph for their draft board records." Even telegrams sometimes did no good. Especially harrowing was the case of a wealthy businessman from New Orleans. His family was on vacation and could not be reached. His draft board, seemingly, was on vacation, too, for repeated appeals brought no response. The New Orleans man offered to pay an officer's round-trip fare to go with him to Louisiana to determine his innocence, but no officer could be spared for such a journey. As a result, the businessman had to languish for days in the bullpen while thousands of other suspects came and went in the continuing roundup.

Just how many thousands were subjected to this rude, cattle-like treatment by the Bureau and its eager-beaver allies was never determined. Official figures subsequently disclosed that 60,187 were picked up in the New York metropolitan area (another 27,000 had been reported taken into custody in the first day in Chicago). But as the *New York World* pointed out at the time, the figures did not include additional thousands who had been picked up, detained briefly at police stations, and then released without ever becoming statistics on the bullpen registers. Even the minimal figures released by the Bureau were sufficient, however, to indicate the enormity of the action.

Just what had been accomplished by this high-handed deed, this trampling of human rights? Once the results were assessed against the awesome totals of dragnet seizures, the fiasco became glaringly apparent. On September 8, 1918, the Chief of the New York Bureau gave the press a breakdown of what had been accomplished by the 60,187 recorded detentions. His figures showed that, of 11,652 men seized in Manhattan, only "about 500" had been judged slackers; of 9,750 held in Brooklyn, only 256; of 38,875 rounded up in northern New Jersey, only 749. But, said the Bureau Chief, struggling for justification, an additional 16,505 cases had been referred to draft boards for "further study." In Washington, an indiscreet clerk in the Justice Department let slip an even more revealing estimate. He told reporters that the Bureau's statistical staff, assessing the results of the nationwide dragnet, had arrived at this proportion: out of every 200 males arrested and jailed overnight, 199 had been mistakes.

Even before this shocking margin of error became known, the callous dragnet procedure had sparked a heated debate on the floor of the Senate. Here attitudes developed that seem significant in our own time. One of the most irate and outspoken senators was William M. Calder, of New York. He had witnessed some of the raids and had protested to the officers in charge against the methods used. His protest had been futile, and so he carried his fight to the Senate, describing to his colleagues the scenes he had witnessed.

"I saw a streetcar stopped and a sailor go to the car and take men out of the car who were sometimes there with women whom they were escorting," he said. "Men were stopped in the street and taken off the corner and crowded into vans, perhaps 50 or 60 packed in like sardines, and taken to the police stations.

"Armed soldiers went into business offices and took men from behind their desks. They went into theaters and took men away from the ladies whom they were escorting. They took men who were over draft age, they took men who were under draft age."

Senator Hiram Johnson, the fiery progressive from California, denounced the dragnet procedure in his best oratory. He likened the action of the Bureau's raiders to "the Law of Suspects" that had existed in France during the Reign of Terror, and he saw in this brash use of authoritarianism a growing American trend toward militarism.

Not all senators viewed with alarm. The attitudes of those who took the happy, constructive view of events still seem significant. Their comments revealed the kind of rationale that has become a virus of our time—the idea that the state's needs must be always paramount, that individual wrongs inflicted in pursuit of the greater good do not really matter, that the ends to be achieved outweigh the methods used.

Miles Poindexter, of Washington, put it this way: "There is nothing to show any serious mistreatment of anybody. It is . . . nothing to arouse the indignation of anyone. . . . I myself am mighty glad it was done, and I hope they will do it all over the United States."

William Fosgate Kirby, of Arkansas, backed the authoritarian principle over democratic individualism in these words: "If in the necessary enforcement of this law in a summary way some individuals are inconvenienced or individual rights are infringed or invaded more or less, they must put up with that rather than that the law shall not be enforced."

Andrieus Aristieus Jones, of New Mexico, added: "We should commend these actions. . . . Under our system of government it is usually the case that some innocent people are called upon to suffer for the crimes of others. . . . Is there a Senator in this body who would not willingly stay in jail a week, if necessary, in order to have justice meted out to even one such criminal?"

It seems hardly necessary to point out that this philosophy is the antithesis of that of the founders of the Constitution. The idea that the many might be properly jailed that one guilty person might be caught would have been anathema to them. Indeed, it was their deep-seated aversion to police-state ideologies that had led them to write into the Bill of Rights specific and unequivocal guarantees of human freedom. Now, however, under the pressures of war, in the blindness and demagoguery of superpatriotism, there were senators of the United States who could see nothing wrong in compromising, in tampering with such fundamentals.

Yet there was something decidedly wrong. On September 7, *The New York Times* reported that the senatorial demands for an investigation of the Bureau and its handling of the dragnet raids had been blocked. It reported, too, that Senator Hiram Johnson had returned to the charge. He told the Senate:

"I got sixty letters in today's mail from men who had been subjected to humiliation and indignity, commending my speech of protest in the Senate. More than two-thirds of these were unsigned. Many of the writers frankly confessed that they were afraid to sign their names."

Senator Johnson was shocked that two-thirds of his correspondents did not dare sign the letters they had written to a United States Senator. And well he might have been. Here, certainly, was a clear sign that the exercise of massive authority was beginning to awe, to daunt, and to intimidate the free American spirit.

The sequel did nothing to encourage the American public to become bolder. The proposed senatorial inquiry died a-borning. Instead, the Justice Department was permitted to investigate itself and to report its findings on its own delinquencies to President Wilson. Even though such a procedure can hardly be expected to plumb the limits of error, Attorney General Gregory's final report contained significant confessions.

The Attorney General condemned the raids as "contrary to law." He had told the detectives "over and over again," he said, what they might and might not do. But they had gone ahead and acted "without consultation with me or with any law officer of the department." They had acted "contrary to my express instructions." Obviously, the close control of the Bureau that Bonaparte had assured the Sixtieth Congress could be so easily maintained was slipping from the hands of the Attorney General. If Gregory was correct in his final report, the Bureau was taking affairs into its own hands and functioning as it willed regardless of the wishes of its titular superior.

This was a highly significant development, and events were soon to show that the Bureau's arrogant use of authority in the 1918 draft raids was not an isolated example of abuse. There was more—and worse—to come.

■ Notes ■

[1] *Congressional Record,* June 13, 1963.

[2] See *Congressional Record,* June 10, 1962, and January 31, 1963.

[3] For much of the material about the Congressional debates that raged around the creation of the Bureau and its early history, I have relied on Max Lowenthal's *The Federal Bureau of Investigation* (William Sloane Associates, 1950). Lowenthal has served under Presidents of both parties. After the publication of his book, critical of the FBI, Congressional committees attempted to spatter him with a pink smear. Nothing came of the charges. His book, while it was denounced, was not factually discredited in any respect.

[4] Don Whitehead, *The FBI Story* (Random House, 1956; Pocket Books, 1958).

[5] Lowenthal, *op. cit.,* p. 15.

[6] J. Edgar Hoover, "Some Legal Aspects of Interstate Crime" (Government Printing Office, Washington, D.C., 1938); and an article in the *Journal of Criminal Law and Criminology,* 1933), vol. 24, p. 480.

[7] Guy Richards in the *New York Star,* Sept. 28, 1948. Second of a series on the FBI.

[8] Whitehead, *op. cit.,* 39.

[9] Burton K. Wheeler, with Paul F. Healy, *Yankee from the West* (Doubleday, 1962), pp. 139–142.

[10] For this description of the New York draft raids, I have relied mainly on the files of *The New York Times* and the *New York World* for the first half of September, 1918, with some minor additions from Lowenthal.

3 Hoover, Palmer and the Red Raids

It was in the era of wartime crisis, when passions ruled and Americans were stirred easily to witch-hunt frenzies by specters of draft dodgers and subversive aliens, that a new personality joined the Bureau—J. Edgar Hoover, whose name was to become, and was to remain, synonymous with the Bureau as we know it.

Hoover was born on January 1, 1895, in a two-story stucco house set in a kind of civil servants' colony in the Seward Park section of Washington, D.C. His father, Dickerson Naylor Hoover, was a minor government employee, and his mother, the former Annie Marie Scheitlin, was a niece of Switzerland's first consul general in the United States. The Hoovers were of British and German stock, and they took root in the capital in the early 1800's. The Scheitlins who settled here were originally Swiss mercenary soldiers, and Hoover's mother, by all accounts, retained many of the traits of a Swiss martinet. She ruled her household and her young son with a strict discipline, punishing disobedience with a military impartiality—a trait that was to become one of the dominant characteristics of her son.[1]

There were two other children in the family, Dickerson N. Hoover, Jr., fifteen years John Edgar's senior, and a sister, Lillian, who was also older. Dickerson, as was only natural considering his lofty seniority, became the mentor and idol of John Edgar's youth, yet the two possessed quite disparate natures. Cheerful, devout, easygoing, Dickerson was to follow serenely in the footsteps of their father as a lesser government employee; John Edgar, evidently more his mother's son, was a martinet and driver, possessed by a restless ambition that goaded him to excel.

71

For those who like to speculate about the imponderables of environment and heredity, the boyhood careers of Dickerson and John Edgar provide fascinating material. Step by step, they were parallel, and yet they led to totally different destinies.

Dickerson, as a youth, was extremely active in the local Presbyterian church, the Church of the Covenant. He practically worshiped at the feet of the pastor, Dr. Donald Campbell McLeod, a rugged man who believed in physical fitness and preached that manliness was a part of godliness. Under the spell of McLeod, Dickerson taught Sunday school, played on the church-sponsored baseball team, and toyed for a time with the idea of entering the ministry. Academically he excelled. He was president of his high school class and won a scholarship to a theological school. This he had to turn down because his father could not afford the campus expenses, and so he got a job as a clerk in a senatorial office and attended night classes at George Washington University Law School. Ultimately he went to work in the Steamboat Inspection Service of the Department of Commerce, and in later life was to achieve one fleeting moment of fame during the investigation of the Morro Castle disaster.

Substitute the name of John Edgar for Dickerson, and you find this early life pattern interchangeable, right up to the moment of entering government service. Trailing Dickerson by fifteen years, John Edgar also fell under the influence of McLeod, who instilled in him a great admiration for Emerson. He sang in the church choir as a boy soprano, taught Sunday school, and played on the church baseball team until a line drive dented his nose and cooled his ardor. Like Dickerson, he was interested in becoming a minister, but finally settled on the law. He was elected valedictorian of his high school class. Like Dickerson, he won a scholarship—this one to the University of Virginia—but had to turn it down because his father could not afford the expense. Like Dickerson, he then entered government service and attended night classes at George Washington University Law School. Never did two careers match more exactly in their externals, but underneath there were subtle differences.

For generations now, the face and figure of J. Edgar Hoover have been as familiar to Americans as the flag. The body is that of a bulky man who packs some two hundred pounds on a five-foot-eleven frame. The head is large, the face square and heavy, with a spatulate nose and with brown eyes so dark and intense they are sometimes described as black. It is a face that now looks its power, and to the millions to whom it is familiar, it must seem incredible that J. Edgar Hoover could ever have given any impression except one of physical force. Yet, when he entered Washington's Central High School in 1909, he was so small and skinny that the football coach rejected him on sight.

Never one to take setbacks lightly, Hoover moped for a time, but his active mind soon perceived an alternate route to distinction. The school had an ROTC cadet corps, which Hoover joined. His small size relegated him to the rear rank of the smallest squad, but this did not daunt him. Once he belonged, he could advance, and he did. Four years later, at the Commencement Day dress parade, he strutted out in all his glory, the captain of the entire company, barking his orders with a proud authoritativeness. He was so in love with his uniform that he wore it to church when he taught Sunday school, and this perhaps says something about his character.

Other Hoover traits, recognizable in the man today, first became discernible in high school years. It was at this time that Hoover acquired the nickname "Speed," by which the more intimate in later years have sometimes referred to him. The origin of the tagline is a bit obscure. Some admirers aver it derived from the fact that he was a swifty on the football field, but the evidence seems indisputable that Hoover's puny boyhood physique barred him from the gridiron. More logically, it would seem, "Speed" got his nickname because, in many ways, he gave the impression of a young man in a hurry to go places. To one admiring chronicler a few years ago, Hoover gave this self-portrait of the boy go-getter:

I started earning money when I was twelve years old by carrying groceries. In those days markets did not hire delivery boys, but I discovered that if one stood outside a store, a customer laden with purchases would happily accept a helping hand and gratefully tip anyone who aided with a heavy load.

The first such commission I got was to carry two baskets two miles, for which I received a tip of 10 cents. I realized that the quicker I could complete each chore, the more money I could earn, so I spent most of my time running. Because I ran back to the market and was outside the Eastern Market every day after school and from 7 A.M. to 7 P.M. each Saturday, I could earn as much as $2 a day. In those days that was a king's ransom.[2]

The boy who exhibited such industry gave other evidences of a burning zest for leadership. In Sunday school, wearing his cadet uniform, he discovered that even older persons listened to him respectfully when he talked. He liked that; he was always to like a forum. This love of the platform, one of the factors that led him to consider the ministry, thrust him into the leadership of Central High's debating team. With Hoover orating in the van, the team scored twelve straight victories on such sensitive issues of the day as "The Fallacies of Woman Suffrage." Hoover, as the title indicates, wasn't in favor of giving women the vote.

His attitude toward women, ambivalent throughout life, was apparent even this early. The boy orator who would not give women the vote nevertheless exhibited a Victorian tendency to put women on a pedestal; and having so elevated them, he admired but did not touch. The same chronicler who reported on his youthful industry also assures us that, in high school, he "had dates the same as the others, except that he never 'went steady.' They all teased him and accused him of being in love with Company A." Hoover was always to be more in love with an organization than with any woman, unless it was his mother. After his father's death in 1922, Hoover lived alone with his mother until she died in 1938, revealing a reverence for her that he frequently expressed. Though he was on rare occasions to appear as the escort of fashionable women, he has remained throughout life one of the nation's more determined bachelors, wedded to his job and his organization.

Summarizing such traits, his high school yearbook rendered judgment in these words: "A gentleman of dauntless courage and stainless honor."

His classmates predicted a great military future for him, but in this, at least, they were wrong. Hoover was to rise so rapidly in government service that he was to be considered indispensable in the offices he held and so was never to see military service in either world war.

On his graduation from Central High in 1913, he went to work in the Library of Congress at a salary of $30 a month, cataloguing new books and learning (information that was to be valuable to him later) the intricacies of card index systems. At night, he attended law classes at George Washington, where, by some accounts, his mother served as unofficial house mother for his fraternity, Kappa Alpha. Both mother and son were apparently straitlaced, and one fraternity brother later recalled: "J. Edgar took a dim view of such antics as crap games, poker, and drinking bouts."

Hoover obtained his degree in 1916, studied for his master's, and the following year passed his bar examination and moved into a clerkship in the Department of Justice, next door to the Commerce Department where brother Dickerson worked. The job paid him only $1,200 a year, but the amount did not matter. Just as with the rear-rank cadet assignment in high school, the significant fact was that Hoover had his foot in the door; given his drive and determination, the future could be expected to take care of itself. Jack Alexander, who later wrote what is probably the most detailed and impartial profile of Hoover ever penned, gives this picture of him as a young-man-about-the-Justice-Department:

> From the day he entered the Department, certain things marked Hoover apart from scores of other young law clerks. He dressed better than most, and a bit on the dandyish side. He had an exceptional capacity for detail work, and he handled small chores with enthusiasm and thoroughness. He constantly sought new responsibilities to shoulder and welcomed chances to work overtime. When he was in conference with an official of his department, his manner was that of a young man who confidently expected to rise. His superiors were duly impressed, and so important did they consider his services that they persuaded him to spend the period of the World War at his desk.

Even at this stage, when young men are usually avid to sample some of the gaudier pleasures of life, Hoover was immersed in the job and in off-hours was solitary and remote. Most evenings, when work did not claim him, he could be found at the University Club— a neat, well-groomed young man seated on a leather sofa, poring over copies of the *National Geographic*. Not for him the foibles of youth.

His dedication and ability so impressed his superiors that they soon gave him charge of an alien registration section of the Bureau of Investigation. It was his first leg up and an important one, for this was a time when, under the pressures of war, an antialien fever swept the nation. It was a fever that was to lead to one of America's most disgraceful, nationwide outbursts of irrationality. And young J. Edgar Hoover, only two years in the Justice Department, was to be a key figure, at the very vortex of the storm.

■ 1 ■

When America plunged into World War I "to make the world safe for democracy," the nation became embroiled in a major foreign war for the first time in more than a century. The Mexican War and the Spanish-American War had been cheap and relatively painless exercises in expansionism and imperialism. The struggle with Germany was a far different matter; it was America's initiation into the desperation of modern total war. It was an initiation that came with shocking impact to an isolationist people, sheltered behind their oceans and accustomed for generations to the serenity of complete security. And so it is hardly to be wondered that this abrupt turnabout from security to insecurity, this sudden and terrible menace in the long-unmenacing world, should shake the national psyche to its roots and produce a trauma such as Americans had never previously experienced.

The Black Tom explosion and other acts of prewar German sabotage had produced suspicion and terror. When war came, the grim evidences of its destructiveness increased the nervous terror and uncertainty. Along the Atlantic Coast, German U-boats torpedoed American ships within sight of land, and tar from the ruptured fuel tanks of sunken ships coated the beaches. The success of the undersea raiders led to wild and irrational rumors that omnipresent German spies ashore were radioing information on ship sailings; along the suddenly imperiled coast, residents who had the misfortune to bear Germanic names became suspect. One can recall a beachfront mansion, surrounded by a concrete wall, its entrance pillars crowned by the heads of concrete lions looking out to sea. The wall and the lions had been constructed long years before the outbreak of the European war, but now, in the rampaging black sickness of rumor and suspicion, the word spread that the lions' heads had been hollowed out and that, in the dead of night, the eyes suddenly lighted and glowed, winking signals to the U-boats at sea. Of such fantasies was the aura of witch-hunt created.

In a panic, victim rather than molder of the national mood, Congress passed a series of repressive acts, so sweepingly phrased that they practically guaranteed the perpetration of injustice. The first, the Espionage Act of 1917, was directed primarily at treason, but it also prescribed a fine of $10,000 and twenty years in prison for anyone who attempted to "convey false reports or false statements with intent to interfere with the operation or success of the military or naval forces of the United States." The Sedition Act of 1918 likewise provided a $10,000 fine and twenty years' imprisonment for anyone who might "utter, print, write, or publish any disloyal, profane, scurrilous, or abusive language about the form of government of the United States, or the Constitution of the United States, or the uniform of the Army or Navy of the United States, or any language intended to . . . encourage resistance to the United States, or to promote the cause of its enemies." Clearly, free speech, if not muzzled, must be muted, for under these elastic provisions almost any criticism of the government or its actions might well be judged an act of sedition.

These two onerous measures were capped by a third, the Alien Act, passed in October, 1918. This Act decreed that all aliens who were anarchists or believed in the violent overthrow of the American government or advocated the assassination of officials should be barred from entering the United States. Furthermore, "any alien who, at any time after entering the United States, is found to have been at the time of entry, or to have become thereafter, a member of any one of the classes of aliens [above mentioned] . . . shall upon warrant of the Secretary of Labor, be taken into custody and deported." This Act was about to become the vehicle of colossal injustice.

Many strands were interwoven in the pattern of coming events. The period that terminated with United States entrance into World

War I had been one of yeasty ferment and of increasing liberalism. American capitalism, which had ruled unchecked, a law unto itself, from the days of the Civil War to the turn of the century, by its excesses had produced its own counteraction. "Fighting Bob" La Follette, Teddy Roosevelt, and the muckrakers typified an era in which big business was pilloried for its sins, and the public called for reform. The national mood that began with Roosevelt culminated in Woodrow Wilson's New Freedom, which brought four years of as active and liberal an administration as the country had ever seen. A series of acts favorable to labor was passed, and membership in the American Federation of Labor zoomed from about 500,000 in 1900 to 4,169,000 in 1919. But, just as was to happen twenty years later when history insisted on repeating itself, there came war—and, with war, the end of all progressivism.

Wilson foresaw and foretold the coming domestic disaster. Just before our intervention in 1917, he had remarked to Secretary of the Navy Josephus Daniels: "Every reform we have won will be lost if we go into this war. We have been making a fight on special privilege. . . . War means autocracy. The people we have unhorsed will inevitably come into control of the country, for we shall be dependent upon the steel, ore, and financial magnates. They will run the nation." [3] In similar vein, on the very night before he called upon Congress for a declaration of war, the President unburdened himself to Frank Cobb of the *New York World* about the authoritarian domestic patterns that he foresaw. War, said Wilson, in Cobb's version of their talk, "would mean that we should lose our heads along with the rest and stop weighing right and wrong. It required illiberalism at home to reinforce the men at the front." Wilson predicted that "the spirit of ruthless brutality will enter into every fiber of our national life, infecting Congress, the courts, the policeman on the beat, the man in the street. Conformity would be the only virtue, the President said, and every man who refused to conform would have to pay the penalty." [4]

No words could have been more perceptive, more prophetic. Wilson's vision was uncanny in its accuracy. It is one of the ironies of history that the liberal President who so correctly foretold the demise of his liberalism should himself become one of the victims of the evils he foresaw, for so immersed did he become in the necessity of winning the war and the peace that he lost all ability, if not all desire, to ameliorate the harsh and tragic course of events.

Once America entered the war, the repressions to produce conformity began. The Socialists were the first victims. Though it seems today to have been virtually forgotten, the Socialist Party in 1912 had polled 897,000 votes for its Presidential candidate, Eugene Debs, and in 1914 it had thirty members in the legislatures of twelve states and some 1,000 members in various municipal offices. From the outbreak of the war in Europe in 1914, the party had opposed it as a crime against humanity and had striven to prevent American involvement—a stand that perhaps today, in the perspective of history, does not seem so radical and irrational as it seemed to many then. American entry into the war did not change this basic Socialist attitude. The Socialists condemned the Espionage Act as "the greatest victory American plutocracy has won over the American democracy," and this condemnation was their undoing. The American public, in the passions fanned by patriotism, just as Wilson had foreseen, was no longer tolerant. The public and the public's officials turned on the Socialists in patriotic fury, and the loosely drafted Espionage Act, which made almost any whisper of disagreement a criminal offense, was invoked against the Socialist leaders in a series of trials that brought convictions and long prison sentences. The Socialist Party in America was broken, never to revive as a serious political force.

This was only the beginning of a period of frenzy and reaction. The conclusion of the war in Europe saw the collapse of a dynastic system that had ruled from the time of Waterloo. Revolution shook the Continent. The Bolsheviks seized control in Russia, established a temporary government in Hungary, and nearly added defeated Germany to their ideological empire. Shock waves from these events ran through all classes of American society, and the trauma they produced among the wealthy and ruling elite became, and was to remain, one of the major facts of life in the twentieth century.

To panic at the top was wedded ferment at the bottom. This ferment, compounded of many elements, took two major forms, one ideological, one eminently practical. While sometimes the components merged and the lines of demarcation blurred, the forces involved were really separate and distinct in identity and purpose. On the ideological front, there were in America a number of Communist splinter groups, their numbers inconsequential, their power generally vitiated by the fact that almost invariably they quarreled as fiercely with each other as they did with the hated capitalists. The more radical and unstable of these factions were composed largely of aliens possessed of only an imperfect understanding of American democracy and the folkways of a people not given to extremism and to violence. In misassessment of the American spirit, such alien fanatics almost instantly concluded, with the success of the Russian revolution, that the worldwide millennium had come. They called for, predicted, seem actually to have expected, the momentary triumph of Bolshevik revolution in America—as complete a fantasy as ever deluded the mind of man.

Far different, more earthy, and more practical, was the second major element that was to contribute to the turmoil of the times. This was labor. The war had brought, as wars always do, a severe inflation. By late 1919, the purchasing power of the 1913 dollar had shrunk from 100 to 45. Food costs had increased 84 percent, and the overall cost of living was 99 percent higher than it had been just five years before. Salaried employees, who were still getting the 1913 dollar, or, at most, increases of only 5 or 10 percent, were caught in a brutal bind. They were actually "worse off economically than at any time since the Civil War." Organized labor suffered less, but it was hurting. During the war, in order to maintain production, labor and management had established an uneasy truce, but when peace came the adhesive of patriotism that had ensured their collaboration was removed. Labor pressed what it felt were its just demands; capital resisted with all its new-gained power; and the collision between them produced a series of some 3,600 strikes in 1919, involving more than four million workers.[5]

Now, as Wilson had foreseen, the relative position of the two antagonists was being reversed. In reaction to war and its hardships, the electorate in 1918 (just as it was to do in 1946) had returned to Washington a Republican Congress, and this Congress, just like its later successor, was to be intent on quickly abolishing all governmental controls and on rolling back, as much as possible, the prewar progressive legislation. Coupled with this re-established beachhead of conservatism in Washington was the new stature of business. By its miracles of wartime production, business—so long the whipping boy—had become the hero of popular imagination. Business seized and made the most of its newfound advantages. During the war, by its support of vigilante organizations, it had discovered what a good thing it had in superpatriotism. And with peace—but a peace in which Bolshevik tremors seemed to be shaking the world—it was in no mood to surrender such an ideal tool for the decapitation of its enemies.

What business wanted, as Robert K. Murray, assistant professor of history at Pennsylvania State University, wrote, was to roll back the present and recent past and to return to "normalcy," but this "normalcy was a special kind. It was the normalcy of the pre-Spanish-American War era. Normalcy (to the businessman) meant freedom from government regulation, from labor unions, from public responsibility—the freedom of laissez-faire." War-created instruments by which business might hope to achieve this flight into the past were at hand. Business-bankrolled organizations like the American Protective League, the National Security League, and the American Defense Society, which had devoted themselves to superpatriotism in wartime, were ideal vehicles for antilabor propaganda in peacetime. Since such organizations, once created, do not willingly expire, they needed for continued existence a new menace—and what menace could be more ideal than a rampaging Bolshevism? "Americanism," in their hands, became a bludgeon with which to attack the character and reputations of groups or individuals whom they hated and feared—to still all dissent and impose conformity.

The America that these pressures created was an America, as Murray wrote, whose "soul was in danger." It was in danger because "the nation was deserting its most honored principles of freedom— principles which had made it great and which had given it birth." The extent of the resulting sickness is perhaps best capsuled in this quotation from the English journalist A. C. Gardiner:

> No one who was in the United States as I chanced to be, in the autumn of 1919, will forget the feverish condition of the public mind at that time. It was hag-ridden by the spectre of Bolshevism. It was like a sleeper in a nightmare, enveloped by a thousand phantoms of

destruction. Property was in an agony of fear, and the horrid name "Radical" covered the most innocent departure from conventional thought with a desperate purpose. "America," as one wit of the time said, "is the land of liberty—liberty to keep in step." [6]

■ 2 ■

The curtain raiser on the scene of national hysteria was the Seattle general strike. A rash of wartime shipbuilding in the Pacific Northwest had caused housing shortages, inflation, economic dislocations of all sorts. On January 21, 1919, some 35,000 Seattle shipyard workers struck for shorter hours and higher pay. Forces quickly marshaled to crush and to win the strike. The Seattle Central Labor Council, in which IWW and other radical leaders played prominent roles, decided to back up the shipyard workers by calling a general strike. From labor's own standpoint, considering the temper of the times, this was certainly an injudicious decision, as was speedily demonstrated when the press and public of Seattle reacted in a frenzy of alarm and excitement. "This is America—not Russia," one editorial cried. A cartoon, entitled "Not in a Thousand Years," showed the Red banner flying over the Stars and Stripes. Ignoring the outcries, some 60,000 workers in various industries walked off their jobs on the appointed day, February 6.

Seattle was paralyzed. Schools closed, streetcar service was discontinued, business nearly expired. Yet the strikers were careful to maintain essential services. Garbage, laundry, milk, and fuel trucks were permitted to roll. At no time was the city without food, water, heat, or light. And amazingly, considering that this was all the doing of the wild Bolsheviki, there was no violence. During the entire strike, not a single arrest was made.

These were the facts, but the fantasy made far more fascinating headlines. Across the nation the press took its cue from the Seattle newspapers and raged with headlines and news stories proclaiming that Seattle was in the hands of lawless mobs. The general strike device—a radical importation from Europe's labor wars—and the presence of IWW leaders in directorial roles were cited as "evidence" that the Bolsheviks were trying to take over Seattle. Generally ignored was the fact that the hierarchy of the American Federation of Labor, traditionally conservative, frowned on the use of the general strike almost as much as big business. Fearing rightly that the tactic would be used to blacken all labor in the eyes of the public, the AFL brought every pressure it could bear on its locals to end the strike. But neither this action nor the orderly conduct of the strikers made any impression on the nation's press, which continued to scream its wild alarums. "REDS DIRECTING SEATTLE STRIKE—TO TEST CHANCE FOR REVOLUTION" ran the headlines.

Into the thick of all this sound and fury now came charging the inevitable man on horseback. He was Mayor Ole Hanson, a maverick politician who had been by turns a Republican, a Progressive, and a Democrat. During an earlier term in the state legislature, he had been regarded as a friend of labor, having sponsored legislation aimed at eliminating labor unrest. But he had an intense hatred of the IWW, whose radicalism appeared to him to be at the root of all labor trouble in the Northwest. There are also indications that Hanson fully appreciated the opportunity the strike offered him to stride before the public in a hero's role. With one motive reinforcing the other, Hanson at once viewed the general strike as a Wobbly (i.e., an IWW) device to establish a soviet and ignite revolution. On the very day the workers struck, he called for federal troops to help him man the barricades of democracy.

Mayor Hanson, riding in a car draped with a huge American flag, led the vanguard of some 1,500 soldiers into his beleaguered city. Backing up the troops with some 1,500 policemen, he then served an ultimatum on the Strike Committee. They would call off the strike or he would crush it by force and use the troops and police to run all essential services. Faced with this frontal threat, pressed from the rear by AFL insistence that the strike be abandoned, the local unions capitulated on February 10, ending the four-day walkout. Good, old-fashioned, forceful Americanism had carried the day, and Ole Hanson, who had draped himself in the flag and become its symbol, overnight catapulted to status as a national hero. He was, to the editorialists, "the man of the hour," "a red-blooded patriot," and a man "with a backbone that would serve as a girder for a steel bridge."

A minority of liberals and radicals viewed Hanson in a different light, dubbing him "the Seattle Clown," and it seems that just possibly there might have been some validity in their viewpoint. Hanson, asked what he thought of all his publicity, commented: "I guess you've got to grab it when it comes along." He soon demonstrated that he was a good grabber. Resigning as Mayor of Seattle, he went on the lecture circuit, and in seven months he cleaned up $38,000, orating on the horrors and dangers of Bolshevism. The evidence seems to say that Ole Hanson, just like many Red-baiters thirty years later, knew a good thing when he saw it.[7]

Understandably, there were some extremists who did not admire the man with a backbone like a steel girder the way the editorialists did. This became obvious on April 28, 1919 when "an infernal machine of sufficient power to blow out the side of the County-City Building was discovered in mail addressed to Mayor Hanson." The bomb consisted of a wooden tube eight inches in length and an inch and a half in diameter. Inside were three dynamite caps wrapped together with thread and attached to about one-third of a stick of dynamite. A vial of sulfuric acid was attached to the top of the package in such a fashion that, when the wrapping was torn open, the vial would break and the acid would set off a detonation. But the vial had apparently broken prematurely and the acid had leaked outward instead of inward; only a few small, insufficient drops had reached the dynamite caps. The entire package, neatly wrapped in straw-colored glazed paper, was postmarked "New York." It bore a return address: "Gimbel Brothers, 32nd and 33rd Streets and Broadway, New York City." And on the address side it displayed a picture of a man with a pack on his back, carrying a staff, and above the figure the word "novelty." [8]

Whether the bomb-mailer had a macabre sense of humor or not, the "novelty" he sent to Mayor Hanson raised the curtain on a new act—a series of bomb plots that in turn triggered fresh waves of public hysteria. Mayor Hanson, who had been in Colorado on a Victory Bond sales tour when the bomb arrived in his office, snorted defiance, demanding: "If they have the courage, why don't they attack me like men, instead of playing the part of cowardly assassins?"

On the same day that the leaky bomb fizzled in Mayor Hanson's office, the explosive temper of the country was illustrated by events that took place across the continent in Chester, Pennsylvania. There the Bolsheviki menace had become so real to Sheriff Albert R. Granger that he proclaimed it threatened "to engulf this city." Determined not to be drowned in the tidal wave, the Sheriff had arrested "sixty-four Bolsheviki" the previous day, and he had marshaled police, state police, special deputies, and the Citizens' Home Guard, throwing a special cordon around the Delaware County Jail.[9]

The next day, April 29, there occurred a shocking incident that seemed to many to justify the fears of Sheriff Granger and other officials. In Atlanta, Georgia, a slim package arrived at the home of former United States Senator Thomas W. Hardwick. A Negro maid tore open the wrapping—and a bomb exploded. It did not have the force of the Seattle bomb "to blow out the side of the County-City Building," but it caused tragedy enough. The blast tore off both the maid's hands and burned Mrs. Hardwick, who was standing nearby, about the face and head. The package was identical in size, appearance, and place of origin with the one that had been sent to Mayor Hanson, but it was more difficult, in Hardwick's case, to understand why he had been selected as a victim. It was true that the former senator had sponsored legislation to exclude alien agitators from the country, but he had never been rabid on the subject and had been considered a liberal on most matters affecting labor. Hardwick himself told the press he had "no idea who the miscreant was." [10]

The Hardwick bombing was a sensation that made headlines throughout the nation. In New York City a young postal clerk, Charles Kaplan, was reading about it as he rode the subway home. Kaplan worked in the parcel post division of the General Post Office, and as he read the description of the Hanson and Hardwick bombs, he felt the hair on the back of his neck prickle with terror, for he recalled that, just three days before, he had laid aside sixteen such packages for insufficient postage. Hurrying back to the post office, Kaplan found the packages right where he had left them. He notified postal inspectors, and they in turn called police. On examination, the packages were all found to contain bombs.

The addresses on the packages showed that the bombs had been destined for some of the nation's most prominent citizens. Some of the names on the "Bomb Honor List," as the press called it, were those of Americans who, by reason of their wealth or activities, would normally be much hated by anarchists and radicals. John D. Rockefeller and J. P. Morgan were two such names. Several others on the list had been active in radical witch-hunts and prosecutions. Senator Lee S. Overman was chairman of the Senate Bolshevik Investigating Committee; Federal Judge Kenesaw Mountain Landis (later to become famous as the strict czar of baseball) had made a reputation as a hanging jurist for the severity of the sentences he had imposed on convicted Socialist leaders during wartime; Postmaster General Albert S. Burleson had banned radical literature from the mails; Senator William H. King was known as a bitter foe of labor; Attorney General A. Mitchell Palmer had been Alien Property Custodian. The prominence and activities of these men seemed to explain their inclusion in the list. But, just as in the case of former Senator Hardwick, there were other names that defied rational explanation. One was Supreme Court Justice Oliver Wendell Holmes, Jr., one of the nation's most independent jurists; another, Secretary of Labor William B. Wilson, who had opposed, and was to continue to oppose, the excesses of witch-hunts.

The mail-bomb plot clearly was the work of a demented mind, or minds, but it seemed too clumsy and illogical in concept and execution to indicate any high-level revolutionary intent to seize control of the nation. The press and the public, however, had no doubts. To them the existence of the bombs showed that we stood at Armageddon. Headlines screamed their alarm, and Mayor Hanson called on Washington to "buck up" and "hang or incarcerate for life all anarchists." Feeling himself the proved master of such exigencies, he added this reassurance to the American people: "If the Government doesn't clean them up, I will."

The May Day parades, with which the bombs apparently had been timed to coincide, resulted in riots in a number of cities as aroused citizens poured into the streets to do battle with the radicals. This was followed by a lull of almost exactly a month. Then the morning papers of June 3 broke out in a rash of glaring headlines as a new and more terroristic wave of bomb plantings and explosions rocked cities across the nation.

The consternation of the hour is still reflected in the four banks of eight-column, war-declaration-size type with which *The New York Times* on June 3 broke the news to its readers. The headlines read:

MIDNIGHT BOMBS FOR OFFICIALS IN 8 CITIES

BOMBERS DIE AT ATTORNEY GENERAL'S HOUSE

TWO VICTIMS AT JUDGE NOTT'S HOME HERE

BOMBS IN BOSTON, CLEVELAND, PITTSBURGH

Clearly, the whole world was being blown up.

The most sensational of the bombings occurred in the nation's capital. Shortly before 11:15 on the night of June 2, Attorney General A. Mitchell Palmer and his family had retired to the upper part of their home at 2132 R Street N.W. to prepare for bed. They had hardly done so when they heard a thump at the front door, followed almost instantly by a terrific explosion. The entire house was rocked, its front was demolished, windows were blown in, the library was wrecked. Up and down the exclusive residential block, buildings shook and windows were shattered from the blast.

Across the street, at 2131 R Street N.W., young Franklin Delano Roosevelt, then an Assistant Secretary of the Navy, stepped through splintered glass, opened his front door, and almost stumbled over a fragment of the bomber's body that had been deposited on his doorstep. Another bit of human debris had been blown through a window of the nearby home of Helmer H. Bryn, Norwegian envoy to the United States, and fell near a cot in which a baby was sleeping. Still a third fragment was found in front of the home of Senator Claude A. Swanson, two doors from Palmer's residence. A large portion of a man's scalp and head lodged in the third-story cornice of a mansion a block north of the explosion. None of the officials in the area had been injured, but the bomb plotter (or plotters) clearly had become, in most gruesome fashion, the victims of their own fiendish device.

Oddly enough, a great dispute developed about whether there had been one bomber or two. Two hats were recovered at the scene and portions of what appeared to be two left legs, but, despite this evidence, police insisted the bombing had been the work of a single man. The *Washington Star* quipped that it was little wonder the bomber had tripped and fallen up the steps of the Attorney General's residence under the handicap of such one-sided pedal equipment, but police continued to strive to identify their one man, two heads, two left legs, and all. Enough fragments of clothing and effects were recovered to show that the bomber (or one of the bombers) was an Italian from Philadelphia. One of the hats had a Philadelphia hatter's trademark in it, but the hatter couldn't remember to whom he had sold it.

Though the identity of the bomber (or bombers) remained obscure, there could be no question about their political faith. Scattered in the street near Palmer's residence were copies of an anarchist tract titled "Plain Words." It proclaimed:

> The powers that be make no secret of their will to stop here in America the worldwide spread of revolution. The powers that be must reckon that they will have to accept the fight they have provoked. . . . There will have to be bloodshed; we will not dodge; there will have to be murder; we will kill . . . there will have to be destruction; we will destroy. . . . We are ready to do anything and everything to suppress the capitalist class.——THE ANARCHIST FIGHTERS

Copies of the same handbill were found at the sites of other bombings. In New York City, a night watchman was killed when a bomb exploded in the vestibule of the home of General Sessions Judge Charles C. Nott, Jr., but this was the only other life that was taken in the series of simultaneous explosions. In Cleveland, the home of the mayor was dynamited. A legislator's home was wrecked in Newtonville, Mass.; a silk manufacturer's home in Paterson, N.J. The dwelling of a municipal judge was demolished in Boston. In Pittsburgh attempts were made on the homes of a federal judge and the city's police inspector. In Philadelphia, the residence of a prominent jeweler was bombed, and the Rectory of Our Lady of Victory was badly damaged.

The public reaction to this outburst of violence was precisely what might have been expected. Here was proof, to most persons, that the Bolsheviki were plotting revolution and were determined to rule the country. Attorney General Palmer asserted that this was so, and the press, ignoring the possibility that the bombings might have been the work of a relatively few crackpots, trumpeted calls for drastic action and "a few free treatments in the electric chair." Governmental response was as lightning-swift as the outbreak of hysteria.

Within forty-eight hours, Palmer acted. He appointed William J. Flynn, former chief of the Secret Service, to head the Bureau of Investigation "with carte blanche to deal with the situation throughout the country in his own way." [11] This was the first in a series of moves designed by Palmer to track down the bomb plotters and wipe out radicalism.

Subsequently he named Francis P. Garvan, of New York, Assistant Attorney General in charge of all investigations and prosecutions undertaken in the probe. And he created under Garvan a new General Intelligence Division (GID) to concentrate on a study of subversive activities—to determine their scope and decide what prosecutorial actions should be taken. Flynn would have full operational control of the Bureau, but GID would be a kind of superagency in the subversive field, and all information gathered by Flynn's agents bearing on radicalism would be funneled to it. To the command of this sensitive center in the radical inquest, Palmer, on August 1, 1919, appointed the 24-year-old "live wire" who, in a mere two years, had so impressed the hierarchy of the Justice Department— J. Edgar Hoover.

■ 3 ■

It has become the fashion to absolve Hoover of all responsibility for any except the meretorious deeds of the FBI. Nothing that happened in the inglorious past has any pertinence now, the thinking runs, for obviously Hoover wasn't, couldn't have been, in charge of the ship. If he had been, things would have been different because Hoover is Hoover—and, well, perfect. Such faith is obviously based on a cult of personality worship, and such cults frequently contain more myth than fact. In Hoover's case, since his image has grown so potent and unchallengeable in our time, it becomes of more than ordinary importance to sift the past. Only by such sifting can one uncover the basis for the current cult of hero worship; only so can one relate the man to his past, separate fact from fancy, and decide whether the myth has any validity.

A favorite tactic by Hoover apologists is to present Hoover in his familiar role of crusader against Communism and to point out that, as head of GID, he first assembled information that made him aware of the importance of the Communist menace. He is credited with masterminding the more respectable court actions that were undertaken against leading extremists, and the impression is given that he had little knowledge and less connection with the crass detective work that raised such serious issues about human rights. This was the pattern followed by Don Whitehead in his best-selling *The FBI Story,* a glowing account published under the aegis of the FBI, with a foreword by Hoover and a replica of the FBI shield on a cover sporting the colors of the American flag. Actually, it was not all so simple. Hoover, when he was given command of GID, had status as a special assistant to the attorney general; his division was a superagency in the compiling of radical dossiers and the mapping of strategy. Anyone who takes the trouble to study the newspaper files or the court records of the period can discover that Hoover emerged as a major and authoritative spokesman—and principal defender, under Palmer —for a performance that was to become known as "Government by Hysteria" or "Palmer's Reign of Terror."

The events of late 1919 and early 1920 probably could have occurred only in a nation that had been deprived of all effective leadership. Woodrow Wilson, who in those last hours before the war had seen so clearly war's devastating effect on democratic institutions, had driven himself to the point of physical collapse in battling for approval of the League of Nations. He lay in the White House, a doomed man, unable to exercise the authority of the Presidency. The ship of state, lacking the direction of a skipper, drifted almost rudderless, at the whim of lesser and avidly ambitious men.

Chief among these was A. Mitchell Palmer. As a boy, he had received a thorough indoctrination in the Quaker faith, a religious grounding that was to influence his actions in later life. A lawyer, Palmer had risen first to prominence in the local affairs of Stroudsburg, Pennsylvania; had been elected to Congress on a reform ticket;

had been Vice Chairman of the Democratic National Committee and head of the Pennsylvania delegation to the Democratic National Convention in 1912. In the hectic nominating battle, he had been chiefly instrumental in throwing the votes of the powerful Pennsylvania delegation to Woodrow Wilson, and for such services he deserved reward. In February 1913, Wilson had offered him a post in his first Cabinet as Secretary of War, but Palmer had declined, saying, "I am a Quaker . . . and the United States requires not a man of peace for a war secretary, but one who can think war."

Wilson understood, and he did not forget his loyal supporter. He appointed Palmer to a judgeship on the United States Court of Claims. In October, 1917, Wilson named him Alien Property Custodian, and in March, 1919, he brought Palmer into the Cabinet by a recess appointment as Attorney General. In this post, Palmer became the man of the hour when the wave of bombings and antialien, antiradical hysteria swept the nation. Shortly after the outburst of June 2, 1919, he asked and obtained from Congress an appropriation of $500,000 to aid the Justice Department in its hunt for the bomb plotters. Aided by this additional bankroll, Palmer began his crusade in earnest.

There can be no doubt that the Attorney General's attitude—his increasing proclivity to discern the hand of the Bolsheviki everywhere—was colored by the bomb attack on his own home. It could hardly have been otherwise. But there are indications too that Palmer, just like Ole Hanson, came to appreciate the role in which he had been cast, and that he hoped, by vigorous exercise of authority in response to popular demand, to propel himself into the Presidency. The same spirit seems to have percolated through the ranks under him. The Red-hunt offered opportunity for everyone. Murray rendered this judgment: "Under the general guidance of bureau chief Flynn and through the unstinting zeal of Hoover, this unit [Hoover's GID] rapidly became the nerve center of the entire Justice Department and by January, 1920, made its war on radicalism the department's primary occupation. In fact, there are indications that both Flynn and Hoover purposely played on the attorney general's fears and exploited the whole issue of radicalism in order to enhance the Bureau of Investigation's power and prestige."

The building of the menace proceeded at a pace that was positively breath-taking. Max Lowenthal (he served for years as consultant and counsel to Congressional committees and was an adviser in the Truman Administration; his research of original records is the most exhaustive that has been done on this period) points out that Hoover's GID, almost from the moment of its inception, compiled and catalogued all kinds of gossip, went in heavily for the use of informers, infiltrated and at times all but captured radical organizations, and undertook the tricky task of identifying just what was a radical idea and just who was a radical. Lowenthal wrote:

> The Bureau of Investigation faced and solved one problem in the first ten days of the existence of Mr. Hoover's division, the problem of the kind of data detectives should send to headquarters. They were going to receive material from undercover informers, from neighbors, from personal enemies of persons under investigation. The detectives were going to hear gossip about what people were said to have said or were suspected of having done—information derived, in some instances, from some unknown person who had told the Bureau's agents or informers or the latters' informants. Some of the information received might relate to people's personal habits and life.
>
> The Bureau's decision was that everything received by the special agents and informers should be reported to headquarters; the agents were specifically directed to send whatever reached them, "of every nature."

To gossip was added the more factual evidence of the printed word. The printing plants of so-called radical publishers were raided; private libraries and accumulations of anarchist and radical tracts were seized. Every inflammatory pamphlet that came into the possession of the bureau, from whatever source, was forwarded to Hoover's division for analysis. The books and pamphlets could have been weighed by the ton.

The speeches of radical orators swelled the tidal wave of data. Informers, agents, even stenographers, covered meetings of suspected radical societies whose memberships were comprised largely of aliens. In some audiences the bureau informers, sleuths, and stenographers were augmented by employees of private detective agencies serving antilabor employers. This concentration of investigators sometimes resulted in comic-opera situations in which the sleuths outnumbered the plotters. Senator Wheeler subsequently estimated that, on some occasions, the snoopers actually comprised 75 percent of the "radical" audiences.

This early, also, light was shed on the tricky business of putting too much trust in informers and secret agents. One of the GID's star informants was a man named Ferdinand Petersen. Petersen was such a master of intrigue that, all the time he was working for the GID, he was climbing the ladder to high rank in the hierarchy of the Communist Party. He eventually precipitated an intraparty crisis by informing the leadership that the Party secretary was actually an informant for the Bureau. The Bureau naturally denied it, and it never became quite clear whether Petersen's charge was or wasn't true. However, the Bureau decided it had better take a close second look at Petersen's activities, and when it did, it made some unhappy discoveries. According to Lowenthal, it developed that Petersen had been giving "the Communist Party leadership a preview of every report he made to the Bureau of Investigation; and he relayed to that leadership facts which he had wormed out of the bureau about its espionage of the Party. The bureau, saying that it had previously concluded that his reports to it were worthless, discharged him."

The Affair Petersen was not to be the last that would raise grave questions about the Bureau's use of informers and its reliance on them.

At the time, of course, no one was in a questioning mood. Correlating the flood of information that poured into his division from all these varied sources, Hoover personally prepared detailed studies of the major radical organizations, with emphasis on the faction-riven Left that had embraced, in one form or another and with varying degrees of commitment, the essentials of Communist ideology. Hoover became convinced that Communism was not just another political party but a revolutionary plot. Whitehead, in his laudatory work on the FBI, claims for Hoover the credit of recognizing at this early date the motif of violence in Communism, the dictatorial dominance by an inner core of leaders, and even the subservience of American Communists to the dictates of Russia. "Here was the most evil, monstrous conspiracy against man since time began—the conspiracy to shape the future of the world and to control the masses on the basis of cold, 'scientific' social formulas conceived in the brain of a few Communists," Whitehead wrote, purporting to give Hoover's views at the time.

This treatment fosters the impression that the FBI always conveys of Hoover's prescience and infallibility. What Whitehead does not say is that Hoover's division was engaged in building up a fantastically bloated picture of a great radical menace. Hoover's analysis of Communism was part of it, but only part. The overall canvas—and this is a truth that has been generally conceded for four decades—was so distorted that it had virtually no contact with reality. Under the circumstances, the accuracy of Hoover's perceptive analysis of Communism is something like finding one solid kernel in a moldy sack of corn.

To get some picture of what was involved, one has to understand the enormous energy expended in assembling a huge secret file on "radicals" in the United States. As Lowenthal pointed out, it is not clear just what standard of measurement was used in cataloguing ideas as radical ideas, for it is obvious that one man's radical may be another's pale liberal and still another's near conservative. In any event, Hoover, with his early training in card-indexing in the Library of Congress, established in the GID a similar card index system to keep track of radicals. The first report of GID on the system showed that 100,000 radicals had made the card index; a few months later, there were 200,000; and a year later more than 450,000. With radicalism building so swiftly into a virtual army, it became necessary to single out for special attention the names that really mattered. Therefore, Lowenthal noted:

> Mr. Hoover directed his Division to write biographies of the more important ones. The writing up of lives and careers proceeded rapidly, so that within three and one-half months of the GID's existence its biographical writers had written "a more or less complete history of over 60,000 radically inclined individuals," according to official information supplied to the Senate. Included were biographies of persons "showing any connection with an ultra-radical body or movement," in particular "authors, publishers, editors, etc."
>
> Rigorous secrecy has been imposed on the list of names of news-

papermen, authors, printers, editors, and publishers who were made the subjects of GID's biographical section. How many additional biographies have been written since the middle of November, 1919, who were the GID's first and later biographers, how they were trained so promptly, and how they managed to write 60,000 biographies in 100 days—these questions have never been answered.

It must be obvious to anyone that, in the mere compiling of these 60,000 biographies, Hoover's GID was invading very precious and fundamental fields of human rights. It was analyzing men's minds. It was preparing dossiers about their private lives, their *beliefs*—and this in a country whose great contribution to the human race had been the proclamation of flat guarantees of freedom of speech and thought to all men! Not by any stretch of the imagination could such dossier-building be justified as a legitimate police activity. Even if every member of the Communist Party at the time had been considered a criminal, there simply weren't anywhere near enough to justify 60,000 dossiers. Hoover, in his *Masters of Deceit* long years later, was to write that Communist Party membership by 1922 had "reached" 12,400. There were, of course, other "radicals" abroad in the land in 1919, especially the anarchists, but 12,400 is still a long way from 60,000. Even in the prejudiced atmosphere of the times, the Department of Justice—wielding all the one-sided power of the wartime Sedition and Alien Acts—was never able to charge more than a few hundreds with anything. Clearly, with the creation of GID, the traditional concept that federal police were to be used to combat crime, to pursue and punish men for their criminal *acts,* had been abandoned, and a whole vast new field of snooping, of dossier-building, of labeling and tarring men for their possibly wayward beliefs, had been opened up.

If this invasion of men's privacy, this authoritarian assessment of the contents of their minds, had resulted in dramatic success in the criminal field—for example, in the arrest and conviction of the bomb plotters—it would still have represented a dangerous and unjustified dilution of basic American concepts of freedom, though the success would probably have been accepted as full justification for such tampering. But one of the ironies of the great Red scare was that not even this excuse could be offered. The tremendous and furious activity—the use of informers, the infiltration of radical meetings, the compilation of mental and personality dossiers—did not advance the real cause of criminal detection one iota. Almost daily during the month of June, 1919, the Bureau of Investigation reported that it was "making progress" in its hunt for the bomb plotters; it was "making good . . . almost fine progress"; it was making "good headway"; it was making slow but sure progress. This steady "progress," however, never really progressed. *The New York Times* became so exasperated that it asked, "Has the gift of skill and genius in ferreting out criminals been denied to our present-day detectives?" In the Senate, Miles Poindexter introduced a resolution demanding an explanation from the Department of Justice for its failure to arrest, to punish, and to deport aliens who advocated the overthrow of the government by force and violence. Something had to be done.

■ 4 ■

The first action was taken on November 7, 1919, when Bureau of Investigation agents were unleashed in nationwide raids against a relatively obscure organization known as the Federation of the Union of Russian Workers. The legal basis for the raids was the Alien Act passed by Congress in 1918. In the light of what was to happen, it seems important to realize just how little the government had to prove to deport an alien. All that was needed was a showing that the alien belonged to an organization advocating the violent overthrow of the government. This showing would be made in an administrative hearing conducted by the Labor Department, which was in charge of deportations. There would be no trial, no judge and jury in the usual sense. A defendant had just two slim chances of obtaining a review of the case against him: The Secretary of Labor *might* personally study the record and reverse the deportation order, or, if the deportation proceedings could be shown to be manifestly unfair, a habeas corpus action might be begun to bring the case before a Federal judge. But ordinarily an administrative judgment that an organization was subversive was sufficient, if backed up by a showing that the individual belonged.

The Federation of the Union of Russian Workers, founded in 1907, was an ideal target for the first test raids. It had made no secret of its radicalism, proclaiming itself composed of "atheists, Communists, and anarchists." Its headquarters were in the Russian People's House at 133 East 15th Street, New York City, and it was here, as Bureau of Investigation raiders struck simultaneously in twelve cities, that the principal blow was delivered. Some two hundred men and women were arrested, and literally truckloads of radical propaganda were confiscated. *The New York Times* reported indications that some of the prisoners had been "badly beaten by the police . . . their heads wrapped in bandages testifying to the rough manner in which they had been handled."

The sequel raised a warning flag that should have been, but was not, heeded. Just as in the Bureau's controversial dragnet draft raids in 1918, the great majority of those roughed up in the process of arrest were poor bewildered innocents. Even though the government in the deportation hearings was rolling with loaded dice, only 39 of the 200 seized in the New York raid were finally held. Some of the 200 were found to be American citizens not subject to deportation; others were simple workmen who spoke little or no English and had gone to the clubhouse for companionship, for recreation, for almost every conceivable reason except the active promotion of revolution.

Across the nation, the same pattern developed. Of hundreds seized in the mass arrests, only a minority were held. Eventually, the worst cases, 249 in number, were gathered at Ellis Island in New York harbor for deportation. The two prize catches in the haul were the admittedly violent anarchists Emma Goldman and Alexander Berkman. According to the government, Emma Goldman's inflammatory speeches had incited Leon Czolgosz to the murder of President William McKinley nearly twenty years earlier. Young J. Edgar Hoover prosecuted both Goldman and Berkman; their deportation was upheld by the Supreme Court; and on December 21, 1919, with Chief Flynn and Hoover watching, the transport *Buford,* dubbed by the press the "Soviet Ark," sailed for Russia.

Though this first offensive against radicalism had been marred by police brutality and by the gross trampling of individual rights, it was hailed by a prejudiced press and public as a great success. Attorney

General Palmer, who only a couple of months before had been attacked in Congress and asked to explain his lethargy, became the new hero of the hour—"a lionhearted man," "a tower of strength." The Senate listened in rapt fascination when Palmer reported to it on November 14, describing the success of the November 7 raid and submitting a report prepared by Hoover's GID that pictured radicalism virtually sweeping the nation. On the basis of this report, Palmer urged the Senate to pass a peacetime sedition act so that American citizens could be subjected to the same kind of dragnet raids that, in his view, had proved their worth against alien agitators.

This initial victory, the chorus of praise, the lack of any effective counterweight except in liberal periodicals like *The New Republic, The Nation,* and the *Dial* (which, of course, could be disregarded), now turned official heads and led to action so rash, so sweeping, and so ill-considered that it was to transform Palmer from hero into villain. With Hoover's GID leading the way, Palmer decided to adopt the same tactics against the Communist and the Communist Labor Parties that had been tested out against the Federation of the Union of Russian Workers. The Labor Department was persuaded to cooperate in the move. Secretary of Labor Wilson (who certainly would have opposed) happened to be ill at the moment; his assistant secretary, Louis P. Post, was occupied with other matters; and so the decision, so vital to Palmer's plans, was made on a secondary level. This, at least at the outset, did not matter. More than 3,000 warrants prepared by Hoover's GID and the Bureau were signed and made ready for service. The new year of 1920 was certainly going to get off to a fast start.

The draft dragnet of 1918 was outdone in brutality by what happened now in a massive roundup of suspected Communists in thirty-three cities from coast to coast. The raids were timed for the same evening, Friday, January 2, 1920, and the bullpens were again packed with human cattle, crowded together in conditions of unspeakable filth and squalor. Scenes that finally outraged the American conscience took place across the nation. They resulted in a number of exhaustive and critical studies.

A group of twelve lawyers and law school professors denounced the raids in May, 1920, in *A Report Upon the Illegal Practices of the United States Department of Justice.* The Interchurch World Movement prepared a denunciatory report that was published by the Federal Council of Churches of Christ in America. The House Rules Committee and the Senate Judiciary Committee, whose moving spirit was the Montana Democrat, Thomas J. Walsh, held hearings. Some of the deportation cases, through habeas corpus action, wound up in the federal courts. From all these sources, this picture emerges: [12]

The raids were planned and synchronized by Hoover's GID and the Bureau, with the help of informers inside the alleged radical cells. The Bureau's instructions to its Special Agents in the field, dated December 27, 1919, read:

"If possible, you should arrange with your undercover informants to have meetings of the Communist Party and the Communist Labor Party held on the night set. I have been informed by some of the Bureau officers that such arrangements will be made. This, of course, would facilitate the making of arrests."

Disclosure of this order subsequently led to much heated debate over the role played by the Bureau's informers. One was shown to have been the actual party leader of his district. Others were influential in the councils of their respective groups; otherwise they could hardly have made "arrangements" to suit the convenience of the Bureau in making arrests. The evidence seems to indicate that the Bureau was treading dangerously close to the vital borderline that separates the legitimate agent from the *agent provocateur*—the line that separates the investigator from the inciter leading sheep to slaughter.

This sensitive issue became apparent almost from the moment the raids broke upon a startled public. In its first account of the proceedings, *The New York Times* noted:

For months, Department of Justice men, dropping all other work, had concentrated on the Reds. Agents quietly infiltrated into the radical ranks, slipped casually into centres of agitation, and went to work, sometimes as cooks in remote mining colonies, sometimes as miners, again as steel workers, and, where the opportunity presented itself, as "agitators" of the wildest types. Although careful not to inspire, suggest, or aid the advancement of overt acts or propaganda, several of the agents, "under cover" men, managed to rise in the radical movement and become, in at least one instance, the recognized leader of a district.[13]

It seems obvious that it would be extremely difficult for " 'agitators' of the wildest types" to refrain from inciting action or for leaders of units to refrain from leading. Bureau agents, it would seem, must have strained their backs leaning over backwards to avoid the odium of becoming *agents provocateurs*.

When the trap was sprung, some 10,000 victims—by a later estimate of the Walsh committee—were swept up in the nationwide dragnet. The shocking actions of the 1918 draft raids were being repeated—on a larger and more vicious scale. The *Times* reporter, observing the first desperados picked up in New York, gave this skeptical judgment:

"They were a tame, unterroristic looking crowd, and their appearance bore out the statements of operatives that not a man had tried to put up a fight. Among the prisoners that came into headquarters late were twenty-five women, half of them apparently girls of high school age."

Some of those arrested were seized in meeting halls; others were tracked down at their homes, which were in many cases entered illegally, without warrants. One witness gave this description to the Interchurch World Movement:

I have lived long enough in Russia under the Czar. I have seen brutality committed there, but I have never seen the brutality that was committed on the Russian people here. In my case, when I was arrested, four men came into the room in the evening, when I was partly undressed and was doing exercises in arithmetic, and asked my name and told me to go along with them. They showed me a badge, but did not tell me the reason for my arrest. When I left the house and at the time I was traveling in the automobile, they were beating me in the sides with their handcuffs, and this continued all the way until they brought me to the Park Row building in New York. In a room where they took me and asked me my name they were beating me again, without any explanation.

The outrages committed in Boston were even more reprehensible. A woman who was among those arrested there described the conduct of the raiders in these words:

There was a man, a gentleman, and there comes some police in uniforms and they make every man "hands up." So every man just stand like that [illustrating] and they fish all the pockets of the men; they don't fish my pockets—of course not—and they get to me, they look over the bag, but there was nothing in it because I don't buy anything yet. So they looked over the hall; they broke the platform, move every chair. . . . They put every man two by two handcuff.

Some eight hundred persons were rounded up in the Boston raids, and about half of them were shipped to Deer Island in Boston Harbor. During the transfer the prisoners were forced to march in chains from the immigrant station to the dock, subjected to the abuse of onlookers. On the island, conditions were primitive. It was winter, but heat was lacking. Sanitation facilities were poor. The prisoners, in accordance with a policy adopted for the raids, were held rigidly incommunicado. In despair, one captive plunged five stories to his death; another went insane; two died of pneumonia.

When the public outcry against such atrocities mounted, the Bureau denied all. In affidavit after affidavit, its agents insisted that they had not beaten anyone, that their conduct had been beyond reproach. On this they insisted, though the mountain of evidence from the various trials and hearings seems flatly to contradict them.

Citizens as well as aliens were subjected to harsh treatment. A dragnet does not discriminate; it is a tactic that sweeps up every unfortunate in its path. Senator Walsh later reported that, of one thousand seized in Detroit, about half were American citizens. The wrongly arrested included all gradations of innocence—and outrage.

The various postraid investigations seem to have established beyond dispute that many of those arrested had assembled in clubrooms and meeting halls for purposes that had nothing to do with subversion. Many were foreigners, lonely in a strange land, who liked to meet with others of their own nation and sing native songs. Others were attending classes, trying to learn English and to study American history and citizenship. One court case involved a man who had been adjudged contaminated by the government agents because he had frequented a clubroom in Lincoln, New Hampshire. It developed that the club was maintained by the lumber company for which he worked and that its purpose was to encourage the firm's foreign-born employees to learn to read and write and to develop some skill in arithmetic. Even more embarrassing as a criterion of detective work was a raid in Lynn, Massachusetts. There thirty-nine men were rounded up. Only one turned out to be a Communist, and he was an American citizen, not subject to deportation. The thirty-nine had been meeting, the government's own subsequent investigation showed, not to plot the overthrow of the national authority but to discuss the formation of a cooperative bakery. How could skilled detectives, backed up by babbling informers, have mistaken a discussion about a cooperative bakery for subversion? The best explanation apparently was that offered by a bureau agent who testified that, after all, these foreigners were jabbering away in a strange tongue and he couldn't understand them. The supervisor who had ordered the raid confessed sadly to Walsh's Senate committee: "It may be that the Lynn Communists were elsewhere that evening, while we expected that they would be at the meeting."

"These people were holding a meeting to discuss the formation of a cooperative bakery," Senator Walsh persisted. "Is there any controversy about that fact?"

"Not now."

Such were the Palmer Red Raids. Walsh's committee later reported that in some cities as many as 97 out of every 100 were picked up without warrants; that some 6,500 were released without prosecution; that the vast majority of those prosecuted were ultimately freed. The official FBI version, as rendered by Whitehead in *The FBI Story,* concedes that the Red Raids were a blunder, then proceeds to minimize their magnitude. Whitehead reported merely that some 3,000 warrants were issued and some 2,500 aliens rounded up. This watered-down version is in irreconcilable conflict with the press accounts at the time. In its second-day story *The New York Times* indicated that meticulous records were being kept and more than 5,000 had been arrested.[14] The belittlement of the event also conflicts with the official findings of the Walsh committee.

The discrepancy is significant if one is trying to understand an FBI that has been placed on a pedestal, whose every statement is accepted on faith, without investigation, without suspicion, without even a normal curiosity. The Whitehead version not only whittles down the magnitude of the Red Raids blunder, but by plain inference absolves Hoover of all blame. Hoover is lauded for his perspicacity on the Communist issue. But as for the raids themselves, it was those other fellows, Director Flynn of the Bureau of Investigation and Attorney General Palmer, who went rampaging around like bulls, trampling on civil rights.

This technique has been employed by the FBI whenever the unpleasant subject of the Palmer Red Raids has arisen. Perhaps the most graphic instance occurred in 1940 when the Bureau engaged in a lengthy altercation with Mrs. Mary R. Beard, the wife of the historian Charles A. Beard, with whom she had co-authored several best-selling histories. The background was this: Hoover's General Intelligence Division had been abolished after the 1919–1920 debacle, but in 1940, as FBI director, Hoover announced that he was reestablishing the old system by re-creating, as a wartime measure, the antiradical bureau and the secret-informer system. Liberals became alarmed at this resurrection of a specter from the past. Mrs. Beard, in a speech before a woman's club in Washington, D.C., criticized both Hoover and the FBI and expressed the fear that old excesses might be repeated.

Alexander Holtzoff, for years one of Hoover's closest assistants and at the time chief law adviser to the FBI, challenged Mrs. Beard's statements. He wrote:

> Mr. J. Edgar Hoover was not in charge of, and had nothing to do with, the manner in which the arrests were made of the so-called radicals under the administration of Attorney General A. Mitchell Palmer. Mr. Hoover at that time was not connected with the Federal Bureau of Investigation but was a special assistant to the Attorney General. His function was at that time limited to the handling of legal matters and the preparation of evidence for presentation to the proper authorities in connection with those activities.

Mrs. Beard refused to accept this statement at face value. In a reply to Holtzoff, she pointed out that, only five years previously, in 1935, the FBI's confidential reports had been made public by Attorney General Homer Cummings. These disclosed that GID had been organized in 1919 "under direct administrative supervision of J. Edgar Hoover" and that Hoover had been "since 1917 in charge of counter-radical activities as a Special Assistant to the Attorney General." Mrs. Beard wondered, in view of all this and in view of the fact that Holtzoff himself had not been in the Bureau at the time, whether he had Hoover's "personal authority" for his statements. Holtzoff replied:

> My statement to you that he did not direct, supervise, participate in, or have any connection with the manner in which these dragnet raids were conducted was based on Mr. Hoover's personal authority to me. The arrests were made under the direction of William J. Flynn, then head of the Bureau of Investigation, who, together with Mr. Palmer, must be regarded as responsible for such excesses as took place. . . . He [Hoover] did not participate in ordering or carrying out the arrests.

Seven years later, Hoover himself in the *Look* Magazine picture book on the FBI denied that he had any responsibility for the raids. The same year, 1947, he told the New York *Herald Tribune:* "I deplored the manner in which the raids were executed then, and my position has remained unchanged."

The well-established, indisputable records of the time tell a different story. They make it clear that, from inception to execution, no man played a more comprehensive role than Hoover. *The New York Times,* in one of its first accounts, pointed out that the warrants signed by the Labor Department had been based on briefs "submitted by J. E. Hoover." In one celebrated deportation trial in Boston, with the district immigration commissioner on the stand, the judge asked some probing questions in an effort to determine just how the raids were born. The immigration official testified: "We had a conference in Washington in the Department of Labor with Mr. Hoover and another gentleman of the Department of Justice."

Such statements seem to indicate that Hoover played an important role in the preraid planning. But this was not all. The documentary evidence is even more explicit about his active participation on the night of the raids and his subsequent responsibility at each phase of the investigation and prosecution. In fact, Hoover emerges from the various transcripts as much of a key figure as Flynn or Palmer. Take, for example, the order for the raids transmitted to all branches of the

Bureau by Assistant Director Frank Burke. The initial order, read into the record at the Walsh committee hearings, informed district agents:

> On the evening of the arrests, this office will be open the entire night, and I desire that you communicate by long distance to Mr. Hoover any matters of vital importance or interest which may arise during the course of the arrests. . . . I desire that the morning following the arrests you should forward to this office by special delivery, marked for the "Attention of Mr. Hoover," a complete list of the names of the persons arrested, with an indication of residence, or organization to which they belong, and whether or not they were included in the original list of warrants. . . . I desire also that the morning following the arrests that you communicate in detail by telegram "Attention Mr. Hoover," the results of the arrests made, giving the total number of persons of each organization taken into custody, together with a statement of any interesting evidence secured.

This seems explicit enough. The Washington headquarters was to be open all night; the agents were to telephone Hoover there and report directly "any matters of vital importance." Subsequent reports were to be sent to Hoover; subsequent telegrams were to be sent to Hoover. Hoover and only Hoover was mentioned as the man to whom the agents were to report their achievements. In final instructions to the Bureau's agents, sent just before midnight of December 31, 1919, Burke again emphasized Hoover's role: "Arrests should all be completed . . . by Saturday morning, January 3, 1920, and full reports reported by special delivery addressed attention Mr. Hoover."

Throughout the long controversy, Hoover emerged again and again as the dominant behind-the-scenes figure in the Red Raids. His disclaimer of responsibility in 1947, his revelation then that he "deplored" the manner in which the raids had been conducted, seems to clash with the impression of fervor for a cause that animated the account of an interview with him that appeared in *The New York Times* more than three weeks after the raids. In this interview, Hoover was defending the department's action. He said flatly that approximately 3,000 of the arrested aliens made "perfect" cases for deportation. (Actually, only 446 ultimately were to be deported.)

He added that it was believed cases against many others could be proved. The *Times* said: "Deportation hearings and the shipment of the 'Reds' from this country will be pushed rapidly, Mr. Hoover declared. Second, third, and as many other 'Soviet Arks' as may be necessary will be made ready as the convictions proceed, he said, and actual deportations will not wait the conclusion of all the cases." [15]

This eagerness to launch a veritable fleet of "Soviet Arks," even without waiting for the conclusion of all the cases, does not accord with the impression so zealously cultivated in later years that J. Edgar Hoover detested the entire proceedings.

The record of Congressional hearings is replete with references to Hoover, with testimony by Hoover, with protestations by Palmer that he didn't know but that Hoover had the answers. The Attorney General, in his appearances before Congressional committees, was always accompanied by Hoover, and on pages 35, 82, and 96 of the Senate Judiciary Committee record, for example, one finds Palmer turning to Hoover to supply the vital information. On one occasion, the Attorney General was being questioned closely about discussions between his department and the Labor Department concerning the status of the Communist Party under the deportation statute. *"Mr. Hoover was in charge of this in the Bureau of Investigation,"* he testified. "He is more familiar with the history of it than I am." Again, asked how many warrants had been issued, the Attorney General replied: "I cannot tell you. . . . If you would like to ask Mr. Hoover, *who was in charge of this matter,* he can tell you." Hoover, who was present, protested that he couldn't say either, since "The search warrants were entirely a matter which the agents in charge of local offices handled." [Italics added.]

The Senate hearings developed evidence on several points that all dovetail into a picture of Hoover, the young martinet, always pressing for extreme action. For example, he argued with the Labor Department that, if a man's name appeared on a membership list, it was sufficient grounds for deportation; it should not be necessary for detectives to prove that the man actually knew and subscribed to the views of the organization. Hoover's position was that "The fact remains that he is an alien and a member of an organization declared to be unlawful, and the same is sufficient grounds to warrant his deportation."

In the matter of bail, Hoover was also an extremist. Most of the aliens seized in the roundup were released in $500 or $1,000 bail until their cases could be disposed of, but testimony showed that Hoover rowed with the Labor Department over the low bail and fought strenuously for a $10,000 figure—an amount which meant, in effect, that an alien would rot in prison until his case was settled. An American Federation of Labor attorney told the Senate committee of a man who was never even brought to trial, but who had been held originally in $10,000 bail. The application for reduction of bail, he said, "was vigorously opposed by Mr. Hoover." When the reduction was won, the man was rearrested on a slightly different charge, and the Justice Department again battled for $10,000 bail.

Another aspect of extremism emerged from a letter Hoover had written to the Immigration Bureau of the Labor Department, urging that it refuse to free any prisoner in bail until he had agreed to answer questions put to him by detectives. Hoover argued that this was "of vital importance," stressed that it was necessary to get prisoners to talk, conceded that it would virtually defeat the ends of justice if prisoners couldn't be induced to give the information necessary for their own deportation. He opposed letting prisoners talk to lawyers or communicate with anyone until they had submitted to questioning. This rule was, indeed, adopted. The Bureau's orders to the branch offices stated that "persons taken into custody are not to be permitted to communicate with any outside person until after examination by this office and until permission is given by this office."

Attorney General Palmer was asked for an explanation of this order, which flouted the basic and vital American principle that a man must not be threatened and coerced into testifying against himself, that he has a right at all times to the advice of counsel. Palmer protested: "At the time, I knew nothing about it. I never heard of it until long afterwards." Hoover was then asked to explain. He did. He said the stringent incommunicado rule had been adopted because subordinates in the Labor Department wanted it that way.

Vital elements of freedom were at stake here—the kind of basic individual liberties for which the founders of the nation had fought the Revolution and which they later sought to guarantee in the Bill of Rights. The entire Red Raids procedure was an exercise in the brutal authoritarianism of the police state. Even in the hysteria of the times, there were some men who perceived this. Francis F. Kane, United States Attorney for the Eastern District of Pennsylvania, submitted his resignation to President Wilson on January 12 because he felt "out of sympathy with the antiradical policies of Mr. Palmer and his method of carrying them out." [16] But Hoover—the man who, by his own later avowal, heartily disproved of everything—remained to the bitter end steadfastly at the helm of GID, and to the bitter end he played the commander's role, defending the actions of the troops.

An example of his deep commitment to the cause of bureaucratic defense developed during the Senate inquiry into the conduct of the Detroit raids. Some 800 persons had been arrested in Detroit and flung for from three to six days into a veritable Black Hole of Calcutta, a dark, windowless, narrow corridor in the city's antiquated Federal Building. For some twenty-four hours, the prisoners had no food. They were packed so closely together that they could not lie down, and there was just one toilet for the lot of them. Such inhumane treatment provoked expressions of outrage from the press, from leading citizens, and from the mayor and other officials. A letter from a Detroit lawyer, read before the Senate committee, charged: "The space allotted to those arrested was not sufficient to even comfortably stand up. . . . The agents of the Department of Justice did not permit either an attorney or the wife of any relative to see the prisoners held. . . . At the Post Office Building the aliens had to sleep on stone floors, there being no bedding or covers, nor any other of their natural needs."

Hoover promptly telegraphed Arthur L. Barkey, Detroit branch chief of the Bureau of Investigation, for an explanation of the charges. The answer, addressed "Attention Mr. Hoover," was submitted to the Senate committee. It insisted that the prisoners had been well treated. The floor on which they had slept wasn't stone but wood, and the corridor in which they had been confined wasn't cramped, but really spacious, measuring "4,512 square feet, which allowed approximately eight square feet for the occupancy of every alien held."

This prettied-up picture of conditions in Detroit received a rude jolt when the Senate committee, still skeptical, summoned before it W. O. Garred, assistant custodian of the building. Under Garred's testimony, the Bureau's spacious 4,512-square-foot corridor shrank to a minuscule 448 square feet. For the 800 prisoners this represented something like half a square foot apiece. There was, said Garred, just one dim skylight opening onto the roof. There was only the one toilet, and men had to stand in line, forty to fifty at a time, waiting for its use. Some couldn't wait. "Before many days . . . the stench was quite unbearable in some parts of this corridor and room," Garred testified.

■ 5 ■

The Red Raids had been conducted to the accompaniment of much patriotic drum-beating and to the applause of an overwhelmingly conservative and generally imperceptive journalistic claque. For a time, in many quarters, the harassment of the Reds, however brutal, at whatever cost to civil liberties, was considered a highly laudable achievement. And Palmer, until sober second thoughts began to set in, seemed to be running a strong race for election by acclamation as every man's hero. But in this flush of achievement, there was one disturbing nettle of failure. The Bureau of Investigation, despite that steady, day-by-day progress it had reported six months earlier, seemed no closer to solving the mystery of the great bomb plots than it had been the night when the front of Palmer's residence was demolished. This was a blot that could hardly be allowed to stand on the federal escutcheon, and detectives now embarked on a desperate effort to remove it.

In trying to track down the origin of the "Plain Words" flier found at the bombing sites, they had received a tip that the type might have been set in a Brooklyn print shop. The printer, Robert Elia, was picked up by Bureau agents on February 25, 1920, and on March 7 Andrea Salsedo, a typesetter in the same shop, was taken into custody. The Bureau later maintained that pink paper—similar to that on which "Plain Words" had been printed—had been found in the

Brooklyn shop and that peculiarities of type faces found there matched the printing of the anarchistic tract. Even so, the Bureau had no evidence on which it could hold the two men on a criminal charge; it had, indeed, no authority under the current laws to arrest them. This, to the Bureau, was a technicality that did not matter. Elia and Salsedo were taken to the New York offices of the Bureau, a suite of rented rooms on the fourteenth floor of the building at 15–21 Park Row. There they were held prisoners without writ, warrant, or charge of any kind preferred against them—and they were held for nearly two months.

One does not have to have a very vivid imagination to be able to picture the pressures that must have been used during this two months' incarceration to induce these supposedly knowledgeable witnesses to talk and so to unlock the secret of the great bomb plot the Bureau was so avid to solve. There is considerable credible evidence that the New York office of the Bureau at the time was especially addicted to brutality. In the January Red Raids, a number of prisoners signed affidavits attesting to violent treatment. One man claimed he had been beaten; a second, that he had been hit repeatedly over the head with a blackjack; a third, that his glasses had been broken off and he had been punched in the face. A fourth, who was ultimately released as innocent of all wrong, testified: "I was struck on my head, and . . . was attacked by one detective, who knocked me down again, sat on my back, pressing me down to the floor with his knee and bending my body back until blood flowed out of my mouth and nose." [17] When such harsh punishment was administered to routine suspects, what must have been the lot of men who—in the Bureau's opinion—possessed guilty knowledge of the great bomb plot?

No final answer to this question was ever to be forthcoming. Elia, who was subsequently deported, signed a statement for the Sacco-Vanzetti defense attesting to some aspects of his and Salsedo's brutal treatment. His statement, on the face of it, evidently disclosed only a part of the truth, for threaded through it are indications of Elia's fear of federal agents and his anxiety not to displease them. Under the circumstances, what Elia did disclose seems of special significance.

His account begins with a scene that took place on the morning of

March 8, the day after Salsedo's arrest. Elia, while being taken to an interrogation room, passed the door of another room in which he saw Salsedo, surrounded by four guards in shirtsleeves. Later, while he was being questioned, he heard Salsedo scream. The following morning he was taken to the office of Director Flynn, who was personally on the scene. He waited in an outer room until Salsedo came in with Narcisco Donato, a lawyer who had offices in the same Park Row building and who was to serve as their attorney. Elia deposed:

> Salsedo's face and forehead were bruised from the beating he had received. He had red spots and scratches on his cheeks and temples and his eyes were vacant. He was depressed. I never saw him normal during all the times after that we were together.
>
> In Mr. Flynn's waiting room Salsedo told me about his interrogation the night before. They showed him a bloody sandal and said, "You see this blood? This is the blood of the man who was blown up. Tell me whose blood that is." He would say that he did not know, and they would swear at him and strike him in the face or body with the heel of the sandal. They did this over and over again.[18]

Salsedo's reaction was that of a cowed and terrified man. "I do not want to die," he told Elia. "We have done nothing, but we are in a trap. What are we to do? I will admit that I printed 'Plain Words,' because I cannot stand any more, and maybe I will help myself."

Questioned on the following day by Flynn himself, according to Elia, Salsedo admitted that he had printed the anarchistic leaflet in May, 1919, but cleared Elia, saying Elia had had nothing to do with it. Elia admitted he had seen Salsedo printing the tract, but insisted he had no further knowledge. This, according to Elia in the most incredible part of his statement, satisfied the curiosity of the federal agents instead of convincing them that men who knew so much must have known more. One might almost be tempted to believe from Elia's statement that the Bureau's agents wanted only the printer, not the bomb planters; for, if Elia can be believed, the third-degree artists now became the most considerate of hosts. His statement continues:

> After that we were not formally questioned any more and we were very well treated. A room was fitted up for us with two beds. We had good meals; we were taken out for walks; once we were taken up to

the movies. When anyone asked me if I was content or if I was willing
to stay at the Department of Justice I always said "Yes," because I
did not want to go to prison and I thought that all depended on the
good will of the agents.

Salsedo refused to be comforted by such glove-handed treatment,
according to Elia. He was convinced that they were going to be sent
to prison. "He would lie groaning and lamenting all the night. He
complained continually of pains in his stomach and head. He was
always nervous. He refused absolutely to eat. He showed clear signs
of an unbalancing mind."

On the evening of Sunday, May 2, after nearly two months (for
Salsedo) of this enforced confinement (the confinement was longer
for Elia), the two men walked up and down in the corridor, and then
Salsedo left to go to bed. Elia sat talking awhile with Bureau agents,
smoking and telling stories in the most friendly fashion. About 11
P.M., when he retired, Salsedo begged him to turn off the light because he had "a terrible headache." Elia, before he went to sleep,
heard Salsedo "groaning and lamenting." When a watchman came to
arouse him in the early morning, he found himself alone. The watchman said: "Your comrade is dead. He has jumped from the window."

It seems incredible that Elia could have slept through the suicide
of his roommate (if suicide it was) or through the hullaballo that
almost certainly would have followed the discovery of a smashed
body on the sidewalk. Wouldn't agents have gone storming into the
room where the men slept to see what had happened? Whether, perhaps, they had quarreled and fought? Whether Elia was still there?
What he could tell them about Salsedo's death? The stillness, the
casual awakening, the almost routine comment that one's roommate
had gone out the window—none of this seems even faintly plausible.

There is another version of events, buried under the years, never
before published. Richard Rohman, who was to become a public
relations man for David Dubinsky's Amalgamated Ladies Garment
Workers Union, was at the time a young reporter on the Socialist
New York Call. Late on this fateful Sunday evening, he recalls, he
wandered into the Park Row offices of the Bureau of Investigation.
He had heard a rumor that the imprisoned men were about to be
deported, and he had come to investigate it.

At that time of night, there was no one in the outer office, and Rohman walked on into the interior of the suite. He recalls:

I became aware of cries coming from an inner office. As I walked on, I could hear these terrible cries, subhuman cries of a man in terrible pain. Suddenly I barged into an inner room from which the cries were coming. Salsedo was slumped in a chair, and he looked as if every bone in his body had been broken. Two or three agents were standing over him, hitting him with blackjacks.

When they heard me, they whirled around, and they recognized me, of course. One of them shouted, "There's that SOB from that Socialist rag, the *Call.* Let's get him." They came for me, and I turned and dashed down some 14 or 15 flights of stairs, with them at my heels. I finally outdistanced them, jumped into the subway, and got back to my office, where I wrote the story.

What became of Rohman's account remains a mystery. His recollection is that the bulldog edition of the *Call,* which carried the bulk of the run, was off the press, and his story, in a replated page one, appeared in only the small remainder of the day's copies. If it did, no trace of it can be found today, for existing microfilms apparently were made from the bulldog edition. Nor, strangely enough, did the *Call,* in its subsequent, multicolumned account of Salsedo's death, refer to Rohman's eyewitness story. Yet Rohman's recollection of the incident seems explicit and clear. "It was," he says, "one of those things you could never forget."*

It is true that there was an expectation that the imprisoned men would soon be released. Donato, their attorney, had been pressing the Bureau to free them, and he had obtained, as he later disclosed, a promise that Elia and Salsedo "would be freed about this time." Only, the Bureau had told Donato, it would have to hold the men until after May Day—after the danger of May Day riots and bomb incidents had passed.

Expecting from this assurance that all would soon be well, Donato was astonished when he went to his law office on the morning of May 3 to find a detective standing by the door.

"Well, your client, Salsedo, is free," the detective told him.

* An official FBI spokesman has stated that the Federal Bureau of Investigation talked with Richard Rohman several times following the Salsedo case; that Rohman always proved most cooperative; and that Mr. Rohman never provided the FBI with information in respect of Salsedo along these lines.

Donato expressed his happiness at the news, and only then did he learn that the detective was playing a macabre game—that Salsedo, in the Bureau's version, had jumped to his death from a fourteenth floor window at 4:20 A.M.

Donato hurried at once to see Director Flynn. The Bureau, badgered by reporters asking about Salsedo's death, had already put up its defenses. It had first put out a "Memorandum of Bomb Plot of June 2, 1919," linking Salsedo to the printing of the pink fliers. Then it had contended that Elia and Salsedo had been held at their own request because "they were afraid of their anarchist friends; afraid that something would happen to them if they were out." Flynn, according to Donato, asked him to back up this story by saying "that the two men had been held with my consent." Donato refused. He declared that both men had been detained against their will and that Salsedo "on at least one occasion" had been beaten up. The Bureau replied to this charge with the righteous statement, hardly credible in view of the earlier Red Raids evidence, that never had "anyone been beaten up in these offices." [19]

Even in the hysteria of the times, the Bureau could not get away with it. When two men could be held illegally for two months, when one could then be killed in a mysterious dive to the sidewalk, even the enthusiastically Red-baiting press began to ask some pointed questions. On May 5, the *New York American,* not exactly noted for its fighting liberalism, asked in a lead editorial where the Bureau thought it got the authority to hold men in such fashion and who had ordered the detention. It demanded a full-scale investigation of Palmer and the Department of Justice.

To meet such criticism, a stout defense was required. On June 1, 1920, when Palmer and Hoover went before the House Rules Committee to justify themselves, Palmer submitted authority's rebuttal in the form of a long report prepared by Hoover's GID. A large section of this report was devoted to the Salsedo case. Criticism of the Bureau was groundless, said the Hoover-GID report, for Salsedo had been "staying in the Park Row building" by his "own choice." He had been given "comfortable quarters," he had been assigned "a clean room," he had been "permitted to occupy . . . clean beds." He had been "given ample opportunity to wash and bathe and change linen." He had been "regularly fed." He had been "taken out for exercise" by his custodians. All in all, he had been "well treated."

The hope of the Bureau had been that Salsedo would cooperate by furnishing clues about the bomb plotters, but, though he had stayed with the detectives for nearly two months "voluntarily," they had been "unable to gather further information voluntarily" from him. The Hoover-GID version of events denied that the Bureau's agents had ever pressed this "likely" source of information against his will. "He was never mistreated at any time and never was struck, intimidated, or threatened," the report said flatly. True, the Bureau agents had pointed out to Salsedo that he had printed a pamphlet they regarded as subversive, and that, as a result, the Labor Department would try to deport him. But, the Hoover division reported, this was not done by way of intimidation or threat. Rather, "the situation was . . . explained" to Salsedo for his own benefit.

After nearly eight weeks of this attempt to gather information, said the Hoover-GID report, "Salsedo put an end to his part of the agreement by jumping from the fourteenth floor of the Park Row building upon the street, committing suicide."

By this act the Bureau had been deprived of "the principal source of information" about the bombings, but it still had "fairly substantial hopes" that "ultimately the plot will be solved." The nature of these hopes was not divulged to Congress, but Hoover noted that he had incorporated them in a private memorandum for the Attorney General. Whatever the hopes were, they were to prove chimerical. The bomb plots were never solved.

This story of Hoover and the Red Raids, as disclosed in the records of the time, is hardly the picture of a man who "did not participate," a man who "deplored."

■ Notes ■

[1] For details on Hoover's boyhood and early background, I have relied on two principal sources: the second article of a three-part profile of Hoover by Jack Alexander, published in *The New Yorker*, Oct. 2, 1937; and one article in a series on Hoover and the FBI published by the *New York Post*, Oct. 8, 1959.

[2] Mildred Houghton Comfort, *J. Edgar Hoover, Modern Knight Errant* (Denison, 1958).

[3] Robert K. Murray, *Red Scare, a Study in National Hysteria* (University of Minnesota Press, 1955).

116　　　*The FBI Nobody Knows*

⁴ Eric F. Goldman, *Rendezvous with Destiny* (Alfred A. Knopf, 1952; Vintage Books, 1958).
⁵ Murray, *op. cit.*, p. 7.
⁶ A. C. Gardiner, *Portraits and Portents* (Harper, 1926).
⁷ This description of the Seattle strike and its aftermath is based on Murray.
⁸ *New York Times*, Apr. 30, 1919.
⁹ *Loc. cit.*
¹⁰ *Loc. cit.*
¹¹ *New York Times*, June 4, 1919.
¹² A detailed account of the testimony uncovered in these investigations is to be found in Max Lowenthal's *The Federal Bureau of Investigation* (William Sloane Associates, 1950), on which to a great degree I have relied.
¹³ *New York Times*, Jan. 3, 1920.
¹⁴ *Ibid.*, Jan. 4, 1920.
¹⁵ *Ibid.*, Jan. 27, 1920.
¹⁶ Murray, *op. cit.*, p. 218.
¹⁷ *Ibid.*, p. 214.
¹⁸ Francis Russell, as quoted in *Tragedy in Dedham* (McGraw-Hill, 1962).
¹⁹ *New York Call*, May 4, 1920.

4 Indictment of a Senator

When Warren G. Harding brought the greedy Ohio gang to Washington, the Bureau of Investigation, like the nation, faced one of its darkest and most shameful hours. Tall, ruggedly handsome, Harding looked the part of a President, but there was precious little substance behind the facade. His cronies were the poker-playing pals and political connivers whom he had attracted during his rise from small-town editor and politician to the loftiest office in the land. And so, when Harding moved into the White House, this swarm of small-time, courthouse leeches descended on Washington and began to feast on the lush pastures of the national preserves.

In their foraging, they scoured every department of the Federal Government with disastrous results. One of the major disasters occurred in the Justice Department, to whose command Harding named his long-time Ohio buddy, Harry M. Daugherty. The new Attorney General was a bombastic type who was to adopt the tactic (employed by Hoover and the Bureau to this day) of equating every criticism of himself and his conduct in office with some dark and devious plot hatched in Moscow. With such a man in command of the department, it became almost inevitable that drastic changes would be made in the hierarchy of its most powerful arm, the Bureau of Investigation. A favorite Washington guessing game evolved around the question: Whom will Daugherty name to head the Bureau?

William J. Flynn tried desperately to hang on to his post as director. In *The FBI Story*, Don Whitehead, who had access to FBI files, reported that members of Congress and four federal judges joined in a Flynn-inspired letter-writing campaign beseeching Daugherty to retain the Bureau chief. But Daugherty had other ideas.

One of the new Attorney General's constant associates was William J. Burns, who had been a boyhood friend back in Ohio. Burns had gone on to found the William J. Burns International Detective Agency, and he billed himself as "the famous international sleuth." In past years, Daugherty had often availed himself of the services of Burns's agents. Burns's hobnobbing with Daugherty and other members of the Ohio gang who had easy access to the White House was like the handwriting on the wall for Flynn.

Powerful business interests were delighted at the prospect. Burns's detective agency had served them long and well. In this service, it had been accused of offering to spy on workers for a price. There had been charges that Burns's detectives, for their own purposes, sometimes fomented labor discord. In one scandal in 1912, Attorney General George W. Wickersham had accused the agency of packing a jury with men who would convict. The prospect of a man with such ties heading the powerful Bureau of Investigation alarmed labor, and rightly so. Protests were dispatched to Washington, but protests did no good. The Harding Administration had a deaf ear where labor was concerned, and on August 18, 1921, Daugherty fired Flynn by telegram and named Burns to succeed him.

Curious, now, was the next act in the drama. Four days after Burns was appointed, Daugherty named a new Assistant Director for the Bureau. Oddly enough, the man he chose was no old Ohio crony. Perhaps Daugherty realized that it would be wise to have in the Bureau's No. 2 command post a man who was familiar with its machinery and personnel. Or perhaps his reason was simply that he had been impressed by the personality and achievements of the man he named. In any event, his benediction fell on twenty-six-year-old J. Edgar Hoover, who as Special Assistant to the Attorney General had been in command of the Red-baiting GID.

For Hoover, it was a gigantic step up the ladder of command.

■ 1 ■

The character of the Harding regime probably was nowhere better exemplified than in the characters of two of its prize pets who now claimed squatter's rights in the Department of Justice. One was a mystery man with the common name of Jess Smith. He had no official status, yet he operated from a private office in the Department of Justice as if he partially owned the place. He was known as Harry Daugherty's closest friend—so close a friend, in fact, that he even lived with the Daughertys in their suite in the Wardman Park Hotel. He was also known as a close personal friend of President and Mrs. Harding, and he was often included among the invited White House guests at exclusive social affairs. It is little wonder that, with such visible evidence of the ties that matter, Jess Smith soon became accepted in Washington, where channels of influence are a bread-and-butter topic, as the man to know when one wanted "to get things done."

The tail of Jess Smith's kite was a big, flamboyant blusterer named Gaston B. Means. Means was a close friend of Burns, and on October 28, 1921, he became a full-fledged agent of the Bureau—the personal appointee of its new director. Never, probably, did an individual appointment typify more clearly the rottenness of an entire regime. Means had been a German agent in 1916. In 1917 he had been accused of murder in the slaying of a wealthy widow, Mrs. Maude A. King, who had been killed by a pistol shot while in North Carolina with Means. Means was acquitted but was subsequently named the defendant in a sensational court action attacking a forged will he had filed—a will that would have given him control of virtually the entire estate of the departed widow. Such was the odoriferous past of the man whom Burns, without an apparent qualm, rewarded with appointment as a Bureau agent.

Means and Jess Smith quickly became a team. The brash, swaggering Means constantly huddled with Smith, used Smith's office as if it were his own, and ignored the hierarchy of the rest of the Bureau as if it were beneath him. Smith engaged in voluminous, secret, semi-official correspondence on behalf of Daugherty; and Means, according to office scuttlebutt, was used to handle confidential investigations of persons whom Daugherty wanted investigated.

The pair, but especially Means with his checkered past, were heartily detested by the more dedicated Bureau personnel. "Means and Hoover clashed almost immediately," Don Whitehead wrote. "Hoover asked Burns to order Means to stay out of his office. Hoover didn't like the man's spending habits or his morals." One does not have to have an idolatrous attitude toward Hoover to believe that a man of his high competence and professionalism would never be able to stomach a character like Means. But more than individual detestation of an obvious rogue was needed to put the Bureau on an even keel.

Means and Jess Smith were the major symptoms of rot, but they weren't by any means the only symptoms. Hoover saw agents' badges handed out to politicians in much the same way as honorary deputy sheriffs' badges in rural areas. One second-rate New York theatrical producer was awarded a badge for bringing to the capital a cheap girlie show that had pleased a prominent Administration figurehead. Another man, a drunken hanger-on, got his badge as a reward for amusing Department of Justice officials with ribald songs and recitations at noontime on the sidewalk outside the building. For a time, as Hoover afterward confessed, he thought of resigning and taking up the private practice of law. But something, perhaps his deeply ingrained religious conviction that right must in the end prevail, restrained him, and he stayed on.[1]

Hoover still headed the General Intelligence Division, which, though the bomb plots and anarchistic excesses had become things of the past, continued to view the future darkly, through Red-rimmed glasses. It could not or would not give up the menace. Palmer and Flynn, who had been, of course, responsible for all past transgressions, had vanished from the Washington scene. Only Hoover remained—the specialist, as he had been since 1918, on alien and radical affairs. So it is perhaps of significance that the Bureau's new chief, Burns, reflecting the consistent and persistent findings of Hoover's GID, kept annually reporting to Congress that radicalism was a greater menace than ever.

In the spring of 1922, appearing before the House Appropriations Committee, Burns was asked: "Do you think it [radicalism] is increasing from week to week and from month to month?" Burns replied: "I think it is." Asked if he thought radical activities were of a "particularly dangerous or violent character at the present time," he answered: "Very. I cannot impress upon you too much how dangerous they are at the moment."

Events persisted in giving the lie to such a dire warning. The ever

imminent violence somehow never erupted, but this fact did nothing
to alter official judgments of its reality. Two years later, in March,
1924, Chief Burns, again before the House Appropriations Committee, pictured the menace in a more horrendous light. "Radicalism is
becoming stronger every day in this country . . . ," he warned. "We
have absolute proof of all this; we have documentary proof showing
that it is absolutely true. . . . I dare say that unless the country becomes thoroughly aroused concerning the danger of this radical element in this country we will have a very serious situation." [2]

The only "proof" that Burns ever adduced was one indisputable
fact—that there were a growing number of serious strikes by American workmen. To the type of probusiness mentality that viewed every
strike as an evidence of rampant radicalism, no other "proof" was
really needed. From this astigmatic viewpoint, the events of 1922
must have seemed justification for the howls of alarm.

The nation was in the throes of a depression. Jobless men walked
the streets by the millions. Harding's battle cry, "Back to normalcy,"
brought the derisive taunt from *The Nation* that the President was
now learning "slowly and painfully" what should have been patent,
"that you cannot turn back the hands of time . . . to McKinleyize
America, to treat it as if nothing had changed since 1896." Yet this
seemed the government's sole desire. The Railroad Labor Board had
ordered a 12 percent wage cut for almost all railroad employees in
1921. When revenues continued to decline, the railroads sought
further payroll slashes, and on June 6, 1922, the Board obliged by
decreeing another 12 percent cut. Congressmen charged that, for
100,000 railroad men, this new ruling meant a rollback of their
income to only $563 a year. Fighting Bob La Follette, Senator of Wis-
consin, charged that railroad wages had a purchasing power no
higher than they had had twenty years earlier. Understandably, labor
was in revolt.

On July 1, though trainmen remained on their jobs, some 400,000
shop workers struck. Railroad management, which in the past had
often ignored recommendations of the Railroad Labor Board as
something less than holy, now held up its hands in horror at the
sacrilege labor was committing. Shaking with righteous indignation,
management proclaimed that strikers would be deprived of all

seniority once they did return to work. This injected a new issue into the dispute, which, for the strikers, became as serious as the original pay dispute, and Harding's efforts at mediation foundered on this new, management-created reef.

When they did, violence broke out. Railroad management imported strikebreakers, many of them gun-toting criminals; railroad guards attacked strikers; and strikers battled both guards and strikebreakers. Engines were sabotaged. The probusiness, antilabor Harding government was shocked to its conservative roots, and it marshaled all the power of the Federal Government to crush the strike.

Daugherty walked into Federal Court in Chicago and, on September 1, obtained what was subsequently called "the most sweeping injunction ever issued" to halt the strike. The Attorney General announced he was going to prevent labor unions "from destroying the open shop." So stringent was the wording of the injunction that any deed—even any word—that could be interpreted as interfering with the railroads' operations could be deemed a violation of the law. Free speech had become suddenly anti-American.

The Bureau of Investigation, in which Hoover occupied the No. 2 command post, and the General Intelligence Division, the bureau's most potent arm, which Hoover directly bossed, were now hurled into the strikebreaking effort. Special Agents were dispatched throughout the nation to infiltrate the strikers' ranks, to worm undercover men into their meetings, to gather evidence of word or deed that would put strikers in jail. Agents operated under code designations, each bearing a letter of the alphabet and a number, and they were instructed to send daily telegraphic reports to Washington, addressed either to Chief Burns or to Hoover, or just to the Director of the GID.

It was a monumental effort that produced miniature returns. Though the Bureau remained firmly convinced that the strike had been ordered and financed in Moscow, all the spies it planted so assiduously in labor's ranks seemed unable to uncover any clinching evidence of the much-sought Red taint. There were scattered reports of IWW sympathy for the strike, and the Bureau's own agents in their reports often mentioned "agitators and radicals." True, one assistant foreman offered to help the government overcome "these

'Yellow Socialists' (they are mostly foreign born)"; but he was obviously just expressing a personal prejudice, not providing evidence. More embarrassingly, some Special Agents reported that they had been unable to uncover any evidence of radicalism at all. One governor charged that the railroads' complaints about violence had been "greatly exaggerated," to the point of being "hysterical." And on the floor of Congress, Senator Joseph T. Robinson (Democrat of Arkansas) denounced the railroads' importation of "desperate characters and noted gunmen" and declared, "Few cases of violence attributable to the strikers have occurred."

This perverse failure of labor to cooperate by furnishing evidence of Muscovite manipulations reduced the Bureau to the censorious pursuit of strikers' vocabularies. Agents ran down cases in which strikers or their wives were accused of offending the sensibilities of strikebreakers by "molesting" them with the rough sides of their tongues. Agents tracked down an offending landlady, a Miss Cooney, because she had banished strikebreakers from her rooming house. "They were called rats and denied the privilege of remaining in her home," the aggrieved agents reported.

Such were the heinous and un-American offenses that the Bureau uncovered. On all kinds of charges, it arrested some 1,200 railroad employees and secured a large number of convictions for contempt of court in violating the no-act, no-speak provisions of the federal injunction. Other convictions were obtained in state courts on evidence turned over to state authorities by the Bureau's agents. And the strike of the railroad shopmen was broken.[3]

■ 2 ■

More laudable, during this period, were the activities of the Bureau in helping to crack the power of the Knights of the Ku Klux Klan, a white-sheeted secret order that had become a national menace. The Klan was frankly anti-Negro, anti-Catholic, and anti-Jew, and it acquired such fanatic power that it came in time to dominate entire legislatures and to wield such political power that, in many states, a candidate simply could not be elected to public office unless he had Klan support.

Of Southern origin, the Klan in the years from 1920 to 1925 swept the nation in an orgy of white-sheeted madness. It was a dominating political force in Indiana; it reportedly controlled the Texas legislature; it marshaled great strength throughout the Middle Atlantic and New England states. Leading citizens in hundreds of communities joined the Klan and masqueraded around at night in bedsheets, cavorting about fiery crosses. Some were perhaps merely kicking up their heels in a second childhood. For others, the Klan was serious—and remunerative—business.

The original Klan had been founded in the South in the Reconstruction period following the Civil War. Its purpose had been to terrorize the Negro, to drive out the rascally carpetbaggers from the North, and to reestablish the supremacy of the Southern white ruling class. In its accomplishment of these purposes, the original Klan had demonstrated that the soul of the fiend and the murderer often took refuge behind its bedsheets and its oaths of secrecy. Eventually, public revulsion at its excesses undercut its power and brought a slow death.

The memory of the Klan, and traces of Klan allegiance and psychology, lingered on, however, in the South. And in 1915 Colonel William S. Simmons, of Atlanta, Georgia, started up a revival movement based on the most virulent kind of racial and religious prejudice. He made little progress until 1920 when he joined forces with Edward Young Clarke, a publicity man who had managed World War I membership drives for such worthy causes as the YMCA and the Red Cross. Simmons made Clarke an Imperial Kleagle, and Clarke sent his salesmen, all suddenly anointed as Kleagles too, out across the land in a drive to drum up membership. Under his contract with Simmons, the Klan's Imperial Wizard, Clarke and his organization kept $8 out of every $10 initiation fee; the other $2 went to Simmons. The pair also divided up the $6.50 they charged the brethren for their bedsheet robes. The loot was stupendous enough to stagger the imagination. Anyone with a memory of those times can recall district Kleagles, previously poor and humble persons, who caught the gravy train of fanaticism, cashed in for a few brief years, and never really had to work again.

This mushroom growth of an order that appealed to man's prejudice and passions had attracted the attention of the Bureau of Investigation, whose agents had checked into the activities of the Klan without uncovering any violation of federal law. Then, according to Whitehead, J. Edgar Hoover was sitting in his office one day in September, 1922, when a journalist came to see him with a fantastic tale. The journalist was Paul Wooton, Washington correspondent for the *New Orleans Times-Picayune,* who had been working on an exposé of the Klan and had just returned from Louisiana. He told Hoover that the Klan was riding roughshod across the state and that even the Governor was its helpless prisoner.

"Do you mean to say the Governor of Louisiana can't even use the telephone, telegraph, or the United States mails because of the Klan?" Hoover exclaimed, according to Whitehead.

"That's just what the Governor told me personally when he sent for me to come to Louisiana," Wooton answered. He handed Hoover a letter given him by Governor John M. Parker. "I brought you this letter because Governor Parker can't trust the mails. His mail is watched by the Klan and his telephone is tapped by Klansmen. He needs help."

Governor Parker's letter was addressed to Attorney General Daugherty. Just as Wooton had said, it asked help. The Klan, the Governor reported, held all of northern Louisiana in a grip of terror. It made its own rules, superior to the law. Men and women who offended it were flogged or jailed on trumped-up charges. Residents who opposed it or incurred its enmity literally were run out of their communities. In one especially vicious case, two men had been reported kidnaped, tortured, and murdered by Klansmen. But the Governor was helpless because, as he later wrote in his formal application for federal intervention, "a number of law officers and others charged with the enforcement of the law in this State are publicly recognized as members of the Ku Klux Klan."

With Hoover playing the leading role, arrangements were made to send Bureau of Investigation agents into Louisiana. It was, for the Klan, the beginning of the end. The cooperation of the Bureau's agents with untainted local authorities led to prosecutions and, more important, to public exposure of the viciousness of the Klan. In New Orleans, the Bureau's agents caught up with Imperial Kleagle Clarke, who was subsequently indicted in Houston, Texas, on a white slavery charge. He pleaded guilty in March, 1924, and was fined $5,000. The Klan, at the time, was at the height of its power, but with the prosecution of Kleagle Clarke and others, the end was in sight.

In a climactic demonstration of its political strength, the Klan paraded 50,000 white-sheeted marchers along Pennsylvania Avenue in Washington in 1925, but already the organization was like a straw man losing its stuffing. Swift as had been the Klan's rise, just as swift was its eclipse. By the end of the decade, the frenzy and force had gone out of the movement, and though remnants were to continue sporadically active for years, the Klan as a disease of the American mind and spirit was dead.

The Bureau's attack on the Klan marked one of its few notable achievements during these years in which, in the mire of the Harding regime, the debit side of the ledger grew to unconscionable length. Ironically, to torture Shakespeare, the good that accrued lives on and is attributed to Hoover; the evil is interred with the past and, anyway, was the work of "those other fellows." Whitehead's handling of the Klan episode illustrates the double standard. Hoover emerges, no doubt deservedly, as the hero of the Klan saga; but it is conveniently overlooked that Hoover at the same time retained the reins of GID and functioned as the No. 2 Bureau commander, usually the man most concerned with the handling of assignments and detail. Jess Smith and Gaston Means were, of course, laws unto themselves and Daugherty; nevertheless, the involvement of the No. 2 chief in many of the less admirable activities of the Bureau would seem all but inescapable.

Congressional criticism that was to build up into a full-scale investigation of the Justice Department first arose in charges that the government had been the victim of multimillion-dollar fleecing on war contracts. Former Supreme Court Justice Charles Evans Hughes had investigated airplane contracts and charged widespread wrongdoing. The Bureau of Investigation took up the trail, followed it, dropped it. Congressmen, suspecting there had been a fix somewhere along the line, endeavored in their probe to find out what had happened. A former agent, H. L. Scaife, who had gathered the evidence on the fraudulent airplane contracts, took the witness stand and testi-

fied that, as soon as he began to get close to pay dirt, "it was apparent
it was going to be blocked." Abruptly, Scaife said, he received an
order to forget all about those dirty old airplane contracts and begin
a bread investigation.

"An investigation of what?" his inquisitors asked in astonishment.

"Of bread—food. . . . I had already dug up cases with audits
complete, showing where the government had been defrauded to the
amount of $25 million at that time. And I got instructions to go
ahead with the bread investigation. I paid absolutely no attention to
those instructions."

"Who gave you those instructions?"

"I think it was Mr. Hoover, of Mr. Burns's office." [4]

The Republicans were so strongly entrenched in Congress that
the Harding Administration was able to fight off several attempts to
launch an investigation of the Justice Department. But when Democratic critics probed Teapot Dome, they struck an oily and irresistible
gusher, one that was to hoist the entire Administration on a black
cloud of scandal. The background was this:

The Navy possessed huge oil reserves in California and Wyoming.
Soon after taking office, Harding had turned the administration of
these reserves over to Interior Secretary Albert B. Fall. He, in turn,
promptly signed a contract with private interests headed by Harry
F. Sinclair and Edward L. Doheny permitting them to pump and
store oil on a royalty basis—a neat little arrangement that, as was
soon to be charged, gave the private oilmen almost carte blanche
authority to loot the naval oil reserves.

Shortly after this official and private meeting of minds, neighbors
in New Mexico noted that Fall's ranch was undergoing an expensive
face-lifting. Montana's Senator Walsh, in one of the most sensational
Congressional probes in history, blew the lid off the Teapot Dome
scandal. And Sinclair and Doheny, in language that seems to have
been preserved in carbon-copy form to the present day, explained
that they had simply "loaned" Fall some $135,000. Doheny, who put
up $100,000 of the "loan," explained (in words that Bernard Gold-
fine would have appreciated) that the money had been "simply an
accommodation to an old friend."

The Teapot Dome disclosures rocked the country. No scandal

since—not the Truman Administration's mink coats, not the Adams vicuña cloth—has created such upheaval. The Attorney General and the Justice Department were squarely in the line of fire, zeroed in by Congressional artillery. Where, asked Congressional critics, had been the watchdog of Justice while the naval oil reserves were being looted? Had he been sleeping? Or had he blinked both eyes shut? The school of thought that favored the deliberate-blinking theory recalled that there had been charges of mishandling funds in the Veterans Administration, and nothing had been done about it; also charges of graft in the Alien Property Custodian's office, and nothing had been done about it. Why?

It was a good question. Too good a question. A lot of people, it became apparent, didn't care to answer.

In the midst of the bursting and brewing scandals, the mysterious Jess Smith committed suicide on May 30, 1923. For an obscure man, he left behind him considerable wealth, an estate estimated at $500,000. Not long afterward, on a trip to Alaska, President Harding became ill, and on August 2, 1923, he died suddenly. Close-mouthed Calvin Coolidge became President. "Silent Cal" was no reformer. He appears to have hoped that the nasty mess would all just go away if nobody said anything or did anything. He appears to have tried to accomplish nothing so hard as to sit on the lid. One prime example of his lid-sitting was his retention of the Daugherty-Burns regime in the Department of Justice.

But the time had passed when the fires of scandal could be smothered. Montana had sent a second fire-breathing senator to Washington to join Walsh—Burton K. Wheeler. On February 20, 1924, Wheeler, a freshman who, according to protocol, should have been seen but not heard, rose in the Senate to make his maiden speech. It was a speech that defied all tradition, and of it one thing can be said with certainty: no maiden speech uttered in that august chamber ever surpassed it for sensation. For Wheeler delivered an all-out attack on the Daugherty regime. He arraigned the Department of Justice for "protecting" instead of detecting "the greatest crooks and those guilty of the greatest crimes against the nation that have ever been perpetrated." It was, wrote the late Paul Y. Anderson of the *St. Louis Post-Dispatch,* "an attack so savage that even the Senate flinched." [5]

The Senate may have flinched—but it could hardly ignore the flat charge that the Department of Justice was in active league with crooks in high places. A special committee chaired by Senator Smith W. Brookhart, of Iowa, with Wheeler acting as counsel and grand inquisitor, was appointed to hold public hearings into the malfeasances of the Daugherty regime. The fat was in the fire, in more ways than one. Daugherty had become the Senate's target—and Wheeler had become Daugherty's.

■ 3 ■

The counterattack against Wheeler—and against other members of Congress who supported him—was launched almost before the echoes of his voice had died away in the Senate chamber. Within three days, a determined smear campaign had begun to paint Wheeler as a "Red."

"Senator Wheeler denies that he is 'socialistic' in his views," said a New York newspaper in a Washington dispatch.[6]

The news item cited partisan attacks made on Wheeler by some of the press in Montana because he had "publicly allied himself with the seditious and treasonable Non-Partisan League"; because as a federal attorney he had failed to prosecute some of the anarchists rounded up in the World War I hysteria; and because he had attacked both Attorney General Palmer and Daugherty for "their campaigns against the Communists." The haymaker was swung in these words: "Last summer Mr. Wheeler made a trip to Russia and later made a speech in Baltimore in which he advocated immediate recognition of Russia. . . . Altogether Wheeler is well known here as a radical of radicals. Probably no man in Congress has such radical tendencies with the exception of Senator La Follette of Wisconsin."

Parenthetically, an obeisance in the general direction of sanity might be made here. If any lesson is needed on the dangers of categorizing ideas, this is it. Senator Wheeler, this "radical of radicals" in 1924, was to become in a short span of years the darling of the conservatives. They loved him when he helped lead the fight on Roosevelt's court-packing plan in 1937; they adored him when he balked at the third term; and when he opposed foreign entanglements on the eve of World War II, the enchantment of America Firsters knew no bounds. Wheeler, *then,* was hailed as a great American patriot, and Republicans even mumbled in their beards about the possibility of making him *their* candidate for the Presidency.

This eminently safe statesman of later years had, however, not yet emerged from the chrysalis of the developing politician in 1924. The Republican National Committee, taking up the theme first planted and tested in the press, tried to disparage any inquiry of Daugherty before it could get started by intimating that Wheeler was a dangerous American Bolshevik. During Wheeler's term as United States Attorney in Montana, the committee declared, that state "became a hot bed of treason and sedition, the leaders in the seditious and treasonable movement being friends of Wheeler's." [7] This propaganda and the desperation that inspired it were transparent. Wheeler and Brookhart, undeterred, drove full speed ahead with the Daugherty probe.

When they did, senators and congressmen became themselves targets of the Bureau of Investigation. The fears of the Sixtieth Congress that the Bureau would become so powerful that it could be turned against Congress itself, the tales of spying and mail-opening in Theodore Roosevelt's time—such events now became the living, glaring, everyday reality. The names of Congressional critics of the Bureau were placed on a "suspect" list, and detectives were turned loose to trail them, to bribe their servants, to ransack their offices. No tactic was too low to be employed in the desperate campaign to dig up some scandal that might be used to silence a critical voice in Congress.

This legislative espionage was subsequently admitted by the Bureau's own operatives. It was described in detail, though no full list of its "subjects" ever became available. "We took testimony," Wheeler wrote in his autobiography, "that Department of Justice agents had ransacked the offices of Senators Thaddeus H. Caraway and Robert M. La Follette and Representative Roy O. Woodruff, a progressive Michigan Republican.

"My own office was rifled during the hearings on several occasions. Government-hired detectives hung around the committee's offices constantly. . . . Some of our witnesses were approached to find out what testimony they would give. Others were shadowed. J. Edgar Hoover, then assistant chief of the Bureau of Investigation, sat next to Daugherty's defense counsels throughout the hearings."[8]

In other accounts of the time, one encounters the omnipresent figure of Hoover. Just as he had sat at the elbow of Palmer during the investigation of the Red Raids, so he now dutifully aligned himself with the defense of the discredited Daugherty during the Brookhart-Wheeler probe of the Justice Department. There are indications that his presence at the defense table could hardly have been reassuring to Bureau personnel compelled to testify before the Senate committee. Samuel Hopkins Adams, in his book on the Harding period, recounted the experience of one female employee of the Bureau who had been served with a committee subpoena. She had to testify or face a contempt citation, but this legal compulsion did nothing to exculpate her in the eyes of her employers. "The next day," Adams wrote, "she received a letter from J. Edgar Hoover, Acting Director of the Bureau, peremptorily demanding her resignation." [9]

Such pressures buttoned the lips of many Bureau employees who wished to keep their jobs, but they could not silence all. One who certainly was not silenced was Gaston B. Means. A brash, blustering, swaggering rogue, Means evidently tried to play both sides of the street, offering Wheeler information at the same time that he was trying to ferret out from Wheeler for the benefit of Daugherty just what moves the committee planned next. Wheeler, telling him nothing, using him for what information he might drop, called Means to the witness stand early in the probe. Preening himself in the spotlight, Means described to the senators, with an obvious relish, the widespread investigation the department had conducted into their official and private lives. Means said he had delivered his reports on this espionage to the departed Jess Smith, now a vital missing link in the chain; he made no secret about the methods he had employed. Describing techniques for spying on United States Senators, he testified:

Oh, [you] search his . . . find out all the mail that comes in, all the papers, anything that he has got lying around. Find out in his home. Just like you would take . . . the same principle that you pursue, Senator, when you make a criminal investigation. There is a servant working in this house. If she is a colored servant, go and get a colored detective woman take her out; have this colored detective woman to entertain her, find out the exact plan of the house, everything they discuss at the table, the family, write it down, make a report. And any information you find that is . . . report what you find . . . and then if it is damaging, why of course it is used. If it is fine, why you cannot use it. It does no damage.[10]

Means said "the next question was" to find what a senator might have in his office," and he acknowledged frankly "I had people" ransack senatorial offices. The committee endeavored to find out how many senators had been honored with such attentions. At one point in the questioning, Wheeler said to Means:

"Senator Moses [of New Hampshire] suggests to me that I can save time by asking you what senators you have not investigated."

"Oh, there are lots of them I haven't," Means replied reassuringly. "They are a pretty clean body. You don't find much on them, either. You don't find very much."

This testament to senatorial virtue, coming from the lips of the rogue on the witness stand, did not exactly mollify the senators. Irate at the shadowing by detectives, at the illegal search of their offices, at the bald-faced attempt to discover scandals that could be used to blackmail them into silence, they erupted in angry outbursts on the Senate floor. Senator Thomas H. Heflin, of Alabama, put it this way:

> These detectives went through the office of the Senator from Arkansas and they read his correspondence; they went through the office of the Senator from Wisconsin; and God only knows how many other offices they went through. That was a general "fishing expedition"; it was fishing in the night, when Senators were at home asleep; but the Department of Justice was awake, and its smooth and alert detectives were quietly going through the offices of United States Senators.

Senator Henry F. Ashurst, a member of the investigating committee, was even more indignant:

> Illegal plots, counterplots, espionage, decoys, dictographs, thousand-dollar bills, and the exploring of Senators' offices come and go in the pages of this testimony; and these devices, these plots, counterplots, spies, thousand-dollar bills, and ubiquitous detectives were not employed . . . to detect and prosecute crime, but were frequently em-

ployed to shield profiteers, bribe takers, and favorites. The spying upon Senators, the attempt to intimidate them . . . are disclosed by this record.

The outcry was too much for Coolidge. Out of his own inertia, out of a sense of loyalty to Harding, out of disinclination to take action and so admit the existence of another major scandal, he had retained Daugherty, but the Wheeler exposures called for action. On March 28, 1924, Coolidge demanded and received the resignation of Daugherty. Burton Wheeler, the hell-raising freshman Senator from Montana, had brought down his powerful adversary. He had scored a sensational victory. But it was a victory for which he was to be made to pay.

■ **4** ■

Weeks before his own enforced departure from Coolidge's Cabinet, Daugherty had set in motion forces which he hoped and intended would discredit Wheeler. Bureau of Investigation detectives had been dispatched to Montana for the express purpose of digging up some kind of criminal charge on which Wheeler could be indicted. Independent testimony on this endeavor is offered by Alpheus Thomas Mason in his monumental life of Harlan Fiske Stone, whom Coolidge selected to succeed Daugherty as Attorney General. In 1951, in preparing the Stone biography, Mason corresponded with Mrs. Mabel Walker Willebrandt, who had been an assistant in the Justice Department during the Daugherty regime.

"I think there is not the slightest doubt," Mrs. Willebrandt wrote, "that Daugherty broke the Wheeler case prematurely in order to *discredit* Wheeler in his charges against Daugherty and Harding."

When rumors broke that Wheeler was about to "blow the lid off" the Harding Administration, Mrs. Willebrandt wrote, "Daugherty came to the Department, summoned Burns and other investigators and the United States Attorney, and worked feverishly with Rush Holland and other political appointees to bring an indictment against Wheeler *before* Wheeler brought his whispered charges out in the open." [11]

Wheeler moved so fast with his committee hearings that it proved impossible for Daugherty to beat him to the punch. But the punch, though delayed, was still to be delivered. Daugherty had been in his forced retirement from public life less than two weeks—and Stone had been Attorney General for just six days—when, on April 8, 1924, a federal grand jury in Montana indicted Senator Wheeler on a charge of violating a federal statute by using his office to get oil and gas leases for Gordon Campbell, a loud-talking Montana prospector who bragged that he had discovered the first oil well in the state.

The indictment was based on Wheeler's admitted retainer by Campbell as one of his attorneys. A flamboyant character, Campbell had become embroiled in some twenty law suits in Montana courts while amassing his oil and gas empire. Two months after Wheeler was elected United States Senator, Campbell paid him a retainer of $10,000 for legal services in Montana courts. Wheeler contended there was nothing secret about the transaction, that it had been widely publicized in Montana, where he had tried one major case for Campbell, and that there was no conflict of interest since he was not representing Campbell on the federal level. The government insisted that, on at least one occasion, he had been in contact with the Department of the Interior to make an appointment for Campbell and that this showed, in effect, that Campbell had purchased a United States Senator to represent him in Washington.

Wheeler, always a good bare-knuckle scrapper, exploded in righteous anger. He stormed before the Senate and demanded that his fellow senators investigate the propriety of his conduct. "The indictment is merely the latest illustration of the corruption of the Department of Justice," he said. He appealed to the Senate "to put a stop to this spy system—to put a stop to this 'framing' of every man." [12]

The New York Times reported that a veritable army of investigators had been sent into Montana for the Wheeler investigation, including detectives from the Department of Justice, the Post Office Department, and "other state and federal" operatives.[13] Daugherty flatly insisted that the Justice Department had had nothing to do with procuring the indictment of Wheeler, picturing it as the zealous and otherwise unmotivated action of the United States Attorney in Montana.

It was a pretense that lasted only long enough for Senate investigators to get William J. Burns on the witness stand. The Chief of the Bureau of Investigation was in an unenviable spot. His departed boss and long-time friend, Daugherty, had laid down the party line, but it was a line to which Burns, under oath, simply could not adhere. A hammering cross fire of questions brought from him a series of damaging admissions. He had sent, he admitted, three Bureau agents into Montana to build the case against Wheeler; he had taken this action "three or four weeks ago" (in other words, after Wheeler had attacked Daugherty); and he had reported directly to Daugherty what the agents had discovered about Wheeler. His testimony made it clear that Wheeler had been the target of a Department of Justice vendetta, and Burns plainly realized the damage his testimony was doing. His "face was ashen when he made the admissions," *The New York Times* reported.[14]

The Senate committee received additional testimony about the plot against Wheeler from W. O. Duckstein, private secretary to Edward M. McLean, then the playboy publisher of the *Washington Post*. McLean had been one of the hangers-on of the Harding Administration, had been rewarded with an honorary Bureau badge, and so presumably had been in a position to learn some inside Administration secrets. It therefore seemed significant when Duckstein, his secretary, testified that two men who identified themselves as Bureau agents had told him, in advance of the event, that they were out to "frame" Wheeler. The agents had added that they were being sent into the home states of other senators, that "they were looking into the records of the members of the committee, watching them all," Duckstein testified.

One member of the committee commented that he thought "the less attention we pay to it the better," but Chairman Brookhart disagreed, saying: "Well, I do not think so, Senator. I think it is time to find out what this government by blackmail is; it is an important thing to know and investigate."

With the Senate committee exposing so thoroughly the vengeful power play that Daugherty had initiated against Wheeler, the deposed Attorney General found it impossible to practice the discretion of silence. In a speech in Columbus, Ohio, on April 23, 1924, he struck

a note that has been sounded many times since whenever the Bureau
of Investigation or the FBI has been exposed to criticism—the charge
that he was the victim of a Soviet-inspired plot. Daugherty noted
that the Brookhart-Wheeler committee had asked for the confidential
files of the Bureau of Investigation. Exhibiting the tender regard for
those files that has been characteristic almost every time the subject
is mentioned, the former Attorney General struck a patriotic pose
and declared that he had refused to open the files. He had resigned
first, he said, because the files "contained abundant proof of the plans,
purpose, and hellish design of the Communist Internationale." Some
might have thought that it would be a good idea to bring such devilish
machinations out into the broad light of day, to expose them—but
not Daugherty. He preferred to tell his listeners about what those
secret files contained. "I would sound a warning note to every American tonight," he thundered. "The enemy is at the gate. He aims at
nothing short of the overthrow of the institutions which are your
protection and mine against tyranny, whether exercised in the name
of a monarchy or in the name of a mob."

This was one cry of alarm that failed to accomplish its purpose.
By the time it was uttered, Daugherty had been so thoroughly discredited that not even a phony Red scare could refurbish him.
Discarded, Daugherty was swept into the backwash of fast-moving
events.

His successor, Attorney General Stone, was from the first dis-
quieted by the performance of Burns and the Bureau of Investigation.
He knew that the Bureau was riddled with incompetents, political
hacks, downright crooks. He recognized the imperative need of a
new broom to clean out the house. The first step was to fire Burns.
On May 9 the new Attorney General called Burns to his office and
asked for his resignation. Burns refused, but Stone was not to be
trifled with. "Perhaps you had better think it over," he warned as
Burns left his office. Burns thought—and resigned.

According to Mason, Stone had been considering whom he might
name to replace Burns. He wanted someone with police experience,
yet a man not steeped in the "more usual police tradition that it takes
a crook to catch a crook, and that lawlessness and brutality are more
to be relied upon than skill and special training." New to the person-

nel of the Bureau, Stone realized that he was handicapped in reaching a decision, and so he sought advice from knowledgeable persons within the Administration. According to Whitehead, one of those with whom Stone discussed his problem was Herbert Hoover, then Secretary of Commerce. Herbert Hoover, after talking with Stone at a Cabinet meeting, returned to his office and mentioned the new Attorney General's problem to his aide, Larry Richey.

"Why should they look around when they have the man they need right over there now—a young, well-educated lawyer named Hoover?" Richey asked.

"You think he can do the job?" Herbert Hoover asked.

"I know he can. He's a good friend of mine," Richey replied.

Herbert Hoover passed the word along to Stone. The Attorney General already had been impressed by J. Edgar Hoover's energy and competence, and he decided to doublecheck his impressions with veterans in the department. One morning he asked Mrs. Willebrandt what she thought of young Hoover. She replied that she "regarded Hoover as honest and informed and one who operated like an electric wire, with almost trigger response."

"Everyone says he's too young," Stone said, "but maybe that's his asset. Apparently, he hasn't learned to be afraid of the politicians, and I believe he would set up a group of young men as investigators and infuse them with a will to operate independent of congressional and political pressure." [15]

The result was that, on May 10, 1924, the day after Burns had been fired, Hoover received a summons to Stone's office. The Attorney General, a huge block of a man, more than six feet tall and weighing more than 200 pounds, studied Hoover impassively for a moment, then told the young man he had been selected to be Acting Director of the Bureau of Investigation.

For Hoover, only twenty-nine, it was an overwhelming honor. It was also a tremendous vote of confidence. But Hoover did not leap instantly to snatch the prize.

Obviously, he had considered this possibility well in advance, and he had made up his mind about the circumstances under which he would take the job. And so he told Stone he would accept, but only under "certain conditions."

Asked to spell these out, Hoover did. He told Stone he must have full authority over hiring and firing; the Bureau must be divorced completely from politics; appointment and promotion must be placed solely on a merit basis.

Stone replied that he would not let Hoover take the job under any other conditions.[16]

It was a historic moment.

■ 5 ■

In a memorandum to Hoover on May 13, Stone outlined a program that was to become virtually the charter of the Bureau and the FBI. Stone stressed six points. The first and perhaps most important provided that "the activities of the Bureau are to be limited strictly to investigations of violations of the law." Henceforth there would be no ransacking of senators' offices; no GID to classify the possibly wayward thoughts in men's minds.

Other reforms on Stone's list called for the reduction of Bureau personnel as far as practical, the weeding out of "the incompetent and unreliable," the dismissal of "dollar-a-year men" and "honorary" badge holders, and the appointment as agents of "men of known good character and ability, giving preference to men who have some legal training." The Bureau at all times was to conduct investigations only under the direction of the Attorney General or an assigned assistant.

In a public statement Stone expressed a philosophy of law enforcement with which it would be difficult to quarrel. He pointed out that the enormous expansion of federal legislation made the Bureau "a necessary instrument of law enforcement." But he added that it was important for the Bureau's activities to be limited to such functions "and that its agents themselves be not above the law or beyond its reach." He continued:

> The Bureau of Investigation is not concerned with political or other opinions of individuals. It is concerned only with their conduct and then only with such conduct as is forbidden by the laws of the United States. When a police system passes beyond these limits, it is dangerous to the proper administration of justice and to human liberty, which it

should be our first concern to cherish. Within them it should rightly be a terror to the wrongdoer.

The Brookhart-Wheeler committee, evidently wanting to make assurance doubly sure, called Hoover before it on May 15, 1924, and questioned him about the Bureau's future role. Hoover told the committee that the Bureau's activities had been cut back and restricted "absolutely" to violations of federal law. Several times, responding in slightly different ways to differently worded questions, Hoover reiterated this assurance.

On the same day that Hoover testified, the separate Senate committee that had been examining the question of Wheeler's personal ethics in the Campbell affair presented its report to the Senate. The committee, headed by the veteran William E. Borah, "wholly exonerated" Wheeler. It reported that he had been careful from the beginning to make it known he was representing Campbell only in Montana courts, and it concluded that "he observed at all times not only the letter but the spirit of the law." This judgment was approved by the Senate by a vote of 56–5, and four of the chamber's leading figures— Borah, Walsh, George W. Norris (the great liberal), and James A. Reed (brilliant and witty and known as one of the Senate's foremost debaters)—volunteered to serve as Wheeler's counsel when the case against him was brought to trial in Montana.

Implicit in the action was a challenge to the ethics of the new Stone-Hoover regime in the Justice Department. Few observers at the time believed there was any validity to the charges. Paul Y. Anderson, one of the most famous Washington correspondents of his day, wrote in the *Raleigh News and Observer* that the federal detectives had simply concocted their charges against Wheeler. The *Philadelphia North American* declared: "It is doubtful if there is presented in the history of government in this country a blacker page than this." Felix Frankfurter and others eminent in the law and public life urged Stone to drop the charges against Wheeler. But, in the face of almost universal sentiment, Stone turned stubborn. (Mason, his biographer, argues that the new Attorney General, with his scrupulous respect for the law, felt that the processes of justice should be allowed to take their course without interference from him; and that, in the face of what appeared to be overwhelming evidence,

Wheeler was not as simon-pure as the Senate's report indicated and legitimate legal issues of major importance were involved. This seems to be partisan reasoning.)

Stone went on to eminence and high honor as Supreme Court Justice and Chief Justice, but his handling of the red-hot political issue posed by the Wheeler case hardly rates as one of his more scrupulous achievements. Instead of administering to the charges the *coup de grâce* they so patently deserved, Stone ordered an entirely new investigation. He appointed Assistant Attorney General William J. Donovan (later known as "Wild Bill" Donovan of World War II OSS fame) to bring the entire Wheeler case before a second grand jury in Washington. This jury, after hearing numerous witnesses and refusing to indict, finally was pressured and persuaded into indicting Wheeler a second time. It was charged, with reason, that this action represented a determination on the part of the Republican administration to hold a second club over Wheeler's head, even if he should be acquitted in Montana. This placing of a United States Senator in double jeopardy for the same offense seemed a clear indication that the supposedly purified Justice Department was going down the line in defense of the skunk cabbage nurtured by the Daugherty regime.

What role did Hoover and the Bureau play in all this?

The question is important since so much of the unquestioning current faith in the FBI rests on the conviction that Hoover himself, though he held sensitive command posts under Palmer and Daugherty, would never have countenanced the least compromise with the principles of pure and impartial justice. Whitehead, in a reference note in *The FBI Story,* presents the Hoover defense. This is simply that he did not know, even after he became Acting Director of the Bureau, exactly what was happening. Whitehead quotes an April 8, 1928, memorandum from Hoover to Donovan in which, he says, Hoover "outlined his views on the misuse of agents in the Wheeler case."

According to the memorandum, the three Bureau agents whom Burns admitted having dispatched into Montana were assigned to John S. Pratt, Special Assistant to the Attorney General. Hoover contended that, during this period when such agents were on special assignment, they were detached from Bureau control. "I didn't know where the accountants or Special Agents were," he wrote. "And it was only after several months that I was able to have orders issued which would at least enable me to know where these men were. . . . I did not even then assume direction of their investigative work nor see any of their reports nor know what they were doing."

It is an explanation that conveniently ignores the federal activity that produced the second indictment of Wheeler. It does not accord with the story that the records of the time seem to tell.

Not until a full year after the first indictment was voted, eleven months after Hoover became head of the Bureau, was Wheeler brought to trial in Great Falls, Montana. On the eve of the trial, *The New York Times* carried an intriguing story. It found Great Falls swarming with federal agents. It estimated the number of agents on hand as ranging from ten to thirty. "What they are doing here and what possible emergency makes their presence necessary are matters of conjecture," the account said. And it added: "From reputable sources, the *New York Times* correspondent has been informed that the Department of Justice sought to work up a case against Senator Thomas J. Walsh. It is said that Justice agents, while working on the Wheeler case, made inquiries as to whether there was any hope of involving Senator Walsh." [17]

Wheeler, in his autobiography, painted a similar picture. He wrote:

> When the first trial opened in Great Falls, Montana, it looked like a Justice Department convention. My friends counted some 25 to 30 agents on the main streets.
>
> I discovered I had many loyal friends in Great Falls. One night I received a telephone call in my hotel room from a stranger asking me if I would be interested in reports of the nightly telephone conversations between the Justice Department in Washington and the special prosecutor in the case. Naturally, I was. The caller said that if I was in the room at a certain time every night he would give me a fill-in. The long-distance telephone calls turned out to be fairly routine progress reports to J. Edgar Hoover; they proved only that the Bureau chief was keeping close tabs on the trial. [18]

Walsh, the brilliant prosecutor of Teapot Dome fame, was Wheeler's defense counsel, and he tore the government's case to shreds. "The evidence such as the government has introduced in this case would not be used to condemn a streetwalker or a jailbird," Walsh told the jury in summation. He pointed out that one main government witness had been convicted of mail fraud in Texas; another, a surprise witness on whom the government had pinned great hopes, had been exposed as an arrant perjurer who had told one story before the Senate committee, another at Wheeler's trial. Significantly, he was also a man over whom the Justice Department held a club when it asked him to testify, since judgments totaling over $300,000 for federal income tax violations had been lodged against him. Of such spurious stuff, a year after Stone and Hoover supposedly had purified the Justice Department and the Bureau, was the case on which the government staked its reputation in Montana. The jury deliberated for less than ten minutes, took one ballot, and acquitted Wheeler. H. L. Mencken wrote an appropriate epitaph to the whole shabby performance in his column in the *Baltimore Sun*. "After filling the newspapers with fulminations for weeks on end," he said, "all the Daugherty gang could produce at Great Falls was a lot of testimony so palpably nonsensical and perjured that the jury laughed at it."

More than a jury's derisive laughter was needed, however, to change the vengeful mood of government. There remained the second indictment voted in Washington, the indictment that had been engineered by Donovan and was the sole product of Stone's regime. Stone had been appointed to the Supreme Court by Coolidge before the Montana trial ended in fiasco, but the Justice Department he had left behind him evidently had no qualms of conscience about the campaign to "get" Wheeler. The government was still hell-bent on a second Washington prosecution of its arch senatorial critic; but a District of Columbia judge, who heard legal arguments brought by Wheeler's defense, quashed the indictment as so defective it never should have been voted. Only then, reluctantly, did the department abandon its campaign of retaliation.

This collapse of the legal vendetta against Wheeler was not the end of the story. When Stone's appointment to the Supreme Court came before the Senate in late January, 1925, Walsh made it clear that he had not been reconciled to the bald-faced attempt to frame

Wheeler and the veiled threats posed against himself. In a series of sharp questions, he drew from Stone the admission that the personnel of the department had not been greatly changed from the days of Daugherty. Walsh named one Daugherty appointee after another, capping the series by demanding: "Mr. Hoover was a subordinate to William J. Burns during all the time the latter was the head of the Bureau of Investigation?" Stone, unperturbed, replied: "He was." The Attorney General took the position that he had retained men on their merits, not on the degree of their relations with the Daugherty regime. Stone's character and evident sincerity impressed everyone; and, despite the bitter feelings the Wheeler case had engendered in the Senate, the Attorney General was confirmed for the high court.

Stone's probity, thus recognized by the Senate, was never afterward to be questioned. This circumstance merely compounds the conundrum: How did a man of Stone's character let himself be enmeshed in the clearly vicious campaign against Wheeler? The answer seems to lie in the bureaucratic pressures that so often operate from beneath to deceive and mold the judgment of the man at the top. In 1950, Wheeler, in a letter to Stone's biographer, A. T. Mason, expressed his conviction that Stone had been duped by his own aides. "He and I afterwards became very good friends," Wheeler wrote. "I think he was an honest, honorable, able man, and I believe that the only way you can account for the handling of the case against me after he became Attorney General was that he was lied to by the people in the department." [19] In his autobiography, Wheeler revealed the basis for this belief. On one occasion, he wrote, Senator John B. Kendrick asked Stone point-blank why he had continued with the Wheeler prosecution. "They lied to me," Stone told Kendrick.[20]

Who was responsible for the deception? On this key question, Wheeler's attitude is strangely ambivalent. For years, in his conduct in the Senate, he appeared to blame Hoover. Now he seems to put the onus on Donovan, who at the time was working closely with Hoover but in the end became Hoover's rival in the field of secret information—and no great Hoover admirer. Wheeler's original attitude, one that endured for years, seems clearly expressed in a Senate speech he made in 1940 when he joined the last Congressional chorus to attack Hoover and the FBI. He said:

When I first came to Washington and began the investigation of the Department of Justice, Mr. Hoover was present at the investigation and hearings, and sat through them during the time the charges against Mr. Daugherty were being heard. Agents of the Department raided my offices; they broke into my offices . . . they stationed men at my house, surrounded my house, watched persons who went in and came out, constantly shadowed me, shadowed my house, and shadowed my wife. . . . During all that time there were in the Department of Justice . . . Burns and Mr. Hoover.[21]

This picture of Hoover at the center of the web seems to accord with the written accounts of the time, with the revelations of the Daugherty hearings, with Wheeler's own discoveries of Hoover's close supervision of the swarm of Special Agents at the Montana trial. But Wheeler now reports that, long years prior to his making this angry Senate speech, he had refused to demand Hoover's head when the Democratic Administration of Franklin D. Roosevelt came to power. Hoover, he writes, came to him and "insisted he played no part in the reprisals against me." Donovan, in this revised Wheeler version, shouldered all the blame.

Much evidence indicates that Wheeler's colleague from Montana, Senator Walsh, was not inclined to such chivalry toward either Donovan or Hoover. Walsh let it be known in 1929 that he would fight Donovan's proposed appointment as Attorney General in Herbert Hoover's Cabinet—and Donovan wasn't named. Similarly, political reports of the period agree that Walsh, who died suddenly before he could take office as Roosevelt's first Attorney General, had intended to remove Hoover from command of the Bureau. One thing is clear from Walsh's actions in the Senate: He never condoned any phase of the Wheeler prosecution or relented toward those connected with it, and he harassed the Republican Administration with a series of denunciations and accusatory resolutions. He demanded to know what the prosecution of Wheeler had cost the taxpayers and what action the Justice Department had taken against its star witness who had been trapped in bald-faced perjury on the witness stand. John G. Sargent, who had succeeded Stone as Attorney General, reported that the prosecution of Wheeler had cost more than $61,000, but he backed up Donovan in the refusal to disclose any information about the status of the government's prize perjurer.

It was not to be the last time that the protective mantle of the United States Department of Justice was to be cast about the person of a perjurer who had perjured in a department-favored cause.

◼ Notes ◼

[1] Jack Alexander in *The New Yorker,* Oct. 2, 1937.

[2] Max Lowenthal, *The Federal Bureau of Investigation* (William Sloane Associates, 1950), pp. 270–271.

[3] *Ibid.,* pp. 284–288.

[4] *Ibid.,* pp. 289–290.

[5] Burton K. Wheeler, *Yankee from the West* (Doubleday, 1962), pp. 213–214.

[6] *New York World-Telegram and Evening Mail,* Feb. 23, 1924.

[7] *New York Times,* Mar. 26, 1924.

[8] Wheeler, *op. cit.,* pp. 227–228.

[9] Samuel Hopkins Adams, *The Incredible Era, the Life and Times of Harding* (Houghton Mifflin, 1939), p. 330.

[10] Lowenthal, *op. cit.,* p. 291.

[11] Alpheus Thomas Mason, *Harlan Fiske Stone, Pillar of the Law* (Viking Press, 1956), see footnote p. 188.

[12] *New York Herald Tribune,* Apr. 10, 1924.

[13] *New York Times,* Apr. 8, 1924.

[14] *Ibid.,* Apr. 11, 1924.

[15] Mason, *op. cit.,* p. 150.

[16] Don Whitehead, *The FBI Story* (Random House, 1956), p. 78 of Pocket Books edition; and Alpheus Thomas Mason (*op. cit.,* pp. 150–151. Both had their versions from Hoover, and they agree on the essentials of this conversation. Whitehead's rendition, which has been largely followed here, is the more detailed and dramatic.

[17] *New York Times,* Apr. 14, 1925.

[18] Wheeler, *op. cit.,* p. 239.

[19] Mason, *op. cit.,* p. 191.

[20] Wheeler, *op. cit.,* p. 243.

[21] Lowenthal, *op. cit.,* p. 365.

5 The New Bureau

Three months after Franklin D. Roosevelt brought the New Deal to Washington, a newspaper article referred to the Bureau of Investigation as a department "little known . . . to the general public." Despite the Bureau's quarter-century of life, despite the sensational controversies in which it had been involved, the description was an accurate one, for the Bureau had made no impact on the public consciousness. Few persons outside official circles knew much about it. Fewer still had any idea that it was to become a household word invested with the trappings of glamour.[1]

Probably the major reason that so little was known publicly in 1933 about the organization was that its more controversial activities had been eliminated and its functions severely curtailed by the reforms Stone had initiated. For nine years, it had confined itself to the relatively limited field of federal law violations that then fell within its jurisdiction. It had had no opportunity to indulge in the dramatic forays against desperados and kidnapers that were to catapult its name into eight-column headlines.

The years out of the public limelight had not been wasted. They had been employed by Hoover—"the electric wire with trigger response" whom Mrs. Willebrandt had recommended to Stone—in a vigorous housecleaning that was to see the Bureau rebuilt in his own image. There can be little question that Hoover, a career man, detested the type of venal political influence that had disgraced the Bureau in the days of Daugherty and Burns. From the moment he took command, he was as anxious as Stone to rid himself and the organization that was now his of the pressures that had so badly corrupted it in the past. It was a program that had a double effect, if it did not have a double motive: it built the Bureau and, in building the Bureau, it built Hoover. Even the abolition of political pull, while salutary, had its side effect, for the Director, once freed from political interference and restraint, became a far more independent and powerful figure than he had been previously.

Whether Hoover foresaw at the outset how greatly a nonpolitical and purified Bureau would redound to his own advantage must remain a mystery, but there can be little question about the tremendous change for the better that he wrought as soon as he had the power of command. Whitehead, with his access to FBI records, convincingly documented the nature and extent of Hoover's Bureau-wide rebuilding.[2]

Whitehead and Mason both tell the story of an early and dramatic test of the no-politics rule. Hoover had transferred an agent who, he felt, had been too active in politics to a post in the Southwest, far removed from the malign influence of his native locale. Almost immediately, a senator came rumbling into Hoover's office, demanding that the agent be brought home because the senator needed him to help in a reelection campaign. Hoover was polite, but adamant. The senator took the matter up with Attorney General Stone, but Stone backed up the Bureau chief all the way.[3]

Such experiences, repeated in infinite variations but with the same invariable result, established Hoover's independent command of the Bureau. Even the skeptics among the Bureau's personnel came to recognize the reality and to understand that, if they wished to continue their careers, they must learn to govern their lives by Hoover's standards. And those standards were strict.

The martinet in Hoover, the meticulous care with dress, the almost religious puritanism regarding personal conduct—all these traits, so recognizable in the young Hoover who had learned discipline from a strict mother and had toyed with the prospect of becoming a minister—were now grafted on the Bureau. Agents were informed in emphatic terms that they must at all times be neat in dress and discreet in their personal habits. They must not drink (this was still the era of Prohibition). They must pay their debts promptly. Not only agents but clerks and stenographers were expected to live by this Spartan code, for Hoover was convinced that the impression employees gave by their appearance and conduct had much to do with the image that the public acquired of the Bureau.

"I am determined to summarily dismiss from this Bureau any employee whom I find indulging in the use of intoxicants to any degree or extent upon any occasion," Hoover wrote in a confidential letter to Special Agents in Charge in May, 1925.

He appreciated, he said, that this was "a very drastic attitude" and that he might be criticized as "a fanatic," but explained: "I do believe that when a man becomes a part of this Bureau he must so conduct himself, both officially and unofficially, as to eliminate the slightest possibility of criticism as to his conduct or actions." [4]

It was this stern regimen that Hoover imposed on the Bureau of Investigation. If it has today been carried to such excess (according to agents like Levine and Turner) that it has become a caricature of its original self, there can be no doubt that Hoover's action in setting high and impeccable standards created a new and much more praiseworthy FBI out of the ashes of the old and scandal-splattered bureau. Good men take pride in their work; they like to take pride in their organization. Hoover, by his tough and demanding standards, gave the men of the Bureau this pride in themselves and the agency to which they belonged. They were an elite outfit. No other law enforcement organization in the land adhered to such exacting standards. And so the man who made the grade in the Bureau under Hoover became, in his own eyes and the eyes of others, a special and higher order of being. Thus was built the esprit de corps that was to distinguish the FBI and that has endured, to a great degree, down to today.

The achievement was perhaps more remarkable in the context of the times. It was hardly an era on which the nation as a whole could look back with pride. The Prohibition Amendment, probably as disastrous a law as was ever enacted by a great nation, had bred cancers that continue to disfigure American life. It laid the foundation that, to the nation's shame, was to make crime and corruption two of the nation's largest enterprises. Of course, crime has always been a social problem, but the individual crimes and the rowdy city gangs of pre-Prohibition days, were kindergarten stuff compared to the modern national crime syndicate, bankrolled by illicit billions, possessed of its own enforcement arm, allotting territories and spheres of influence, decreeing life and death through its own tribunals—in a word, governing a clandestine and illicit underground life of America even as the national government governs legally by established rule. This development, then not yet fully apparent, was the outgrowth of of an unpopular law that it had become popular to flout. In the flouting, fantastic revenues poured into the laps of gangdom. Official life on every level became corrupted. Every town of any size had its speakeasies. The identities of the chief bookleggers were items of common knowledge. And the immunity of both speakeasies and bootleggers to the law meant simply that law enforcement officials in virtually every echelon, from the flatfoot on the beat to the district attorney in his plush office, were on the payroll of the mob.

Against such a background, in such an atmosphere, the incorruptible law enforcement agency stood out like a solitary powerful beacon on a black and stormy night. It was unique; it was tailor-made for hero worship.

■ 1 ■

Hoover's energy in face-lifting the Bureau had convinced Stone that he had made one of the wisest choices of his life in naming the young man acting director. After observing Hoover in action for seven months, Stone had made his appointment as Director permanent on October 10, 1924, and he never afterward wavered in his conviction that, in Hoover, he had given the Bureau a veritable genius as its commander. On January 2, 1932, long after he had left the Justice Department for the Supreme Court bench, Stone wrote Hoover a lavish testimonial of the younger man's great services.[5]

There were others, however, who were not so completely convinced. Many Democrats and independents, persons of liberal persuasion, looked askance at Hoover and the Bureau. They had not forgotten the Bureau's role in the attempted framing of Wheeler. They had not forgotten its strikebreaking activities and its tendency to pin the "radical" label indiscriminately on all progressive thought. And, though Stone had abolished Hoover's GID and brought a halt to the probing of men's minds, these critics recalled that, when the "bonus army" marched on Washington, President Herbert Hoover had denounced it as composed largely of "criminals or Communists." This statement reportedly had been based on information furnished the President by J. Edgar Hoover's Bureau.[6]

The result was that, when the New Deal came to Washington, there were persistent rumors that Director Hoover's days were numbered. Even after the death of Senator Walsh, who almost certainly would have replaced him, his tenure was by no means secure. His personal call on Wheeler, his disclaimer of personal responsibility in Wheeler's case, was an indication of his concern. So strong did the tide against him seem to be running that one news dispatch from Washington in mid-June 1933 flatly reported that the Bureau would be abolished and all federal investigative activities merged in a small, compact unit to be headed by Louis R. Glavis, then chief of the Interior Department's investigative divisions. "Mr. Hoover may be transferred to some field office, despite powerful political pressure to keep him at the head," the dispatch noted.[7]

This prospect, by all accounts, drove Hoover nearly frantic. He developed a positive phobia about Postmaster General James A. Farley, who, he felt, was out to get his scalp. The Washington political grapevine kept reporting that Farley, who had a close coterie of friends inside the New York Police Department, intended to bring some of his favorites to Washington to take over the high command of the Bureau. Even the name of the man whom Farley favored to step into Hoover's shoes was freely bruited about the capital. Hoover, according to the veteran New York journalist Guy Richards, who wrote a series on the FBI in 1948, reacted to the threat with counterthreat vigor. From agents who had been in the Bureau at the time, Richards obtained some insiders' views of the tense power struggle. One former agent told him:

> I think he [Hoover] got an obsession that Farley was somehow a sort of walking symbol of his chances to keep or lose his post. I don't even know now whether Farley ever hoped or tried to have Hoover removed. All I know is that Farley hadn't been in Washington more than a couple of months before Hoover threw the works at him.

> A tap was put on Farley's office phones. Others were put on his homes in Washington and New York. Not only that—on several occasions a rotation of different agents was assigned the job of trailing Farley to dinners and nightclubs in New York and into the steam room

and swimming pool of a midtown New York hotel where he was fond
of going on Saturday afternoons. . . .

Of course, in those days, agents tapping or tailing big shots like
Farley often were told that their assignments were for the security and
protection of the subject—that there had been threats on their lives,
and stuff like that, and that it was being done for their own good. If so,
I wonder why the agents were required to report everything that Farley
said, and to whom? Was Hoover afraid Farley was going to talk himself to death?

Even after Hoover had weathered the worst of the storm and it
appeared almost certain that he would retain his grip on the Bureau,
the fixation with the Farley threat, according to the former agents,
showed few signs of abating. The tapping and tailing continued until
it finally reached the ludicrous climax in the late 1930's. Farley was
scheduled to attend a convention in New Orleans. His trip, as it happened, coincided almost perfectly with the timing of FBI plans to
raid one of the city's more famous bordellos. Some executive in the
Bureau (forever unidentified) evidently conceived the idea that the
two events might dovetail, and so a Special Agent was assigned to
keep close tabs on Farley and his party. This agent subsequently told
Richards:

> Much as I didn't mind going to New Orleans, it struck me as being
> plain dumb. I expressed that opinion to my immediate boss—I won't
> say who he was—telling him that anyone who knew Jim Farley knew
> he was about the most simon-pure guy in public life and that women
> were strictly out of his range. What do you suppose the reply was?
> The reply was that Farley's job required him to be tolerant of all
> kinds of people with all kinds of tastes and that some of those people
> were his close friends. Didn't I understand, asked the boss, that it was
> just as important to get something on Farley's friends as on Farley?

The agent went to New Orleans and did his duty. Phones were
tapped to keep check on the bordello's clientele and on the call-girl
business the house conducted with the city's swankier hotels. Some
of the names that registered in listeners' ears were those of politicians,
but none were any of Farley's close friends. When the agent returned
from his unproductive assignment and reported to his boss, the latter
commented: "Too bad it was no dice." [8]

This account gives some view of the nature of the in-fighting that developed when Hoover's job was threatened. It is interesting on two counts: the violence of the reaction and the relatively temporary nature of the threat that produced it. Whatever may have been the original inclination of the Roosevelt Administration toward Hoover, it did not take it very long to see the light. Though Wheeler in his autobiography gives the impression that Hoover might have been fired had he [Wheeler] demanded it, there are some valid grounds to doubt this. They are to be found in the rather marked antipathy of Roosevelt for Wheeler and in the conservative influences that never ceased to exert considerable pressure inside the liberal Roosevelt Administration.

One of the channels through which such pressures operated was Homer Cummings, named Attorney General after Walsh's death. One of Cummings' close friends was J. Bruce Kremer, the Democratic national committeeman from Montana. Kremer, whom Wheeler described as "a reactionary and a lobbyist for the Anaconda Copper Mining Company," had fought both Walsh and Wheeler, but now, through Cummings, he began to exert more influence on patronage matters than Wheeler could. So it was perhaps no coincidence that, with the growth of Kremer's influence, Hoover grew stronger and became more secure than ever in his hold on the Bureau.[9]

The turnabout was effected with almost lightning rapidity. Just six weeks after the *New York World-Telegram* mid-June report that the Bureau would be abolished and Hoover possibly relegated to a field office, *The New York Times* announced that Cummings had appointed Hoover director of what he called his "new Division of Investigation." From the instant of the announcement, it was obvious that Hoover and his Bureau were to be cast in a new and more powerful role. The account in the *Times* concluded with this significant line: "The new division of the Justice Department will conduct the nation-wide warfare against racketeers, kidnapers and other criminals." Obviously, that "powerful political pressure" noted in June as operating in Hoover's behalf had done its work—and done it well.[10]

For anyone who wonders about the identity of the power that works such miracles, it is perhaps important to note that the tracks of conservative dinosaurs are traceable in the agitation of the period for ever stronger federal participation in the field of crime control. The hand of big business and ultraconservatism had been apparent in the witch-hunts and the antistrike activities of the Palmer and Daugherty eras, but there was, in addition, covert agitation for the creation of an ever more powerful federal police force that could be used, if necessary, to preserve the status quo. William Seagle, in an article in *Harper's* in 1934, gave a detailed picture of the behind-the-scenes personalities that long had championed an augmented federal force. He wrote:

> The story of the drive for federal crime control centers in the activities of an organization known as the National Crime Commission which was organized in 1925. The N.C.C. must not be confused with the later Wickersham Commission. It owed its existence not to governmental initiative but to a gentleman by the name of Mark O. Prentiss, who had had the singular privilege of accompanying Mussolini in his march on Rome, and who naturally became an admirer of the methods of the dictator. Incidentally, Prentiss believed that a majority of crimes of violence were committed by aliens. Prentiss interested the late Judge Gary of the United States Steel Corporation in the formation of a small national association of prominent men for the purpose of combating crime. The N.C.C. was organized at a meeting held in the directors' room of the United States Steel Corporation. The first executive committee consisted of several prominent captains of industry, two brigadier generals, several educators, and a number of nationally prominent statesmen. The chairmanship was offered to Richard Washburn Child, who had been American Ambassador to Italy, and who in this capacity had struck up a firm friendship with Mussolini, coming to believe that there was more democracy in Italy than in the United States.
>
> From the very first the Commission championed "vigorous measures." It definitely supported the treat-'em-rough school of penology. [So, it may be noted in passing, does Hoover, on occasion.] . . . Two years after its organization the Commission was in a position to assemble a tremendous national conference at the Willard Hotel in Washington. It was attended by a throng of law professors, criminologists, prison officials and representatives of associations including the American National Retail Jewelers' Association, the Furriers' Security Alliance of the United States, the Jewelers' National Crime Committee, the Salvation Army and the Rotary International.

. . . A member of the executive committee of N.C.C. and an enthusiastic supporter of its program of national attack upon the crime problem was then a comparatively obscure state governor by the name of Franklin Delano Roosevelt who within a few years was to become the thirty-second President of the United States.[11]

With a President so committed in advance, with a nation wracked by Prohibition crimes and corruption, America was primed to welcome the ride to the roundup. Its fever and impatience were increased by one heart-tugging, catalytic event. This was the kidnaping on March 1, 1932, of Charles Augustus Lindbergh, Jr., the infant son of the nation's first air-age hero. When the baby was spirited from his crib in the family home in Hopewell, among New Jersey's brooding Sourland mountains, national horror and outrage reached a peak. The demand to "do something," *anything,* resounded through the land. And since law enforcement on the local level had brought itself into disrepute, since local and state authorities seemed to be making a perfect botch of the Lindbergh case, the public focused its attention and its hope on Washington, the last recourse.

Herbert Hoover's Administration, prone to inaction, not wanting to create a possible states' rights squabble in an election year, had withstood the mounting pressure for vastly expanded federal police powers. It had looked with considerable and justifiable skepticism on the national hysteria that, in the wake of the Lindbergh kidnaping, saw this baby-snatching crime as a new national menace. The St. Louis police department, in a survey conducted in 1932, discovered only 285 kidnapings in the nation's largest cities, compared with 15,000 murders. But the emotional impact of kidnaping could not be equated in statistics, and the Department of Justice, making use of the new menace (just as it had done earlier when it set out to protect every man's wife, mother, and daughter from white slavery), drafted what it called a twelve-point program to meet the need of the hour. Attorney General Cummings, spoon-fed this heady program, bought the entire parcel, and in a speech before the Daughters of the American Revolution, proclaimed: "We are now engaged in a war that threatens the safety of our country—a war with the organized forces of crime."

No nation that stands at Armageddon, with its very existence at stake, can refuse to act, and so with a great whoop and holler, the Roosevelt Administration drove through Congress a crime-busting package that put the Bureau of Investigation into action in an unprecedented way. The first measure to be passed was the so-called Lindbergh Law, which gave the Bureau jurisdiction in kidnaping cases if the kidnapers crossed a state line. Another statute made it a federal offense to send a ransom demand or a kidnaping threat through the mails. As Jack Alexander later wrote: "These measures were revolutionary. They put the government, for the first time, into the business of punishing crimes of violence. Previously this had been the exclusive function of local authorities, except in cases of crimes committed on government reservations." [12]

This was only an opening wedge. The following year, 1934, with Congress acquiescing, the Administration further broadened the scope of federal police powers. It added the death penalty to the Lindbergh Law. And it put a whole host of new crimes under federal jurisdiction for the first time: the robbing of a national bank, the flight of a defendant or a witness across state lines to avoid prosecution or giving testimony; the transmission of threats by any means whatsoever; racketeering practiced on businessmen engaged in interstate commerce; transporting stolen property across a state line; resisting a federal officer.

All these new headline-catching crimes fell under the purview of just one federal agency, the Bureau of Investigation. And J. Edgar Hoover, its chief, only a few months before a man worried about keeping his job, was transformed almost overnight into the champion of the nation, the knight on the white charger riding down the forces of evil.

■ 2 ■

The first thriller broke just at the time when Hoover was most on tenterhooks about his job. On the morning of June 17, 1933, a group of Bureau of Investigation agents and local police escorted a recaptured, top-ranking desperado into Kansas City's Union Station. Their prisoner was a man named Frank Nash, a convicted mail robber with a twenty-five-year sentence hanging over his head.

Nash had broken out of the federal penitentiary at Leavenworth, no inconsiderable feat, and he had enjoyed nearly three years of liberty. Just the previous morning, Special Agents F. J. Lackey and Frank Smith, accompanied by Police Chief Otto Reed, of McAlester, Oklahoma, had spotted him as he stood in front of the White Front Pool Hall in Hot Springs, Arkansas, drinking a bottle of beer.

The officers had spoiled Nash's drink for him, and they had hustled him out of town as fast as their car would take them. Hot Springs in those days was a hotbed of gangdom, a watering place for top echelon racketeers and a refuge for lesser hoods seeking a place to lie low until the heat had cooled. Since Nash had high status as a criminal brain, the Bureau agents anticipated that the underworld legions in Hot Springs might make a desperate effort to rescue him —and they were right.

Hardly had the agents and their prisoner zipped out of town before Nash's cronies went into action. Their first gambit consisted of putting out a false alarm that Nash had been kidnaped; they even described the agents as the kidnapers and gave police the license number of their car. The ruse almost worked. Some twenty miles from Hot Springs, local police halted the supposed "kidnapers" and were astonished to find that they were in reality Bureau of Investigation agents. Once convinced of their identity, the police let them proceed.

At 8:30 that night, at Fort Smith, Arkansas, the agents and their prisoner caught the Missouri Pacific flier, bound for Kansas City. They plunked their prisoner in a stateroom, guards beside him, other guards in the corridor outside the door. Throughout an uneasy night, they kept watch as the train roared across the dark plains. They were to arrive in Kansas City's Union Station at 7:15 in the morning. There other agents and police would meet them, and they would transfer their prisoner to a waiting car for the final leg of the trip back to Leavenworth.

The train arrived on schedule, and Nash's captors were met at the station by reinforcements. In a tight little knot, with Nash handcuffed in the middle, they hustled through the slowly awakening station to the eastern entrance. Across the street Special Agent Raymond Caffrey had parked his Chevrolet coach. Behind it was a covering and escorting car that was to be manned by two Kansas City detectives, W. J. Grooms and Frank Hermanson. Nash was so surrounded now by the little army of agents and police that it seemed nothing could prevent his delivery to Leavenworth.

"Get into the front seat," Caffrey told Nash. "Slide over behind the wheel and sit in the middle."

Nash, handicapped by his handcuffs and fumbling with a toupee that kept slipping off his bald pate, meekly obeyed. Bureau agents Lackey and Smith and Chief Reed climbed into the back seat. Reed E. Vetterli, Special Agent in Charge of the Kansas City office, moved around the rear of the car to get in the right-hand front door. Caffrey stood by the door on the driver's side. He took one last look behind him and saw Grooms and Hermanson covering his party from the rear. Everybody, it seems, was preoccupied with these moves; everybody was watching Nash and the dispositions made for his security. Nobody was watching the street.

A file of six nuns in sober black habits started to walk across the front of the station on their way inside. At the same instant, three men materialized as if they had popped up out of the pavement. Two were armed with Thompson submachine guns; the third, with a revolver. A voice shouted:

"Get 'em up! Up!"

There was a split-second's pause, not time enough for the startled law officers to obey or to refuse. Then another voice called: "Let 'em have it!"

At the word, on the instant, the machine guns opened up spraying a lethal rain of fire. Methodically, the machine gunners walked around the car, pumping out such a steady stream of lead that the car top was nearly severed from the car body. In that scythe-like hail, men were literally cut to pieces.

Caffrey was killed instantly by a bullet that ripped through his head from front to back. Hermanson and Grooms were riddled by the flock of bullets that caught them where they waited by their covering car. A slug caught Vetterli in the left arm and spun him to the pavement. In Caffrey's Chevrolet, the interior was transformed into a shambles. Police Chief Reed slumped forward, dead. Lackey collapsed, desperately wounded, two forty-five-caliber slugs lodged in his spine, a third near his pelvic bone. Only Agent Smith escaped unscathed. Sitting there in the back seat, glass splintering, bullets zinging all around him, men crumpling and dying, Smith saw Frank Nash's head whip back as if he had been clipped with a right to the jaw, and his toupee, as if flung by some irresistible force, sailed back and splatted against the rear window. Nash slid forward, dead, the victim of the men who had come to rescue him.

In less than five minutes, five men had been gunned to death in the full light of day in front of Kansas City's Union Station. It was an outburst of savagery that became known as the "Kansas City Massacre," and it made headlines that stunned the nation.

In Washington, J. Edgar Hoover hurled all the resources of the Bureau into the hunt for the killers. It did not take the Bureau long to piece together the story of what had happened. The underworld grapevine had flashed the word of Nash's capture ahead to Kansas City, where a criminal brain trust plotted the rescue. The key man in the scheme at the outset had been Vern Miller, as cold-blooded a killer as the Oklahoma badlands ever spawned. Miller, knowing he would need help, had issued a call to a couple of distant confederates—Charles ("Pretty Boy") Floyd and Adam Richetti, who were at a remote spot in Missouri. They sped to Kansas City in answer to Miller's summons, leaving a tell-tale trail of crime behind them— a string of stolen autos and one sheriff whom they kidnaped at gunpoint when he got in their way. They arrived in Kansas City about 10 o'clock on the night before the massacre, met Miller, and canvassed the streets, setting the scene for slaughter.

With the identity of the killers established, the Bureau clung doggedly to the trail, and one by one the lethal trio fell by the wayside. In Vern Miller's case, the underworld itself lent a helping hand. Miller reportedly committed the indiscretion of knocking off a henchman of the powerful New Jersey underworld czar, Longie Zwillman, and on November 23, 1933, his body was found on the outskirts of Detroit, where he had been gunned to death.

Richetti and "Pretty Boy" Floyd gave the FBI a longer chase. They were finally traced to Ohio, and on October 21, 1934, Wellesville, Ohio, police arrested Richetti, who was later executed in the Missouri gas chamber. The following day, Special Agents of the FBI and local police caught up with "Pretty Boy" Floyd on a farm between Sprucevale and Clarkson, Ohio. Floyd elected to shoot it out with the posse, for him a fatal error. On his body, officials found a watch and fob on which he had etched the number of his killings. It was an impressively bloodthirsty tally—ten notches.[13]

■ **3** ■

Only a little more than a month after the "Kansas City Massacre," there occurred another famous headline case, the Urschel kidnaping.

On the night of July 23, 1933, Mr. and Mrs. Charles F. Urschel, of Oklahoma City, were sitting on their screened porch, playing bridge with friends, Mr. and Mrs. Walter R. Jarrett. Suddenly the screen door was thrown open, and two men, armed with machine gun and pistol, stalked through it onto the porch.

"Which one of you is Urschel?" one gunman asked.

Neither Urschel, a wealthy Oklahoma oil man, nor Jarrett answered.

"All right, we'll take both of them."

The gunmen warned the two women not to use the telephone, not to give the alarm. Then they faded back into the night, herding their captives before them.

As soon as they were gone, Mrs. Urschel telephoned the Bureau of Investigation. Hoover, having recently been given jurisdiction in kidnaping cases, had had a special kidnap wire installed on the Bureau's switchboard in Washington. When this line came alive with light shortly after midnight, the operator switched the call directly to Hoover's home. Awakened by the ringing phone, Hoover found himself talking directly to Mrs. Urschel.

Hoover at once threw all the investigative machinery into action. He volleyed orders to the Bureau office in Oklahoma City. He rounded up agents from surrounding Bureau offices and sent them hurrying on the roads to Oklahoma City. Agents were instructed to cooperate with the local police and with the family, leaving the decision as to whether any ransom should be paid strictly to the Urschels.

About two hours after the kidnaping, Jarrett returned home. The kidnapers, he said, had driven to a spot about ten miles northeast of the city. There they had stopped, taken $50 from him, and put him out. Then they had sped away with Urschel on a road leading toward the south.

Three days of silence followed. On the fourth day, a Western Union messenger delivered a package to a friend of the Urschels. The package contained four letters, one in Urschel's handwriting. One of the letters was addressed to E. E. Kirkpatrick, of Oklahoma City, a friend of the Urschels. It demanded $200,000 for Urschel's safe return. Precise directions for communication were spelled out in the other letters. If the Urschel family agreed to pay the demanded ransom, they were to insert a classified ad in a local newspaper, ostensibly offering for sale a small farm and its equipment.

The Urschels, feeling they had no choice, agreed to all the kidnapers' demands. The ad was inserted. Another letter of instructions, this one mailed from Joplin, Missouri, was received. Kirkpatrick, acting on it, left Oklahoma City carrying $200,000 in $20 bills stuffed in a handbag. The Bureau of Investigation had taken the precaution of recording the serial numbers of all the bills.

Kirkpatrick went to Kansas City and registered at a designated hotel. Soon he received a call from the kidnapers. Following their instructions to the letter, he took a cab to the La Salle Hotel, got out, and started to walk along the street to the west. As he did, a man came up beside him and said, "Mr. Kincaid, I'll take that bag." Kirkpatrick started to protest, but the man said: "The title deeds to the farm will be delivered within twelve hours." Kirkpatrick, reassured, surrendered the bag and its $200,000.

The next night, Urschel returned home, unharmed but exhausted from his eight-day ordeal. Bureau agents, their hands freed by his safe return, now took up the trail in earnest. They found that, in Urschel, they had a man who, throughout his captivity, had kept all his wits about him. True, Urschel could not give them any direct clues to the identity of his kidnapers, but he had observed little details that in the hands of skilled detectives might point the way.

One minute but tell-tale incident had occurred when the kidnapers, after driving for several hours, had stopped at a gas station. Urschel was lying out of sight, bound and gagged, on the floor of the big kidnap car, and the woman who came to fill the gas tank noticed nothing suspicious. Acting like casual tourists, the kidnapers engaged in idle chitchat with her.

"How are crop conditions?" one of them asked.

"The crops around here are burned up," the woman said, "although we may make some broomcorn."

Leaving the gas station, the kidnapers had driven for hours. Finally, after spending the night in a house that Urschel could not identify, he was taken to a farmhouse that was to become his prison. Urschel had been carefully blindfolded all the time, but he knew he had been held on a farm because he had heard all the familiar sounds —chickens cackling in the morning, cows lowing, and hogs grunting. He had also heard water being drawn by a bucket from a well that, he judged, must be northwest of the farmhouse, and when he had been given water to drink, it had been from a tin cup without a handle. The water, he recalled, had a distinctive mineral taste.

Throughout his confinement, Urschel had been handcuffed to a chain, but he had managed to work his blindfold loose enough so that he could glimpse his watch. This, as it turned out, was a feat, because each day Urschel heard a plane pass over the farmhouse at 9:45 in the morning and 5:45 in the evening. There had been just one interruption in this regular schedule. On Sunday, July 30, the day before Urschel was released, the area had been drenched by a heavy downpour, and Urschel had not heard the morning plane.

Such were the slender threads of clues that Urschel furnished to the Bureau agents. What the Bureau did with them was to make a tale that enthralled the public and greatly enhanced the Bureau's stature.

Agents decided that the best clue to the location of the kidnapers' farmhouse was contained in Urschel's account of the regularly flying plane and its one missed trip. Hoping to obtain a fix, they began to check airline schedules for a radius of six hundred miles around Oklahoma City, and they began to compare the schedules with meteorological data on recent rainfall. The combination produced some startling results.

On July 30, the agents learned, an American Airways plane on the Fort Worth–Amarillo run had been forced to make a wide detour to the north to avoid a heavy rainstorm. United States Weather

Bureau records in Dallas showed that this entire Texas area had been suffering from a heavy drought and that corn had begun to burn in the fields before the July 30 rains came. The two major clues that Urschel had given dovetailed with these facts. It seemed almost certain that he had been held in a Texas farmhouse located in the drought area.

Concentrating on the American Airways schedules, agents calculated that the morning plane leaving Fort Worth for Amarillo and the evening plane leaving Amarillo for Fort Worth would pass over a point near Paradise, Texas, at just about the morning and evening hours recalled by Urschel. So Paradise became the focal point for the agents' attention. A search of the countryside located a farmhouse that matched the description given by Urschel. There was a well to the northwest of it, and in the bucket was a tin cup without a handle. The water from the well had a distinctive mineral taste.

Bureau agents swooped down on the suspect farm. It was, they learned, the property of Mr. and Mrs. R. G. Shannon. The Shannons were the stepfather and mother of Kathryn Kelly—and Kathryn Kelly was the wife of the notorious "Machine Gun" Kelly, renowned for his fondness for tattooing his initials in the sides of barns with his machine gun.

The Shannons, questioned, confessed that they had helped to guard Urschel. The actual kidnapers, they said, had been Kelly and a confederate, Albert L. Bates.

The Bureau of Investigation, working with the most meager of clues, had cracked the case. Its performance had been brilliant, and the American public at the time, not accustomed to such achievements by the law, got a thrill out of this cops-and-kidnapers tale. Overlooked in the general chorus of praise were some subtle overtones that went into the furbishing of the Bureau's image. Among other things, the phrase "G-men" was coined—by "Machine Gun" Kelly.[14] When the agents heard it, they asked Kelly what he meant, and the cowed desperado explained that "G-men" was underworld parlance for "Government men" and that it was a dread term conveying to a crook the certainty that his jig was up. The phrase was short, colorful, ideal for headline purposes. The press seized upon it avidly. Magazines and the movies took it up.

It seems almost indecent in the circumstances to ask: Did it really all happen that way? Perhaps it did, but there is at least one other version of the trapping of "Machine Gun" Kelly that should be considered. In an article in *Harper's,* Howard McLellan rendered a quite different version, one evidently based on information gleaned from the Memphis police. Here is the way McLellan described the final taking of "Machine Gun" Kelly:

> In Memphis, Tenn., the local police were advised that Kelly and his wife were living in a bungalow in that city. Police detectives and Department of Justice agents kept the house under observation all night. On a dining-room table at which Kelly sat was an automatic pistol; on the floor were several sawed-off machine guns, his favorite weapon. At six in the morning, Detective Sergeant W. J. Raney (of the Memphis police force), slipped into the house. The bedroom door opened and there stood Kelly, a gun in hand, ready. The detective, who had been trained to look at a quarry's hands and not at his face, made one move. He shoved his shotgun barrel into Kelly's stomach and said, "Drop that gun." And Kelly dropped it.
>
> "I've been waiting all night for you," said Kelly, grinning.
>
> "Well," said Raney, "here we are!" [15]

This dramatic, but more prosaic, account of the grand finale may impress some as having a more sober ring of truth, but one thing is certain: It could never cope with the vividness of the Bureau of Investigation's third-act sensation that pictures the groveling hoodlum pleading with his captors: "Don't shoot, G-men! Don't shoot, G-men!" Sergeant Raney, the hero of McLellan's account, has faded completely from the historical record, but the Bureau agents, so colorfully christened by "Machine Gun" Kelly, have ridden on to glory.

Few Americans would begrudge that ride, but it may perhaps be permitted to begrudge its excesses. If it is undeniably good for a nation to glorify the deeds of its law-men heroes against the forces of evil, it is just as undeniably necessary to be ever on guard against the so easily cultivated conviction that an agency so enshrined can do no wrong. The sequel to the case of "Machine Gun" Kelly points up this moral.

The government's prosecution of all the fringe conspirators in the

Urschel kidnaping was relentless and phenomenally successful. The "hot money," those marked ransom bills, was traced with meticulous care. Some of it was dug up in a Texas cotton patch. Some was traced to St. Paul, Minnesota; some, to Oregon. In all some twenty persons, including those who had merely touched the ransom money, were prosecuted and sent to prison. It was one of the most thorough, across-the-board clean sweeps that federal prosecutors had ever made. Yet, unknown at the time, unknown for more than twenty-five years, was one deeply disturbing circumstance.

The trials of some of the defendants had been started before "Machine Gun" Kelly and his wife were trapped in Memphis. The Urschels, key government witnesses, received two letters, postmarked Chicago, threatening dire reprisals against them if they testified Subsequently, at the trial of the Kellys, the government contended they had sent the threatening letters, and so the documents became important in the government's arsenal of evidence, especially in the attempt to establish the deep personal involvement of Mrs. Kelly in the plot. Edward Bennett Williams, a famous Washington defense attorney, disclosed what happened in his book *One Man's Freedom,* published in 1962:

> At the trial of the two Kellys, the prosecution offered damaging evidence against her. A local handwriting expert testified that she had signed the two threatening letters. "I did not!" she testified. She insisted her husband had signed them. . . .
>
> Counsel for Mrs. Kelly concentrated on trying to convince the jury that she was coerced by her husband, much against her will, into participating in the crime. She took the stand and asserted that she had begged her husband to release Urschel when she found out about the kidnaping. She testified that Kelly told her it was "none of (her) business" and that he would kill Urschel if no ransom were paid. The jury convicted her along with Kelly. Both received life sentences. Kelly died in Leavenworth penitentiary in 1954.
>
> Mrs. Kelly remained in prison from 1933 until her case was reopened in 1958. An attorney new to the case then argued that her trial was unfair and that she should have been permitted to bring in another handwriting expert to give his views.
>
> The Federal judge who heard this argument ordered the prosecution to produce the twenty-five-year-old records of the case so that he could

ascertain whether there was substance to the defense's claims. The Department of Justice refused to produce the files. Thereupon the judge set aside Mrs. Kelly's conviction and freed her on bond pending a new trial. The U.S. Court of Appeals for the Tenth Circuit later reversed this ruling and sent the case back to the lower court for a continuation of the hearing before that court.

Although considerable time has passed, at this writing there has been no hearing. Perhaps the reason is that the FBI had in its possession in 1933, during Kathryn Kelly's trial, evidence that she had not signed the letters in question. Charles A. Appel, the FBI's top handwriting analyst at the time, examined the letters and concluded that the signatures were *not* those of Kathryn Kelly, but might well have been written by George Kelly.

This evidence was kept from the jury that tried Kathryn Kelly. If the jury had known that the local handwriting expert was wrong, according to the FBI's own expert, and that Mrs. Kelly was undoubtedly telling the truth when she denied signing the letters, the verdict might have been different. This, of course, can be small consolation for twenty-five years in prison.

But the most disturbing fact of the case is that this evidence *was not even disclosed in the 1958 hearing.* Instead, the Government chose to keep the file closed and forget the case.

This case therefore is a classic example of the need for a change in pretrial procedures to give the defense a fair opportunity to discover the evidence confronting it. If Mrs. Kelly . . . had known that the FBI's own expert had concluded after extensive analysis that she had not signed the letters, she could have called him as a witness. But the procedure of combat by surprise had dealt a lethal blow to her chance to defend herself.

It is ironical, but important to bear in mind, that the Urschel kidnaping case, representing one of the FBI's most brilliant pieces of detective work, also stands as a monument to the intrinsic danger of elevating a detective agency to sacrosanct status. Every time there is an outcry—and such outcries have been a hallmark of our times— about the sanctity of the FBI's secret files and the necessity to keep them closed and guarded for the preservation of the flag, it might be well to recall the case of Kathryn Kelly, with its deliberate suppression of vital evidence that would have disproved a key element of the charges against her. The police state, in its authoritarianism, does not hesitate to adopt such tactics in convicting the innocent whose guilt it has predetermined. But such procedures must ever be held anathema in a democratic society whose principal glory is its protection of the individual, its guarantee to the individual of the principles of justice. Those principles, as Kathryn Kelly's case demonstrated, are not advanced when a detective agency is permitted to establish secrecy as a supreme cause, transcending the far more vital cause of justice itself.

■ Notes ■

[1] Washington dispatch to the *New York World-Telegram,* June 14, 1933.

[2] Don Whitehead, *The FBI Story* (Random House, 1956), pp. 79–80 of Pocket Books edition.

[3] *Ibid.,* p. 85.

[4] *Ibid.,* pp. 82–83.

[5] *Ibid.,* p. 87.

[6] *New York World-Telegram,* June 14, 1933.

[7] *Loc. cit.*

[8] This account is taken from Guy Richards' article, "FBI Spied on Farley," in the *New York Star,* Sept. 28, 1948.

[9] See Arthur M. Schlesinger, Jr., *The Politics of Upheaval* (Houghton Mifflin, 1960), pp. 138–139.

[10] *New York Times,* July 30, 1933.

[11] William Seagle, "The American National Police," in *Harper's,* November, 1934.

[12] *The New Yorker,* Sept. 25, 1937.

[13] Like all famous FBI chases, the story of "Pretty Boy" Floyd and the Kansas City massacre has been told many times. In this version, I have relied mainly on the account by Ken Jones in *The FBI in Action* (Signet, 1957), pp. 39–45.

[14] Whitehead, *op. cit.,* p. 120.

[15] Howard McLellan, "Shoot to Kill," in *Harper's,* January, 1946.

6 Building the Image

The FBI now began to stride—in a blaze of gunfire, heroics, and publicity—across the pages of the nation's press as had no other police agency in history. In the short space of two years, 1934 and 1935, FBI agents engaged in innumerable shoot-downs with tough, machine-gun-toting hoodlums, and, though some agents were killed in the process, the hoodlums always bit the dust in the end. "Pretty Boy" Floyd. John Dillinger. "Baby Face" Nelson. Clyde Barrow. "Ma" Barker and her son, Fred. Alvin Karpis. There seemed no end to the scroll. No sooner had Public Enemy No. 1 been gorily eliminated than a new No. 1 sprang up to take his place—and to be in turn rubbed out. It was all more thrilling than the last act of a Grade B Wild West thriller on the movie screen, and the best part of this thriller was that it was really happening. It was as real as the latest headline.

A nation disgraced by the corruption of Prohibition, a nation that had become accustomed to seeing the toughs of the underworld gunning each other down on the streets—and sometimes killing small children and innocent bystanders in the process—responded with a wave of adulation for the FBI and its director. G-man movies usurped the place of gangster movies; "the magazines bloomed with sagas of aggressive federal purity"; children abandoned gang-warfare games and began to make up their own dramas in which the G-man always triumphed over the wrongdoer.[1]

This was what Jack Alexander later called "a spontaneous phenomenon." Both he and Whitehead agree that Hoover, at first, did nothing to promote it. Whitehead pictures Hoover as a man who actually detests personal glorification, as one who embraced his own deification reluctantly because he felt, in the 1930's, that some countersymbol was needed to expose the phony glamour with which mobsters were gilded in the popular imagination. For this reason, says Whitehead, Hoover finally decided to promote the image of the G-man as the incorruptible fighter against crime. Alexander, in his more balanced portrait, also accepts the thesis that Hoover at first shied from publicity. In fact, he wrote, Hoover at first refused to cooperate with movie companies or fiction writers eager to promote the G-man symbol. However, "when he got thinking of it, he was unable to resist the temptation to capitalize on it. Somehow the Kansas City massacre had shocked the Director worse than anything that had happened before in that line." An all-out crusade against crime was needed, Hoover felt, and Alexander sees his final decision this way: "Someone had to become a symbol of the crusade, and the Director decided that, because of his position, it was plainly up to him. As he tells of it now, he was reluctant to accept the role because it meant sacrificing the personal privacy he had enjoyed before the G-man excitement began, but he felt that he was not justified in refusing it simply because it was distasteful. So he acted."

Once Hoover's ever-so-reluctant decision had been made, there began that spate of publicity that has continued unabated for almost thirty years. All possible media of information that could be used to build the image have been tapped. Newspapers, avid for sensation, have gloried in displaying cops-and-robbers features, with Hoover and the men of the FBI cast in infallible heroes' roles. Magazines have followed in the footsteps of the press. Comic strips have featured the FBI in daily sequences of derring-do. Radio and television have dramatized the great manhunts. Books bearing Hoover's name or, if not his name his blessing, make the best-seller lists. Movies have poured out documentaries and full-length feature dramas, lending visual impact to the promotion of the legend. The barrage has been overwhelming. Never before, on any level of government, have the American people been subjected to such brainwashing on behalf of any agency.

A lesser man than Hoover might have taken advantage of the situation to build himself a private fortune, but, from all indications, greed of money is not one of Hoover's faults. His record on this score began early and seems to have been consistent. Alexander lists specific details. When editors mailed him checks for as much as $1,000, he mailed them right back. All the profit of the "War on Crime" comic strip, the first of a long line, went to the writer, Rex Collier, a Washington newspaperman and friend of Hoover. The Director spurned the offer of an automobile manufacturer to pay him $2,000 for each of the twenty-six weekly radio talks; he refused to sign an endorsement for a cigarette company that offered him $2,500 for the use of his name (the going rate for Senators was then $1,000). When suppliers offered a rebate to the FBI for the privilege of advertising that the G-men used their products, Hoover's answer was to write a clause into each purchase contract specifically forbidding such promotion. "We are engaged in the midst of a crusade of law enforcement, and it would be a mistake to cheapen it by any kind of commercialization," Hoover told Alexander. The most that Hoover has ever been willing to do, by all accounts, is to turn revenue received from his books or movies over to departmental welfare funds.

This lofty attitude served only to provide the public with another vivid example of the FBI's incorruptibility. It added another strand to the legend, helped to foster the impression that Hoover was superior to all mundane considerations. At the outset, the effect may have been beneficial, helping to nourish a healthy public regard for the law and contempt for criminals, but there is always danger when such excessive praise, lacking the counterweight of effective criticism, is lavished on any man or any agency over a period of decades. When a man becomes the convert to his own heroic image, when he embraces the idea of his own infallibility, he rapidly becomes to himself an issue and a cause more important than any other. In Hoover's case, the evidence of the years plainly says that, however reluctant Hoover may have been in the beginning, he came to revel in his role and to become one of the first and greatest victims of his own publicity.

This is a fact, one of the most ignored of our time, that has been demonstrated in many ways. It is especially notable in two strongly pronounced Hoover characteristics: his tendency to lap up praise the way a cat does cream, and the way he reacts to the first whiff of criticism by indulging in condemnation that almost invariably ends by consigning his critic of the moment to the most convenient Communist doghouse.

The ego that is revealed by these contrasting but complementary reactions certainly must rate as one of the most formidable of our day. Its appetite for praise seems insatiable. As long ago as 1940, Senator Norris paid acid tribute to this facet of Hoover's character. Norris told his colleagues of a Midwestern editor who "receives an average of one letter a week from Mr. Hoover. Whenever anything of a commendatory nature, or anything which could be construed as commendation of anything the FBI has done appears in the newspaper, the editor receives a letter of approval from Mr. Hoover." No publication was too obscure or too cheap to receive a royal pat on the head if it had seen and done its duty by praising the FBI. Alexander, in his *New Yorker* profile, gagged a bit at the delight Hoover expressed at one outrageous puff. "Last June [this was in 1937] *The Feds,* a pulpwood thriller magazine, began a series of articles about Hoover and his Bureau in which he was lionized as 'Public Hero No. 1.' Anyone who expected him to repudiate or ignore the puff must have been surprised to read in the September issue excerpts from a letter the publishers received from Hoover. In the letter, Hoover expressed himself as 'particularly happy' about the series, which he described as one of the best treatises of its kind he had ever read." [2]

The other side of the coin, the extreme sensitiveness to criticism, seems from earliest days to have been a Hoover trademark. Even as a young man, in charge of GID, he was outraged by the widespread criticism by ministers, writers, and lawyers of the deportations on the *Buford* and the Red Raids. In 1920 his GID, in language compatible with some of Hoover's own later effusions, had prepared for Attorney General Palmer a defense marked by this censorious passage:

> There would have been no vicious and hurtful criticism of the administration, but rather free praise from all reasonable sides for its promptness and good effect, had it not been for the press agents of the Reds and their hallucinated friends among the parlor bolsheviks, and even a certain class of liberal writers from whom better discretion might have been expected, who drenched the newspapers and magazines with malicious and false descriptions of the raids, of the deportations, and the policy of the administration. They particularly accused

the Department of Justice of a spirit of Bourbonism, and an animus against free speech. There was no justice in the screeds.[3]

In 1940, under attack by Senator Norris and others for some of the activities of his Bureau, Hoover let loose a full-scale barrage of vituperation. His critics, he said in speeches and statements, were "un-American"; they were "vipers" who "have sought to wash away our national foundation in an ink stream of vilification." They were "confidence men, seeking to steal our wallets." The FBI was being "vilified by the scum of the underworld."

In 1941, the critics were "the rabble-rousing Communist, the goose-stepping bundsmen, their stooges and seemingly 'innocent' fronts, and last but not the least, the pseudo liberals. . . . By whom have these persons been set upon us? By persons whom we have trusted the most—by certain teachers in our public schools and institutions of higher learning, by certain writers, fattening upon the royalties paid by the American people while fostering class hatred and discontent, by some prattle-minded politicians, grabbing for votes with one hand while waving the flag of pseudo-liberalism with the other, and worst of all by some ministers of the Gospel who have loudly proclaimed the Communist's right to destroy America and its God-fearing way of life. . . .

"That word 'liberalism' is something we should weigh carefully during these dark days that confront our nation."

Study well such statements. In them, one may discern most of the seeds of the McCarthy era—the patent anti-intellectualism and anti-liberalism; the suspicion of the seemingly innocent, of those whom we have trusted most, our teachers and our ministers; the blanket denunciation of all critics as "un-American" and Communist-tainted radicals. Such eruptions seem plainly to mark an ego that has identified itself with the nation—and not in any subordinate capacity.

The effects have been far-reaching. Hoover has become in the popular mind—indeed in fact, as Whitehead writes—the FBI. Even relatively minor arrests of second-grade hijacking rings must be announced in his name. No agent of the FBI may tell his experiences in magazine articles or books—only Hoover. In the retelling of the famous manhunts, the blunders and failures, if mentioned at all, must

be glossed over; the recital must adhere to the legend of FBI infallibility leading to a typical, untarnished FBI triumph. The hoodlums
must stand ten feet tall until the FBI cuts them down (which, of
course, makes the FBI stand even taller); and all the credit for that
final scything must go to Hoover and the FBI, never a crumb to local
police who, as in the case of "Machine Gun" Kelly, often had more
to do with the final outcome.

Such is the pattern. Such are the demands of self-glorification and
press-agentry. Perhaps as good a place as any to see the pattern working out is in the FBI's most famous chase, the hunting of John
Dillinger.

■ 1 ■

Mention the name of John Dillinger to almost any American who
has been reading the press and the magazines during the last thirty
years, and it's a safe bet that certain images will flash through his
mind: The prince of desperados—"the most brazen killer this nation
has ever known," as some FBI literature puts it. The Woman in Red
who betrayed him. The trap set at the old Biograph Theatre in Chicago. And the sharp, accurate fire of FBI agents dropping the nation's
No. 1 menace dead in his tracks before the startled eyes of gaping
theatergoers.

But mention the names of St. Paul and Little Bohemia, of Matt
Leach and Sergeant Martin Zarkovich, and it's almost a cinch the
reaction will be a bewildered "Who were they?"

Yet St. Paul and Little Bohemia, Leach and Zarkovich, are as
integral parts of the Dillinger melodrama as the Woman in Red and
the Biograph. And the fact that only the triumphant half of the story
has registered in the public consciousness seems a tribute to the art
of propaganda, to skillful manipulation of half-truths by storytellers
serving media of information interested only in giving the public what
they think the public wants—a bedtime thriller cast in the heroic
mold of gallant knights tilting with evil.

To understand what Dillinger means to the FBI, one must appreciate the importance that the FBI itself has attached to what is

probably its most famous single case. In the anteroom of the office of J. Edgar Hoover in Washington, millions of Americans, doing the tourist's round of the capital, have found Dillinger enshrined as the No. 1 scalp in the FBI's massive collection, and they have been chillingly titillated by the macabre Dillinger memorabilia clustered at the very threshold of the throne room. Jack Alexander described the scene:

> In the anteroom where visitors wait to be admitted to the Director's presence the most compelling decorative object is a startling white plaster facsimile of John Dillinger's death mask. It stares, empty-eyed, from under the glass of an exhibit case. There are other exhibit cases in the anteroom, but this one, like a prize scalp, is significantly located closest to the Director's office. Grouped around the mask are souvenirs of the memorable night when the spectacular outlaw was cornered and shot down after he had emerged from the motion-picture theatre in Chicago. There are the straw hat he was wearing, a wrinkled snapshot of a girl which was fished from his trousers pocket, and the silver-rimmed glasses he was wearing to heighten his disguise, one of the lens rims snapped by a bullet. There is the La Corona-Belevedere cigar he was carrying in his shirt pocket that summer night, still banded and wrapped in cellophane.

Let's take a close look at the Dillinger story. Was he really the prince of desperados, the most brazen killer in the nation's history? Definitely not. What Dillinger was, as the record makes quite clear, was a daring poseur who was deliberately built into a legend by police and who came to glory in the role detectives had created for him.

Dillinger was the wayward son of a prosperous grocer. His mother died when he was three; his father was so busy that he paid scant attention to the boy's upbringing. And John, in his teen-age years, set out on a familiar path—petty thefts, girls, a stolen car. Serious trouble, the kind that sends a man to prison, did not really come his way, however, until the summer of 1924, when he attempted his first holdup and was so nervous he botched the job.

His father, who had remarried, a circumstance in Dillinger's brooding resentment of life, had moved to a farm outside Mooresville, Ind., the home town of his second wife. John Dillinger had walked away from a short hitch in the Navy, had held various machinist's jobs, and this summer was amusing himself by playing shortstop on a local baseball team. One of his fellow players was a weak-witted drunkard who suggested that they might make themselves a bundle by holding up the owner of the town's grocery store. This store owner made a habit, when he went for a haircut on Saturday nights, of taking the store's receipts with him, and all that was necessary, said Dillinger's friend, was to hit him over the head and take the money. Dillinger fell in with the scheme and was elected to do the deed. He accepted the honor.

Fortifying himself with liquor, Dillinger lay in wait for the grocer. When the quarry came along, Dillinger jumped him and hit him over the head with a bolt wrapped in cloth. The evidence seems to say that Dillinger's heart really wasn't in such personal violence, for he delivered only a couple of ineffectual swats that, far from silencing the grocer, only stimulated him to loud outcry. Instead of killing the man on the spot (Dillinger, it seems, could have, for he had a .32 caliber revolver in his hand), this prince of desperados fled off into the night, went home, and calmly waited for the police to come.

They did. Dillinger was arrested. Not knowing any better, he accepted police assurances that, if he pleaded guilty, he would get off with a light sentence. What he got was ten to twenty years.

Dillinger felt he had been double-crossed, especially since his baseball-playing confederate, the man who had suggested the holdup in the first place, escaped with a two-year sentence. Bitterness ate him. He became an obstreperous prisoner, tried repeatedly to escape, was caught each time, and had additional months added to his sentence. Resentment of injustice, hate of the world, filled him with bile, and prison gave him a liberal education in crime. He came to know and admire two really first-grade toughs, Harry Pierpont and Homer Van Meter. By the time nine years had passed, Dillinger felt that society owed him heavy reparation, and when he was finally released from prison on May 10, 1933, he had no intention of going straight. Indeed, he had made a pact with Pierpont and Van Meter that he would join their former gangs and embark on a series of bank robberies to raise sufficient money to buy guns, pay bribes, and help them break out of prison.

Now began the real criminal career of the prince of desperados. A month to the day after his release from prison, on June 10, 1933, the bookkeeper of the New Carlisle National Bank unlocked its front door—and was promptly jumped by three men, faces masked by handkerchiefs, who had sneaked in through an unlocked window during the night. The bookkeeper was so unnerved that he fumbled and failed twice while trying to open the safe, and one of Dillinger's companions growled: "Let me drill him. He's stalling." Dillinger vetoed this. "Take your time and open it," he said to the bookkeeper in a soothing voice.

While the bookkeeper was still struggling with the safe, a woman bank clerk entered. Dillinger told her to come into the office and lie down, gallantly spread a banker's smock on the floor for her, and apologized as he trussed up her hands and feet with wire. Two more men, a cashier and a customer, were similarly bound when they put in an appearance, and Dillinger and his robber pals escaped with $10,600 in cash.[4]

During the next three weeks, Dillinger helped loot some ten banks in five states. In the middle of July, he and two confederates were planning to rob the Daleville, Indiana, bank, but before they could put their plans into effect, Dillinger's partners were caught by police. So Dillinger decided to tackle the job alone.

He walked into the bank at 12:45 P.M. Monday, July 17. Teller Margaret Good was the only bank employee on duty at the time. Though she had been held up twice previously, she suspected nothing when Dillinger, looking like a prosperous businessman, strolled up to her cage and asked to see the bank president. She told him that the president was no longer active in the affairs of the bank and that the cashier had gone to lunch.

"Well, honey, this is a holdup," Dillinger said.

He whipped out his gun, used the ledge of the cage as a step, and vaulted over the six-foot barrier with the athletic agility of a Robin Hood. The teller wondered why he had gone to such trouble when he could simply have walked through the door. The answer seems to be that Dillinger was a great fan of Douglas Fairbanks and was simply acting out a role.

This Fairbanks-like leap over the barrier of the Daleville bank marked Dillinger as a bank robber with a certain distinctive flair and brought him to the attention of the detective who was to spend more time than any other trying to track him down, Captain Matt Leach, commander of the Indiana State Police. Leach had already obtained a confession from one of Dillinger's arrested confederates, who had told of plans to rob the Daleville bank in cooperation with one "Dan" Dillinger. Leach deduced that the high-vaulting bank robber must be Dillinger. He sent pictures to the Daleville bank and got a tentative identification of Dillinger. Muncie newspapers broke out with head-lines about "Desperate Dan." It was Dillinger's first taste of fame—a purely local fame.

In the Midwest, outside of Indiana, hardly anybody had yet heard of Dillinger. The blackest headlines at the moment were being preempted by Clyde Barrow and his gun-toting, poetry-writing girl friend, Bonnie Parker. Barrow and Bonnie, and Barrow's brother Buck and his wife, Blanche, shot their way out of ambush after ambush in a gaudy career across the Midwestern states in flaming defiance of the law. Everybody was preoccupied with the menace and latest doings of "the Barrow gang," and hardly anybody except a man named Matt Leach worried that a bank robber named Dillinger was on the loose.

This was soon to be changed. Dillinger, true to his word to Pier-pont and Van Meter, smuggled guns to them in Michigan City prison, and on September 26, 1933, Pierpont led ten convicts in a successful break. However, by the time they reached the hideout Dillinger had arranged for them, Dillinger himself had been trapped by the law. He had gone to visit a girl friend in Dayton, Ohio, not knowing that detectives were aware of his romantic interest. The result was that the law caught him with his guns down, looking at some snapshots in his girl friend's room at 1:30 in the morning. Docile as a kitten, Dillinger was hustled off to the Lima, Ohio, jail.

Pierpont, who owed his freedom to Dillinger, decided to effect a rescue. At 6:20 P.M. October 12, he and two confederates, all armed with revolvers, walked boldly up to the red brick building in Lima that served as the county jail and the home of the sheriff. The sheriff and his wife had just finished dinner when the trio barged in.

"We're officers from Michigan City, and we want to see John Dillinger," Pierpont told the sheriff.

"Let me see your credentials," the sheriff answered.

"Here are our credentials," said Pierpont, pulling a gun.

The sheriff, instead of surrendering, made a lunge for the gun. Pierpont shot him.

Dillinger, who had been playing cards in the next room, hopped up and grabbed his hat and coat when he heard the shots. Then, always the poseur, he strolled slowly out of the unlocked cell door. In the sheriff's living quarters, he paused for a moment, knelt, and examined the dying man's wounds. Then he rose and, not meeting the eyes of the sheriff's wife, went out into the night with his rescuers. He was still, in his own mind at least, more debonair Robin Hood than heartless killer.

Two days afterward, Dillinger led a band of his followers in a raid on the Auburn, Ohio, police station. They got a submachine gun, two steel vests, and over 1,000 rounds of ammunition. On October 20, Pierpont, with Dillinger at his heels, led a raid on the City Hall in Peru, Indiana, and walked off with enough lethal hardware to equip a small army. The Lima jailbreak, and the series of bold depredations that followed it, now impressed the name of Dillinger on the general consciousness of the law enforcement fraternity.

While headlines screamed the alarm and pictured the Pierpont gang as conducting "open warfare" on the law, Captain Matt Leach, the first man to appreciate the potentialities of Dillinger, plotted a devious stratagem. Knowing that Pierpont was proud of his underworld status and reputation, he figured that, if police publicly proclaimed Dillinger as the gang's leader, internal dissension would be stirred up, and the rats would soon be killing each other off. Leach took reporters into his confidence, and almost as fast as typewriter carriages could swing into action, out popped stories describing Dillinger as the leader of the gang and the new Midwest menace.

It was a clever scheme, but it didn't work quite the way Leach had hoped. Pierpont read the stories and laughed at them. He was grateful to Dillinger for springing him from prison, but he knew that Dillinger knew who the leader of the Pierpont gang really was. Dillinger, on the other hand, savored the accounts and hoarded the press clippings. He was becoming almost as big a man as Douglas Fairbanks.

Leach's propaganda ploy, though it hadn't succeeded in its original objective, had at least one important effect. It built up Dillinger, and from this point on, every major heist committed in the Midwest was attributed to "the Dillinger gang." Today it's almost impossible to determine which of the various deeds "credited" to the "Dillinger gang" by police in the rapidly developing hysteria were actually performed by Dillinger.

In this uncertain category lies a New Year's Eve raid on a Chicago roadhouse that netted close to a quarter of a million dollars and led to the wounding of two highway patrolmen. This was followed on January 15, 1934, by the robbery of the First National Bank in East Chicago, Indiana, in which Patrolman Walter P. O'Malley was shot and killed. Dillinger was identified as the machine gunner who held the bank terrorized while Pierpont looted it, and he was accused of firing the shots that felled O'Malley when the patrolman came upon the gang as it was making its getaway.

These developments raised official fevers. Rumor had it that the raided roadhouse had been one of the prize preserves of Al Capone; and Chicago police, who hadn't done much about the 127 murders Capone was supposed to have committed, suddenly were possessed of a righteous zeal to lay the Dillinger mob by the heels. Orders went out to shoot to kill Dillinger on sight.

Only, at the time, Dillinger wasn't there to be sighted.

He, along with the entire Pierpont mob and their girls, had gone south for the winter. They stayed for a time in Daytona Beach, Florida, then traveled on to New Orleans, and finally wound up in Tucson, Arizona, enjoying the desert air. Here disaster struck. A fire broke out in the Congress Hotel, where the mobsters were staying, and all guests had to be evacuated. Firemen who helped to lug out the baggage of the obviously well-heeled gentlemen were impressed by its inordinate weight and developed suspicions, which they communicated to police. The Tucson cops swung into action and accomplished with relative ease a feat that police of the entire Midwest had failed to effect. They nabbed Pierpont, Charles Makely, Russell Clark—and Dillinger, who was captured when he walked unsuspectingly into a police trap that had been set at the apartment of Clark, who had already been captured. Half a dozen waiting cops got the drop on him, and he meekly surrendered. In the entire roundup, not a shot had been fired.

For Pierpont and Makely, it was the end. They were sent back to Ohio to be tried for the murder of the Lima sheriff. Both were doomed. Makely died later in an attempted prison break, Pierpont in the electric chair. As for Dillinger, he still had a course to run. Arizona shipped him back to the Crown Point County Jail in Indiana, where he was held on a murder charge for the slaying of Patrolman O'Malley. With the truculence of the committed gangster, Dillinger righteously insisted on his innocence, realizing at the same time that —considering his reputation—he didn't have much chance of establishing it.

"Let them prove I'm guilty," he said. "Don't the law consider a guy innocent until he's proven guilty? Well, I'm innocent, but it looks like I'll get the works though. They got me charged with everything from strangling gold fish to stealing the socks off a blind man. Why, they've even got me tagged with bank jobs I couldn't have committed. Two and three bank jobs in different states at about the same hour on the same day when I couldn't have been in all the places at the same hour."

The Crown Point jail had a lady sheriff, who had been appointed to fill out the unexpired term of her deceased husband. There was some agitation for transferring Dillinger to the more secure Michigan City State Prison, but the lady gaoler took umbrage at this reflection on her capabilities, hired twenty extra guards on an around-the-clock basis, and announced that she would see to it that Dillinger didn't get out of *her* prison. Unfortunately for the lady, she didn't know Dillinger.

He had no intention of remaining quietly in prison until the electric chair claimed him. Early on the morning of March 3, 1934, he suddenly whipped out a pistol, cowed a guard, then cowed a whole succession of guards. With the help of a Negro inmate, Herbert Youngblood, who was also facing a murder rap and had nothing to lose, he locked the guards in the prisoners' cells, strolled out of a side entrance of the prison and into a garage, took the lady sheriff's own car, and headed for Chicago.

This second jailbreak by Dillinger created an enormous sensation.

The legend was born that Dillinger had brazened his way out of the Crown Point Jail with nothing more lethal in his hands than a piece of wood that he had carved into the shape of a revolver. Dillinger himself, always happy to embroider his legend, went along with the myth, having his picture taken holding the supposed "wooden gun" in his hand. Actually, his break had been made possible by a real gun, smuggled into the prison by confederates on the outside.

More important than the jailbreak was an indiscretion that Dillinger committed during his flight to Chicago. He drove the lady sheriff's car across the Indiana state line and into Illinois, where, on the outskirts of Chicago, he abandoned it. This crossing of a state line in a stolen car was a federal offense and made Dillinger, on the instant, legitimate game for the FBI. J. Edgar Hoover, seizing the opportunity, swung into action.

Now the headlines were filled with the clamor of the great all-out federal war on the new national menace, John Dillinger. "Act first, talk afterward," Hoover said, ordering his men "to shoot straight and get the right man." Joseph B. Keenan, Assistant Attorney General, picking up the cue, declared: "I don't know when or where we will get him [Dillinger], but we will get him and I hope we get him under such circumstances that the government will not have to stand the expenses of a trial." And Attorney General Cummings, who seemed to have fallen into the habit of echoing Hoover, put the federal determination into focus succinctly when he said, "Shoot to kill— then count ten." [5]

The G-men's war on Dillinger now began to crowd even Roosevelt out of the headlines. Hoover threw a veritable small army into the hunt. Policemen and agents took constant target practice, warming up their revolvers by aiming at silhouettes of Dillinger—and the papers printed the pictures for Dillinger to see. No doubt about it, we were riding to the last roundup, and the FBI was hogging the entire road.

Through the years Hoover has given lip service to the ardent desire of his Bureau to cooperate with local police, whom he likes to flatter by calling them the backbone of law enforcement. But in the Dillinger case, as in other notable investigations, cooperation with the FBI was strictly a one-way proposition. It was all take, no give. In fact, local authorities were kept in such ignorance of the FBI's intentions that time and again FBI flying squads were mistaken for Dillinger's gang, and it was one of the lesser miracles of the drama that police and FBI agents managed to avoid being drawn into a tragic shoot-down with each other.

Captain Leach, the policeman who had been earliest and hottest on the Dillinger trail, found himself completely frozen out. He later claimed that only his own caution "averted the slaughter" of FBI agents on more than one occasion. In one instance, Leach recalled, a citizen reported that an automobile loaded with armed bandits was speeding eastward through northern Indiana. The "bandits" turned out to be FBI agents. Another time, Leach said, he had a report that Dillinger and his gang "were bound for Mooresville in two machines. Those machines were found loaded with armed members of the Department of Justice." Leach declared angrily that "these fool-hardy methods by J. Edgar Hoover made it necessary for me to lodge a formal complaint with Governor Paul V. McNutt against the policies of the Department of Justice." [6]

It was certainly a cross-purposes way to conduct a great investigation, and some of the results were predictably disastrous. The G-men tangled first with Dillinger in St. Paul, Minnesota. Dillinger and an aide, Eugene Green, were trapped in an apartment, usually a hard place to get out of. There was a furious machine-gun battle, and Green was mortally wounded, Dillinger less seriously so. Amazingly, both men got clean away.

This first encounter was followed by a fiasco even more embarrassing. The prince of desperados took several of his bad men, with women for all, and on Friday, April 30, 1934, holed up in a road-house known as Little Bohemia Lodge in a secluded area some nine miles from Mercer in northern Wisconsin. They had hardly taken possession of the lodge, terrorizing the proprietors, Mr. and Mrs. Emil Wanatka, before a tip went out to the FBI. Henry Voss, of Rhinelander, Wisconsin, Mrs. Wanatka's brother-in-law, put the call through to Melvin (Little Mel) Purvis, the FBI special agent in charge of the Chicago office.

"The man you want most is up here," he said.

"You mean Dillinger?" Purvis asked.

Voss said he did. Dillinger, five other men, and four girls, he said, were staying at the Little Bohemia Lodge, some fifty miles from Rhinelander.

Purvis rounded up eleven FBI agents, packed them into two chartered planes, and took off for the northern Wisconsin wilds. Before leaving, he had talked with the St. Paul office, from where another FBI contingent, headed by Assistant Director H. Hugh Clegg, set out to meet Purvis in Rhinelander. There the two forces borrowed five automobiles and set out along wood roads with which they were totally unfamiliar in search of their quarry. Significantly, and typically, they didn't bother to seek the help of local law enforcement officials, whose intimate knowledge of the area, as it turned out, might well have been invaluable.

On the trip to Little Bohemia, three of the borrowed cars conked out, and the agents finished the ride clinging to the running boards of the other cars. The attack plan called for five agents to close in from the left side of the lodge, five from the right; three others, wearing bullet-proof vests, would storm the front door. This left only the rear of the lodge uncovered, but since the lodge backed on a lake and there were no boats, the agents did not worry about that. What they didn't know was that there was a steep bank along the lake shore that would effectively mask the flight of fleeing men around the ends of the FBI pincers. The agents were also unaware of the fact that there was a deep ditch along the left side of the lodge and a barbed-wire fence along the right, and that the lodge was guarded by a couple of husky watchdogs.

Into these pitfalls, a little before nine at night, the FBI raiders plunged headlong. The dogs began to bark furiously. All chance of surprise gone, the agents left their cars and dashed for their assigned stations on the wings of the lodge. Those on the left plunged into the ditch. Those on the right became entangled in the barbed-wire fence, and while they were trying to extricate themselves, the front door of the lodge opened and three men came out. Two bartenders also stepped outside to see why the dogs were barking. Seeing five men emerging from the lodge almost together, the FBI agents concluded they must be the Dillinger gang, and they called on them to halt.

The first three men, actually only drinking customers on their way home, either were too groggy to pay any attention or didn't hear. They got into their car and started away. Clegg shouted to his men to fire at the tires, and at his order a fusillade broke out. Bullets riddled not only the tires but the car. Two of the customers were wounded; one was killed. And inside the lodge, Dillinger and his gang were at last alerted.

They grabbed their guns and sprayed a deadly fire into the woods around the lodge. For a time, bullets zinged back and forth, hitting nobody. Then Dillinger, having deterred the FBI rush on the door, led the way out of a second-story window at the back of the lodge. He and his gang partners jumped from the roof into a pile of snow, crept about twenty-five yards, and slid down the steep bank to the lake's edge. Concealed by the bank, they slipped off into the night, leaving the FBI raiders none the wiser. When day broke, the FBI men made their final rush—and found the nest deserted. Only the gang molls were huddled in the roadhouse, waiting to receive them. Dillinger and his crew had vanished.

The Dillinger gang, once clear of Little Bohemia, split up to make their escape. They commandeered cars and made their way out of the woods with little trouble—all except Lester Gillis, alias "Baby Face" Nelson, the most ruthless killer of the lot. Nelson became confused in the woods, finally wandered out to a house some distance from the lodge, and walked almost into the arms of Special Agent W. Carter Baum and two other officers. Without warning, Nelson opened up on them with his submachine gun, killing Baum and wounding the other two. Then he seized their car and escaped.

Dillinger, John Hamilton, and Van Meter, all veterans of the Pierpont gang ever since the days of the Michigan City prison break, had made their way out of the wilds together. Hamilton had been wounded by one of the wild-flying bullets during the gun battle at the lodge. His wound went untreated for days, gangrene set in, and he died. They buried him, Dillinger pouring lye on Hamilton's face and hands to prevent identification should his corpse be found. Then Dillinger and Van Meter, having had enough of the north woods, headed back for Chicago. This was the hottest city on the continent for Dillinger, and that was precisely why he went there. He reasoned it would be the last move the law would expect.

Dillinger found a room and holed up. He underwent plastic surgery, hoping to have his features so altered that he would not be easily recognized, but the surgeon who did the job succeeded only in inflicting on Dillinger's features a mass of lumps and bruises without significantly altering their contours.

The Pierpont gang had now been whittled away by arrests and death until only Dillinger, Van Meter, and "Baby Face" Nelson were left. Dillinger felt, as he confided to friends, that his own time was coming, that indeed he must be a jinx. And he wasn't at all reassured when on June 22, 1934, his thirty-first birthday, the FBI publicly proclaimed him Public Enemy No. 1.

To keep himself in funds, Dillinger pulled an occasional bank robbery. But the old touch seemed gone; the proceeds were small for the risks he took. Probably he needed Pierpont, who had always been the real brains of the gang but who was now in prison. Dillinger, a hunted and hounded man, was strictly on his own.

He cheered himself up by acquiring a new girl friend—Polly Hamilton, 26, an attractive waitress. Polly had sublet a room from Anna Sage, 42, a husky Slavic woman of Rumanian origin, and Dillinger, a constant caller in Polly's room, came to know Anna. What was more important, she came to know him.

Though Dillinger didn't know it, Anna Sage was a woman in deep trouble. A bawdy-house madam, she had operated establishments in Gary and East Chicago, Indiana. She had been twice arrested and convicted for running disorderly houses, and she had been twice pardoned by the governor. A third arrest, however, had exhausted the patience of the law, and the federal government was at the moment threatening her with deportation. Anna, who didn't want to go back to Rumania, needed bargaining power to keep from being sent. And, as fate would have it, into her lap at just this critical juncture dropped the most wanted man in America, John Dillinger.

The result was that, one day in July, Anna Sage made a little trip into East Chicago and discussed her problem with Police Sergeant Martin Zarkovich, whom she had known for two years. Her proposition was simple: she would deliver Dillinger to the law, but she wanted two things—a promise that she would not be deported and the $10,000 reward that had been placed on Dillinger's head. Zarkovich took her proposition to his superior, Captain Timothy O'Neill, and O'Neill telephoned "Little Mel" Purvis.

Hoover, in his anxiety to catch Dillinger, had sent Special Agent Samuel N. Cowley from Washington to take supreme command of the FBI's special Dillinger squad, but Purvis still retained charge of the Chicago office. Conferences were now set up with Cowley and Purvis, and, with Hoover's approval, Purvis met Anna Sage. He pointed out to her that deportations were handled by the Labor Department, not the Justice Department, but he promised that, if she would help, he would do all he could to help her. Though he could make no guarantee about the reward, here, too, he promised to try to see to it that Anna Sage got her just deserts. With this, Anna had to be content.[7]

Events now moved swiftly. Anna told investigators she often accompanied Polly Hamilton and Dillinger to small neighborhood theaters. They were going, she thought, the next night. She would wear a vivid, red-looking dress.

Cowley summoned all the FBI agents in the Chicago area and briefed them on the trap. John Toland, in *The Dillinger Days,* wrote: "The plan had one astounding aspect. America's Public Enemy Number One was to be captured in Chicago without the knowledge of the Chicago police."

Since it was uncertain whether Dillinger would go to the Marbro or the Biograph, Purvis led a squad to the Biograph while Sergeant Zarkovich went with other FBI agents to the Marbro. Cowley and the main squad waited at headquarters for the final word. As it turned out, Dillinger selected the Biograph. Cowley phoned Hoover in Washington, and they discussed the possibility of taking Dillinger in the theater, but decided against it because gunplay there would endanger others. They would wait and take him as he came out.

Some fifteen FBI agents now descended on the Biograph. They were stationed at every exit, in the mouth of an alley just to the left of the theater, across the street in front of the theater, and up and down the street on both sides of the main entrance. Purvis took up his station in a doorway just to the left of the entrance, in the direction in which it was figured Dillinger would turn on his way back to Anna Sage's apartment. In his hand, Purvis held a cigar, and as soon as he spotted Dillinger coming out, he was to light the cigar as a signal to the agents to close in.

This concentration of strange men around the Biograph was so obvious and so ominous that theater employees began to get jittery. They feared a holdup, and the manager telephoned Chicago police to come and investigate. The police, not aware that the FBI was on the prowl for Dillinger, dispatched patrol cars and plainclothesmen to the danger scene.

About 10:20 P.M. one patrol car swung into the mouth of the alley near the theater where two of the strange men were standing. A Chicago detective jumped out and aimed a shotgun at Special Agent Ray Suran. "Find out who he is before you shoot," the detective at the wheel advised. Fortunately, the shotgun wielder heeded this precaution. Suran had a chance to identify himself, and slaughter of lawmen by lawmen was averted. The patrol car got hastily out of sight.

Other plainclothesmen, however, had arrived at the theater and talked to the manager. They came out, turned to the right and accosted some of the strangers loitering there. It was now 10:30, and the feature picture, "Manhattan Melodrama," with Clark Gable and William Powell, had finished. Just as one of the FBI agents on the right-hand side of the theater was presenting his credentials to the suspicious Chicago police, Dillinger and his two companions strolled out. They turned, as had been expected, to the left, not noticing the strange give-away tableau at the right. As they walked past Purvis, he raised a match and lighted his cigar. The ring of FBI agents started to close.

Dillinger, with the acute instinct of the hunted, instantly scented trouble. He cast one frantic glance about him, stooped, and started to run toward the mouth of the nearby alley, clawing for the gun in his right-hand trouser pocket. The pursuing agents fired a fusillade. One bullet ploughed through Dillinger's left side; another struck his bent back and tore upward, passing out through his right eye. Dillinger plunged face downward, as if chopped from behind by a poleax, his feet still on the sidewalk, his head in the edge of the alley, the gun he had drawn popping into the air from his lifeless hand.

The FBI's most dramatic chase had ended in final and gory

triumph. Dillinger, dead, had become a priceless exhibit for the FBI showcase in Washington.

There can be no doubt that Dillinger was a desperado. Cornered, he would no doubt kill the way a rat kills. But the evidence seems to say that he was not a man who savored or sought killing. He may or may not (since there was never a trial to prove it) have killed Patrolman O'Malley, but this seems to be the only murder directly attributable to him. His was not the notched gun butt of a Clyde Barrow or the gory and boasted record of a "Baby Face" Nelson. Dillinger was as much actor as desperado; he played a role; he lived a fiction, finding relish at times in deliberately taunting the cops, even in walking up to a policeman and asking him a question. This was needless risk, such as no coldly calculating mastermind of the underworld would ever court; but Dillinger was no mastermind. The real brains of "the Dillinger gang" seems to have been Harry Pierpont.

What was Dillinger then? He was a police-created symbol of menace, and when he went down in death, he went down in the cause of the FBI's glory. He became a foundation stone in building the myth of infallible success.

The fact is that the FBI's performance in the Dillinger case had been something less than perfect, less than brilliant. Its insistence on preserving Dillinger for itself and its own glory had led to situations in which, except for Providence, FBI agents and local officers could have become embroiled in deadly shooting matches. It had led to the fiasco at Little Bohemia and the slaying and wounding of innocent bystanders. These misadventures, in the determination to preserve the Dillinger legend and the FBI legend, are now usually glossed over. An example of such whitewashing is Whitehead's rendition of the St. Paul and Little Bohemia episodes in *The FBI Story:* "On two occasions, FBI agents thought they had Dillinger trapped. Each time he escaped in a barrage of machine-gun fire." And that is all he reported about these two gun battles, except for a brief reference in the "Notes" section at the end of the book.

Actually, when Attorney General Cummings and the FBI embarked on a campaign of "Shoot to kill—then count ten," Dillinger had committed no offense under federal law except to drive a stolen car across a state line, for which, as Turner Catledge (then Washington correspondent of *The New York Times*) acidly noted, "the offender is seldom shot on the spot." There can be little question that Dillinger was a headline means to an end—the building up of the greater, the infallible FBI. And in this context, he served this purpose well. So well, indeed, that Hoover and the FBI, almost from that shot-punctuated instant in front of the Biograph, have ruled the American law enforcement roost.

The fantastically swift accretion of power that was Hoover's was exhibited for all to see three years later when Captain Matt Leach was fired as head of the Indiana State Police. The State Police Board announced that the action had been taken at the request of Hoover. The FBI director, the board said, had accused Leach of refusing to cooperate in the hunt for the Brady gang of killers and had sent two of his agents to lodge a complaint against Leach and to notify the board that the FBI was severing relations with the state police. Leach responded by disclosing what had occurred during the Dillinger chase. He also said he had information that the FBI deliberately had warned witnesses not to talk to state police about the Brady gang. In Washington, Hoover and the FBI refused all comment and maintained a lofty detachment regarding the Leach affair, but somehow word got out to newsmen that the official decapitation of the veteran Indiana chief was "the first result of a drive" by Hoover to get the cooperation of local police forces.[8]

The Director, who just four years earlier had been worried about his own job, had become so powerful that he could lift the scalp of local police chiefs who had incurred his disapproval.

■ 2 ■

The FBI's credit-grabbing propensities showed in other famous cases during this glory-building period of the mid-1930's. No matter what agencies uncovered vital clues, it was almost invariably the FBI that rode to the final roundup and claimed all credit for itself and its director. Sound detective work, it seemed, was sometimes subordinated to the cause of propaganda—for example, in the celebrated capture of Alvin Karpis, Hoover's personal bête noire among the bad men of the era.

The Barker-Karpis mob was as precious a band of cutthroats as American gangdom ever spawned. Their depredations made the much-heralded feats of Dillinger look almost amateurish. Bank robbery. Kidnaping. Murder. The Barker-Karpis mob, or some individual member of it, had personal acquaintance with practically every crime in the book.

Kate ("Ma") Barker and her precious brood of four sons formed one wing of the mob; Alvin Karpis, whose right name was Francis Albin Karpavicz, the other. Fred Barker (one of "Ma" Barker's sons) and Karpis (nicknamed "Old Creepy" because his fish-eyed stare made other mobsters shudder) were introduced to each other while serving time in the Kansas State Penitentiary, and they formed a great mutual admiration society. Once let loose, they teamed up to comprise the heart and brain of a criminal combine that, from 1931 to 1936, was credited with ten murders and robberies that produced almost one million dollars worth of loot.

In July, 1932, the Barker-Karpis combine knocked off the Cloud County Bank at Concordia, Kansas, and escaped with more than $240,000. In a pre-Christmas raid the same year, they scored heavily at the Third Northwestern Bank of Minneapolis. As they were decamping with their loot, two policemen got in their way and were cut almost to pieces by a spray of machine-gun fire. One of the mob, spotting a civilian who seemed to be trying to memorize the license number of the getaway car, turned his machine gun on the observer and loosed a stream of bullets that eliminated this potential witness.

Anyone who looked at the Barker-Karpis mob courted death. "Ma" Barker's lover, suspected of possible disloyalty, was taken for a typical gangland ride and dumped, horribly perforated, by the shore of a small lake, with a woman's blood-stained glove left beside him as a memento of his fatal love affair. An attorney who had failed to secure the acquittal of one of the mobsters (the mob suspected him of not having done his best) was lured to a golf course north of Tulsa and there dispatched. If Dillinger represented a propaganda-created image of menace, the Barker-Karpis mob represented the grim reality.

Two of the more successful kidnapings of the era were attributed to the gang. The FBI finally decided (it had first tried to hang this crime on the Touhy bootlegging gang, but a jury wouldn't convict) the Barker-Karpis mobsters were responsible for the snatching of William A. Hamm, Jr., of the Hamm Brewing Company of St. Paul, which netted a $100,000 ransom. In January, 1934, the gang kidnaped Edward George Bremer, president of the Commercial State Bank of St. Paul, held him prisoner for almost a month, and released him after collecting $200,000 ransom in five and ten dollar bills.

The FBI, with its special interest in kidnaping, the crime that had catapulted it into the big-league crime-busting business, rode hard herd on the mob. One by one, some of the lesser desperados—and a number of their political and police protectors in corrupted Midwestern cities—were picked off, tried, and jailed. But "Ma" and Fred Barker and Alvin (Old Creepy) Karpis seemed to lead elusive and charmed lives. The persistent pursuit by the law was making them edgy, however, and Karpis, in a fine flight of megalomaniac rage, concluded at one point that his only salvation lay in the virtual liquidation of the FBI. According to Hoover, "Old Creepy" mapped a truly creepy chain of high-level murders. His battle plan called for the use of fast cars and airplanes to speed him from one slaying to the next. First, he would knock off the top FBI agent in Los Angeles; next, the agent in charge in Chicago; then, the principal agent in New York; and finally, Hoover himself. Whether Karpis was insane enough to do more than dream about such an incredible scheme isn't quite clear. When word of it reached Hoover, he demanded that every tidbit of information about Karpis' whereabouts and activities be expedited directly to his personal desk.[9]

In January, 1935, FBI agents got on the trail of "Ma" and Fred Barker. They were hiding out in a cottage on the shores of Lake Weir, near Ocala, Florida. FBI agents surrounded the cottage and called on the Barkers to surrender. The answer was a burst of machine-gun fire. A pitched battle followed. The FBI agents hurled tear gas bombs and riddled the cottage with machine-gun bullets until the Barkers' guns were silenced. The raiders then rushed the hideout and found both "Ma" Barker and her son dead, the guns they had dropped as they expired lying beside their bodies.

One wing of the mob had been liquidated, but Karpis was still on the loose. And Karpis was a power to be reckoned with. On April 24, 1935, he and two heavily armed confederates held up a mail truck in Warren, Ohio, and escaped with $70,000. Shortly afterward, in an even more lurid robbery, his gang raided Erie Train No. 622, bound from Detroit to Pittsburgh, at Garrettsville, Ohio. They held up postal employees, seized some $30,000 and escaped in a waiting airplane.

Such violations of United States mail brought a second powerful federal detective force, the postal inspectors, into the nationwide hunt for Karpis. According to the subsequent report of the Postmaster General, the postal sleuths made the next big score. In March, 1936, in cooperation with Kansas state police, they tracked down one member of Karpis' mob, and from the speed with which the searching agents got on Karpis' trail, it would seem that the postal men must have uncovered vital information.

Hoover, in the meantime, had been treating Karpis with denunciation and contempt. Karpis, he said, headed the "shrewdest, most cold-blooded gang in America"; he was "Former Enemy Number One" who had become "Public Rat Number One." And Hoover and the FBI were going to exterminate this "rat."

Soon after the postal sleuths had scored their coup in Kansas, in this same month of March, 1936, Hoover and the FBI learned that Karpis and one of his trusted triggermen had sought refuge in Hot Springs, Arkansas, the wide-open haven of mobsters on the lam. Hoover says that they were "afforded protection by the chief of police and the chief of detectives" and that "Karpis took unto himself a dexterous woman who managed to divide her attentions between him and one of Hot Springs' law enforcement officers." Hoover and a squad of his agents rushed to the Washington airport and were prepared to take off to interrupt Karpis' affair with the dexterous one when they got the message that Karpis had fled, tipped off apparently by the police in Hot Springs who had been protecting him.

Hoover, in disgust, returned to his office and waited for his agents to pick up Karpis' tracks again. While he waited, he became involved in what for him was becoming an increasingly rare experience—a head-butting contest with a powerful Congressional committee. Senator Kenneth D. McKellar, Democrat, of Tennessee, had made no secret of the fact that there was little love lost between him and Hoover, and in late April, 1936, he took advantage of his position as chairman of the Senate Appropriations Committee to subject Hoover to a severe grilling. As his questions made clear, his purpose was to show that Hoover had never personally made an arrest, that he had little personal experience in crime detection—that he was, in a word, a virtual amateur. As *Time* Magazine recounted it, McKellar "wanted to know why G-man Hoover wasn't out risking his own neck. Hoover had to admit that he had never personally made a pinch." Hoover, said *Time,* was "boiling mad." Don Whitehead wrote (years later) that Hoover's "face was flushed with anger." Determined to show up McKellar for the slur on his personal courage, Hoover raged for his agents to flush out Karpis. Soon they did.

The word was flashed to Hoover that Karpis had been traced to New Orleans. Posing as a "Mr. O'Hara," Karpis was living with a henchman and the henchman's kept woman in a pleasant apartment on Canal Street. Just how the FBI had learned all this, Hoover has never said. Much-miffed postal inspectors intimated after the event that the G-men had been acting on leads developed by the inspectors. Hoover denied it, but offered no counterexplanation. In any event, Hoover, with McKellar's jibes acting as a goad, lost no time beating the postal inspectors to the pinch.

Hoover, with a raiding party he had marshaled, took off by airplane from Washington on the evening of April 30, 1936, and the following morning, after an all-night flight, swooped down on New Orleans. Here other agents were assembled, and plans were drafted for the raid on the Canal Street apartment. Hoover himself and four assistants were to crash the front door while his men ringed the apartment house and guarded all possible exits.

The agents had hardly taken up their posts when Karpis altered their plans. The front door of the apartment house opened, and there was Karpis, accompanied by his hoodlum pal, striding down the front steps. They walked toward their car, parked at the curb. Before Hoover and his men could move or fire, a small boy riding a bicycle passed between them and Karpis. They had to wait for the boy to get out of harm's way before they could act, and by that time Karpis and his aide were seating themselves in the car. The FBI men rushed forward. Hoover, running to the left side of the car, grabbed Karpis before his surprised "Public Rat Number One" could reach for a rifle lying on the back seat.

It had all been ridiculously easy. Under the circumstances, with McKellar breathing caustic fire down his back, Hoover's personal nabbing of Karpis represented a great triumph. But now, in the moment of victory, came a strange denouement. Hoover himself later described the event for one of his favorite writers, Frederick L. Collins. This is Hoover's first-person account as rendered by Collins: [10]

" 'Put the cuffs on him, boys,' I said.

"Then it developed that not one of us had a pair of handcuffs. They were in the other cars. A crowd was gathering and we had to move fast, so the two agents bound the hands of the hoodlum with their neckties.

" 'To the Post Office Building,' I instructed the driver.

"The car, with four of us, turned into Canal Street. After it had gone a few blocks, I asked the Oklahoma agent who was driving:

" 'You know how to get there in a hurry, don't you?'

" 'No, sir,' he replied, 'I was never in New Orleans before in my life.'

" 'Mr. Hoover,' broke in Karpis, who hadn't said a word up to then, 'if you mean the new Post Office, I know where that is, because I was just goin' to rob it.'

"Fortunately for the dignity of the Federal Bureau of Investigation, it was the old Post Office where the prisoners were to be taken, and we didn't have to accept the proferred guidance. We did, however, have to ask the way from a passing pedestrian."

These details, which seem to indicate that even in this major headline case some of the FBI's arrangements were less than perfect, didn't all come to light at the time. What was immediately obvious was that Hoover had personally made an important arrest and that, by doing so, he had neatly turned the tables on Senator McKellar. The arrest of Karpis was a dramatic answer to McKellar's barbs, and the red flush of embarrassment had been neatly transferred from the face of the Director of the FBI to that of the chairman of the Senate Appropriations Committee. The result: Hoover rode higher than ever—so high that it would be a bold Senator indeed who, in the years to come, would risk the fate that had been McKellar's. [11]

■ 3 ■

The widely ballyhooed Dillinger and Karpis episodes, plus the almost weekly exploits of FBI agents riding to other exciting if slightly less notable roundups, enshrined Hoover and the FBI on such a lofty pedestal in the popular imagination that hardly anybody asked questions about the claims the Director advanced concerning the Bureau's achievements. If Hoover said it was so, it was so. This became, and remains, the popular attitude, and no one critically examined the Hoover technique of credit-claiming. Kidnaping, a major preoccupation of the Bureau, was the offense that first had broadened the FBI's crime-hunting range; as a result, the FBI devoted to it a major portion of its effort. In his annual reports over a period of years, Hoover always emphasized the fact that almost every kidnaping case had been solved. He may not have said so explicitly, but the clear impression he gave was that the FBI, single-handed, had done the perfect clean-up job. Newspapers headlined this deft suggestion as unassailable fact, and nobody asked the obvious questions: Should all the credit in all these cases go to the FBI? What about the local police departments that worked on the same crimes? Did they, perhaps, do the key detective work—furnish the vital clues?

In September, 1935, Milton S. Mayer, who had had the advantage of observing firsthand some of Hoover's celebrated cases, wrote an article that he called, "Myth of the 'G-Men.' " [12] He pointed out that the McElroy, Lindbergh, and Weyerhaeuser kidnapings were broken by other agencies, not by the Bureau. Two years later, Jack Alexander, in his *New Yorker* profile of Hoover, made acid note of the manner in which the FBI indoctrinated thousands of tourists in the belief that it alone had broken the Lindbergh case. Alexander described how an FBI guide, with a line of running patter and graphic physical exhibits, carried his gaping audiences right into the heart of the recreated chase for criminals. Elaborately prepared maps and charts, on which blinking lights picked out the course of action, helped make each tourist feel like Dick Tracy, hard on the heels of the malefactor. Alexander described the overall effect:

The tourists also get the impression that the FBI has been responsible for the solution of most of the recent major crimes. In dilating upon the Lindbergh case, for example, the tour leader tells how "we" solved it, and directs attention to a large map of New York City on which the G-men, using colored pins, kept a geographical record of the trail of the spent ransom notes. No mention is made of the fact that New York police kept a similar map, or of the fact that Treasury agents really set the trap which caught [Bruno Richard] Hauptmann. Perhaps few of the tourists realize that the ransom packets as originally made up by J. P. Morgan & Co. contained no gold notes, and that it was only because Treasury agents insisted that the packets were remade to include $35,000 worth of them. The passing of one of the gold notes at a filling station led directly to Hauptmann's arrest.[13]

Even more striking than the Lindbergh case as examples of Hoover's publicity techniques were a couple of 1936 captures in which Hoover emphatically took all credit for the Bureau, and in which facts popped up that seemed most embarrassingly to contradict him.

The first contretemps arose over the May 11, 1936, arrest of Thomas H. Robinson, Jr., in Pasadena, California. Robinson had been the object of a nationwide hunt as the kidnaper of Mrs. Alice Speed Stoll. When he was nabbed in his apartment with an arsenal of five guns around him, Hoover personally announced his arrest and claimed full credit for the FBI. The United Press paraphrased Hoover's remarks this way:

> Mr. Hoover said trailing the ransom money as it turned up across the country was one of the major factors in apprehending Robinson, but declined to reveal details of the hunt or exactly what had led to his final apprehension.
>
> He did say, however, that the capture was entirely the result of work by FBI agents and that *no tips had been received from any outside source* which were of the slightest value in the hunt. [Italics added.]

The same day that newspapers were publicizing this claim by Hoover, the United Press tracked down a source who, it appeared, must have been of some assistance to the G-men. He was Lynn Allen, a lunch-counter manager in a Pasadena drug store. Allen described in graphic detail how, two weeks earlier, "a stylishly dressed young woman" entered the drug store, "gracefully seated herself at the soda fountain and asked for orange juice." Just one thing had been wrong. The "woman" had a man's voice, and Allen had subjected "her" to close, covert scrutiny and had thought he recognized the much-hunted kidnaper, Robinson. "He [Allen] telephoned police. Police notified the G-men," the United Press reported.

In a separate, by-line story, the news agency carried Allen's own account of how he had become suspicious of Robinson. He wrote:

> The thing that attracted my attention was his extreme height. Only a few women as tall as 5 feet 11 or 6 feet come into the store. I started scrutinizing him carefully when I waited on him. . . . I remembered a description of Robinson. This man fitted the description even to a dimple on his chin and a disfigured ear. He was heavily painted, apparently to conceal the stubble on his face. The only time he spoke was when I asked him if he wanted grapefruit juice or orange juice. He said, "Orange juice."
>
> His voice was that of a man, although he tried to conceal it by making it high-pitched. I called police as soon as possible and told them I believed I had seen Robinson. They brought me to the police station and after seeing the photographs there was no question in my mind that it was Robinson.[14]

This account seems to establish that the G-men hadn't made their score all by their own little selves, as Hoover had claimed, but that they had received a major and vital assist from Allen in pinpointing the very area in which Robinson was nabbed. And the tip had come not directly to the FBI but through routine police channels.

Even more specific in its refutation of an all-out claim by Hoover was the case of Harry Brunette. Brunette and his partner, Merle Vandenbush, had been hunted as suspects in a series of bank robberies. After November 11, 1936, they had been wanted for kidnaping, too, for on that day, in escaping from Somerville, New Jersey, they had kidnaped State Trooper William A. Turnbull and had held him prisoner for a short time. The kidnaping naturally made headline news, and the hounds of the law were soon hot on Brunette's trail. They ran him down just after midnight, early on the morning of December 15, 1936, when Hoover personally led a squad of ten agents in a raid on an apartment at 304 West 102nd Street, New York City, where Brunette was holed up.

The raid was not staged with maximum stealth. G-men began the action by trying to shoot the lock off Brunette's apartment door. Brunette, not taking kindly to the idea, grabbed his guns and shot back. Bullets began to ricochet around the walls of the apartment building, where twenty families lived. Unable to outshoot Brunette, the federal agents hurled tear-gas bombs, trying to smoke him out. One of the bombs set fire to the building. Firemen were summoned.

The fire-fighters found themselves caught in a cross-fire of bullets, and it seems a miracle none of them got killed. *Newsweek,* in describing the battle, wrote:

> Amid the hubbub, a flustered G-man poked a submachine gun at a husky fireman. "Dammit, can't you read?" growled the fireman, pointing at his helmet. "If you don't take that gun out of my stomach, I'll bash your head in." For thirty-five minutes, the shooting continued. Then a lull. "Give up, or we'll shoot," shouted a G-man—as if they had been throwing spitballs up to then. A young woman, the wife of Harry Brunette, staggered out, shot in the thigh. Then came the unharmed Brunette—twenty-five-year-old bank robber.

The New York Times reported that both the New York City police and the New Jersey State Police were incensed at Hoover for the manner in which the raid had been staged and accused him "of violating an agreement with them in order to steal the glory that was rightfully theirs." Brunette, they charged, had been run down through their efforts alone, and if Hoover hadn't rushed in prematurely in a glory-grabbing raid, there was an excellent chance that Vandenbush might have been trapped in the apartment with the Brunettes.

Hoover, in Washington, expressed the surprise of a man back on his pedestal at such picayune carping. His attitude was that everybody should be deliriously happy because a bad man had been caught. He explained that he had written letters to all the aggrieved police officials, thanking them for their cooperation. As for their charges, he insisted he had never double-crossed anybody and added: "Hindsight is better than foresight." Hoover refused to disclose where he had obtained the information that led to the trapping of Brunette, but he denied that it came "from any law enforcement agency."

This denial got some rough handling from Colonel Mark O. Kimberling, commander of the New Jersey State Police, and from Commissioner Lewis J. Valentine of New York, one of the most famous police executives in the country. Both Kimberling and Valentine, quoting from basic day-to-day investigative reports that dovetailed and told a devastating story, made it clear that their detectives had located Brunette and that they had told the FBI the details only after they had Brunette under surveillance.

The first part of the investigation belonged to Colonel Kimberling's State Troopers. A car had been left in a Philadelphia garage and hadn't been claimed by the owner. The garage people, believing that the vehicle answered the description of the one used in the Turnbull kidnaping, had notified police. New Jersey State Troopers went to Philadelphia and dusted the car for fingerprints. They raised one showing that Vandenbush had been an occupant. More important, in the glove compartment, detectives found an old garage bill. The garage was located in New York City. And so Colonel Kimberling had briefed Commissioner Valentine on the information that the New Jersey detectives had gathered.

Taking up the recital at this point, Valentine supplied step-by-step details of the hunt. According to *The New York Times,* he quoted from detective reports so specific that they left little doubt. A number of detectives had been assigned to the case. Garage employees had been questioned, and they had identified pictures of Brunette and Vandenbush as the men who had used the car. More important, garage attendants recalled that they had often seen the car parked on 105th Street and that Brunette was known in the neighborhood as the boy friend of Arline LaBeau, who lived with her parents in an apartment there.

The detectives had followed this lead. They had learned that Arline LaBeau had recently married her boy friend. The newlyweds were understood to be living in an apartment of their own in the same general neighborhood. Hoping to spot them, Trooper Turnbull himself drifted about the area in plain clothes. The girl had been in the car with Brunette and Vandenbush when the trooper was kidnaped, and Turnbull felt sure he would recognize her. Luck was with him. He actually spotted Arline on the street, trailed her, but lost sight of her near 102nd Street.

At this point, Commissioner Valentine said, the FBI was notified that city detectives and New Jersey troopers had developed a lead in the Brunette case. But the investigation was still handled, in its entirety, by the cooperating New York and New Jersey detectives. The commissioner went back to reading the detailed daily reports that showed this.

The detectives had made a house-to-house canvass along 102nd Street. At 304 West 102nd, Detectives James Cotter and James A. O'Brien, of the New York police, and Trooper Sergeant Gustave Albrecht, of the New Jersey force, had learned from the superintendent that a new couple had registered in the building under the name of Mr. and Mrs. Robert Lake. The superintendent had identified a picture of Brunette as the man he knew as Lake.

The detectives had made a careful study of the building. They had noted all possible means of escape. They had even gotten into the Brunettes' apartment while the couple was out and had mapped its physical layout. They had set up a plant in another apartment inside the building. The Jersey troopers had set up another plant in an adjoining building from which they could watch the entrance. At this point, said Valentine, Hoover had been notified again—this time that the quarry had been run to earth and was being watched.

Brunette could have been seized at any time, but the New York and New Jersey police, like good detectives, wanted to get Vandenbush too. They were content to wait until they could catch the confederates together. The FBI, it appears, was more impatient. But Valentine and Kimberling both insisted that an ironclad agreement had been made with the G-men. It provided that all information would be shared, that the three agencies would act in concert. After the pact had been concluded, there were some rumbles of discontent from the FBI, Valentine admitted. As a result, a conference, with the three agencies represented, had been held in New York police headquarters on a Monday afternoon. Again, after some argument, the G-men had agreed to concerted action, and a specific time had been set for the raid: two o'clock on Tuesday afternoon. Valentine explained that there were two reasons for this timing: first, Vandenbush had been reported in the vicinity and might turn up at the apartment; second and most important, surveillance had established that Brunette was a night owl who prowled in the dark, slept all day. Two o'clock in the afternoon would be the best time to take him with his guns down.

Notwithstanding this explicit agreement, Hoover personally led the G-men on the raid shortly after midnight—some fourteen hours before the agreed time. Detectives Cotter and O'Brien had left their plant for a coffee break, Valentine acknowledged, but Troopers Albrecht and Meade, of the Jersey force, were on watch. Startled when Hoover and his raiders showed up, they rushed out into the street to ask what he was doing, but, according to *The New York Times*, "he merely shrugged his shoulders, one of the police officers said." While Albrecht stayed on the scene remonstrating with Hoover, Meade dashed around the corner and dragged Cotter and O'Brien from their coffee. By the time the three detectives got back, the G-men and Brunette were making war.

This precipitate action by Hoover cost authorities the chance to catch Vandenbush at that time. The sequel showed that, had Hoover waited, had he honored the solemn pact the FBI had made with New York and New Jersey police, Vandenbush as well as Brunette might have been bagged. Jack Alexander wrote:

> An ironic epilogue to the raid was enacted two months later when the fugitive Vandenbush and two other hoodlums were captured by village police in Armonk. Vandenbush told his captors that he had come to 102nd Street to see Brunette just as the federal siege was starting and that he got so close to the excitement he could almost have leaned over and touched the Director on the shoulder. After rubbernecking in the crowd of other citizens for a few minutes, Vandenbush said, he strolled off. His captors received this message from Hoover: "Your work in apprehending Vandenbush constitutes a material contribution to the advancement of the cause of law enforcement." It had done all of that and more; it had furnished a striking lesson in contrasts. The rustic cops had not found it necessary to fire a shot or throw a single tear-gas bomb, despite the fact that the men they were stalking were armed and were trying to escape with $17,626 in loot.[15]

What was Hoover's explanation? The record shows that newspapermen kept after him for several days, but Hoover wasn't saying much. The official silence in Washington was broken first by Attorney General Homer Cummings, who, as always, was Hoover's champion. He proclaimed that the arrest of Brunette had been "a necessary job well done" and added: "Everybody ought to be happy, and it is too bad to have all this talk." [16]

Three days later, Hoover himself followed the lead of his titular boss. In contrast to the detailed reports of Kimberling and Valentine, Hoover spoke in generalities. He charged that the New York detectives, instead of taking a coffee break, had goofed off on the job for four hours. One of his own agents, Hoover said, had seen Brunette on the street with a woman, evidently his wife, about midnight and had seen them go back into the 102nd Street building. So? As for the Jersey troopers, they couldn't see the front of the building adequately in the dark, Hoover said, ignoring the fact that they seemed to have spotted him quickly enough. As for the charge that his men had fired "hundreds" of bullets, it wasn't so at all—they'd fired only sixty-two. As for the rest, it was all "unjustified and petty criticism," the New York and New Jersey cops were indulging in "kindergarten stuff," all that mattered was that the public had gotten its money's worth when the FBI grabbed Brunette. And anyway what was needed was less of this bickering and more genuine cooperation between local and federal law enforcement agencies.[17]

■ 4 ■

We are left with a picture that seems quite different from the portrait of FBI supermen riding flawlessly to glory. Obviously, the Hoover who was building his legend and his Bureau's legend on the gunfire of agents in wild scenes reminiscent of the frontier West was a man who was arrogating to himself tremendous power. He could not decently share credit with local police where credit was plainly due. He could not cooperate, even when lack of cooperation risked the defeat of his purpose and (as at Little Bohemia and the Biograph and again in the Brunette case in New York) the lives of his agents and of innocent bystanders. He was a man who could brook no opposition, no criticism. In such cases, as Matt Leach had learned, as others were to learn, he could lash about with a heavily punitive hand.

In 1938, smarting from the FBI's failure to solve the kidnaping of young Peter Levine, of New Rochelle, New York, who was beheaded by his captor, Hoover teed off at the press in an article in *Collier's* Magazine. He plainly implied that the press was responsible for the Levine boy's death because it had hindered the efforts of the FBI by breaking out in a rash of page-one stories that had alarmed the kidnaper. Lou Wedemar, the *Daily News* reporter who had broken the barrier of silence on the case and forced the first publication, responded with an account that plainly implied Hoover was trying to make the press the scapegoat for his own bureau's delinquencies. He wrote:

> The first ransom note warned the parents against notifying the authorities. Nevertheless, the first steps taken inevitably insured publicity. And what happened then? Within a few hours two youthful G-men were clambering over a wall and setting up headquarters in the house; window shades were pulled mysteriously up and down; linesmen began installing special telephones; guards skulked on the terraces of the residence. Investigators began going from house to house in the neighborhood; G-men's automobiles roared through the little city. Confusion and hysteria were so evident that the news reached the press within a short time. Even before it was published, however, the kidnaper could not have failed to know that his injunction had been disobeyed.[18]

Westbrook Pegler, who was then a highly regarded columnist, not the vitriolic man of journalism that he later became, observed the dispute from the sidelines and rendered judgment. Sure, he said, perhaps the activities of reporters sometimes did embarrass the FBI, but this did not mean that reporters must be held responsible for the murder of the Levine boy. He pointed out that Hoover had made a wild charge without offering a shred of evidence. He continued:

> It would seem more likely that in this case and in the Mattson case the criminals never had any intention to return the victims, and killed them as soon as they conveniently could. A captive, living child is a dangerous handicap to a criminal who knows that a murder adds little, if anything, to the penalty he has already deserved. Mr. Hoover, who boasts that many of his agents are lawyers and that all of them, himself included, know evidence, makes an emotional accusation against

the reporters in these two instances, but does not support it with anything that even resembles proof.

Do you want to know something about Mr. Hoover? He is spoiled. The American press has treated him as a sacred cow. . . . He has been praised in proportion to the very fine feats of detection which his bureau has achieved, and a little beyond, for the G-men have received entire credit for some jobs in which other agencies took part. He is a great personal press agent, and he has pet writers, or stooges, with access to big newspaper and magazine circulation, who scratch his back in return for material that glorifies Edgar Hoover and the G's.[19]

■ Notes ■

[1] Jack Alexander, *The New Yorker,* Sept. 25, 1937.

[2] Publishers persisted in the Hoover accolade. In 1958, after I had written for *The Nation* a critical assessment of the FBI, one of the popular men's magazines, finding that the issue was selling out on the newsstands, asked a writer friend of mine to refurbish my prose in man's magazine style, keeping in some of the criticism along with the dramatic chases. As the manuscript went through the editing process, the items of criticism disappeared one by one and the glowing words of praise became more glowing. The publisher confessed that what he wanted was a personal letter from Hoover commending him for his patriotic services to the nation, and so the manuscript was tailored to this end. The final distortion may not greatly have served the ends of truth, but at least it achieved its purpose.

[3] Page 239 of memorandum, "The Revolution in Action," prepared for Palmer by Hoover's GID and submitted by Palmer to the House Rules Committee, 66th Congress, 1920, under the headings, "Attorney General A. Mitchell Palmer on Charges Made Against the Department of Justice by Louis F. Post."

[4] This account of the Dillinger saga is based to a considerable degree on John Toland, *The Dillinger Days* (Random House, 1963).

[5] See McLellan article in *Harper's;* also Milton S. Mayer, "Myth of the G-Men," in *The Forum,* September, 1935.

[6] Leach's angry statement denouncing FBI tactics was carried at considerable length in the *New York World-Telegram* and other papers on Sept. 4, 1937.

[7] In the end, Anna Sage's treachery where Dillinger was concerned availed her little. She received only $5,000 of the reward money, and, despite her help to the FBI, was deported to Rumania, where she died in 1947.

[8] United Press dispatches in the *New York World-Telegram,* Sept. 4 and 8, 1937.

[9] See Hoover's own by-lined account, "The Toughest Mob We Ever Cracked," in *The FBI in Action,* by Ken Jones.

[10] Frederick L. Collins, *The FBI in Peace and War* (Putnam's, 1940). With an Introduction by J. Edgar Hoover.

[11] The devastating sequel was described by Jack Alexander in *The New Yorker,* Oct. 9, 1937, in these words: "The Senate appropriations committee recommended a cut of $225,000 [in Hoover's budget] and when the matter was brought up on the floor, Senator McKellar . . . spoke in favor of the cut. Senator (Arthur H.) Vandenberg arose and denounced McKellar as a miser who would cause the threat of kidnaping to hang once more over every cradle in America. . . . While he talked, Democratic leaders gathered in an excited knot and decided to abjure McKellar's cynicism. Obviously, it would not do to permit the Democratic standard to wave on the side of the underworld. When Vandenberg sat down, one Democrat after another got up and lavishly eulogized the G-men for their work. After the echoes of the oratory had died down, an amendment embodying the proposed cut was defeated by a throaty roar of noes and the Senate voted the full appropriation. McKellar sat apart in Catilinian silence, shunned by friend and foe alike."

[12] *The Forum,* September, 1935.

[13] Alexander in *The New Yorker,* Sept. 25, 1937.

[14] United Press dispatches from Washington and Pasadena in the *New York World-Telegram,* May 12, 1936.

[15] *The New Yorker,* Oct. 9, 1937.

[16] *New York World-Telegram,* Dec. 17, 1937.

[17] *New York Times,* Dec. 20, 1937.

[18] Lou Wedemar, "The Press Agent Takes Over," in *Scribner's,* 1939.

[19] Westbrook Pegler in the *New York World-Telegram,* Aug. 8, 1938.

7 Efficiency – and Science

Just how efficient is the FBI? It is impossible to answer that question without first cutting through the fog of propaganda with which Hoover's highly organized publicity staff has shrouded the activities of the Bureau. The trouble is that FBI propaganda has not been recognized and treated as propaganda. Instead, it has been accepted as one of the verities of the ages, because it is disseminated under the FBI's impressive imprimatur. To question a release by the Bureau, to doubt an assertion by Hoover, to challenge a Hoover interpretation of the problems of our times, has become an exercise in *lèse-majesté* that can brand the man attempting it as something less than a 100 percent American.

Everyone knows that figures can be made to lie. But when Hoover dogmatically asserts that the FBI maintains a 97 or 98 percent conviction record, no one doubts or challenges his figures or speculates about the insidious effect of this kind of reiterated propaganda on the minds of a jury sitting in judgment on a man accused of crime by the infallible FBI. Everyone knows that the cataloguing of men's minds is a dangerous and uncertain business, that one man's pale liberal is another man's shouting radical. But when Hoover pictures Communism as riddling the framework of democracy—and takes off on attacks against "fellow travelers" and "pseudo liberals" and Communist "dupes" and "stooges"—an entire nation listens and quakes, and each man begins to look askance at his neighbor. The influence of the FBI and its Director has been deep and permeative, and it is hardly possible to see ourselves or our times in any kind of clear perspective unless we can also see Hoover and the FBI with clarity and understanding.

205

The issue is not academic; it is basic to any contact with reality. If Hoover's glory-grabbing—his propagation of superhuman stature for himself and his Bureau—had served only to add to his own reputation and to build the image of the FBI as the nemesis of crime, little harm would been done. But if the history of the twentieth century proves anything, it is that the effects of propaganda are never confined. The myth of superman inevitably conditions the society that renders him obeisance, as Hitler and Mussolini demonstrated. In a democracy, if it is to endure as a democracy, myth must not become confused with reality; the word of the superman must not be blindly accepted as the last word, closing all debate.

Is the FBI record really so infallible? How does it compare, for example, with the much less publicized sleuths of the Secret Service who guard the President and have all but eliminated the crime of counterfeiting? Or with the postal inspectors? Or agents of the Federal Bureau of Narcotics? Does the FBI even begin to justify that image of spotless perfection that the great majority of Americans have of it?

■ 1 ■

Back in 1937, one aspect of Hoover's unrestrained publicity campaign struck Jack Alexander as conflicting sharply with basic requirements of sound detective work, as flying in the face of all common sense, all logic. Alexander wrote:

> The ways of the FBI have been so exhaustively publicized, in the writings of Hoover and in books and articles by outsiders published with his blessing, that a moderately literate criminal ought to be able to avoid capture indefinitely. The books and articles, by implication, tell him what mistakes to shun, and some of them, in addition, give him an interesting slant on himself which he would be unlikely to reach by introspection. For example, one of Hoover's prides is a modus-operandi file, something which describes the characteristic touches by which the techniques of specific public enemies may be recognized. In cases in which none of the witnesses is able to identify the criminals from rogues'-gallery photographs, the G-men are frequently able to identify them from descriptions of their handiwork. Thus it is possible to get started immediately on the trail of thugs who

think they have made a clean getaway and who are therefore apt to be careless. But a criminal who takes the time to read *The Feds* or *Farewell, Mr. Gangster!*, a book about the FBI published last year with a foreword by Hoover, can learn all about the modus-operandi file. Then, unless he is immune to suggestion, the wisdom of varying his technique from time to time must inevitably occur to him.

The FBI policy of disclosing how it works differs sharply from the secrecy which other federal detective bureaus, notably the postal inspectors and the Treasury units, throw about their activities. No one learns how the Secret Service guards the President, and only rarely, usually through local police sources, does the public learn how it catches counterfeiters, how the postal inspectors trap perverters of the mails, or how the Treasury agents discover those who defraud the government of revenue. When these agencies work in conjunction with local police, they withdraw after a capture and let the police tell the story. In informed circles, their detective work is rated above that of the FBI. Their style resembles the homely style of first-rate police detectives, who dislike gunfire and tear gas and prefer to get a fugitive by slipping in quietly by way of the fire escape while he is visiting his mother.[1]

Alexander's report that "informed circles" rated the work of some of the other federal detective agencies as superior to that of the FBI doubtless will come as a shock to a nation brainwashed for decades into believing that the G-men represent the epitome of detective art. Can this belief possibly be valid?

In the attempt to find an answer, there is an important guideline. More than twenty-five years ago, the Brookings Institution, of Washingon, D.C., was hired by a Senate committee headed by Senator Harry F. Byrd, the veteran conservative Democrat from Virginia, to make an impartial survey and comparison of all federal law-enforcement agencies. The Institution's findings were published in 1937, in a volume titled *Crime Control by the National Government,* by A. C. Millspaugh of the Brookings staff.

Anyone who has become conditioned during the years to accept Hoover's statement that the FBI achieves from 94 to 97 or 98 percent of convictions in its cases, a nearly perfect batting average, almost certainly will be shocked at the Brookings Institution's findings for the 1935–36 period. Instead of accepting the Hoover statement as bona fide because Hoover made it, the Brookings researchers cross-checked with the reports of federal attorneys, as incorporated in the U.S. Attorney General's own report, on the disposition of cases developed by the different federal detective agencies. They found that the FBI's record of convictions for the 1935–36 period was 72.5 percent— trailing the Narcotics Bureau, the Secret Service Division, the Alcohol Tax Unit, the Post Office Inspection Service, and the Internal Revenue Bureau. The only agency that ranked below the FBI in percentage of convictions was the Customs Bureau, with 71.5 percent.[2]

Millspaugh turned a critical spotlight on the manner in which Hoover played the numbers game to promote the belief that the FBI was virtually infallible. In a footnote, he pointed out that Hoover, in a speech to the United States Conference of Mayors in November, 1936, had boasted: " . . . the Federal Bureau of Investigation . . . is proud of its latest record which shows that only three out of every hundred men walk free from the court-room once this organization has assembled its evidence and placed that evidence before a judge and jury. In other words, it averages 97 per cent of convictions." [3]

The gimmick here, which would never occur to the average citizen listening to such a claim by the impressive J. Edgar Hoover, is that not all men who are arrested wind up in court. Bad cases may be discarded by federal prosecuting attorneys, or grand juries may fail to indict. A claim based on the percentage of convictions obtained in cases that actually go to court is one founded on partial and favorable statistics. Even so, Millspaugh found, Hoover and the FBI were greatly over-rating their perfectibility by advancing a 97 percent conviction claim. Their own statistics did not justify it and would not even stand critical examination. Millspaugh wrote:

> For example, the Bureau of Investigation states that 117 persons were convicted in the federal courts in 1935–36 under the federal bank-robbery statute and *only three persons* were acquitted. In the same official report, the Attorney General's statistics show only 114 defendants tried for national bank robbery, only 53 convicted, and *no less than 31 acquitted.* Again, in his testimony before the House Appropriations Committee in January 1937, the Director of the Bureau of Investigation stated that "the percentage of convictions obtained by the Bureau in cases which we investigated was 94.35." Although this

figure apparently represents the percentage of defendants who were not acquitted after trial, in order to obtain it the cases which were otherwise disposed of must be treated as if convictions had been obtained. As we have seen, the percentage actually convicted was 72.5.[4] [Italics added.]

The Brookings Institution pointed out also that the FBI's statistics on its own performance were greatly improved by the practice of taking credit for a tremendous amount of work performed by other agencies. For years, a major factor in boosting FBI figures has been the recovery of stolen automobiles that have been driven or shipped across state lines. The FBI always claims full credit for the recovery of such cars and for the apprehension of the thieves. It annually points to the millions of dollars it has saved the taxpayers through the recovery of such stolen property. Yet, in many, if not in most instances, such stolen automobiles are found and recovered by local police, and even in the tracking down of car theft rings the FBI receives vital assistance, not only from local police, but from detectives of private agencies like the National Board of Fire Underwriters, which represents the insurance industry. Private detectives, who frequently perform the key work in such cases, always fade from the picture when the FBI compiles the statistics on its achievements.

Commenting on this pattern, Millspaugh sharply criticized the Bureau's 1935–36 figures as being obviously and grossly inflated:

> In a considerable number of cases attributed to federal agencies, a part—and in some cases a substantial part—of the work of investigation, apprehension, and collection of evidence is performed by other law-enforcement agencies, federal, state, and local. For example, of the 3,905 convictions reported to have been obtained by the Bureau of Investigation in the fiscal year 1936, 1,570 or 40.2 percent were under the national Motor Vehicle Theft Act; and it would seem that in many such cases substantial assistance must have been rendered by state and local law enforcement officers.[5]

The numbers game, though the public seems not to realize it, should never be taken literally, because it is an essential ingredient of bureaucratic propaganda. Federal bureaus like the FBI must go to Congress for funds. To get the funds they want—and they always want more—they must show a crying, if indeed not a desperate, need. The more urgent the need, the more grandiose the figures, the more likely is it that the bureau standing on the brink of crisis will get the cash it wants to help it avert some horrible national disaster. In one prophetic paragraph, the Brookings report turned a searchlight on such uses of bureaucratic propaganda. "In order to obtain the appropriations which they consider necessary, a law-enforcement agency, like any other administrative service, finds itself between the horns of a dilemma," Millspaugh wrote. "On the one hand, it must reveal tangible accomplishments; on the other hand, it must show its inadequacy. It must report progress, but not too much; for, if it demonstrates that its problems are disappearing, it will be arguing in effect for a cut in its appropriations. Government bureaus rarely do that." Had Millspaugh been privileged to know Jack Levine, he could not more perceptively have described the Bureau's need to maintain a dying domestic Communism as a menace.

In the years since Millspaugh's description of bureaucratic need was written, there has always been a crisis, always a Menace. The original menace was, of course, the white slavery that threatened every man's mother, wife, and daughter. Next came war and spies; then, with peace and the demise of spies, the Red Menace of the Palmer era. Kidnaping gave the Bureau its next great shot in the arm, and no sooner did kidnaping begin to wane in popularity than we had the great bank-robbery menace. This in turn was to yield the stage to sabotage and espionage. And with the second peace and the Cold War, the Red Menace, with its threat of internal subversion and betrayal, was with us once again, only this time in more aggravated and insidious form. We have had other menaces. Juvenile delinquency was pretty big for a while, but nothing has been quite so good, quite so enduring, quite so scary as the Red Menace. That's the one that really builds a protective bureaucracy.

Just what should one believe when one hears the Director of the FBI thundering about such menaces? Obviously, it should be recognized, as generally it is not, that a perpetual need of the Bureau, for its own preservation in the manner of life to which it has become accustomed, is an imminent menace. And the techniques used by Hoover in shocking the public into an awareness of his menace of the moment should be properly understood. Millspaugh, writing at a time when Hoover had nothing more dramatic than mere crime to work with, analyzed the pattern (in two paragraphs far back in his book that escaped the attention of the press at the time and seem to have been almost ignored):

> The Director of the Bureau of Investigation referred in March, 1936, to the "armed forces of crime which number more than three million active participants." Three months later he stated that "the criminal standing army of America" numbered 500,000, "a whole half-million of armed thugs, murderers, thieves, firebugs, assassins, robbers, and holdup men." About six months afterward he gave the total criminal population as 3,500,000, and the number of crimes as 1,500,000. Five months later he stated that 4,300,000 persons were engaged *by day and by night* in the commission of felonies, and estimated that 1,333,-536 major felonies were committed in the United States during the year 1936. In these estimates, he refers only to major infractions and disregards "the millions of petty crimes which are often not even reported, the pilfering of possessions from an automobile, the theft by a servant of a few dollars, the filching of supplies from commercial houses, the stealing of trinkets from the desks of office employees."
>
> What is the basis of his estimates of the criminal population? Presumably, convictions and records of arrest. In an address about a year ago, he stated that "the files of the Bureau of Investigation show that there are actually three million convicted criminals. Beyond this there are enough more with police records to demonstrate that an average of one out of every twenty-five persons in the United States of America has had at least his brush with law enforcement agencies and is inclined toward criminality." In the same address he declared that "there are today in America 150,000 murderers roaming at large"; but it appears from the Uniform Crime Reports [issued by Hoover's own FBI] that in 987 cities with a total population of 35,450,666 the police were cognizant of only 3,582 cases of criminal homicide, and, of these, 2,936 or 81.9 percent had, according to the police, been cleared by arrest.[6]

This analysis would seem to demonstrate in devastating fashion that, when the Director of the FBI takes the stump to expatiate on the horrors of crime, he gets carried aways by his theme until his figures lose all contact with reality. And this is precisely the point. The infallible policeman should never be out of touch with reality. Just how often such exaggerations have been accepted by press and public as gilt-edged facts because Hoover uttered them, it is impossible to say, for there has not been another thorough and impartial study like the 1937 Brookings survey, and the record that has been accepted is the record as the FBI says it is. However, one indication that FBI figures should still be subjected to critical evaluation was provided by *The New Yorker* in the spring of 1958. This was at the height of the juvenile delinquency hysteria, and *The New Yorker* had been shocked by a headline in *The New York Times* reading "Youth Charged with Nearly Half Major Crimes in '57, the FBI Reports." The headline was based on the FBI's annual crime survey in the nation. *The New Yorker* made this analysis:

> If you took a "group of serious crimes classified separately—murder, manslaughter, rape, robbery, aggravated assault, burglary, larceny, and auto theft," the FBI reported, "those under eighteen made up 47.2 percent of persons arrested for such crimes."
>
> "Separately" to us seemed to mean "singly" or "one by one." We were astonished that JD's (juvenile delinquents) had committed 47.2 percent of all murders, 47.2 percent of all aggravated assaults, and the rest. In the next paragraph, though, it developed that "separately" referred to "group of serious crimes," which was to be considered separately from another group of (more, less, equally) serious crimes, not listed. In the group of serious crimes separately considered as a group, the FBI had taken the percentage of persons arrested for each type of crime who were under eighteen, and then averaged all the percentages. Sixty-seven percent of the persons arrested for auto theft during 1957, for example, were under eighteen. Auto theft is and has always been a typically adolescent crime; adolescents take autos because they are too young to own any themselves or to have driving licenses, and in most cases the autos are found within a week. Thus the 67 percent figure is not very exciting news. Six percent of persons arrested for murder were under eighteen. If you average 67 and 6, it is plain that 36.5 percent of the persons arrested for auto theft and murder, considered separately as a group of serious crimes, were under eighteen. This sounds more ominous; the 36.5 might give the fast reader the impression that one out of every three murders, like one out of every three auto thefts, was committed by a JD. Actually, if you cut burglary—which technically includes breaking into a locked summer house at the shore—larceny, and auto theft off the end of the

separately considered group, the JDs came out inconspicuously. For instance, they have been arrested for 9 percent of all aggravated assaults (which is far too much, of course), but that doesn't make as good a subhead as "nearly half." The facts are disquieting enough; nobody has to improve on them with statistics.[7]

Such criticism has had no perceptible effect on the FBI. In the spring of 1963, it was viewing hitchhiking with alarm and warning motorists against picking up strangers on the highways. To make its point, the FBI came up with what the *Charleston Gazette* called "the unverifiable statistic." It solemnly announced that two out of every five thumbs raised to cadge rides had been fingerprinted in police files. Since there is no electronic Seeing Eye watching every highway in the nation and registering on a computer the number of hitchhikers, such a statistic is patently ridiculous. The *Gazette* pointed out that it wasn't in favor of hitchhiking; that "enough robberies, highjackings, and murders have been committed by hitchhikers to convince us that they are in the main bad risks." It added:

"But that's not the issue. What is is the reputation of the FBI—the nation's foremost crime-busting agency. To maintain that reputation it should be scrupulous about being able to document everything it reports and asserts. Loose contentions, absurd on their face, hardly enhance the agency's credibility ratings." [8]

Nor do such contentions accord with the image of the infallible policeman whose every utterance must be accepted without challenge, in the faith that it must be true because he said it.

■ 2 ■

Neither Hoover nor the FBI today really needs the Madison Avenue approach. There is abundant evidence that the Bureau, if it could be content just to do its job without scare headlines, without trying to swing the nation by the tail, would be a highly valuable organization. One of Hoover's valid accomplishments, one that no honest critic should belittle, may be found in the great change he has wrought in law enforcement by his emphasis on scientific detective work. The scientific achievements of the FBI under Hoover fall into three main categories: the establishment of a huge fingerprint collection, a principal resource of every police department in the nation in tracking down criminals; the creation of a skilled laboratory to make the most delicate scientific tests on minute physical clues; and the establishment of the National Police Academy, which trains selected officers from police departments throughout the country in the latest scientific methods.

All are Hoover's creations. On the fingerprint collection alone he must share partial credit with others, but he is certainly the man who gave the technique its present importance. The value of prints, no two of which have ever been found to be identical, had long been accepted in Europe and by the principal law enforcement agencies in this country before Hoover became Director of the Bureau in 1924. The police chiefs of the nation had wanted a national clearing house for prints, and a couple of centralized collections had been made. William J. Burns, when he was head of the Bureau, had brought these files to Washington and had attempted to establish a fingerprint center, but he had run into opposition in Congress and use of the collections had lapsed. Hoover, taking over from Burns, gained the support of his superiors in the Justice Department and with their aid managed to get from Congress the appropriations to set up an Identification Division. Some 800,000 of the old prints that had been placed in storage were sorted out and filed as a starter, and Hoover began a nationwide publicity campaign to get local departments to send him the prints of all arrested men.

The advantages of a central fingerprint bureau have been demonstrated in thousands of cases during the years. For example: A man calling himself John Johnson is arrested in Seattle, Washington, in an armed holdup; his prints are taken by local police and forwarded to the FBI in Washington, D.C.; a check of FBI fingerprint files quickly discloses that John Johnson is really Everett Smith, who has been sought for murder ever since his prints were lifted from a car used in a ride-killing in Boston. Thus a murder is solved, a hunt is ended, simply because the FBI fingerprint nerve center could connect two crimes an entire continent apart.

The Identification Division is open around the clock, with service available to police departments throughout the nation at all times. If speed is essential, prints can be transmitted to the department on a device known as the Speedphoto Transceiver, similar to the equipment used by news agencies to transmit pictures to newspapers. An answer can be sent back within minutes.

The only criticism that has ever been made of the Bureau's fingerprinting activities stemmed from Hoover's urge to gather more and more prints, to amass the most colossal fingerprint collection in the world. Tourists passing through the FBI headquarters were urged at the end of the tour to let themselves be fingerprinted. Women's clubs, business and civic groups, even school organizations have been encouraged to conduct local campaigns for fingerprinting. In 1936, the Bureau publicized that it had acquired the prints of John D. Rockefeller, Jr., Edgar Guest, and Walt Disney, and it urged everyone to follow these distinguished examples by being fingerprinted. The result of this campaign, conducted over a period of years, was that by mid-1956, according to Whitehead, the bureau had 141,231,773 fingerprints on file. Of these, 29,215,596 prints, representing 11,336,712 persons, were in the criminal file. The remainder, 112,016,177, representing 60,753,062 persons, were in the separately kept civil file.

This all-out effort to corral every fingerprint in existence contrasts rather sharply with the emphasis placed on prints by that other famous police agency, Scotland Yard. There the effort is concentrated in the other direction: to weed out prints, to keep the collection down to manageable and efficient size. Sir Harold Scott, commissioner of London's Metropolitan Police, has stated Scotland Yard's theory:

> The main fingerprint collection at Scotland Yard, consisting of the prints of all ten fingers, includes more than a million and a quarter, and increases at the rate of 50,000 a year. Although the collection is weeded out regularly by removing the prints of people who have died or have reached an age when they are unlikely to indulge in further serious crime, an even more drastic weeding is necessary, and as soon as enough staff is available, all cards relating to offenders who have not come to notice for thirty or even twenty years will be removed. This will involve some risk of missing an occasional case, but in the interests of speed and efficiency that is a risk which must be faced. In any event, the weeded forms are not destroyed but only removed to a "dead" section.

Weeding is essential, for the time required to make a search depends on the number of prints to be examined, and time is often vitally important, since to be of any practical value a prisoner must be linked with his previous criminal record by the time a case comes into court. Fingerprint work also requires a large and expensive staff and demands great accuracy and concentration. If the collection is allowed to grow too large, the output of each worker will be reduced and the cost of administration will go up.[9]

Cost, of course, has never been a consideration with Hoover, who has always been able to get every dime he asked for from Congress. As for Sir Harold Scott's contention, logical on its face, that hoarding unnecessary millions of prints only makes identification more difficult and slows the work, there has been no indication of sluggishness in identifying prints in the FBI's Identification Division. Local police departments seem well satisfied with the speed and efficiency of the service.

The question remains whether the FBI's nearly universal fingerprint collection serves any purpose comparable in value to the cost and effort that has gone into collecting and maintaining it. While the fingerprints of criminals are invaluable in the performance of detective work, what is the purpose of hoarding the prints of millions of law-abiding citizens?

Liberal thinkers have long been suspicious of this particular phase of the FBI's fingerprinting activities, insisting that the fingerprinting of an entire population would be one of the best means by which a police state could keep tabs on its people. This danger, if danger it is, remains potential. No one can tell what might happen if, in the event of serious trouble with Russia, the FBI put its "Operation Dragnet" into action, rounding up all suspect thinkers and agitators. Its use of dragnet procedures in the past, in the draft and Palmer Red Raids, do not provide a happy augury for the future, but until the event itself occurs, if it ever should, the whole issue remains speculative.

Hoover has always insisted that such apprehensions are a lot of tommyrot. What has an innocent, law-abiding citizen to fear? he asks. On the other hand, he argues, fingerprints are a protection to the citizen. They have been used to identify victims of amnesia and return them to their families; to identify the bodies of disaster victims who would otherwise have gone to unmarked graves; and, in rare cases, to reunite long-separated families. While such peripheral effects of the huge civil fingerprint collection are doubtless beneficent, they are still peripheral, and one may reasonably question whether the amassing of such a collection, some four to five times as large as the criminal file, can ever justify the enormous effort and expense that has gone into it.

The files in the criminal fingerprint section, aside from their value in catching crooks, have proved to have another use. Local police departments, in weighing candidates for appointment, take their prints and check them with the FBI's criminal fingerprint collection. In an amazing number of cases, the fingerprint check establishes that men who have been arrested for breaking the law are the same ones who want to acquire the right to wear the uniform.

A dispute over this kind of fingerprint check arose in New York City during Works Progress Administration days. The fingerprinting of all WPA workers was ordered, and in two years, according to Whitehead, some 46,663 sets of WPA fingerprints were checked through FBI files. Of these, 4,205 persons were identified as having criminal records, 2,506 of them for serious crimes. Of those applying for jobs as watchmen or as workers in the child recreation program some four dozen had records of sex crimes.[10] This is the positive side of the picture.

On the other side, a fingerprint record sometimes scars and hounds a man who has atoned for a long-ago transgression. Lowenthal cited this example:

> The FBI meticulously checked all persons connected with such depression-period agencies as the WPA, and reported all cases in which it found any adverse record. An example was the case of a man who had been in the Rainbow Division in World War I, had been sent back to the United States after being wounded in battle, had lost his wife in childbirth, had gone from his home in Brooklyn to Detroit looking for a job, and had there bought a ring on the instalment plan and pawned it to raise fare for his return home. The young man was sentenced to prison and served time. This was his only offense. Twenty years later, the FBI traced his criminal record and reported it to the WPA, with the result that he lost his WPA job. In the meantime, he had become a construction engineer, was the father of two grown daughters, and the head of his American Legion Post.[11]

In such cases, Hoover contends that the FBI merely reports what it finds to the hiring authority; it does not recommend. But it is an indication of the police-mind virus of our times that such negative reports from an agency as widely revered as the FBI seem to call for drastic action on the part of the recipient authority. To fail to act on such reports seems to put the responsible executive in an untenable position. And so, at times, gross individual injustice is done.

Not as well known as the Identification Division but equally important in furnishing the scientific solution of many crimes is the work of the FBI laboratory, established on a shoestring basis in November, 1932. Large city and state police departments, of course, have their own scientific laboratories, but for many smaller departments the FBI laboratory is a godsend—the authoritative word on the scientific evidence connected with a crime. In ballistics tests, guns can be fired and linked—or not linked—to a murder. A fleck of blood on clothing can be analyzed and identified as either human or animal. A bit of hair clutched in a dying fist can often be traced to the head from which it came. A speck of dirt on the clothing of a suspect may match the dirt at the scene of a murder, placing the suspect there. Type specimens of virtually every known make of American typewriter, and many foreign makes as well, are indispensable in tracking typed records to their source. Some 42,000 different watermarks help to trace and identify paper. Treads of every tire turned out by Canadian and American manufacturers help to link a specific car to a specific crime. This is only a fragmentary list, but it is enough to show the importance of the emphasis Hoover has placed on the scientific side of crime detection.

In extension of this interest, the FBI Director in 1935 established the National Police Academy. In its first twenty-one years, the Academy gave training courses to more than 3,200 law enforcement officials. Whitehead's breakdown shows that 28 percent of these have since climbed to "positions as executive heads of their departments with such titles as chief of police, sheriff, and state police chief." The training given by the Academy has been credited with raising the standards of local police work, and it has the additional advantage, from the FBI's standpoint, that the Bureau acquires influential contacts in local departments.

These scientific functions of the FBI under Hoover represent major achievements. They have contributed greatly during the years to better law enforcement. This is indisputable.

■ 3 ■

Any efficiency rating of the FBI must take into account not only the loose use of statistics for propaganda purposes and its undoubted scientific skills but also the *kind* of criminals it catches. On this aspect, one of the nation's profoundest mysteries is encountered. The mystery is that Hoover has never challenged the real lords of the underworld. He built two-bit desperados like Dillinger and Karpis into national menaces and flourished their scalps from the FBI totem pole, but all the time he ignored, with a persistent perversity, the growth of organized, multi-billion-dollar underworld power. It was a power that was symbolized in names like the Mafia, the Combination, the Syndicate. The semantics were not important, but the reality was. Every detective who knew his business, every crime reporter with any kind of contacts, appreciated the reality of big-league underworld organization, with its own kangaroo courts, its own murder-enforcement arm, its colossal bribery of police and politicians. It was this reality that Hoover ignored. He even at times denied its existence.

Compare the rosters. On Hoover's scroll of achievement one finds names like "Pretty Boy" Floyd, "Machine Gun" Kelly, Dillinger, Karpis, "Baby Face" Nelson. But where are the names that have really mattered? Charles (Lucky) Luciano. Frank Costello. Joe Adonis. Albert Anastasia. Meyer Lansky. Al Capone. Tony Accardo. Buggsy Siegel. Mickey Cohen. Jack Dragma. Tony Bender. Vito Genovese. The roll of the dark emperors—the underworld czars bankrolled by millions and hobnobbing with politicians—goes on and on, but hardly one was ever scratched by the FBI. Capone did suffer a rap on the knuckles, and Louis (Lepke) Buchalter was picked up by Hoover himself at a time when Buchalter wanted to escape the local law and seek refuge with the Feds. But, with the exception of these two far-from-heroic deeds, the FBI's record against the real powers of the underworld is startlingly blank.

This picture is the very antithesis of the publicity-induced image of the FBI as the nemesis of crime. Didn't Attorney General Cummings and Hoover proclaim in the 1930's that the FBI, with its broadened powers, was going to get the big shots of the underworld? They certainly did, but their conception of what constituted a big shot was exceedingly naïve.

The extensive powers given to the FBI by the first Roosevelt Congress in 1934 were predicated on the idea, valid enough in itself, that crime was becoming interstate in character, for the automobile and the airplane gave gangsters mobility, enabling them to commit a crime and then hop across state lines to far-distant hideouts. For this reason, the FBI specifically was given jurisdiction in cases in which a person crossed a state line to avoid prosecution or to avoid giving testimony—a sweeping provision that seemingly would cover a multitude of cases and would embrace, if the effort were made, most of the major activities of the Syndicate.

But Attorney General Cummings and Hoover weren't so much concerned at the time with the secretive and important machinations of the underworld. They were preoccupied with the sensational, the spectacular. In speech after speech, Cummings proclaimed the thesis that huge underworld gangs, built up by bootlegging millions in Prohibition days, would become desperate when deprived of their principal source of revenue and would turn to kidnaping. This was a patently false and ridiculous theory, as Milton S. Mayer pointed out in his September, 1935, *Forum* article:

> Kidnaping is largely an amateur sport. Unlike bootlegging, it is desperate and dangerous. It attracts two kinds of men: nuts and the kind of person who shoots up banks. It does not attract the kind of man who peddles illicit goods or murders fellow hoodlums for hire under the tolerant eye of both police and public. "Good" criminals, the foundation blocks of the underworld, avoid it because it's a one-shot racket; kidnaping is easier to solve than any other major crime; the life of a "kidnaping gang" has never been shown to be more than one kidnaping.

William Seagle in *Harper's* expressed the same thought:

> The opinion of at least the New York Police Department is that kidnaping is an amateur crime, and this impression is certainly borne

out by most of the front-page stories of kidnaping. . . . It is true that the record of the Division of Investigation of the Department of Justice has been very brilliant in the kidnaping cases in which it has assumed jurisdiction. But it has been conveniently forgotten that the record of local police forces has been brilliant, too, the Lindbergh case to the contrary notwithstanding.

Time has proved the validity of these analyses. The famous kidnapers were not the big names of the underworld. Hauptmann was an impoverished carpenter; Angelo John LaMarca, executed for the kidnap-murder of the Weinberger baby on Long Island in the late 1950's, was an impecunious laborer driven to the border of insanity by the crushing pressure of debts. The record of the years makes it obvious that the dreaded powers of gangdom, the men who directed vast enterprises and held life and death in their hands—Luciano, Genovese, Costello, Adonis, Anastasia, Lansky—were never so stupid as to mess with a cheap thug's crime like kidnaping. While the FBI was garnering headlines in its wild and gory battles with desperados, these real criminal brains of the nation quietly went about the business of amassing fantastic and untold millions—their rackets such lucrative fields as narcotics, the numbers, bookmaking, and gambling casinos that rivaled the plush of Monte Carlo and ran as openly.

As far back as the early 1940's, the Murder Inc. probe in Brooklyn exposed the ramifications of Syndicate organization for all to see. When Abe Reles told his lurid tales of murder, it became apparent that the ghoulish and sadistic killers of Albert Anastasia (the Lord High Executioner of the underworld) had been acting as the enforcement arm for gang lords across the nation. The enforcers had enforced so often that, when Reles and others came to sing, their minds were taxed to recall all the places where they had dumped the bodies. But, incomplete as was their saga of murder, it demonstrated beyond dispute one cardinal fact: the New York killers had left a trail of corpses that stretched all the way to California. This was interstate crime on a colossal scale—interstate murder that was bought and paid for and delivered. But the FBI, the watchdog of interstate crime, never expressed any passion to interfere.[12]

During the entire decade of the 1940's the Syndicate ran the widest-open gambling empire in the nation in Bergen County, New Jersey, just across the Hudson River from New York. In plush casinos that speckled the Bergen countryside, it flushed the wartime profits out of the pockets of the bigwigs of New York. Fleets of Cadillacs made the nightly trip across the George Washington Bridge, ferrying well-heeled players from Park Avenue penthouses to the houses of chance run by Joe Adonis and the Moretti brothers. On one occasion, during the gasoline-rationing days of World War II, agents of the Office of Defense Transportation tracked the Jersey-bound Cadillac fleet right to the doors of the Bergen gambling halls. Finally, in the investigation of a local "charity" gambling game, New York's District Attorney Frank S. Hogan, who had no jurisdiction in New Jersey, gathered the evidence that showed the underworld had been running a colossal (and conservatively estimated) $13,500,000-a-year gambling business along the brink of the Jersey Palisades. Senator Estes Kefauver, in his 1950 crime-busting role, picked up Hogan's disclosures, gave them a headline whirl, and forced the sluggish and reluctant officials of New Jersey to clean out the Bergen racket nest. In this decade-long flouting of the law—when agencies that had no jurisdiction and even newspapermen were running down clues that were as glaringly obvious as a lighted advertising extrava-ganza above Times Square—it seems legitimate to ask where, oh where, was the FBI, the watchdog of interstate crime? He was, it seems, the guardian who slept, who never twitched his tail—and never emitted one single, disturbing, anguished woof.

It is axiomatic that the management of such vast illegal enterprises, run in open defiance of the law and needing *sub rosa* arrangements to placate the law, requires at least as skillful direction as the manage-ment of a legitimate enterprise like General Motors. Just as one would not expect General Motors to schedule car production and shipment without a human headquarters staff to decide on details, so one could hardly expect interstate Cadillac fleets to run by themselves, or casinos to pop up out of the ground complete with ankle-deep rugs, modernistic décor, charming and scantily clad waitresses, and a cuisine prepared by some of New York's best chefs. This kind of enterprise takes some doing. It requires planning, financing, and man-agement just like any other business—and since it is illegal, perhaps even more so. In such a setup there had to be an active, everyday, operating headquarters, and in the New Jersey gangland haven of the 1940's there was just such a headquarters. It was in a tavern known as Duke's in Cliffside Park, almost opposite the entrance of the Palisades Amusement Park.

Here, in a closely guarded inner sanctum, the Syndicate established a regularly functioning Council of Five to administer the affairs of crime. Joe Adonis was chairman of the board, and his fellow councilors were Willie and Solly Moretti, Albert Anastasia, and Anthony (Tony Bender) Strollo, a lieutenant of Vito Genovese. When major decisions were to be made, underworld minions would be summoned from New York and New Jersey; they would congregate in the bar and wile away the hours as the Council of Five deliberated, decided, and ultimately issued its orders. So autocratically did Adonis and his fellow chieftains operate that frequently three times as many hoods would be summoned as were needed—just to make certain the right men were present to handle any chore that might arise.

This governing nerve center of gangdom was as well known to the minions of the underworld as the corridors of City Hall to the ward heeler. Protected by a security screen worthy of the FBI itself, Duke's became famed as a secure haven to the masterminds of crime across the nation. Tuesday, according to Federal Bureau of Narcotics agents who shadowed the premises, was the regular meeting day for the major lords of crime. On that day, Frank Costello would be chauffeured across the bridge from New York to meet with the Council of Five. Or Abner (Longie) Zwillman, the old bootleg czar, might drive across from Newark. Or Meyer Lansky, on occasion, would fly in from his swank gambling casinos in Hollywood, Florida, and Saratoga Springs, New York. Interstate crime? Duke's was the nerve center, the brain and the heart, of interstate crime that crosshatched the nation. But did the FBI, with its broad jurisdiction, attack it? Or did Hoover, with his enormous prestige, expose it and demand more sweeping laws, if they were needed to enable him to deal with such a mammoth conspiracy? He did not. The FBI was silent.

Anyone studying the FBI's record against the genuine masterminds of the underworld is struck by the paucity of entries. In 1929 it did move against Al Capone on a minor issue. Capone was the ruthless dictator of the Chicago underworld; he bribed, murdered, flouted the law at will. And no law enforcement agency, local or federal, had taken any effective action against him until he committed the strategic error of failing to answer a subpoena to appear as a witness in a Chicago Prohibition case. Capone argued, with a doctor's affidavit to support him, that he had been too ill to appear, but the FBI's investigation showed that at the time he was supposed to have been bedridden he had been enjoying himself at the races and even taking off by air to the Bahamas. A contempt-of-court charge was lodged against Capone, the first of his legal troubles. He was subsequently arrested in Pennsylvania on a charge of carrying a concealed weapon, and while he was serving a year in jail on that charge and another six months on the FBI's contempt rap, the sleuths of the Internal Revenue Service delved into his records and uncovered the evidence that jailed him for ten years and put an end to his career.

The other major exception to the FBI's generally inconsequential record in tackling big-league crime is the Lepke Buchalter case. Lepke's had been a dread name in the New York underworld for years. He sat in the inner council of Eastern crime; he was the Syndicate's specialist in industrial racketeering and extortion; he was said at one time to own nearly half the garment industry in New York; and his take-home pay, after financing his mob and ladling out heavily for protection, was reputed to be a million dollars a year. It was a bankroll that had made him one of gangdom's top-flight untouchables until Thomas E. Dewey began to ride herd on the New York rackets. Dewey wanted Lepke's scalp in the worst way, and the City of New York posted a $25,000 reward for Lepke's capture. Even this kind of folding money wasn't enough to induce anyone in the mob to betray Lepke, who went into hiding protected by Albert Anastasia, bankrolled by the hundreds of dollars a week that continued to flow to him from his garment industry businesses and his rackets. Authorities suspected that Lepke must have hopped across state lines to some far-distant hideout (actually, he was holed up in Brooklyn most of the time), and so the FBI was drawn into the chase. The Bureau announced that it would pay $25,000 if in-

.formation leading to Lepke's capture came to it *first;* otherwise it would pay merely its standard $5,000 reward for the apprehension of a top fugitive.

For nearly two years, Lepke thumbed his nose at everybody. The FBI had no more success than Dewey and the New York police. Lepke was making its reputation for infallibility look ridiculous, and this could not be borne. Burton B. Turkus, the prosecutor of Murder Inc., who afterward had the story from some of his song birds, described the denouement:

> The FBI felt it had to beat state authorities to Lepke in order to "save face" after two years of futility. So, J. Edgar Hoover sent a flat fiat to Joey Adonis and Frank Costello, the ranking "brass" of Unione Siciliano: Unless Lepke came out of his hole and gave up *to the* FBI, every Italian mobster in the country would be picked up. Mr. A. and Frank C. could not afford to let this happen. They sent an ultimatum to their old pal, "Sorry, chum—surrender to the Feds or we'll have to deliver you personally." [13]

The next act in the drama was performed by Walter Winchell. Long an admirer of Hoover and personally close to the No. 1 G-man, Winchell went on the radio and pleaded with Lepke to give himself up. Lepke, it would appear, had no choice. And if he had to surrender, he obviously preferred Hoover to Dewey. Dewey had proclaimed publicly that he had enough evidence on Lepke to pack him away for five hundred years, but all that federal authorities had was a case that had been perfected not by the FBI but by the Federal Bureau of Narcotics. A narcotics rap might jail Lepke for ten years, but that was a lot different than a lifetime. The result was that Lepke made contact with Winchell, was assured he wouldn't be double-crossed by being handed over to Dewey if he surrendered, and so on August 24, 1939, at a designated rendezvous, Lepke walked up to Winchell's car, sat down beside the columnist, and was driven away to be delivered personally to Hoover.

Federal agents questioned Lepke for hours, then booked him on the narcotics charge. New York's Mayor Fiorello H. La Guardia and the local gendarmes were furious, because they learned of these interesting developments only by reading their morning newspapers. Dewey, too, was highly chagrined, because his detectives were firmly barred from the presence of the prisoner. The only way he could get access to Lepke, Dewey was told, was to develop a charge so serious it would take precedence over the federal narcotics rap. Ultimately, Dewey did just that. He had Lepke indicted for murder, tried him, convicted him, and sent him to the electric chair in Sing Sing.

Two aspects of the Lepke case are worth noting. It brought Dewey and Hoover into a direct power clash, and for years it was an accepted article of faith in political circles that, if Dewey ever became President, Hoover would be replaced. In 1948, however, with this prospect seemingly inescapable, there appears to have been a rapprochement between the two men. The second curious circumstance of the case, if Burton Turkus is correct, is that Hoover, in forcing the surrender of Lepke, used the apparatus of the underworld—an apparatus whose very existence he spent years in denying.

Contrasts are invidious, but anyone who compares the record of the FBI with that of the Federal Bureau of Narcotics cannot help being shocked at the difference between myth and grim reality. While the FBI seemed to be living in a dream world with its Dillingers, the narcotics bureau was recognizing and wrestling with the sanguinary reality of the Mafia, the dread Sicilian secret society transplanted here by immigrants. Based on the family ties of chieftains, founded on a system of murder and terror and extortion, the Mafia became the cement of the American underworld. Its American branch has been called at different times by various names—Mafia for one, the Unione Siciliano for another. And since gangsters not of Italian or Sicilian origin have also risen to high levels in the American underworld (Longie Zwillman was a prize example), broader terms like the Combination and the Syndicate are often used. But the murder-enforcement arm, the guts of the system, has always been Mafia-like in organization and control. The terms do not matter. What does matter is the reality of underworld organization on a national basis: running an invisible government that has repeatedly demonstrated, in the murder of key witnesses and the intimidation of others, its immunity and its superiority to the law. It is this reality that makes the fighting of Syndicate crime, under any logical interpretation of the facts, the FBI's major responsibility in the criminal field—and it is this reality that Hoover has persistently denied. While he builds FBI statistics with the recovery of stolen cars that are taken across state lines, he consistently belittles the specter of the Mafia and insists that crime-fighting is a local business to be handled strictly by local and state police.

The contention became patently absurd on November 14, 1957, when the Mafia called a national convention in the obscure New York town of Apalachin. Just how many Mafia dons gathered at the hilltop mansion of Joseph Barbara, Sr., probably will never be known, but some sixty were stopped, questioned, and identified when New York State Police Sergeant Edgar L. Croswell discovered the rally and flushed out the delegates. The event should have converted the last skeptic about the sweep of gangland power and its close-knit organization, for the delegates identified by Croswell came from the Eastern Seaboard, from the Midwest, from California, from Cuba, from Puerto Rico. And at least two were recent arrivals from Italy, where they were believed to have had contact with the international narcotics czar, Lucky Luciano.[14]

Though Croswell obtained no evidence on the details of the Mafia agenda at Apalachin, his discovery of the meeting triggered investigations and created a shock wave from coast to coast. Here was the reality of underworld organization, of gangland's "invisible government." The cry to "do something" resounded from all sides. The New York *Herald Tribune* felt that the FBI should handle the job and that the only reason it hadn't done so probably was that it lacked men and money. Even the *Herald Tribune* was a bit puzzled, however. It acknowledged that "Congress has never yet refused anything J. Edgar Hoover said he had to have. Let him demand the funds to take on this job. Let Congress provide them, plus stronger laws on national crime." Hoover, who had never been reticent about heeding such calls, turned a tin ear to this plea. His attitude, as the sequel was to demonstrate, was that the status quo was perfect and should be maintained.

The McClellan Senate Rackets Committee, confronted with the undeniable fact of Apalachin, toyed with the idea of creating a National Crime Commission. This would be a permanent kind of Kefauver committee to keep track of the doings of mobsters and to

keep a public spotlight focused on them. Two rather prominent per-
sonages thought, at the time, that this was a good idea: Senator
John F. Kennedy, a member of the committee, and his brother
Robert, the committee counsel. In the executive branch of the Federal
Government, Attorney General William Rogers decided that something should be done, and so he created the Special Group on Organized Crime, headed by Milton R. Wessel, a young and energetic
former Assistant United States Attorney.

What hadn't been realized before Apalachin, what indeed was
not too widely realized even after it, was that there was simply no
clearing house, anywhere in the law enforcement system, for information on organized interstate crime. What information the FBI
had, the FBI kept for the FBI. There was no central source to pull
together the ties of gangdom, to keep track of the movements of
Mafia dons. And so, as Apalachin had demonstrated, it had been
possible for underworld czars across the nation to leave their home
pads and travel to Apalachin without anyone, including the FBI,
having any knowledge of what was occurring. Except for the chance
discovery by Sergeant Croswell, neither the public nor law enforcement agencies on any level would have had the slightest suspicion
that Apalachin had even happened. The Wessel group was designed
to put an end to this haphazard system, to gather all available information from local and federal agencies, to build cases wherever
possible against the emperors of gangdom, and to keep tabs on their
future movements.

It was a big order—too big an order, especially considering the
type of cooperation the Wessel unit got. Though Wessel always
leaned over backwards to avoid criticizing Hoover and though he
never intimated that he got less than 100 percent cooperation from
the FBI, some of his aides were less restrained. Richard V. Ogilvie,
who was in charge of Wessel's Midwestern office, put it bluntly:

> Hoover was very cool to the whole idea of the Attorney General's
> special group. He ordered that the FBI files, containing the very infor-
> mation we needed on organized crime, were to be closed to us. . . .
> Criticizing Hoover is a dangerous thing for anyone to do. . . . But
> honesty compels me to say that some of Hoover's ideas are sadly
> behind the times. . . . The FBI is still organized to fight a crime pat-

tern of the '20s and '30s. It is not set up to do battle with the criminal syndicate—the organized conspiracy that drains $22 billion a year from the United States.[15]

Another Wessel aide, Gerard L. Goettel, wrote that the special crime group had to fight not only mobsters, but bureaucrats in entrenched positions in Washington. "The FBI was the coolest agency of all," he declared. "J. Edgar Hoover at a national meeting of United States Attorneys decried the need for 'special groups' to fight organized crime." The Special Group, in investigating the Apalachin meeting, found everywhere they went, according to Goettel, that the FBI had been there before them. Not being able to prove the criminal purpose of the conspiracy, the FBI had quietly shelved the reports, and when the Special Group asked for them, "the G-men acted as if they had never heard of Apalachin. This aloofness was due in part to their mistrust of us. It also reflected an internal dilemma—the FBI has long taken the position officially that large criminal syndicates do not exist—or if they do, they are a state and local law-enforcement problem." [16]

The result was that Wessel's Special Group was doomed almost from the start. After less than two years of life, it was abolished. And though it had achieved much—deporting some criminals, jailing others—its major prosecutions (the conviction of the Apalachin conspirators and of Tony Accardo for income tax evasion) were later thrown out by the courts. Wessel and many others were convinced, however, that the Justice Department should establish a small, permanent, functioning unit to act as a clearing house on syndicate crime for law enforcement agencies across the nation. Advocacy of such a heretical notion roused Hoover to wrath.

In early October, 1960, the International Association of Police Chiefs held its annual convention in Washington, D.C. A special committee of the association, headed by Police Chief Edward J. Allen, of Santa Ana, California, in the past one of Hoover's favorites, submitted a recommendation urging the establishment of such a nerve-center on organized crime. Wessel appeared at the convention to urge support of the recommendation. Many police chiefs seemed sympathetic; they inclined to the view, later expressed by Captain James E. Hamilton, of the Los Angeles police department, that "the definite lack has been on a Federal level in furnishing local departments information as to the movements of national figures." However, Hoover and the FBI were adamant in opposition. The FBI, whose influence with the police chiefs is always strong, did tremendous spadework among the membership to block the proposal, and Hoover himself in a speech to the convention denounced the idea.

The man who heads the most powerful police bureaucracy in the nation, an organization that cows congressmen and senators and makes even Presidents pause, raised the specter of a national police force and a "gestapo" that might rob all of us of our liberties should such a task force be formed to fight organized crime. Hoover said:

> The persons who endorse these grandiose schemes have lost sight of some very basic facts. America's compact network of state and local law enforcement agencies traditionally has been the Nation's first line of defense against crime. Nothing could be more dangerous to our democratic ideals than the establishment of an all-powerful police agency on the Federal scene. The truth of these words is clearly demonstrated in the experience of nations ruled by ruthless tyrants both here in the Western Hemisphere and abroad.[17]

These words from the master pointed out to the assembled police chiefs the clear path of duty, and they saw it. The Allen recommendation was shelved, and Allen, who had been a devout worshiper of Hoover, was almost read out of the lodge. He offered to resign as chairman of the association's committee on organized crime, but urged that the committee continue its work. The board of officers of the IAPC, however, met on December 12, 1960, and deactivated the too-active committee, which had drawn Hoover's ire. The Kennedys, in power, listened to Hoover and abandoned their plan to establish a National Crime Commission. And that was that. Or almost.

An outstanding trait of Hoover's is that he never forgets a critic. Appearing before the friendly sounding board of the House Appropriations Committee in the spring of 1961, he was asked a leading question by Representative John J. Rooney (Democrat of New York) about the performance of the Wessel Special Group. He seized the opportunity to square accounts with Ogilvie, Goettel, and the ever silent Wessel. Criticism of the FBI for lack of cooperation, said Hoover, had been "unwarranted and unfair." He added: "My only conclusion is that some individuals look at . . . TV too frequently and absorb some of the fantastic panaceas as to how to solve *local crimes.*" [Italics added.] The Wessel group prosecutors, he said, had indicated by their activities that "their chief preoccupation is the quest for nest-feathering publicity." They had asked the FBI to assign special agents to the group "to be used on 'fishing expeditions' " but "obviously, we have neither the manpower nor the time to waste on such speculative ventures." [18]

His explanation ignored the obvious fact that if you don't embark on fishing expeditions you don't catch fish. The press of the nation however, wasn't thinking in these terms. All that registered with it was that the head master had delivered a public spanking to Wessel's Boy Scouts.

Clearly, Hoover not only has failed to exhibit any eagerness to lead the fight on organized crime where it really counts, against the top echelons of the Syndicate, but he has resented, fought, blocked every proposal that might have set up a rival federal agency to perform this most important chore. Why? Certainly not because the FBI itself is not willing. Both Jack Levine and William Turner asserted that the agents in the ranks are only too eager, in most instances, to be let loose in an all-out campaign against top-level racketeers. But so far these willing agents have generally been kept on a tight leash. Again one asks: Why?

The reasons are not clear, but those who have had close contact with law enforcement suggest what seem like logical possibilities. The estimated twenty to twenty-two billion dollars' worth of loot the rackets filch out of the American pocketbook each year buys a lot of influence. Wessel estimates that half the multibillion-dollar take of top-level gangdom is funneled right back into payoffs and the purchase of political influence. Many a political machine is bankrolled by such tainted money, and in devious ways the purchased pull makes itself felt on Capitol Hill.

Another possible reason: If a central clearing house on syndicated crime ever should be created on a permanent basis, Hoover's FBI would be compelled to share its information—and the glory. This it has never been willing to do.

Lastly, it's much easier to catch car thieves than Frank Costellos. Hoover's FBI has grown to mammoth proportions by use of statistics and propaganda. An enormous number of arrests and 97 percent convictions are impressive when the Director goes before Congress and asks for more money. As the veteran agent, William Turner, put it, "a large portion" of the FBI's conviction statistics represent "misdemeanor offenses, not felonies." The stumblebums of crime are easy to convict. "These people usually can't afford attorneys when they're caught. They usually figure, well, the FBI's got me, and they invariably plead guilty—with few exceptions." [19] They are a factor in building statistics. Hunting the overlords of crime is quite another matter. A great number of agents would have to put in a great number of man-hours, and they would have to build airtight cases that could stand the battering of the highest-paid defense attorneys in the land. Results might be extremely minimal, and the FBI, instead of the universal praise it gets, might well reap the whirlwind of hostile criticism.

Whether these are the actual reasons that have restrained Hoover and the FBI from an all-out assault on major citadels of crime is less important than the undeniable fact of that restraint. The names of Costello, Adonis, Luciano, Anastasia, Accardo, Genovese, are names that do not even appear when the FBI, through Whitehead, tells *The FBI Story*.[20]

■ Notes ■

[1] Jack Alexander, in *The New Yorker*, Oct. 9, 1937.
[2] A. C. Millspaugh, *Crime Control by the National Government* (The Brookings Institution, Washington, D.C., 1937), p. 256.
[3] *Ibid.*, p. 258.
[4] *Ibid.*, pp. 257–258.
[5] *Ibid.*, p. 261.
[6] *Ibid.*, pp. 271–272.
[7] *The New Yorker*, May 3, 1958.
[8] *Charleston Gazette*, Apr. 17, 1963.
[9] Sir Harold Scott, *Scotland Yard* (Penguin Books, 1957), pp. 153–154.

[10] Don Whitehead, *The FBI Story* (Random House, 1956), p. 163 of Pocket Books edition.

[11] Max Lowenthal, *The Federal Bureau of Investigation* (William Sloane Associates, 1950), pp. 380–381.

[12] For an excellent account of the entire gory Murder Inc. saga, see Sid Feder and Burton B. Turkus, *Murder Inc.* (Farrar, Straus & Young, 1951).

[13] Feder and Turkus, *op. cit.,* pp. 369–370.

[14] For an account of the Apalachin meeting, the organization of the Mafia, and the Federal Bureau of Narcotics war upon it, see Frederic Sondern, Jr., *Brotherhood of Evil: the Mafia* (Farrar, Straus & Cudahy, 1959).

[15] Interview with Harry Singer and Gerold Duncan in the *New York Mirror,* Apr. 3, 1961.

[16] Gerard L. Goettel, "Why the Crime Syndicate Can't Be Touched," in *Harper's,* November, 1960.

[17] From the text of an address by J. Edgar Hoover to the International Association of Police Chiefs, Oct. 3, 1960.

[18] These quotes are taken from a special release put out by the FBI publicity bureau after Hoover testified, evidently in a determination to make certain no one missed his testimony.

[19] Turner. From the text of the Pacifica station radio interview.

[20] As this is written, there is a great public furor about the disclosures of one Joseph Valachi, a former cellmate of Vito Genovese. Valachi, believing he had been marked for death by the Syndicate, decided to bare his soul to a Federal Bureau of Narcotics agent who originally had arrested and questioned him—a man whom he evidently trusted. He revealed the Mafia-like ties of gangland chieftains, whose organization, he said, was known by the boys as the "Cosa Nostra," or "Our Thing." Valachi's information was turned over to the FBI to investigate. Attorney General Robert Kennedy subsequently called the Valachi data "the biggest intelligence breakthrough we have ever had," and William Hundley, who heads the Justice Department's section on organized crime, made the amazing statement that he had always previously felt that rumors of Syndicate organization were "a lot of hogwash." The Valachi story was leaked first to the *Saturday Evening Post,* then to the press—a procedure that obviously antagonized Hoover. Indicative of Hoover's tremendous power is the fact that he did not hesitate promptly and publicly to contradict and dress down his boss, the Attorney General. In a personally signed editorial in the FBI's September, 1963, law enforcement bulletin (see the *New York Herald Tribune* and the *New York Times* of Aug. 31, 1963), the FBI director did two things: he denied emphatically Robert Kennedy's assertion that the Valachi information constituted the "biggest breakthrough," and he took the Attorney General politely to task for having divulged the information. The disclosures, he said, had served only "to magnify the enormous task that lies ahead," and Valachi's tale merely "corroborated and embellished the facts developed by the FBI as early as 1961, which disclosed the makeup of the gangland horde." Hoover said that in January, 1962, he had disclosed that the FBI had made "a successful penetration" into "the innermost sanctums of the criminal deity." If so, such a premature disclosure of the presence of a working informant inside the top level of the Syndicate would have been even more reckless and foolhardy than Kennedy's disclosure of the story of Valachi, who

after all was in protective custody. At this writing, the full importance of the Valachi revelations remains to be assessed. But it seems evident that Hoover, who so long had denied the reality of the Mafia and whose influence in this respect has been reflected in the thinking of men like Hundley, does not intend to be outdone in credit-grabbing, not even when such grabbing brings him into conflict with his titular boss, the brother of the then President John Fitzgerald Kennedy.

8 The Man, the War and the First Spies

As the decade of the 1930's drew to a close, the FBI was established as a national institution. It had won its gun battles with desperados. It had tracked down kidnapers. The image of Hoover and the Bureau as the incorruptible and infallible fighters of crime had been implanted in the consciousness of the American people. Now the scene was about to change. The greatest war in history loomed on the European horizon, and inevitably this meant new tasks, new emphases for the FBI and its Director.

Stone's dictum that the FBI should be used only to investigate violations of the law was to be discarded, and the Bureau was to begin once again to catalogue the "radical" thoughts of men. It was to become not just a law enforcement agency but an organization deeply involved in espionage and counterespionage. It would check up on the loyalty of men. Careers would depend upon its verdict. Since enormous power was to be concentrated in the hands of the FBI and its Director, it seems relevant to ask: What had success done to that young "live wire with trigger response" whom Stone had placed in charge of the Bureau?

■ 1 ■

The Hoover who emerges from the portraits of the 1930's is a natural outgrowth of the earlier Hoover. The strait-laced young man who didn't drink or play poker; the austere, lonely bureaucrat immersed in his job; the ambitious, capable, hard-driving martinet —all of these traits of character had become accentuated in the personality of the powerful Director of the FBI. Hoover remained a confirmed bachelor, living with his mother until her death in the modest civil servant's home in Washington in which he was born. Even after his mother's death, it was some years before Hoover moved into more elaborate quarters in a home in Washington's fashionable Rock Creek Park section.

The man whose name was a household word was a man about whose personal life little was known. Russell Turner, writing a Hoover profile for the United Press in 1938, commented on this anomaly. "His name has probably made more headlines than any other except President Roosevelt's," Turner wrote, "but those who know that he is a stamp and antique collector, that he is a baseball fan and an expert fisherman could be assembled in a small drawing room."

Turner described the Hoover of the late 1930's as "of medium height, inclined to stoutness, sharp-featured with coal-black curly hair. He speaks with sharp, clipped, staccato phrases. He dresses like a magazine fashion plate. Mr. Hoover's acquaintanceships are innumerable, but those who could be classified as intimate or close friends are few."

A more detailed portrait of a man remote and powerful, with parochially narrow interests, was drawn by Jack Alexander in his *New Yorker* profile:

At home in Washington, D. C., Hoover spends most of his free evenings puttering around in his study. He lives in the house in which he was born, a small stucco dwelling in the unpretentious Seward Square section. All about it are rows of similar dwellings, mouse-like in their lack of distinction and occupied mostly by government clerks and their families. In his study, Hoover is surrounded by paintings, etchings, and bronzes, which he collects in a modest way. He reads all five of the Washington newspapers. His primary interest in them is the G-man strips and his favorites are "Dick Tracy," "Secret Agent X-9," and "War on Crime." He considers them highly important influences in creating a public distaste for crime and derives a keen inward satisfaction from seeing their flinty-jawed detective heroes prevail over evil. Among other types of newspaper strips, the one he likes best is "Tarzan." Hoover's book-reading is apt to be of the inspirational type. He has read Emerson since boyhood, and in maturity has turned also to Vash Young and Edgar Guest, both of whose works he has in collected sets, and to Robert W. Service, the he-man poet. He also finds inspiration in "Verses I Like," a collection of poems which Major Bowes has read over the radio and which are described on the book-jacket as heart-warming. On the desk in the study is a framed copy of Kipling's "If." Hoover knows "If" by heart. His radio taste runs to softly played dance music. If he happens to tune in a symphonic program accidentally, he will listen to it no longer than he has to, for the meaning of highbrow music has always evaded him.

At 8:30 in the morning a Pierce-Arrow sedan stops in front of the modest Seward Square house and with a brisk, military step, Hoover comes out and gets in. The sedan, which is a government car, rolls downtown and deposits him in the courtyard of the handsome classic-modern Department of Justice building, on whose fifth floor the FBI offices are located. The FBI is one of the most popular shrines in the capital for the tourist trade, and if Hoover happens to pass a sight-seeing party in the corridor, he is likely to hear the tour leader point him out, not as Mr. Hoover, but, remotely and impersonally, as the Director.

The Director's office, the center of a felon-snaring web which covers the United States, is a large, stately room, carpeted in cherry red. From the doorway to the desk, which is at the opposite end of the room, is a walk of thirty or thirty-five feet. A few paces to the rear of the Director, as he sits down at his desk, are two tall brass standards, topped by brass eagles and clingingly embraced by furled American flags. Much of the Director's time is spent alone in the impressive quiet of this room, framed by the flags, and in other quarters than the underworld there is uneasiness over what he may be thinking. Some persons of liberal and leftist beliefs are uncomfortably reminded by the symbolic eagles, and the magnificent distance between door and desk, of the official lair of Mussolini. They cite this in support of a suspicion they have that the Director has Fascist leanings and is preparing himself to be the secret police chief and the spearhead of a Fascist dictatorship. The Director gets wry amusement out of this. He insists that the idea of any non-democratic form of government for the United States, fascism included, is repellent to him, but he doesn't expect his critics to believe him, because, he says, they have "mental halitosis." He uses this difficult phrase for anyone who he thinks deliberately distorts his motives.[1]

The martial impression that Hoover created against the backdrop of the flag and the eagle standards dovetailed with another facet of his personality. Though the great Communist threat Hoover and Palmer had trumpeted in the 1920's had failed to materialize, Hoover was still preoccupied with the specter of Communism as a domestic danger, and he made little secret of the fact that he didn't look with favor on Stone's rigid ban on the FBI's meddling in ideological issues. Alexander pointed out that "the pinks and some liberals," remembering Hoover's "sturdy service in Palmer's red-baiting orgy," were apprehensive lest the FBI Director launch another similar purge. Alexander continued:

> One hears in Washington that Hoover has secret dossiers on all left-wingers and is just awaiting a chance to clap them in concentration camps. Hoover pooh-poohs such stories. In discussing them, he points out that the Sedition Act has long since been repealed and that it is now anyone's privilege to advocate overthrow of the government, so long as no overt act is committed. He doesn't believe that the law should be so broad-minded, but says that as long as it is, he considers it no business of his to gather evidence on agitators, and insists that he has not done so. The supposed secret dossiers, he says, do not exist. Privately, Hoover is frankly disturbed by Communist activities, particularly on college and university campuses. "Youth is unable to evaluate such theories properly," he says. . . .
>
> The American Civil Liberties Union has long kept its eye on Hoover but has never once caught him in the act of abridging anyone's sacred rights. Yet there remains an undercurrent of feeling that somehow he is doing something to undermine the citadel of liberty. Washington newspaper correspondents are, in general, hostile to him because of a similar vague feeling. A few assert nervously that they have even more specific reasons. One, who represents a Middle-Western paper, swears that while he was gathering material for an article on Hoover, which Hoover knew would be unfavorable, he was shadowed. Another is similarly positive that he, too, was followed while he was preparing an article on Hoover for a magazine. This one says that a shadower watched him post his manuscript in a Washington mailbox and that the next morning a man purporting to be from the FBI visited the office of the magazine, in New York, and asked to see the manuscript. Hoover vehemently denies the allegations of both writers and insists he has never had any writer shadowed. When the subject is brought up, he makes a point of recalling that the morbid fear that one is being followed is a classic instance of pathological behavior.[2]

Hoover, Alexander wrote, was unpopular on other counts. Washington hostesses considered him "a cold fellow" because he shunned their parties. Men sometimes disliked him "because he seems to lack the traditional male vices." On those rare occasions when he was seen in a bar, he might have one drink (the youthful teetotaler had weakened this much) but never more than one. His cronies were all bachelors with whom he attended baseball games and wrestling matches and went off on fishing trips. For an abstemious man and one who detested large parties and frenzied gaiety, Hoover at this period developed one idiosyncrasy: he became an habitué of the nightclubs, with the result that his name kept popping up in gossip columns.

Alexander pictures Hoover as a man so preoccupied with his work that he sometimes went about his nightclubbing in an almost grim fashion, as if determined to enjoy himself in spite of himself. His favorite stamping ground was New York's Stork Club, with whose proprietor, Sherman Billingsley, his relations certainly verged on friendship. During the 1940's, Billingsley, Hoover, and Paul Lockwood (at the time confidential secretary to Governor Dewey) posed for one buddy-buddy picture that later was enlarged and prominently displayed in the Stork. As was later revealed, when Billingsley applied for a pistol permit, he gave Hoover and Lockwood as his references.[3]

This was Hoover in his forties, a man growing accustomed to the taste of fame and savoring that taste. There has been little change in him since. In later life, he developed one penchant that seems a bit unusual for a man who in his youth eschewed poker-playing and adhered to an almost Puritanical code of ethics. Hoover became a great racetrack fan and an ardent defender of the fine art of betting on the horses "in moderation."

In an unusual interview with Oscar Otis of the *Morning Telegraph,* Hoover explained that he went to the races every Saturday if possible because an afternoon at the track "gives me complete relaxation from a grueling week in the FBI." He saw no harm in betting, he said, "if it is done in moderation. . . . Actually, from a law-enforcement standpoint, a well-conducted racetrack is a help to a community if only for the reason that the people at the track are finding an outlet for their emotions, which, if they weren't at the track, they might use for less laudable escapades."

Though betting on the horses has been disclosed time and again as a major underlying cause of embezzlements, this aspect appeared to have made no impact on Hoover in this interview, which furnished excellent propaganda for racing interests. Hoover, who had become quite simpatico with Texas tycoon Clint Murchison, usually spending his annual vacation at a Murchison motel at La Jolla, California, was asked about his intimate knowledge of the manner in which racing was conducted at Murchison's Del Mar track. Rising to the lure, Hoover assured the *Morning Telegraph* that there were "wonderful people" in racing and that Del Mar's charity racing days, in which the net profit went to boys' club work, "helps directly in making the nation sturdy, for Communist penetration is currently directed mainly at labor organizations and youth organizations."

He was the same old Hoover, preoccupied as he had been all his life with the insidious influence of Communism, but now offering racing—and betting—as an antidote. Recognizable Hoover traits cropped up, too, in the concluding quote of the interview, in which Hoover, discussing his enthusiasm for sports, commented:

"I tried tennis, but to play well took too much time. I took three golf lessons and got high blood pressure from not being able to master a good swing. I like baseball and football as spectator sports and I even look at the wrestling matches on TV—because it's a good show and that's what I like—a good show." [4]

■ 2 ■

At 9:15 on the morning of August 24, 1936, J. Edgar Hoover, having received a summons to the White House, was shown into the President's office. Franklin D. Roosevelt looked up, smiled, and said: "Sit down, Edgar." Then the President pushed himself back from his oval desk, lit a cigarette, and said:

"I called you over because I want you to do a job for me and it must be confidential."

Though this conference occurred more than a year before Jack

Alexander's profile of Hoover, there was no knowledge of it at the time of his writing (1937). It was to be years before Don Whitehead, with his access to Hoover memoranda, supplemented by Hoover recollection, was to disclose the full details for the first time—in *The FBI Story.* The reason that Roosevelt had summoned Hoover was his deepening concern about the ominous state of world affairs. In Europe, Mussolini and Hitler were on the march; Spain was torn by civil war; Stalin was pressing his bloody internal purges. In the United States, Fascist and Communist sympathizers were stirring, and the President felt he had been getting insufficient information about their activities.

"Mr. President," Whitehead quotes Hoover as saying, "there is no government agency compiling such general intelligence. Of course, it is not a violation of the law to be a member of the Communist Party, and we have had no specific authority to make such general investigations."

Roosevelt, never a man to be balked by a technicality, insisted that "there must be some way this could be done," and asked Hoover for suggestions. Hoover was ready with an answer. He pointed out that the FBI had authority to undertake investigations for the State Department, if specifically requested to do so by the Secretary of State. Roosevelt frowned. He feared a "leak" about what he was contemplating doing, and he didn't like the idea of having to appeal to the Secretary of State. He told Hoover to come back the next day.

The second conference took place at 1:45 P.M. August 25. Cordell Hull, the Secretary of State, was present. When Roosevelt told him what was wanted, Hull turned to Hoover and said: "Go ahead and investigate the ———— ———— ————!"

There was further discussion. Roosevelt analyzed the international nature of both the Fascist and Communist movements. (In view of subsequent assertions, to which Hoover contributed so much, that the Roosevelt and Truman Administrations were riddled with Communism, it seems important to note here that the President's major concern at this meeting seemed to be with the Communist menace.)

According to report, Constantine Oumansky, counselor for the Soviet Embassy in Washington, had been traveling widely around the country and was rarely to be found at his desk in the embassy.

Roosevelt felt it was important to find out whether this strange activity had any possible connection with Oumansky's duties as a foreign diplomat or whether it indicated a more devious purpose.

In a third meeting, a week later, on September 1, Roosevelt, Hull, and Hoover agreed on the final arrangements that were to put the FBI into undercover work. The Bureau was to investigate for intelligence purposes only, not for prosecutions in court. On this understanding, Hoover on September 5 sent "Personal and Confidential" letters to his Special Agents in Charge, notifying them that the Bureau desired "to obtain from all possible sources information concerning subversive activities being conducted in the United States by Communists, Fascists" and others advocating the violent overthrow of the government.

Though it was the Fascist and Nazi dictators who were to bring the world to war, Hoover's major preoccupation from the very outset seems to have been with the Communist threat. On September 14, William Bullitt, American Ambassador to France, conferred with Attorney General Cummings and Hoover. Bullitt was concerned about the travels of Oumansky in the United States. According to the memorandum that Hoover prepared after this talk, Bullitt warned that Oumansky was in direct contact with groups engaged in subversion against the United States. Bullitt also advised that the Communists would try to place spies in organizations involved in the investigation of subversive activities—even in the FBI itself.[5]

For an administration that later was to be so virulently accused of being "soft on Communism," Roosevelt and his aides seem to have been strangely alert to the dangers of Communist intrigue. Paradoxically, they seem to have been far less concerned about the blatant activities of Nazi movements like the German-American Bund. The Bund was holding public rallies, with displays of the swastika and the Heil-Hitler salute, but nobody on any level of government appears to have been greatly concerned about *this* type of subversion. In March, 1937, columnist Heywood Broun charged that the Bund was conducting "actual recruiting" and that it had already raised "a considerable body of storm troopers here in America." These troops, Broun wrote, were drilling and holding rifle practice, and "their loyalty is palpably directed toward Hitler and the homeland."

This column caused a belated stirring of interest about the Bund. President Roosevelt saw it and called for an investigation. The War Department, to which he sent his request, passed his letter along to Justice, and the FBI was given the job. Its findings were incorporated in a 14-volume study that was transmitted to superiors in the Justice Department. The study revealed that the Bund had a membership of between 6,600 and 8,300; that Fritz Kuhn, its leader, had participated with Adolf Hitler in the abortive Munich beer-cellar *putsch* of 1923; that the Bund conducted military drills without the use of firearms, raised and lowered the swastika and the Stars and Stripes together at Bund camps, and made German mandatory speech in Bund schools. On the basis of this report, the Justice Department decided the Bund had committed no overt act in violation of the law, and the probe came to a dead end. Subsequent disclosure of the FBI's findings, however, did help to arouse public sentiment and focus it against the Bund.[6]

As war neared in Europe, the first of many bureaucratic head-buttings developed in Washington over what agency was to have the glamorous job of catching spies. Hoover was determined to preempt the stellar role for the FBI, but every department with a detective force at its disposal wanted to get into the act. Roosevelt threw his support to Hoover and the FBI in a memorandum that gave the FBI and the intelligence divisions of War and Navy complete authority over all espionage, counterespionage, and sabotage matters. All other government agencies were instructed to report any information on subversive activities to the nearest office of the FBI. As for foreign intelligence, spheres of influence were marked out. The FBI was to be responsible for the entire Western Hemisphere; Naval Intelligence, for the Pacific; Army Intelligence, for Europe, Africa, and the Canal Zone.

The tensions of the time and the fantastically swift expansion of the FBI's functions are reflected in a staccato-like succession of news reports from Washington during 1939. On May 18, Hoover told the House Appropriations Subcommittee that spy cases had averaged about 35 a year prior to 1938, but that 634 cases were investigated in 1938, and he anticipated about 772 in 1939. The preciseness of this anticipation might seem suspicious to the skeptic, but there was nothing dubious about the action that Congress took. It appropriated another $300,000 to finance a counterespionage program by the G-men.

In less than a month, events had outstripped Hoover's estimate. On June 16 the United Press reported from Washington that "the government has mobilized for the most extensive spy hunt since the World War. More than 1,000 cases of alleged espionage are to be investigated." The figures continued to ascend like a hydrogen-filled balloon. On July 24, *The New York Times,* quoting from Hoover's annual report, noted that 1,651 espionage cases had been investigated during the fiscal year.

With the outbreak of war in Europe in September, 1939, the spy fever soared into the stratosphere. On January 5, 1940, appearing before the House Appropriations Subcommittee, Hoover predicted that espionage complaints during 1940 might reach an average of 214 a day, or more than 70,000 a year. He made the further remarkable statement that comparatively few complaints were without substance, and he raised a specter from the past when he testified that, as a result of Roosevelt's directive assigning the FBI to a broad field of espionage and counterespionage work, he had revived the General Intelligence Division. The division, Hoover said, would have "supervision of espionage, sabotage, and other subversive activities." It would investigate persons reported active in subversive activities *"or in movements detrimental to the internal security.* In that connection, we have a general index, arranged alphabetically and geographically, available at the Bureau, so that in the event of any greater emergency coming to our country we will be able to locate immediately these various persons who may need to be the subject of further investigation." [Italics added.]

This statement was to touch off one of the bitterest fights of Hoover's entire career.

■ 3 ■

Hoover's revival of his once-discredited, much-hated General Intelligence Division and the card index system caused agitation among liberals, but the outburst of criticism that followed his announcement might have been less severe had it not been for a series of raids in early February, 1940. The raids were aimed against veterans of the Abraham Lincoln Brigade—American volunteers who had fought on the side of the Loyalists during the civil war in Spain.

The Loyalist government, the legitimate government of Spain, had been supported by Communist parties throughout the world in its battle against Generalissimo Francisco Franco, who had been backed to the hilt by Hitler and Mussolini. It was obvious at the time that, if the dictators were not stopped in Spain, they would go on to World War II, but the democracies of the world and their purblind statesmen had cut off aid to the Loyalist forces. In the resulting one-sided contest, Hitler and Mussolini battle-tested the weapons they were to use in World War II, crushed all opposition in a Spanish blood bath, and imposed on Spain the dictatorial rule of Franco. The American volunteers who had gone to Spain to fight for the Loyalists, either out of Communist fervor or detestation of dictatorship, had returned home—that is, those who had survived. Their one-time involvement in a war already lost and finished seemed a dead issue in the light of the much more horrible holocaust already raging. But not to the FBI and the Justice Department.

In 1937, during the height of the Spanish Civil War, the FBI office in Detroit had received reports that the Young Communist League "and others" were recruiting volunteers for the Loyalist forces. Information was gathered, and in January and April, 1938, the FBI filed reports on the Detroit recruiting with the Criminal Division of the Justice Department. When no action was taken on these reports, according to Whitehead, Hoover instructed his agents in Detroit to drop the investigation. Later, according to this Hoover-sponsored version, the Justice Department revived the probe. First it ordered prosecution of the offenders; then it backed off and withheld action. Finally, after extended vacillation, in December, 1939, Justice gave the green light to the prosecution.

The key suspect in Detroit was Philip Raymond, who had been the Communist Party's candidate for Governor of Michigan in 1937. Raymond, according to the FBI, had promised recruits for the Abraham Lincoln Brigade $300 a month and all expenses. Medical examinations had been given to volunteers by doctors on the staff of the Detroit Health Department, and the doctors' fees for their services had been billed to the city. Volunteers who had qualified physically had been supplied with bus and railroad tickets to New York. Raymond, the FBI charged, had obtained the tickets through World Tourists, Inc., a Communist-front travel agency operated by the well-known Communist Jacob Golos—an important name to keep in mind, for in the postwar Communist hysteria this was the agency and this the man who were supposed to have operated a Russian spy web unsuspected by the FBI.

The heinous offense involved in the recruitment of volunteers for the Loyalists was a technical one: a violation of the federal penal code prohibiting the raising of a foreign army in the United States. This is a violation that is committed every time volunteers assemble to attack Castro, and prosecutions are hardly ever undertaken unless it suits the political purposes of authority to undertake them. In the case of the Spanish Loyalists, it would seem that, with the Civil War in Spain ended, and with the recruiting ended, the technical violation of the penal code had been rendered academic by events.

However, the United States Attorney in Detroit, acting on orders from Washington, submitted evidence of the offense to a federal grand jury and secured indictments against eleven men and one woman. The FBI was given the task of rounding up the suspects.

The Whitehead-Hoover apologia details the extreme care taken by the FBI director to treat the defendants with kid gloves and so vitiate the inevitable Communist cries of police brutality. The defendants were all to be picked up at the unnerving hour of 5 A.M., it is true, but this was only because they might be more easily found at that hour. A federal judge would not be available for their arraignment before 3 P.M., a gap of ten hours, but these ten hours were not to be used for extended third degrees, but simply for the photographing, fingerprinting, and questioning in the gentlest fashion of the suspects. Breakfast and lunch were to be served to the prisoners; if anyone wanted more food and drink, his wants were to be supplied; agents were to be courteous at all times and to avoid arguments. And this, according to the FBI, is just the way it happened.

In the predawn of February 6, 1940, FBI agents picked up ten men and a woman in Detroit and the twelfth defendant in Milwaukee.

In a couple of instances, when defendants refused to unlock their doors after the G-men had identified themselves, the raiders broke down the barriers. All the defendants, according to Whitehead, "were either admitted Communists, members of known Communist-front organizations, or openly Communist sympathizers," a defining that, as can be seen, grows more elastic as it goes along. On arraignment of the main group in Detroit, United States marshals, who took over custody from the FBI, handcuffed the prisoners to a long chain as they were led from court to prison, and photographers took pictures of the "chain gang." Though the FBI was not responsible for this particular incident, the storm broke about the FBI's head.

It was fanned by an offshoot raid in New York. Though no one there had been indicted, FBI agents hunting for evidence barged into the New York headquarters of the Veterans of the Abraham Lincoln Brigade at 55 West 42nd Street. Milton Wolf, national commander of the organization, charged in *The New York Times* on February 9 that the agents "rifled desks, emptied wastebaskets, and took many notes." When Wolf refused to give his name, he said, he was told: "It doesn't matter anyway; you'll soon have a number."

Such were the actions that touched off the most critical barrage Hoover has had to weather since his acquisition of real power. Hoover and the FBI have always insisted that the outcry resulted from a Communist plot to blacken Hoover and destroy his Bureau. In support of this contention, Whitehead quotes a February 6 memo from an informer to the FBI to the effect that Communist leaders had met in Washington and concocted a plan to attack Hoover and the Bureau for violations of civil liberties. In March another informant reported that Communist leaders had met in New York and had agreed to turn the Detroit case into a national issue. An anonymous writer prepared a seventy-six-page document attacking Hoover for his performances in the Palmer Red Raid era and predicting similar dire tramplings on human rights. Resolutions were mimeographed and dispatched to labor groups for adoption.

There is probably little question that the Communists used the issue for all it was worth, but this does not mean that all the criticism was tainted and unjustified. Hoover's inveterate tactic, when attacked, is to link his critics to some devious Communist conspiracy, thus foreclosing any rational discussion of the issues that have been raised. But this technique hardly applies to Senators Norris and Wheeler, who now spearheaded the attack in Congress, or to organs like *The New Republic* and the *Milwaukee Journal*. These, certainly, were honest and rightfully inflamed critics. The predawn knock on the door reminiscent of totalitarian methods, the inflated size of the Bureau and its activity in preparing card indexes and secret individual dossiers, the attack on a left-wing activity that had already expired, were the features that aroused legitimate fears. *The New Republic* blast, headlined "American OGPU," said: "The glamour that surrounds him [Hoover] conceals the growth of a power inconsistent with our conception of democratic institutions." The *Milwaukee Journal,* declaring that the tactics of Hoover's men were "to be outright condemned," deplored the damage done (to an agency it supported) through the creation of an impression "of a 'Gestapo' that can haul citizens off to prison and court in ignominy, imposing any kind of conditions the captors wish without accountability."

The uproar was such that Attorney General Robert H. Jackson, a liberal, who had succeeded Frank Murphy after the prosecution had been ordered, acted on February 16 to quash the indictments. He noted that the Spanish struggle had ended, that "some degree of amnesty at least is being extended in Spain," and that it seemed pointless to revive the issue in harsher terms in America, and, in doing so, to limit prosecution to one side of the Spanish war sympathizers. This common-sense decision, which, it seems, should have been made in advance of the action, did little at the moment to quiet the controversy.

Some of the severest criticism came not from Communist-tainted or liberal sources but from writers usually deemed conservative in their orientation. In late February, when the controversy was at its height, Hoover was in Miami heading the last of his big Mann Act raids, the controversial performance that caused such an outcry that it practically put an end to this favorite Bureau endeavor. This second detested action of the Bureau, coming so closely on the heels of the uproar over the Loyalist raids, added fuel to the flames. The *New York Daily News* gave some prominence to a speech in Congress in which Representative Vito Marcantonio blasted Hoover as "a Stork Club detective."

The Marcantonio crack inspired Westbrook Pegler to level a couple of roundhouse swings at Hoover and the FBI. He pointed out that Hoover might retort that Marcantonio was a "Communist Congressman," but then he took out after the chief G-man. Hoover's worst fault, Pegler wrote, was not that he "hangs out in the glamour jukes," but that "he is sensational. For a file of trashy personal publicity, he has permitted the prestige of his Bureau to be exploited commercially by a following of self-elected junior G-men and himself to be identified in the public mind with gents'-room journalism."

In a subsequent column, Pegler returned to the attack, commenting on a proposed investigation of the FBI in these words: "It would shock most of us, but it would subdue our inquisitiveness, because it would smear so many of us. The FBI has more dirt on more Americans, including Senators, Representatives, labor leaders, Governors, Mayors, and members of some of the political families of the New Deal government, than the foulest whelp of an open-air grand jury bred to a professional blackmailer of the press, radio, and screen could reefer up in a thousand and one nights under the goofy spell of the toxic weed."

Having delivered himself of that philippic, Pegler continued:

The files of the FBI in Washington contain legal proof of perfidy by hundreds of thousands of Americans. . . . The files of the FBI include not merely confirmed criminal data but a vast amount of background on individuals who have never formally been accused of any crime. . . .

The FBI cooperates with police departments which tap wires of family telephones and even, in one incredible case of which I am, nevertheless, positively aware, took phonograph records and moving pictures, on suspicion, of conversations and scenes within the bedroom of a husband and wife. That happened in Los Angeles. And how do you like that? [7]

In Congress, the criticism was equally heated. Senator Norris had called on Attorney General Jackson to study the FBI's conduct in the Detroit raid. Even as Pegler was writing his second scorching column, Jackson was reporting on March 1 that he had found "nothing to justify any charge of misconduct against the Federal Bureau of Investigation." Norris was not satisfied. He had talked to one of the defendants, had received letters from others, and was convinced the prisoners had been subjected "to third-degree methods from the time they were arrested." He called for a further investigation. Once more Jackson yielded.

While this re-examination was under way, Senator Wheeler, chairman of the Interstate Commerce Committee, joined the attack. He denounced the "spying psychology in this country" and added: "Persons who have committed no crime, but whose economic and political views and activities may be obnoxious to present incumbents of law enforcement offices, are being investigated and catalogued." Wheeler wanted a thorough investigation of FBI wiretappings. Hoover replied that wiretapping was limited to cases of "kidnaping, extortion, and flagrant white slavery." Jackson sought to quiet this part of the furor by banning all tapping and instructing United States Attorneys not to try cases in which information was developed by taps.

Henry Schweinhaut, chief of the Civil Liberties Unit of the Department of Justice, next submitted the report on his three-week investigation of the Spanish Loyalist raids. Jackson said the inquiry had completely absolved the FBI, but Senator Norris was not appeased. He called the performance "a whitewash," charged the Justice Department had "ignored the admitted facts," and launched into a four-hour denunciation of Hoover and the FBI.

Norris called Hoover "the greatest publicity hound on the American continent today," and he tore into the FBI-maintained publicity staff that constantly ground out speeches, magazine articles, and books glorifying the FBI. Norris saw a clear threat to liberty as long as this flood of publicity continued on the one hand and was coupled with "universal adulation" on the other hand. "Unless this is stopped," he said, "there will be a spy behind every stump and a detective in every closet. . . . It is my humble judgment that Mr. Hoover is doing more injury to law enforcement in this country by his publicity-seeking methods than any other one thing in his department. It is not true that we can resort to the methods he resorts to and have success with the efforts to preserve human liberties. It is just as necessary that we give a Communist a fair trial as we give a Methodist charged with a crime." [8]

Analyzing the dispute, Scripps-Howard's conservative Ludwell Denny pointed out on May 8 that Roosevelt himself was responsible. It was the President "who decreed the drive on alleged subversive activities and who authorized revival of the discredited Hoover system for that purpose." Denny agreed that Jackson had submitted to Norris a second whitewash. He noted that the Supreme Court in three decisions had thrown out convictions in cases where defendants did not have the benefit of adequate counsel "or were subjected to prolonged police questioning before trial." Denny added: "The Jackson report admits that the agents broke into at least two homes, and that some papers taken by them 'would not come within the catalogue of seizable matter as outlined by the Supreme Court.' "

The next day, May 9, Roger Baldwin, director of the American Civil Liberties Union, said that the report offered no justification for the 5 A.M. arrests, for searching homes without warrants, for not permitting defendants to get in touch with counsel, for impounding the indictment so that it could not be seen by counsel, for giving defendants insufficient time to confer with counsel (only about 15 minutes before the 3 P.M. hearing), for using handcuffs and a chain, and for demanding "excessive bail."

The FBI had its defenders, both in the press and in Congress. Most important, it had as its champion the one man who really mattered, Roosevelt. The President was, as Denny had written, fundamentally responsible for what had happened. He had also been the champion, ever since his days as Governor of New York, of a strong national police force. He had taken vicarious pride in the FBI's war against the desperados, the headline feats which had incidentally redounded to the glory of his Administration. So Roosevelt was a Hoover partisan, and he made his position clear, as Whitehead tells it, at the annual dinner of White House correspondents on March 16, 1940. The President, who was the guest of honor at the head table, singled out Hoover for special and flattering attention.

The word sped swiftly through Washington.

After that, though the final Jackson report was yet to be made, everybody knew that Hoover had weathered the storm.[9]

■ 4 ■

Its critics defeated, if not silenced, the FBI now rode to the roundup of spies much as it had ridden to the roundup of desperados. Of the numerous spy cases that the FBI successfully broke, one that exhibited the Bureau at its skillful best developed in 1940—the same year that had been marked by the Loyalist civil rights furor. William Sebold, a naturalized American citizen, returned from a visit to his native Germany an acutely disturbed man. His grandfather was a Jew, and while he had been abroad, the Gestapo had threatened to exterminate his relatives unless he agreed to become a German spy when he returned to the United States. Sebold pretended to agree. The Gestapo gave him the details of a secret code. He was trained in the use of short-wave radio and given instructions concerning the use of microphotographic equipment that he was to pass on to other German agents when he returned to America. Once back in this country, Sebold went directly to the FBI.

Given this ideal opening wedge for counterespionage, the FBI made the most of the opportunity. It instructed Sebold to play his role of Nazi spy to the hilt. It helped him in the stage-managing and carefully baited the bear trap.

FBI agents built a short-wave radio station at Centerport, Long Island. From this station, on May 20, 1940, a message purportedly coming from Sebold was sent to the Gestapo station in Hamburg, Germany. The Gestapo was delighted. With contact thus established, FBI agents fed the Gestapo a line of spurious information. Each message contained a grain of truth—nonvital truth, as the FBI made certain by clearing the details with Army and Navy Intelligence officers in advance. The Gestapo, deluded by the apparent success of its plot, never suspected the ruse. In return, it sent instructions and advice to Sebold, who was operating out of a mid-Manhattan office that the FBI had helped him procure to serve as a front for the spy ring.

Never was an office more thoroughly booby-trapped. A looking-glass on the wall was actually a one-way window through which agents could observe everything that went on in Sebold's office without themselves being seen. Through the same aperture, movie cameras, grinding away quietly in secret, filmed each unsuspecting visitor. Hidden microphones picked up every whisper and carried it to recording devices. For months, the FBI watched, identified, and tailed the unsuspecting German spies. During this period, some five hundred radio messages were sent back and forth to the Gestapo in Hamburg. So skillfully was the counterespionage handled that the agents of the Gestapo suspected nothing until the FBI sprang its trap.

The prize catch was Fritz Duquesne, a German agent whose spy career dated back to the early 1900's. Thirty-two others were corraled with him. All were prosecuted and convicted.

The Duquesne ring was the largest to be uncovered before Pearl Harbor, but it represented no isolated success. Again and again, the FBI demonstrated its ability to nip Nazi espionage before it could accomplish its purpose. The record that the Bureau established in such cases was a proud one.

At the very time that the FBI was embarking on the Duquesne-ring spy case, which it carried to such a brilliant conclusion, it was demonstrating that it could be led far astray by investigative enthusiasm. This second case broke on January 15, 1940, when FBI agents, in carefully synchronized raids, swooped down on seventeen members of a Christian Front Sports Club in Brooklyn. The details, as given out at the time by the FBI and the United States Attorney's office, were of the shocking, sensational kind that automatically makes eight-column headlines.

The seventeen arrested Christian Fronters, the government said, actually had been plotting the overthrow of federal authority. They had been stealing arms and ammunition from a National Guard Armory. They had been making bombs. Hoover, personally announcing the arrests, put his own prestige directly on the line in painting a picture of a horrendous conspiracy. He said he had wanted to wait until the FBI could catch the plotters in some overt act, but that he had been compelled to move when he learned they were plotting to blow up a public building. William Gerald Bishop, the alleged ring-leader, was described by Hoover as a man who intended to place a dictator in the White House. Bishop planned to accomplish this, said Hoover, by instituting a reign of terror and violence—blowing up bridges, seizing and destroying communications centers, confiscating the gold in government vaults. In support of these allegations, the FBI detailed an impressively long list of the weapons seized with the plotters—such items as 15 partly made bombs, 12 Springfield rifles, 4 22-caliber rifles, an automatic, a shotgun, 750 rounds of machine-gun ammunition, and 3,500 rounds of ammunition for the Springfields.

"It took only twenty-three men to overthrow Russia," Hoover told startled newsmen, and added: "We have evidence to substantiate every claim we have made." [10]

The roundup caused a great furor because of the possibility that the plotters might be linked to the Reverend Charles E. Coughlin, extreme right-wing clergyman of the era. Coughlin announced that he had repudiated the group, but letters written by some of the leaders spoke of the necessity of defending Coughlin "with the last drop of our blood." They pictured the dangers of a Communist revolution in America and stressed that the only way to prevent it was to act the way Franco had acted in Spain.

The government's presentation of its case in the newspapers certainly carried conviction. The evidence seemed airtight. And yet, as in the case of the Palmer Red Raids, there was a faint sense of unreality about the whole performance. In its first story on the roundup, the New York *World-Telegram,* paralleling the skepticism of *The New York Times* in the Palmer era, noted: "Although the men were taken to court in handcuffs, guarded with care by deputy marshals and G-men, they looked anything but dangerous. They were a shame-faced lot of low-paid white-collar workers and laborers."

The trial opened in Brooklyn Federal Court in April, 1940. In early testimony, the prosecution added seemingly impressive details to its case. One FBI agent testified that he had made recordings of conversations held by the plotters in the home of Denis Healy, the government informer who had helped to break the case. The recordings, the agent insisted, proved unintelligible, but he testified he had overheard Bishop brag that "175 policemen in New York were ready to join the revolution" and that the plotters had "300,000 men under arms in the United States." A second FBI agent testified that another of the plotters had suggested "knocking off at least a dozen congressmen." The arsenal seized in the raids was introduced into evidence. And a striking, seemingly clinching bit of evidence was produced—a film secretly made by FBI agents. This showed the Christian Fronters actually drilling with arms, sprinting across open spaces, flopping to the ground, and practicing rifle fire.

The mounting weight of the evidence was impressive until the government ran into a couple of stumbling blocks—the self-defeating activities of its own star informer and the recordings that agents had made of the plotters in conversation—recordings that turned out to be intelligible enough to put an entirely different complexion on the menace.

The unraveling of the fantasy began with the exposure of Denis Healy. The government's star informer, it developed, had been rather well paid for informing. At first he had been put on the payroll at a salary of $25 a week; later, as his information got better, he had been paid $75 every two weeks. His wife, too, had been compensated. In all, it was admitted, the FBI had paid out some $1,300 to the Healys since the previous October 10—compensation, it was explained, to reimburse them for time lost from their regular jobs and to pay them for expenses they had incurred in aiding the government.

These details suggested the possibility that the Healys might have informed for pay, but more damaging was Healy's admission that in his enthusiasm for the cause he had aided and pushed the plotters onward in their plot, helping to create some of the evidence against them. The matter of the arsenal the plotters had amassed was a key item. Healy testified that he had gone to his National Guard commander and had obtained his cooperation (Healy understood the FBI had paved the way for this) to let him "borrow" rifle and machine-gun ammunition to give to the Christian Fronters. Even the ammunition used in the rifle practice the FBI had filmed had been obtained not by the plotters but by Healy. He had used FBI funds to purchase it. He had used FBI funds, too, he conceded, to treat the conspirators well; they had dined on pheasant at $2.50 a head and had been supplied liquor—all courtesy of the FBI. The testimony at this point began to take on the odious overtones of the activities of an *agent provocateur*. The line between the activities the Christian Fronters had undertaken on their own initiative and those they had undertaken on Healy's active stimulation and encouragement became blurred.

Recordings of one of the conspiratorial sessions in Healy's home were introduced into evidence. Instead of proving the desperate character of the plotters, these transcripts established only that they had indulged in a lot of wild talk while under the influence of FBI-supplied liquor. The clink of glasses and the clunk of falling bottles punctuated a long, rambling talk between one of the defendants and Healy. "I want to be a revolutionist, I really do," the poor boob said at one point plaintively, as if trying to convince himself. And Healy remarked: "You drink too damned much of that stuff." As the evening progressed, one of the bottles fell off the table with a loud crash. There was some maudlin talk about "a girl with a little hat." Finally one of the desperate characters who was going to put a dictator in the seat of power in Washington remarked: "Oh God, I feel kind of lousy; give me a cigarette."

The defense scored some telling blows in cross-examining FBI agents about the methods used to extract statements from the defendants. The arrests had been made on a Saturday night, and the prisoners had been questioned during the weekend prior to their arraignment on Monday. The FBI vehemently denied it had used tactics smacking of the third degree. The denial became suspect when one agent conceded that the questioning had continued for fourteen uninterrupted hours, with the longest interval between questions "about four or five minutes." Another agent acknowledged that one of the defendants had been questioned continually and had had no food for eleven hours, and that he had complained of headaches. Defense attorneys charged that such methods constituted at least a mental third degree.

When the case went to the jury in late June, 1940, the fate of only fourteen defendants remained to be decided. One defendant had committed suicide in his prison cell, and charges against two others had been dismissed by the trial judge for lack of proof. The evidence against the remaining fourteen was weighed for forty-seven and one-half hours, but the battle over the verdict did not indicate, as it usually does, great doubt in the jury's mind. The impression made by the government's case is clearly shown by the fact that, on the first ballot, nine of the jurors voted to acquit all the defendants. The final verdict was a compromise. Eleven of the jurors wanted complete acquittal, but one holdout refused to go along with them on five cases. The result was that nine were acquitted, and the government was left with the necessity of re-trying the other five if it wanted to persist with the case. It didn't. All the charges were finally dropped.

It was an outcome that provided its own comment on Hoover's initial boast: "We have evidence to substantiate every claim we have made." [11]

■ 5 ■

With a world war raging, there was no containing the FBI. Hoover and the Bureau, by Roosevelt's direction, had been given charge of espionage and counterespionage only in the Western Hemisphere; but, with glory up for grabs, there was literally no possibility of setting a line of demarcation that the FBI would respect. Its agents fanned out worldwide. In their brashness, they didn't hesitate to devote their attention to high American officials abroad as well as to the potential enemy.

In early 1941, shortly after Roosevelt had been sworn in for a third term, the thin, sickly, brilliant, and vibrant man who was his shadow—Harry Hopkins—made a trip to London to confer with the heads of the British Government. Though Pearl Harbor was still months away, Roosevelt and Hopkins felt war for America would ultimately be inevitable, and they wanted to lay the groundwork to synchronize our scientific and military information and skills with those of the British. Lord Beaverbrook, who was then in charge of British airplane production, gave a private dinner for Hopkins in Claridge's. It was an off-the-record meeting with British publishers and journalists. Hopkins impressed them all with his brilliance and his broad grasp of issues. Lurking in the wings of Claridge's that night, however, were some unscheduled guests, agents of the FBI, who forwarded their impressions of Hopkins' performance to the Bureau in Washington. Hoover himself then dictated a memorandum that he forwarded to the White House for Roosevelt's private information. It read:

> At the conclusion of the dinner it appeared from facial expressions that all the guests were quite happy as a result of the dinner and discussions. Small groups of them stopped in the coffee room, where representatives of this Bureau were seated at the moment, and the gist of the conversations related to the very charming manner of Mr. Hopkins, his keen insight into current problems, and the very remarkable fact that he combined a very charming but almost shy personality with a very vigorous and dynamic mentality. In no instance was any unfavorable comment made and the entire gist of their conversations relative to Mr. Hopkins was positive and commendatory.

This strikes one as both a fawning and a presumptuous performance. It was a police-state type of checkup on the man who, above all others, was Roosevelt's favorite and confidant, and though the result was laudatory, the fact of the checkup remained. Were we to have a government of suspicion and checkup and secret reports on the conduct of even a Harry Hopkins? This is a question, it appears, that never occurred to the President. The mighty Hoover ego had flattered Roosevelt's mightier ego. "It delighted Roosevelt to know that the G-men were checking up on his personal representative." [12]

The man who didn't hesitate to shadow Harry Hopkins was the type who naturally wouldn't hesitate to stretch his authority to the outermost limits—and at times a bit beyond. Overweening vanity seemed to show in his desire to grab every espionage and counterespionage chore for the FBI, and this at times brought him into sharp conflict with rival agencies, even to the extent of interfering with their plans.

In 1940 Hoover struck up a partnership with William Stephenson, a "quiet Canadian" deceptively posing as a businessman, who was actually the head of the British Secret Intelligence Service (SIS) in New York. Stephenson, who was subsequently knighted for his great undercover work, himself approached Hoover and sought a pooling of the resources of the FBI and SIS. Hoover was willing, if not eager, but he pointed out that he had no authority to enter into such an arrangement and could not do so without the private O.K. of Roosevelt. Even then, he stressed, the relationship between himself and Stephenson would have to be kept a secret, even from the State Department, which was committed at the moment to carrying out the official American policy of strict neutrality. Stephenson, through a mutual friend, approached Roosevelt, and the President gave his enthusiastic approval to the secret collaboration of the FBI and SIS. So a powerful partnership, which was to harass Axis agents throughout the Americas, was formed.

The story of the Hoover-Stephenson teamwork has recently been told by H. Montgomery Hyde, a British author who was a wartime agent under Stephenson and had access to all of Stephenson's personal records. Hyde clearly admired Hoover's courage and ability, but at the same time, as repeated references in his account show, he recognized the FBI director's abnormal ambition, a trait that made him hostile to potential rivals in the field of intelligence.[13]

At the outset, as Hyde points out, Hoover had "no legal right to employ any agents outside United States territory," and he was "forced to act surreptitiously without the knowledge of the State Department and the official United States missions in Latin-American countries." Since there was "no domestic censorship of mails and cables . . . FBI agents were reduced to purloining letters from Post Offices. Had this illicit action been exposed, and proved unjustified in any particular instance, it would have caused political repercussions of sufficient magnitude to place in jeopardy the continued existence of the organization or at least of Hoover as its Director." [14]

The SIS helped the FBI at this difficult juncture by bringing it up to date on the latest techniques of postal espionage. An experienced FBI agent was sent to Bermuda and instructed in British-developed methods of mail examination. In America, the FBI laboratory was made acquainted "with the various methods of examining letters in such a manner that their recipients were not aware that they had been opened. This highly secret process included the unsealing and resealing of diplomatic and other privileged mail so that the seals appeared absolutely intact and were impervious to the ultra-violet ray and other chemical tests."

Hoover's cooperation with Stephenson in this prewar period often extended far beyond the mere gathering of intelligence and involved active warlike roles. "Indeed," Hyde writes, "it may fairly be said that he [Hoover] was in the war from the moment that they began their collaboration." On occasion, Hoover even undertook to plant "strategic deception material" in the German Embassy in Washington. One example was a message designed to deter Hitler from embarking on any large-scale military campaign. It read: "From highly reliable sources it is learned U.S.S.R. intend further military aggression instant Germany is embroiled in major operations." Another message, designed to keep the Germans from using poison gas, reported that, in this event, the British would unveil their "secret weapon," said to consist of "some kind of glass balls containing chemicals producing such terrific heat that they cannot be extinguished by any known means."

Such assistance to the British, Hyde writes, was "willingly given" by Hoover, but it "was always conditioned by Hoover's great ambition for the Bureau which he directed. Unhappily this was to lead him, after his country entered the war, into the untenable position of insisting in effect upon retaining for the FBI, among United States Intelligence agencies, monopoly of liaison with BSC [as the American wing of the British intelligence setup was known]. It was an untenable position which Hoover was with some reluctance eventually brought to realize." [15]

Hoover's nose was put sadly out of joint when Roosevelt moved to set up a rival undercover agency. The President obviously reasoned that the FBI had enough to handle with its enormous domestic law enforcement duties, its full responsibility for the protection of war plants against sabotage, and its jurisdiction over espionage and counterespionage in the entire Western Hemisphere. It should have been clear to any reasonable man, though it was not to Hoover, that another agency would be needed to gather information and conduct the worldwide clandestine operations that the exigencies of war were soon to demand. In mid-June, 1941, the President called to the White House General William J. (Wild Bill) Donovan, the former Assistant Attorney General who had served in the Department of Justice with Hoover during the days of the Wheeler prosecution. Donovan yielded to the President's urging and agreed to set up an agency to be known as COI (Coordinator of Information), the nucleus of what was soon, with American involvement in the war, to become the Office of Strategic Services.

Stephenson, a close friend and admirer of Donovan (when seen together, they were often called "Little Bill" and "Big Bill"), had been anxious to have the Americans establish just such a super-intelligence agency, and he did his best from the start to furnish Donovan's COI with the kind of help and information that would keep it alive. His assistance was pivotal, because the intrusion of this new interloper in the intelligence field created animosities in existing agencies, which feared, in Stephenson's words, that COI "would infringe on their own prerogatives. This was particularly true of the FBI, and to a lesser extent of the Service Intelligence Departments." [16]

British intelligence continued to supply Hoover and the FBI with information, sending it some 100,000 reports on a wide range of subjects during 1941. But Hoover keenly resented Donovan, and "his resentment was inevitably extended" toward Donovan's British collaborators. In January, 1942, with the United States at war, a committee was set up to coordinate all Anglo-American intelligence operations in the Western Hemisphere. At its first meeting, Assistant Secretary of State Adolf Berle proposed that Stephenson's organization should maintain liaison with no United States organization other than the FBI. This would have blacked out Army and Navy Intelligence as well as Donovan. Stephenson could not agree to this and held many discussions with Berle "in an effort to temper his hostility." He finally succeeded, but Hoover remained obdurate. The sequel is told by Hyde:

> In June, 1943, a memorandum from the Department of Justice to Stephenson, which bore unmistakable signs of having been composed at Hoover's instigation, directed BSC to desist from direct contact with the U.S. armed services and maintain liaison only through "approved military channels." Since Stephenson knew this directive was diametrically opposed to the wishes of U.S. services intelligence, he referred it to General George Strong, head of G.2, who stated unreservedly that "he was not prepared to submit to an FBI censorship."

A meeting of all the interested services was held, and at this Berle finally endorsed General Strong's view and ruled that the British should be free to decide for themselves which American agencies they should contact and how they should transmit their information. "Hoover had no choice but to accept this ruling," Hyde writes, "and thereafter, it is only fair to add, he abided by it without apparent demur." The strained relations between Hoover and Stephenson's BSC lasted "for about eighteen months," a period that was "a difficult time for Stephenson." [17]

A less temperate picture of Hoover's animosity and its results was drawn by Donald Downes, an undercover agent who worked first for Stephenson's organization and later for Donovan's OSS. In January, 1942, Downes was summoned to Washington and told the OSS wanted to penetrate some of the neutral embassies that, it was suspected, were secretly collaborating with the Axis powers. American military intelligence was especially anxious to obtain the key to the embassies' secret diplomatic codes, so that, if a neutral embassy sent messages for the Germans, American experts might be able to decipher the communiqués. Donovan had been asked to handle the delicate assignment, which, of course, would be disowned should any of the operatives engaged in it ever be discovered. Downes had been selected to head this particular OSS embassy-cracking endeavor, and he assembled about him a team of experts for the performance of his assignment.

One embassy was a relatively soft touch, and Downes managed to place a couple of girl secretaries on the staff to keep OSS informed of all vital messages that went out. A second embassy proved much more difficult. It had a modern electronic coding machine, which it kept locked up securely in a massive safe. Though Downes had managed to place a girl linguist on this embassy staff, she hadn't been able to obtain the closely guarded combination. The only solution was to steal into the embassy like a burglar in the night, get that safe open, and so gain access to the coding machine. But how? Downes consulted a veteran safecracker, who was also a safe expert, and, following his advice, he obtained a small hard-rubber hammer, which his girl spy slipped into her handbag. At a propitious moment, when no one was looking, she whipped out the hammer and delivered a blow with all her might at the dial of the safe. The rubber-muffled stroke was enough to put the safe's mechanism out of order, and the embassy had to summon a safe expert. Downes, of course, had prepared for this eventuality in advance, and when the expected call came to the company that had supplied the safe, his veteran safe-cracker was ready to appear in the role of repair man. After that, though the adventure remained extremely risky, the safe offered no problem, for Downes' safecracker possessed the necessary knowledge of the combination.

This preliminary intrigue successfully completed, Downes' squad stole into the embassy in the dead of night, unlocked the safe, and gained access to the coding machine. His electronics expert and his photographic expert, working furiously against time and chance dis-covery, dissected the machine, took some 3,400 photographs, locked everything up just as they had found it, and decamped before dawn without leaving behind them any traces of their clandestine presence. For the next month, until the settings of the coding machine were changed, American intelligence would be able to read all the tele-graphic messages dispatched by this embassy.

It was a great intelligence coup. But all the time Downes and his team had been working to pull it off, they had been beset by a secret worry. Downes described their problem in these words:

> We had taken all imaginable precautions—that is, all except one— against the possibility of betrayal by someone high enough in the American Government to know what we were doing. . . .
>
> But apparently Edgar Hoover was out for Donovan's scalp and any type of co-operation was pretty well one-sided. Not only OSS, but the British Secret Intelligence, many of whose investigations were bound to lead to America, were constantly being hounded by the FBI.
>
> "Bob" and "Dick" [two members of Downes' team] both told me that they thought their apartments in Washington had been searched and they were certain that on several occasions they had been followed. I assured them it was only the FBI checking on strangely behaving individuals in Washington.
>
> A friend of ours in the Department of Justice had warned us that Edgar Hoover believed we were "penetrating" embassies and that he was annoyed.

For a time, nothing happened. For three straight months, Downes' safecracking and decoding team entered the embassy and came out with the information that would enable American intelligence to decipher the embassy's messages for another month. Then the fourth month rolled around, and they made still another attempt. Downes gave this account of the last try:

> At 11 o'clock the phone rang. It was "Dick."
> "We had to get out. We had just got in and were preparing to open the safe when two FBI squad cars pulled up outside the building and turned on their sirens. It woke everybody. All the lights . . ."
> "Tell me later. If you are sure you're not being followed come here immediately."
> In five minutes they came in. They had seen a car following them and had stopped to check on it, but recognizing the FBI car which had often followed them before, they had gone on, parked two blocks from the embassy and walked to the janitor's door. The janitor had just given them their suitcases, and they were actually in front of the safe beginning to open it when the sirens had been turned on. "No one saw us. We scrammed."

Downes called his OSS superior, who was incredulous. Together they went to see Donovan at his home. "I don't believe any single event in his career ever enraged him more," Downes wrote.

"The next morning," his tale continues, "Donovan went to the White House to protest.

"On that level the case was clearly over my head and out of [my] hands. Donovan was in-fighting with the man of whom I had often heard it said in Washington that no President dare discipline him, let alone dismiss him."

The result was inevitable. Downes was told a couple of weeks later to go to see a "Mr. Brown" in the FBI's Washington field office and to turn all his projects and their personnel over to him.

"The personnel, almost to a man (and woman), came back later to protest," Downes wrote. "Instead of being treated as patriotic people making war for their country, Mr. Hoover's Mr. Brown treated them as so many stool-pigeons, as inferior people who had sunk to the depths of being police spies and informers—the classical cop attitude toward the underworld weakling whom they use to trap gangsters." [18]

■ 6 ■

Fortunately, Hoover and the FBI were not always fighting with their own service competitors and allies, and when they were not, their accomplishments were of a high order. The immense importance of the collaboration between Hoover and Stephenson, when it was not marred by petty interservice animosity, was demonstrated most vividly perhaps by the manner in which the two services dynamited Nazi plans for a coup that would have set up a dictatorial, pro-Axis government in Bolivia.

Hoover was the first to get wind of the danger, and in May, 1941, he notified Stephenson of his discovery. He had information that Major Elias Belmonte, the violently pro-Nazi Bolivian Military Attaché in Berlin, was in touch with Nazi elements in his own country. The FBI information indicated that Belmonte and his fellow conspirators at home were planning a coup to overthrow the pro-British government of President Peñaranda. President Roosevelt was most concerned, because Bolivia was the principal American source of wolfram, the ore from which tungsten is derived. Should a pro-Axis government in Bolivia cut off this source of supply, a body blow would be delivered to United States steel and arms manufacturing industries.

Since the FBI was handicapped by the prewar neutrality stand of the United States on taking positive action outside the country, Hoover sought Stephenson's help. The Canadian spy master promptly dispatched Hyde to Bolivia, and Hyde returned with information that confirmed all the details in Hoover's original report. Stephenson's next step was to alert his agents in South America to watch out for and try to intercept couriers traveling between Berlin and the German legation in La Paz. The surveillance that was set up finally resulted in a British agent's snuggling up to a Nazi courier while they were crowded together in an elevator in the German Bank Building in Buenos Aires. Helped by the crush, the light-fingered British agent managed to lift a sealed document from the pocket of the messenger.

This expert pocket-picking produced all the evidence the Americans and their British allies needed. The purloined letter, dated June 9, 1941, had been dispatched from the Bolivian legation in Berlin. It bore the signature of Belmonte, and it was addressed to Dr. Ernst Wendler, the German Minister in Bolivia. It discussed plans for a coup in the middle of July, when Belmonte planned to fly back to Bolivia to take personal command of a revolt spearheaded by younger elements in the Bolivian army. Once successful, Belmonte wrote, his government would "rescind the wolfram contract with the United States, and also substantially modify the tin contracts with England and the United States." But this was not all. Belmonte confidently predicted "the other countries [of South America] will quickly follow our example, and then with one sole ideal and one sole supreme leader, we will save the future of South America and will begin an era of purification, order, and work."

No document could have been more damaging. Stephenson passed the purloined letter over to Hoover, who in turn gave it to Secretary of State Cordell Hull. Hull apprised Roosevelt of the find, and the Bolivian government was given a photostatic copy. Forewarned, the Peñaranda government took drastic action. On July 19 it proclaimed a nationwide state of siege, ordered Dr. Wendler, the German Minister, to leave Bolivia, and rounded up army officers and German and Bolivian civilians suspected of complicity in the plot. Belmonte's conspiratorial plans were balked, and Bolivia was saved from revolution. More important, the Axis was denied a foothold in the Southern Hemisphere. It lost the opportunity to foment other coups, and the solidarity of the Americas was preserved.[19]

Throughout the war, the FBI and its British secret service partners consistently foiled Axis plots in South America. Except for Argentina, which had a pro-Fascist government, enemy agents were never able to gain a secure toehold south of the border.

The secret services also foiled Axis plots against the United States. German efforts to land saboteurs on our coasts all ended in ignominious failure. One reason seems to have been that the men recruited by German intelligence lacked any real stomach for the job. As in the case of the major body of saboteurs landed at Amagansett, Long Island, there seemed to be almost always at least one man in the group who lost his nerve and communicated with the FBI as soon as he got ashore. So tipped, agents quickly launched nationwide man-hunts that tracked down their prey. The Long Island saboteurs, others landed on the Florida coast, and a final pair put ashore in Maine, all were apprehended before they could place their first dynamite stick.

Equally perfect was the FBI's guardianship of America's sprawl-ing industrial plants. Long before America became embroiled in the war, Army and Navy Intelligence had agreed that the FBI should have sole responsibility for guarding against sabotage and espionage. A system of plant security had been set up with specially designated workers in each plant serving as volunteer undercover agents and informants for the FBI. This plant spy system drew much criticism in labor and liberal circles, but it seems to have been designed, as Whitehead says, solely for the protection of the plants and the coun-try, not for antilabor purposes.[20]

To Hoover's eternal credit, he also staunchly resisted superpatriotic attempts to recreate the vigilante system of World War I. This would have been extremely easy to do. In the hysteria that followed the treacherous attack on Pearl Harbor, the FBI was practically inun-dated with offers from patriotic citizens who wanted to join the hunt for spies and saboteurs. Cecil B. DeMille, the Hollywood mogul, through the President's son, James Roosevelt, made an offer almost identical to the one that had led to the creation of vigilante organ-izations in World War I. He offered to organize, direct, and finance an "FBI unit" in the motion-picture industry. Hoover diplomatically replied that he greatly appreciated the "very generous and patriotic offer," but he felt the FBI had "the situation well in hand," and there was no need to establish "any so-called auxiliary."

More difficult to reject was the offer of the American Legion. Dur-ing the summer of 1940, the Legion came up with a plan under which some 11,000 posts throughout the nation would organize their own special investigative bodies to help combat subversion. Attorney General Jackson, with a liberal's sensitiveness to civil rights issues, frowned on the suggestion. He felt that investigative work should be carried out by professionals, not left to the discretion of amateurs, and he suggested that any information the Legion gathered should be turned over to the FBI. Some Legionnaires were miffed at this cold reception of their proposal, but Hoover, who has always been one of their idols, mollified them by suggesting a liaison system between Post Commanders and Special Agents in Charge. Whenever a post commander felt he or his Legionnaires had gathered information that might be helpful, he was to communicate it to the SAC in his district. Then the FBI, not the Legion, would make the necessary investigation. Hoover, who has never wanted to share his investigative powers with anyone in any case, seems also to have been motivated by a determination to avoid the vigilante excesses of World War I. There were not to be, this time, any lynchings like the hanging of Frank H. Little at Butte, Montana.

Under such conditions, Hoover and the FBI guarded the home front. They guarded it well. According to statistics quoted by Whitehead, FBI investigations of 19,649 cases of suspected sabotage during the war years turned up not a single case that was the work of enemy agents. This is a typical FBI presentation of its own perfection, but even one who is skeptical of such 100 per cent claims can agree that, in this instance, the boast was justified. One thing is clear: the tragic events of German sabotage in World War I were not repeated in World War II. There were no incidents like the disastrous 1916 Black Tom Island and the 1917 Kingsland, New Jersey, explosions.

◼ Notes ◼

[1] *The New Yorker,* Sept. 25, 1937.

[2] *Ibid.,* Oct. 2, 1937.

[3] This fact came to light in the mid-fifties when Billingsley, incensed at some workmen who, he felt, were creating a nuisance in his neighborhood, rushed out with his pistol, firing it into the air. In the subsequent investigation, his use of the names of Hoover and Lockwood as references on his permit was revealed by one of the veteran Associated Press police reporters.

[4] In April, 1962, when a drive was under way to legalize racing in Texas, the *Racing Times,* which devoted most of an entire issue to whooping up the campaign, reinforced its arguments by reprinting most of the Hoover *Morning Telegraph* interview.

[5] For these developments that placed the FBI in a new undercover role, see Don Whitehead, *The FBI Story* (Random House, 1956), pp. 188–193 of Pocket Books edition.

[6] Associated Press dispatch from Washington, Apr. 3, 1939.

[7] See the *New York Daily News,* Feb. 28, 1940; and the Westbrook Pegler columns of Feb. 29 and Mar. 2 in the *New York World-Telegram.*

[8] *New York Times,* May 8, 1940.

[9] Whitehead devoted a full chapter to this controversy (pages 204–217 of the Pocket Books edition), completely exculpating the FBI. Max Lowenthal, in *The Federal Bureau of Investigation* (William Sloane Associates, 1950), pp. 319–322, dealt with the attack in Congress in greater detail. I have also relied on the almost daily running accounts of the *New York Times* and the *New York World-Telegram* for the months of February, March, and May, 1940.

[10] Lowenthal, *op. cit.,* p. 317; *New York Times,* Jan. 15, 16, and 17, 1940; *New York World-Telegram,* Jan. 15, 1940.

[11] For accounts of the Christian Front spy trial, see the *New York Times,* the *New York Herald Tribune,* and the *New York World-Telegram* for April, May, and June, 1940.

[12] Robert E. Sherwood, *Roosevelt and Hopkins* (Harper & Brothers, 1948), p. 250.

[13] H. Montgomery Hyde, *Room 3603* (Farrar, Strauss & Cudahy, 1963).

[14] *Ibid.,* pp. 54–55.

[15] *Ibid.,* pp. 58–59.

[16] *Ibid.,* p. 155.

[17] *Ibid.,* pp. 163–167.

[18] Donald Downes, *The Scarlet Thread* (British Book Centre, New York, 1953). See pp. 87–102.

[19] Hyde, *op. cit.,* pp. 139–144.

[20] Whitehead, *op. cit.,* p. 251.

9 Hysteria — and More Spies

History was now about to repeat itself. As World War I had ended in turmoil and revolution, so did World War II. Communism, born in the first conflict, seemed for a time about to engulf the world as an aftermath of the second. Americans reacted to the prospect much as they had reacted a quarter of a century earlier. Just as the Bolshevist revolution had led to fear and shock and a period of witch-hunt, so the stresses of the post-World War II era led straight to McCarthyism. Only now there was this vital difference: the witch-hunt was not just the aberration of a moment; it was to taint politics and public attitudes for more than a decade.

A difference in technique produced the difference in effect. The Palmer Red Raids of 1919–1920 had been a blatant and brutal exercise in authoritarianism. Their excesses had laid them open to swift exposure; reason quickly had rejected fantasy, and sanity had reestablished itself. The second witch-hunt of the post-World War II era could not be unmasked so easily, for this was a more insidious campaign, one that shunned direct collision with observable fact.

It was a campaign based on the hypothesis not of overt acts, but of secret treason; not so much on men's deeds which might be subject to proof or disproof, but upon the predilections of their minds as these might be deduced from their ties and associations. Demagogues, abetted by a largely partisan press, developed the thesis that America had lost the fruits of victory and found herself menaced in a largely hostile world simply because there had been treason in high places. If this interpretation of current events could not be factually demonstrated, it did not need to be factually demonstrated—for what traitor would admit his treason? So his denials could be disregarded. So we came to have just one guidon of truth—the word of the turncoat who supposedly had suddenly discovered conscience, the tale of the informer who supposedly had been on the inside of horrendous conspiracy and had come out to tell all and, of course, to tell all truthfully. Those who espoused this pernicious doctrine in the name of the greater patriotism disregarded, if they perceived—and many of them must have perceived, for they were not all unintelligent men—the subversion they themselves were practicing on the most precious fundamentals of the American system.

That system, above all else, has had from the days of its founding one supreme benison to offer all mankind—the concept of individual freedom, of individual justice. The two are, of course, inseparable, and they rest upon one cardinal principle—that every man, no matter how low or how high, must be presumed innocent until proved guilty. Strike out that one pillar, and you destroy America's noblest reason for being. Yet it was this pillar that the witch-hunt that was now to sweep America would most seriously undermine. Under the virus of suspicion, in a time when a man could be condemned by phrases not susceptible of exact definition, let alone positive proof—phrases like "fellow traveler" and "pseudo liberal" and "dupe"—presumption of innocence would be discarded and superseded by a new doctrine, presumption of guilt. The accused still had the right to try to defend himself, if he dared and if he could, but the creeping authoritarianism that pinned prejudicial labels upon his character and his mind defied him to do it.

In the production of this national evil that was to enthrone innuendo and make the word of the informer sacred doctrine, no man in America was to be more influential than J. Edgar Hoover. His role was basic; his interpretation of fact, unchallenged; his word, in effect, superior to that of any court in the land.

■ 1 ■

The postwar witch-hunt was based on an interpretation of the events of the critical war years. The events themselves seemed to say that the war, considering its global nature and the massive effort required, had been fought to its victorious conclusion with a maximum of speed and efficiency. But disillusionment with a victory that had brought not peace but the frustrations of the Cold War rapidly began to alter this common-sense view. The theory was industriously promulgated, and widely adopted, that the new insecurities of the age were attributable to treason and sell-out in high places. To lend substance to the theory, a campaign began to convince the American public that, all during the war years, Communists and "fellow travelers" had been stealing our most precious secrets.

Implicit in this demagogic endeavor was a crowning irony. J. Edgar Hoover and the FBI had been specifically entrusted with the task of ensuring American security. Either they had performed well and efficiently, as most persons supposed—or they had not. All during the war years Hoover insisted that the counterespionage record of his Bureau was one of absolute perfection; then, suddenly, the war won, Roosevelt dead, and right-wing hysteria building, Hoover altered his tune to lend support to the thesis that, throughout the war, spies had been having a veritable field day in Washington. In this rewriting of history, no opprobrium ever attached to the FBI. It remained the infallible agency. Only the mantle of J. Edgar Hoover, a man sacrosanct, could have covered without seeming strain such opposite poles of alleged fact.

Yet it is basic that truth cannot lie simultaneously at such incompatible extremes. If Hoover's first assertion of FBI perfectability is correct, his amended picture of virtually unlimited and successful espionage becomes automatically suspect. And so does the entire substructure of the witch-hunt.

To appreciate the conflict and its importance, let's take a look at a long sequence of unvarying Hoover statements. From the earliest days of the war, Hoover repeatedly assured the American people that the FBI had everything under control. Typical was a story under his by-line—and so presumably his own free effusion, with no one prodding him—that the United Press distributed on October 17, 1940:

> The nation is safer from spies and saboteurs than ever before. . . .
> The activities of spies and saboteurs have long been scrutinized. Their names and activities have been carefully indexed and filed geographically for future reference. Added to these are *the names of leading*

agitators in the German-American Bund and Communist Party. Your
government knows their identities and activities. [Italics added.]

Throughout the war, Hoover claimed credit not just for the lightning roundup of German spies and saboteurs landed on our coasts but for *all* internal security, for the guarding of our atomic secrets, for the thorough checking-out of the loyalty of government employees. On October 9, 1943, in his annual report, Hoover presented some astronomical figures. He said his Bureau had handled 390,805 national security matters during the year, a 50 percent increase from the preceding year. "As in the past," he added, "a keynote of the FBI's work in this field was the prevention of espionage, sabotage, and *other activities inimical to the nation's security. . . .* The only test of investigative efforts in this field is the absence of sabotage and the futility of the efforts of enemy espionage agents." [Italics added.] Hoover further asserted that "the counter-espionage program of the FBI has brought activity of enemy agents within the United States under control."

Spies and saboteurs were being confounded with infallible success more than a year later. On December 30, 1944, Hoover reported, according to *The New York Times,* that there had not been one act of foreign-directed sabotage and that espionage had been kept under control. Again, on February 11, 1945, the *Times* published Hoover's report that "espionage activity has been kept under control," but that he worried because there was "no assurance that we are going to be as successful tonight or tomorrow."

On August 8, 1945—three months after the German surrender— the FBI summarized its achievements. No sabotage had occurred at any atomic plant, it said, though German spies in the United States had had orders to get information on the bomb and on uranium. A Bureau spokesman emphasized that no contacts had been made by German agents with atomic personnel.

The FBI advanced the claim that it had played a key role in the preservation of our atomic secrets. In an Associated Press dispatch this statement was made: "The FBI studied 269,303 applicants' finger cards for the 'Manhattan District Project' and found that 31,-223 persons had criminal records worth investigating by the Army, the spokesman said. In addition, *the FBI investigated every person employed by the atomic-bomb development.*" [1] [Italics added.]

During the war, of course, Russia was our ally, and it could conceivably be argued that Hoover and the FBI were not paying special attention to Russia as a menace, but anyone familiar with Hoover's Red-menace fixation, dating back to 1919 and the days of GID, might doubt this. Indeed, the records of the times make it abundantly clear that, despite wartime brotherhood, Hoover remained intensely distrustful of Communist motives.

The extent of his concern is evident in the manner in which he sought from Stephenson's Secret Intelligence Service a full report on Communist activities in Great Britain. Hyde reports that "a good deal of correspondence" took place before Hoover "was provided with the complete and exhaustive survey which he desired." This material he later used with devastating effect.

In February, 1944, Hoover learned that Donovan's OSS favored an agreement with Russia for an exchange of secret service missions. An OSS team would be sent to Moscow, and in turn a squad from the Soviet Security Service (NKVD) would be permitted to establish itself in Washington. Hoover determined to scotch the proposal, and on February 10, 1944, he sent a confidential letter to Harry Hopkins. He wrote:

> I think it a highly dangerous and most undesirable procedure to establish in the United States a unit of the Russian Secret Service which has admittedly for its purpose the penetration into the official secrets of various government agencies. The history of the NKVD in Britain showed clearly that the fundamental purpose of its operations there was to surreptitiously obtain the official secrets of the British Government.

Hoover also sent a memorandum to his superior, Attorney General Francis Biddle, advising him of his action and adding that secret agents of the NKVD had been attempting to get confidential War Department secrets.[2]

Hoover's action effectively blocked the proposed OSS–NKVD exchange of missions. Clearly, the FBI watchdog had not snoozed where the threat of Communist subversion and espionage was concerned. Therefore, Hoover's claims of perfectibility in protecting the homeland and its secrets must in all logic have applied to Communists as well as to Nazis. Indeed, from an entirely independent source came the assertion that the FBI had been the nemesis of Communist spies.

In a 1948 speech before the New Jersey Association of Police Chiefs in South Orange, New Jersey, William A. Consodine, former deputy chief of Manhattan District Intelligence—and so a man in a position to know—described the difficulties and the success we had had in keeping the A-bomb secret from the Communists.

"We had no Jap spies to deal with, no German spies either," Consodine asserted. "The Communists kept us busy. They tried to work through people in the project wherever possible. We were forewarned only by the complete reports of the people in the FBI. The FBI and other government agencies stopped Communist espionage dead in its tracks." [3]

Hoover himself, in public speeches that certainly were the expressions of his own opinions, began stressing at this time the reality of the Communist menace, even as he kept insisting on the perfect manner in which the FBI had guarded us. Two speeches made within a month of each other in 1945–46 illustrate both his fierce Red-menace style and his proud boasts of FBI achievements.

On January 8, 1946, speaking to the New York Catholic Youth Organization on the occasion of his being presented with the 1945 Club of Champions Medal by the then Cardinal-designate Francis J. Spellman, Hoover delivered a warning against "the conversion of our haven of liberty and freedom to worship as we choose to a Godless, totalitarian state."

A month earlier, on December 10, 1945, he had spoken to the International Association of Police Chiefs in Miami. He had told them, in tones reminiscent of the forecasts of 1919, that the nation's police, on top of all their other duties, would be hard pressed to stop the wave of Communism. "Panderers of diabolic distrust already are concentrating their efforts to confuse and divide by applying the Fascist smear to progressive police departments like the FBI and other American institutions to conceal their own sinister purposes," Hoover declared. Yet, at the same time, he proclaimed that the FBI during wartime had met the menace, eyeball to eyeball, and turned it back. He said:

"Early in the war skeptics proclaimed that we were open to espionage. . . . The record is exactly the contrary. We knew from the very outset of the war that espionage was under control. . . . Foreign *powers* tried to steal not only the atomic bomb, but other military secrets. . . . The counterespionage program which we developed did more than encircle spies and render them harmless. It enabled us to learn their weakness and their aims."

The timing of this speech was remarkable—because already the campaign of hysteria had begun. Six months earlier, a press dedicated to the eradication of the last vestiges of the New Deal had whooped up the first postwar spy sensation, the *Amerasia* case. And in August, 1945, Elizabeth Bentley, on whose complete reliability Hoover was later to stake his own prestige, had given the FBI an "inside" picture of wartime Communist espionage on high levels in Washington. In fact, almost a month before Hoover uttered his proud boast to the police chiefs in Miami, he had prepared a secret memorandum, based on the Bentley disclosures, that accused thirty-seven officials in government of betraying their trust by passing information to a Communist spy ring. If Hoover believed Bentley and the contents of his own memorandum, how could he be so certain that not a single spy had succeeded?

The question serves only to highlight again a thread that runs throughout the story of the FBI—the duality of Hoover's operation. Incompatible poles of fact are harmonized to look like twin kittens. The FBI's perfection when it becomes imperfection is still perfection because the imperfection wasn't the FBI's fault. There is always a scapegoat; other, less-than-perfect agencies must take the blame.

This was to be the case now. The persistent refrain of years that we had been absolutely secure because the FBI was guarding us was about to be changed to the shocking, the frightening, assertion that the Russians had stolen everything but our short pants. It is one of the most amazing paradoxes of history that the infallible policeman, who had been taking all the bows for guarding us perfectly, was to take none of the blame for guarding us imperfectly. Houdini himself never wrought greater magic.

■ 2 ■

The great about-face began on June 7, 1945. On that day, eight-column headlines in the New York press informed readers of the great *Amerasia* spy case. The Scripps-Howard press, the Hearst press, and other organs with almost rabid anti-New Deal fixations trumpeted in wild alarum, even though some of their most capable reporters, exhibiting more balance than their editors, recognized from the start that there were some glaring flaws in the great spy sensation.

Amerasia was a little-known magazine, published in New York and devoted to Asiatic affairs. It had a circulation of only about 1,700 copies, but, it was later to be charged, a disproportionate influence. Some officials in the State Department were said to follow it avidly and to consider it the bible on China and the Far East.

Behind the headlines that erupted in June, 1945, was a months-long investigation. Early in March, an official in the New York branch of Donovan's OSS happened to be reading a copy of *Amerasia*. What he saw in print almost made him fall out of his chair.

The article that had attracted his attention was one criticizing the British occupation of Thailand. In substance, it was virtually identical with a secret report the OSS had forwarded to the State Department. In fact, some of the language in the report appeared to have been lifted almost verbatim.

This discovery sent the OSS into action. Frank Bielaski, New York regional director, established a round-the-clock surveillance of *Amerasia*'s headquarters at 225 Fifth Avenue. The watch wasn't very productive, and so on the night of March 11, 1945, Bielaski led his raiders in a search of the editorial sanctum.

The OSS agents discovered six documents marked "top secret" from the Office of Naval Intelligence, the original OSS report on Thailand, five other original OSS documents, which nobody had suspected were missing, and finally a bulging suitcase crammed with scores of documents ranging in importance from "restricted" to "top secret." The documents had originated in the offices of Naval Intelligence, Military Intelligence, Censorship, the State Department, and OSS.

Bielaski, taking a few samples that he hoped wouldn't be missed by *Amerasia,* left everything else just as he had found it and hopped a plane for Washington. Donovan at once notified top Navy and State Department officials. A conference was called and a decision made to call in the FBI for a thorough secret investigation. Three months of intensive surveillance followed.

The principal figure in *Amerasia* was Philip J. Jaffe, its editor, a greeting-card manufacturer. On several occasions, FBI reports later revealed, agents tailed Jaffe on visits to the Soviet Consulate in New York. Three times they followed him on trips to the home of Communist boss Earl Browder in Yonkers, New York. And on April 22, 1945, they watched while Browder brought a prominent Chinese Communist to Jaffe's Greenwich Village apartment, where the three conferred for five hours. The FBI attached significance to this long meeting of minds because one of the documents Bielaski had spotted in Jaffe's stuffed suitcase was a complete report on the size and disposition of Chiang Kai-shek's Nationalist armies, then battling the Communists.

Probing into the history of Jaffe (a determined Marxist theoretician), the FBI identified him as a long-time supporter of Communist fronts, especially those devoted to promoting the Soviet foreign policy in China and Asia. On March 21, 1945, the FBI obtained what was later described as its first big break in the case. On that day Jaffe left New York for Washington, where he registered in the Hotel Statler. Though he evidently had no suspicion of the fact, FBI agents were swarming all around him.

They were watching when Emmanuel Sigurd Larsen, a specialist in the China Division of the State Department's Office of Far Eastern Affairs, strolled into the lobby of the hotel with his wife and met Jaffe. They were watching when another couple, Lieutenant (USNR) and Mrs. Andrew Roth joined Jaffe and the Larsens. They were watching when the five had luncheon in the Colony Room. They were still watching when, the luncheon over, Roth drove Jaffe and Larsen to the latter's State Department Office. In the parking area, they saw Roth and Jaffe examining some papers spread out over the steering wheel. The day-by-day chronology of FBI shadowing is replete with details like this. Larsen, Roth, and Jaffe were seen in constant association, with much exchanging of papers and manila envelopes. When Jaffe headed back to New York, he carried bulging luggage.[4]

In late May, having developed this detailed information by its constant surveillance of Jaffe, the FBI laid its cards on the table in a discussion with Justice Department officials. It recommended immediate action. The decision initially was in its favor, to go ahead and make the arrests. But before this decision could be implemented, it was countermanded. Qualms developed because the San Francisco conference for the establishment of the United Nations was in progress, and it was felt this would be an undiplomatic time to accuse the Russians of widespread espionage.

Julius C. Holmes, Assistant Secretary of State, balked at this decision. He discussed the *Amerasia* affair with Acting Secretary of State Joseph C. Grew, who asked to be reassured on just two points: Was the FBI convinced the evidence was airtight? Did the FBI believe a prosecution would be successful? The answer was an emphatic "yes" on both counts, and so Holmes, with Grew's blessing, carried his protest directly to President Truman. Though the Truman Administration was soon to be maligned as "soft on Communism," Truman promptly and personally intervened. He ordered the FBI to go ahead with the case, and he gave Hoover a wide-open invitation to go over everybody's head and appeal to him personally if he encountered any further obstructions. In that event, Truman made clear, he wanted to know who issued the obstructing orders and just what those orders were. With this full backing by the White House, Hoover acted swiftly.

On the night of June 6, Jaffe and five others were arrested. FBI agents, in serving the warrant on Jaffe, found four filing cases crammed with documents ranging from "confidential" to "secret" and "top secret." The total count numbered some 1,700 documents—the vast bulk inconsequential, but a significant number—some seventy in all —dealing with such vital subjects as the disposition of American submarines, the schedule and target for bombing Japan, the disposition of the Japanese fleet after the Battle of Leyte, and plans for bombing barge traffic on the Danube.

The initial charge against the *Amerasia* defendants was conspiracy to violate the federal espionage statutes through the theft of highly secret documents. This sounded highly portentous. Yet, despite the FBI assurance to Holmes and Grew of the solidity of its case, even a cursory examination of the facts disclosed one obvious and serious flaw. It would seem that about the stupidest method the human brain could invent of committing espionage would be to write articles in a magazine based on documents the spy has stolen. This public flaunting of the existence and success of espionage, one of the most secretive of all human pursuits, defies rationalization. In addition to this implausibility, the *Amerasia* case had a gaping hole in the chain of evidence. The FBI had absolutely no proof—and later sadly acknowledged it—that information had actually been passed to the Russians. The case lacked, in other words, the essential ingredient of a bona fide spy case: a courier conveying the secret information.

The result was that the great *Amerasia* spy case ran into trouble when it was presented to federal grand juries. One jury heard most of the evidence, then went out of session without acting and without asking for an extension of time so that it could act. A second jury refused to indict three of the defendants, but did indict Jaffe and two others on a greatly reduced charge of conspiracy to embezzle and steal government documents. Even this was not the end of the watering-down process.

Of the three indictments, the one against Roth was later dismissed for lack of evidence. This left Jaffe and Larsen as the sole defendants in what had started out as a six-person espionage ring. Even against them, the government did not have clear sailing. The original OSS snooping in the *Amerasia* office without benefit of warrant had been conducted in clear violation of the Constitution. Furthermore, there was some indication, though the FBI vigorously denied it, that Larsen's apartment had been invaded illegally by FBI agents before a warrant was obtained. These illegal searches, according to the later official alibi, jeopardized the entire proceedings. And so, in an unusual Saturday court session on September 29, 1945, with hardly anybody present, Jaffe pleaded guilty to conspiracy and was fined $2,500. Subsequently, Larsen entered a *nolo contendere* plea (meaning merely that he did not choose to contest the charges), and he was fined $500. Both the fine and his $2,500 in legal expenses, he said later, were paid for him by Jaffe.

This disposed of the *Amerasia* case from the legal but not from the propaganda standpoint. Republicans and powerful Republican-oriented elements of the press, eager to get the Democrats out of the White House at whatever cost, were already toying with the treason label, and the *Amerasia* case was filled with potential explosives. The battle cry became the charge that the *Amerasia* defendants had escaped only because the Administration had put in the fix. One of the first indications of this tactic came from an amazing source—Larsen, the State Department Far Eastern specialist. In September, 1946, less than a year after his case had been settled, with a crucial Congressional election coming up, Larsen charged into print with the thundering accusation that the *Amerasia* case had been characterized by "a mysterious whitewash of the chief actors."

Larsen's opus appeared in the first issue of a new magazine called *Plain Talk,* edited by Isaac Don Levine, who, as the confidant of Whittaker Chambers, was to become a shadowy figure in the wings of the Alger Hiss case. Larsen's article, entitled "The State Department Espionage Case," charged that the State Department was infiltrated with Communists, that only part of the evidence in the *Amerasia* case had even been presented to the grand jury, that the case had been killed because "further probing . . . might assume proportions even more far-reaching than those of the Pearl Harbor investigation."

It was an astounding broadside coming from a man who had himself been one of the only two defendants remaining in the case. How could Larsen, in these circumstances, charge a "whitewash"? He, of course, had been entirely innocent. His association with Jaffe, he insisted, was an innocent social one; they both liked to talk about China and the people they knew there. Jaffe, Larsen admitted, had bailed him out by paying $3,000 for his fine and legal expenses; but then, biting this hand of generosity, he accused Jaffe of having had dealings with Earl Browder and of having dined on more than one occasion in the Soviet Consulate in New York. "For some unaccountable reason," Larsen wrote, "the government attorneys presented to the grand jury only part of the evidence in their [the FBI's] possession." He was highly critical of the fact that when the case of Jaffe, his benefactor, came up in court, the government prosecutor said he could summarize it "in less than five minutes."

Such was the man, such were the sweeping assertions made in a new magazine no one had ever heard of. Yet these charges were picked up by the New York press as if they had gilt-edged authenticity and were made the basis of lengthy stories hinting at a smelly Administration cover-up.[5]

In retrospect, few of the sensational *Amerasia* charges appear to have been valid. This was simply not a genuine spy case. The writers and editors who got the secret information from government files wrote, edited, and published the details, certainly not characteristic activity for spies. The case stands, like the spurious Christian Front subversion case, as a glaring example of a pernicious FBI habit of overestimating and overdramatizing the importance of its investigations in this field.

On the other hand, the *Amerasia* case did demonstrate the incredibly loose practices that prevailed at the time concerning the handling of government documents. The 1,700 official papers that had found their way so easily into *Amerasia*'s files were proof that security arrangements in government departments were not what they should have been. It was, indeed, a fact, as almost any Washington newsman worth his salt could testify, that it was no great feat to come into possession of secret documents. This availability of supposedly restricted materials, something never truly appreciated by the public, is perhaps significant in view of the Alger Hiss case that was soon to erupt.

One other major point of the *Amerasia* spy sensation seems to have been established beyond cavil: it was not whitewashed. Probably no man in America was ever less sympathetic to Communism than Harry Truman, and the action that he so promptly took in the *Amerasia* case was a characteristically decisive Truman action. Truman's open-door invitation to Hoover to appeal to him at the first sign of a roadblock discredits the subsequent loud shouts of whitewash. And it must be borne in mind that the final court action, the acceptance of pleas to drastically reduced charges, was taken only, according to the local prosecutor, after consultation with Attorney General Tom C. Clark (now as a Supreme Court Justice quite the darling of the FBI).

The sequence makes it devastatingly clear that the *Amerasia* case was an exaggerated menace, and the eagerness of some of the great media that form public opinion to tar the Truman Administration seems little less than despicable. They exhibited a Barkus-is-willing attitude to make the Democrats the scapegoats for each and every real and fancied failure of security. They capitalized on this attitude when the second major development of 1945, long kept secret, burst on the public consciousness. This was the spy saga told by Elizabeth Bentley, who asserted that, as a courier for a Communist spy ring, she had had access to a freight car full of secrets.

■ 3 ■

Miss Bentley was to become the queen bee of the informer sect, but when she first brought her information to the attention of the FBI, events moved in an almost incredibly dilatory fashion. The sequence, as established in later court actions, went this way:

About August 21 or 22, 1945, Miss Bentley walked into the New Haven, Connecticut, office of the FBI with the sole purpose, according to her, of telling agents about her role in filching America's secrets. Documents later introduced in court show that she was also inquiring about an American captain whom she had dated and who had told her he was a secret agent. In any event, whether the mysterious captain or the mysterious spying was the major topic of conversation, the FBI's initial reaction to Elizabeth Bentley was not a startled and excited one. The agent to whom she talked, she says, simply took her name and address, told her to go home and wait. The Bureau would get in touch with her later.

Weeks passed, and it was not until October 8, 1945, that the FBI office in New York wrote Miss Bentley to come in for an interview about the captain. The letter was sent to a temporary address, had to be forwarded, and it was two or three weeks before it caught up with Miss Bentley. Even then, when she went to the New York FBI office, she was told by an agent to whom she talked that the Bureau's "expert" on Communism wasn't available. Would she please come back later when he was in the office?

It was November 7, 1945—nearly twelve weeks after she first

approached the FBI in New Haven—before Miss Bentley got her story across. The date is fixed by testimony Hoover gave before the Senate Internal Security Committee on November 17, 1953. He said:

"On November 7, 1945, Miss Elizabeth Bentley advised special agents of the FBI in considerable detail of her own career as an espionage agent. In November 8, 1945, a letter bearing that date was delivered to Brigadier General Harry H. Vaughn."

Hoover described this letter as "a preliminary flash," a warning of possibly impending danger. The letter stated that "information has recently been received from a highly confidential source indicating that a number of persons employed by the Government of the United States have been furnishing data and information to persons outside the Federal Government, who are in turn transmitting this information to espionage agents of the Soviet Government." Hoover added in the letter that the investigation was being pressed vigorously, "but I thought the President and you would be interested in having the foregoing preliminary data immediately."

In his 1953 appearance before the Senate committee—eight full years after his first flash on the Bentley disclosures—Hoover placed his entire personal prestige and the prestige of the FBI on the line in one of the most complete endorsements ever given by a top police executive to a prize informer. He testified:

> From the outset, we established that she [Miss Bentley] had been in a position to report the facts relative to Soviet espionage which she has done. All information furnished by Miss Bentley, which has been susceptible to check, has proved correct. She has been subjected to the most searching cross-examination; her testimony has been evaluated by juries and reviewed by the courts, and has been found to be accurate.

In the light of this blanket endorsement, it seems essential to understand just who Elizabeth Bentley was and just what her story was. A graduate of Vassar, she had studied abroad; she had been revolted by the Fascism she encountered in Italy; she had returned home and had joined movements opposing Fascism's brutality; and so in time she had drifted into the Communist Party. In 1938, through Communist headquarters in New York, she met a man known to her at first only as "Timmy," with whom she was to develop a common-law husband-and-wife relationship. "Timmy," Miss Bentley learned in the fall of 1939, was actually none other than Jacob N. Golos—in her words "a famous person." A Russian who had left a wife and child behind him in the Soviet Union, Golos had been extremely active in the Communist Party in America; he had been one of the editors of a Communist newspaper in New York; and since the early 1930's he had owned and headed World Tourists, a travel agency set up by the American Communist Party to promote travel in, and closer ties with, Russia.

At the time of Golos' romance with Miss Bentley in 1939, the travel agency was to figure in one of the strangest aspects of the entire affair. On October 20, 1939, representatives of the United States Attorney General's Office, the State Department, and the United States Marshal's office served a subpoena on Golos requesting that he produce all of World Tourists' records and books before a federal grand jury. Papers and documents in the office were examined by detectives, impressions were taken of the keys of all the office typewriters, and guards were stationed at the door to prevent the removal or destruction of records.

In subsequent months, Golos made some twenty appearances before federal grand juries. He handed over nearly two truckloads of records. He was compelled to supply all the telephone-number indexes in his office. The exact nature of all this evidence remains an FBI secret, but Miss Bentley acknowledged at a subsequent trial that, as the result of the investigation, "there were found a lot of things on the premises which gave away a great deal about the underground organization."

It will be recalled that, in the Detroit Loyalist raids that broke at this same time, the FBI disclosed it had established that Golos and World Tourists had handled the arrangements to send recruits to the army in Spain. Clearly, Golos was a key operative in the communistic apparatus in America. This point was further emphasized on January 3, 1940, when *The New York Times* reported from Washington that Attorney General Murphy had accused "eight persons and three business houses, all alleged to have Communist Party connections, of military espionage." Among those named were Jacob N. Golos and World Tourists. On March 14, 1940, Golos was indicted for failing to register as a foreign agent, and the following day he pleaded guilty. He was given a suspended sentence of four months to one year in prison and fined $500. World Tourists was fined $500. Golos and World Tourists were the only ones on the list originally accused by Murphy to be indicted and convicted.

This encounter with the law would seem to establish conclusively that Jacob N. Golos and World Tourists were well known to American authorities. Their names—and the names of innumerable contacts who appeared on their records—must inevitably have gone into that card-index file in which, as Hoover repeatedly told the country, all espionage records, all persons of suspicious or dangerous tendencies, were registered. Certainly, the one man and the one agency that had been convicted in a Soviet espionage case would seem to have been marked for continued FBI surveillance; their usefulness as an espionage conduit would seem to have been terminated. Yet, according to Miss Bentley, Golos went right back to his old role of master spy, filching government secrets, operating with perfect impunity, attracting not the slightest suspicion.

Miss Bentley insisted that she had played a key role in all this. She became a courier for Golos, traveling to Washington to meet Communist contacts there, lugging back information. Yet one would think that Miss Bentley herself would have been a marked woman, even as Golos was a marked man. She had been Golos' girl friend at the time of his arrest. Even more obviously, she worked for a subsidiary of his World Tourists, the U.S. Service and Shipping Corporation. She spent, as she later wrote, "at least half" her working time in the office of World Tourists, and for one period of a year and a half she actually ran the parent concern.

These were nakedly visible ties, but amazingly the catalogue of obviousness does not end here. Miss Bentley wrote that she made personal trips to consult with Earl Browder, and that she used World Tourists' telephone, a dandy instrument, to call the office of the *Daily Worker* and set up personal meetings with the *Worker*'s editor of the moment, Louis Budenz. The lack of secrecy, the lack of "cover" in all this activity, poses the horns of a most uncomfortable, but inevitable dilemma: either Miss Bentley's subsequent sensational spy-ring disclosures were exaggerated and concocted in large measure of fantasy, or they were completely valid—in which case, with all the wide-open opportunities for discovery, with the FBI's unremitting zeal in tracking down Communist ties and contacts, the Bureau would seem to have been exposed as a most incompetent watchdog. Either alternative might be correct; both cannot be.

The Truman Administration, which was developing a hard anti-Communist line in foreign affairs, had had knowledge of the Bentley disclosures—and opportunity to investigate them—for more than two years before the case erupted into the blaze of page-one publicity that was to convince many Americans a Communist lurked under almost every bed. Yet the Justice Department had taken no action. This lack of action was now to be branded a coverup in blithe disregard of the other obvious possibility—that the charges may have lacked sufficient substance. The time was not a time for reason. It was the year 1948, and the Presidential campaign pitted Dewey, with all the advantages in his corner, against an embattled Truman, the definite underdog. Republicans, banished for fifteen years from the White House dining board, were slavering to get back. The 1946 Congressional elections had sent to Washington a hard core of ultrarightist congressmen, and these hard-right Republicans and the equally conservative Southern Democrats were in complete control of the committee machinery. Truman, as perceptive Washington newsmen commented at the time, did not have a single friend at court when the House Un-American Activities Committee and its senatorial counterpart began to dissect his administration.

The prejudice and partisan purpose were obvious in the House committee before which Elizabeth Bentley and Whittaker Chambers testified. Its chairman was J. Parnell Thomas, an archconservative New Jersey Republican who was ultimately to go to federal prison, convicted of operating a kick-back racket with his office payroll. Thomas never made any secret about the overriding partisan purposes that impelled his official inquiry. Long afterward he wrote that the Republican National Committee chairman "was urging me in the Dewey campaign to set up the spy hearings. At the time he was urging me to stay in Washington to keep the heat on Harry Truman." [6] Even during the hearings, Thomas made little pretense of being an impartial chairman. For him, New Dealers and Communists were cut from the same bolt of cloth. At one point during Elizabeth Bentley's testimony he almost audibly licked his chops as he commented: "We have been unearthing your New Dealers for two years, and for eight years before that." [7]

The bias of Southern Democrats on the committee was equally pronounced. A shining example was Representative John E. Rankin, of Mississippi, who equated the civil rights movement in the South with Communism. He kept interjecting into the Bentley testimony the comment that the departed Mississippi political boss, Senator Bilbo, "dying of cancer," had been compelled to stand on his feet, "wearing his life away fighting this so-called 'civil rights,' this Communist program." It was enough for Rankin that some of the men named by Miss Bentley had supported civil rights and were among those who had "trumpeted up a persecution" of Bilbo "because of his fight against this communistic movement." [8]

Among other members of the committee, two of the most active were Representative Karl Mundt (Republican of South Dakota) and Representative Richard M. Nixon (Republican of California), a product of the class of 1946, in Congress by virtue of his first "pink sheet" smear campaign against the veteran Democrat Jerry Voorhis. And in the background, half-concealed in the shadows but more important than any of the front-line hatchet men, bulked the massive and powerful figure of the one man who really mattered, J. Edgar Hoover.

There can be little question that Hoover at this period, though he held his post at the pleasure of the Democratic Truman Administration, though he sedulously guarded his nonpolitical image, actually was playing a covert game of footsie with Truman's fanatical Republican opposition. The material that fueled the Republican-dominated investigating committees clearly was funneled to them straight from FBI files, and anyone familiar with the kind of storms Hoover can kick up about the sanctity of these files knows full well that such leaks would not have been possible without his collaboration. Even so, the case does not rest alone on such hard-reasoned speculation. At one point during the Hiss affair, the hearing record shows, Mundt chuckled over some private morsel of knowledge and revealed that he had been the beneficiary of some private advices from the FBI.

At another point, when Nixon proposed that the committee ask Hoover to give "any corroborative evidence" he might have, Thomas forestalled the move and, in doing so, made a frank statement regarding the love affair between his committee and the powerful Director of the FBI.

"The closest relationship exists between this committee and the FBI," Thomas declared. "I cannot say as much as between this committee and the Attorney General's office, but the closest relationship exists between this committee and the FBI. I think there is a very good understanding between us. It is something, however, that we cannot talk too much about." [9]

Years later, Jack Levine would be told that the FBI acted as a law unto itself, independent of the Justice Department of which technically it was a part. Here was the prize historical example. It is clear from Thomas' statement that the Attorney General, Hoover's titular boss, was taking one position. Hoover, undercutting both his immediate boss and the Administration of which supposedly he was a part, was taking another. The Sixtieth Congress had worried lest the Bureau became so powerful that it might turn on Congress itself. Now, in collaboration with a witch-hunting committee of Congress, it had turned on the President.

Its action conceivably might have been justified if there had been any great overriding moral or patriotic principle involved—if the Truman Administration had been truly a treasonous administration, betraying American interests. Only the most extreme fanatic would be prepared to argue for that proposition in the calmer perspective that the passage of time has brought to the issue. Yet the scare that the scare headlines of 1948 created was to have a deep and lasting effect on the psyche of the nation. It was to lay the groundwork for McCarthy. It was to leave a residue of deep suspicion and uncertainty and to help impose on a nation of individualists a distrust of dissent and a passion for conformity. How valid was the frenzy?

Elizabeth Terril Bentley was called to the stand before Thomas' House Un-American Activities Committee on July 31, 1948. After describing her early life, her commitment to Communism, her association with Golos, she came to the heart of her story: her activities as a spy courier, a contact agent for Golos in meeting government employees and officials in Washington. Anyone reading the transcript in the sober afterlight can hardly fail to be struck by one vivid impression: This was a most queasy and uncertain witness, one who characteristically shunned the flat statement in preference for implication, one who exhibited a positive eagerness to agree with her august inquisitors.

Asked if mail had come for Golos from one Fred Rose, Miss Bentley disclaimed all knowledge, then obliged the committee in this two-sided statement: "I can't state of my own knowledge, Mr. [Robert E.] Stripling [chief investigator], because I didn't look inside the envelopes, but I suspect it may have been." Asked whether Golos had set up an espionage apparatus to obtain information from government employees and officials just prior to her first being sent to Washington, her answer was: "I think that he set it up. I rather doubt that he had operated it before that. Of course, I can't state definitely." More positive knowledge might have been expected from the woman who had lived with Golos in a common-law relationship; but, with a witness so eager to oblige, much could be forgiven. Miss Bentley's one original contact in Washington had been with a man named Nathan Gregory Silvermaster, an employee of the Farm Security Administration and later, briefly, of the Bureau of Economic Warfare. Silvermaster, Miss Bentley testified, was a Communist. This wasn't enough for Rankin, who wanted to know if he wasn't also "an agent of the Communist International." Miss Bentley, so cued, promptly gave the Congressman the horror picture he so obviously wanted. "Probably an agent of the NKVD would be more correct," she said.[10]

Her testimony was patently woven of large strands of hearsay. Her direct contact, she said, was with Silvermaster; he collected information and acted as the agent of his "group." As for other members of the group, she knew only what she had been told by Silvermaster and others whom she met. She had "heard" that this man or that man was a member of the Silvermaster "group" and was contributing information to it. She collected Communist Party dues from Silvermaster for the "group." But the committee's repeated efforts to find out just how these dues were determined, just how much was paid, met with the reply that she never knew. They were just in an envelope, she just took the envelope to Golos, Golos just turned it over to the Com-

munist Party, and no one, so far as she knew, ever checked on the
amount to see if the right sum of money had been paid for the right
number of people. Yet by such indirect testimony a lot of men were
to be named, a lot of reputations and lives ruined. Typical testimony:

Q. (by Stripling) May I ask you, Miss Bentley, was one Solomon
Adler a member of this group?

A. Yes, he was.

Q. Was he a rather active participant?

A. Rather remotely, Mr. Stripling, because at the time I had charge
of the group he was in China. . . .

Q. Miss Bentley, did you collect the Communist Party dues from
Mr. Adler and turn them over to Mr. Silvermaster? Do you recall
doing that?

A. Mr. Silvermaster gave me the dues for his complete group and
I take it for granted those included Mr. Adler. Since he was in China,
I am not too sure about it. [Italics added.]

Q. Did you ever meet Mr. Adler yourself?

A. No, I never did.

In similarly inconclusive fashion, this spy queen injected into the
proceedings a name that was to precipitate a political storm a few
years later—that of Harry Dexter White, Assistant Secretary of the
Treasury.

Q. (by Rankin) Is he a Communist?

A. I don't know whether Mr. White was a card-carrying Communist or not.

Q. (by Stripling) What was the extent of his cooperation with your
group?

A. He gave information to Mr. Silvermaster which was relayed on
to me.[11]

Such testimony makes clear why, after more than two years, the
Truman Administration had not initiated criminal actions against
any of these named in the Bentley tales of espionage. This stuff simply was not evidence. It was a concoction composed of what a woman
who claimed she had been a spy-ring courier said she had been told.
It was a quicksand of innuendo, lacking in solid specifics and, even
when specifics were offered, barren of any possibility of proof.

For her lack of detailed knowledge, Miss Bentley had a ready explanation. The material she had collected from Silvermaster had been on microfilm; she had carted the film home to Golos; and, just as in the case of the dues payments, she couldn't be too certain what she had carted. Occasionally, it is true, she had picked up a few details. One item that seemed to stick prominently in her mind (she mentioned it in her testimony several times) dealt with the timing of the D-day invasion of Normandy. Her spies in government knew well in advance of the event the exact date of the D-day landings, Miss Bentley asserted. She made a reference to this first on page 522 of the House hearings; she referred to the remarkable feat again on page 525; and she spelled it out in more explicit detail on page 560. The information about D-day had been squirreled out by William Ludwig Ullman and passed along to Silvermaster, she testified. Chairman Thomas asked why she made a special point of mentioning this incident, and there followed this colloquy:

Miss Bentley: I suppose because it stuck in my mind out of all the other things.

The Chairman: Well, did he know about D-day many days before or . . .

Miss Bentley: Yes; it came actually from Mr. Ullman, not from Mr. Silvermaster.

The Chairman. And Mr. Ullman said that Silvermaster knew all about D-day before?

Miss Bentley: No; Mr. Ullman was in the Pentagon with the Air Corps, and through his connections with General Hildring's office he had learned the date, and I remember it distinctly because with that knowledge he was betting with a friend of his when D-day would be and, of course, he won the bet, since he knew it ahead of time.

Since the infallible policeman himself subsequently was to stake his prestige on the statement that "all information furnished by Miss Bentley, which has been susceptible to check, has proved correct," it is interesting to see what happens to this D-day item when one takes the trouble to check it. It was as full of flaws as a mouse-eaten bit of cheese is of holes.

Some of these flaws were pointed out in 1955 in a brief filed with the Civil Service Commission's Loyalty Board by William Henry Taylor, one of the federal officials accused by Miss Bentley. He strenuously denied her charges. According to the brief, one of the lesser errors in Miss Bentley's D-day intelligence report was that General Hildring, the supposed source of the marvelous information, was never in the Air Force. In 1944 he was attached to the Civil Affairs Division of the War Department. An even more serious flaw from the standpoint of credibility: We were at the time of the D-day landing in Normandy an ally of Russia. For allies, it was important that attacks on Germany from the East and West should be coordinated. It therefore served our patriotic purpose to inform Russia in advance just when the invasion would begin. And this is what we did.

Winston Churchill has described in his history of the Second World War how he made a special trip to Moscow for the explicit purpose of briefing Stalin as fully as possible on Allied plans for the opening of a second front. Churchill wanted to make certain that Stalin and the Russians would mount a tremendous offensive in the East to prevent the Germans from reinforcing their armies in the West. But so uncertain were Allied logistics and the weather, that even he could give Stalin only an approximate invasion date.

Subsequently Major General John R. Deane, head of the United States military mission in Moscow, related (in *The Strange Alliance*) that he received instructions on April 7, 1944, to notify the Russians that the invasion had been set for May 31, with a two- or three-day margin on either side, depending on tides and the weather. Even this official information wasn't specific. It didn't pinpoint the exact day— and for one very good reason. It couldn't.

As anyone who has read Dwight D. Eisenhower's *Crusade in Europe* and other official books on the subject must realize, D-day was a variable date, and even Eisenhower himself couldn't have given Miss Bentley's spy ring the information in advance. In fact, the invasion was originally scheduled for June 5 but was postponed at a staff conference at 4 A.M. on June 4 because meteorological reports were "discouraging." The actual decision to invade on June 6 was not made until the last possible minute, at another staff conference at 4:15 on the morning of June 5—a sequence that ridicules Miss Bentley's claim to specific prior knowledge.

The historical record thus dynamites Miss Bentley's testimony on this one hard nugget of espionage achievement that had stuck in her mind above all others. The point has a double significance. The significance lies not in just the doubt it casts on the Bentley testimony but also in the reflection it casts on the type of mind that is prepared, in the face of such evidence, to give full credence to the tale of the informer. Though the true details of the manner in which D-day had been determined had been revealed by Eisenhower and others long before Hoover took the witness stand in 1953 on Miss Bentley's behalf, they did nothing to shake his faith or the faith of others predisposed to believe. Rebecca West, the well-known British author, wrote a lengthy defense of Congressional committee inquisitions in which she accepted at face value the Bentley disclosures. The espionage ring, she wrote, "had done serious business" and had discovered and transmitted "such genuine secrets as the date of D-day." [12] Closed minds persisted in ignoring the fact that the secret had been too genuine for discovery and transmittal.

One striking feature of the Bentley testimony generally overlooked was the manner in which it buried a sharp harpoon in the hides of Hoover's arch rival, General Donovan, and Donovan's organization, the OSS. This aspect of the testimony developed the instant Karl Mundt asked a leading question. Mundt wanted to know if Miss Bentley, in her tours of Washington, had become acquainted with other collaborating Communists outside the Silvermaster ring, and if she had, had she included their names in the list to which she had already testified?

"No," Miss Bentley replied; "Mr. Stripling has not asked me for them yet. *I was waiting for him to ask.*" [13] [Italics added.]

Then, in the space of two pages of testimony, she named five OSS employees who, she said, had collaborated with the spy ring.

The principal name that she dropped was that of Duncan Chaplin Lee. Lee had been an attorney in Donovan's New York office, had followed his chief to Washington, had become a legal adviser in OSS, had served throughout the war, had risen to the rank of lieutenant colonel. If Lee had truly been a collaborator, this was striking close to Donovan.

According to Miss Bentley, the Communist Party's original contact with Duncan Lee had been made through Mary Price, for a time secretary to the columnist Walter Lippmann. After Lee moved to

Washington with OSS, "Mary took care of him for awhile, and then Mary left Washington, and I took him over at that point." She testified that Mary Price, before leaving Washington, told Lee about Miss Bentley, who was to be known to him only as "Helen," and "I just walked into his apartment and said, 'I am Helen,' and spoke about things only the two of us would know, and that is how we made our contact." [14] She testified about subsequent meetings with Lee and his wife in their apartment, about cokes in drug stores, dinners in restaurants, numerous meetings, at all of which, according to her, information was passed.

Duncan Lee took the stand and denied her story. It was true, he said, that he and his wife had known Miss Bentley. They had known her as Helen Grant, and they had met her in October, 1943, at the apartment of Mary Price. Lee denied that he had ever been a Communist, a member of the Young Communist League, or any other Communist group. He denied that he had ever paid "Helen Grant" Communist Party dues, that he had ever passed her information. As he told it, the contact he and his wife had had with "Helen Grant" had been purely social. They had seen each other for perhaps fifteen times over a period of a year and a quarter. The relationship developed, Lee said, because Miss Bentley attached herself to them like a leech, professing that she thought they were the most marvelous people. Since people so flattered find it hard to reject the flattery and since Miss Bentley seemed to be an intelligent woman, they maintained for a time a fairly close acquaintanceship. But then, he testified, doubts began to set in.

"We came to the conclusion," he told the House committee, "that she was a very lonely and neurotic woman, that she was a frustrated woman, that her liking and apparent liking for us was unnaturally intense. We began to feel she was an emotional weight around our necks and that really there was nothing in the acquaintance that justified the intense way she did follow us up."

Lee added that Miss Bentley had posed at first as a mild liberal, but that on further acquaintance he became disturbed because her views seemed to be much farther to the left than he had thought. This, he said, was a secondary reason that reinforced the decision he and his wife had made to break off the relationship, which, he said, they did as considerately as possible. What explanation could he give for Miss Bentley's charges? This:

> It is hard for me to believe that Miss Bentley's statements are those of a rational person. In trying to recall my acquaintance with Miss Bentley I have been puzzled that I do not remember that she ever tried to get any information out of me. In view of that fact I am tempted to believe that Miss Bentley used her social relationship with me merely to help her misrepresent to her employers for her own personal build-up that she had access through me to someone of the importance of General Donovan.[15]

Faced with this conflict of testimony, the House committee brought Miss Bentley back to the stand, and she now embroidered her original account with some specifics. Her major specific dealt with an undisputed fact—the Donovan proposal for an exchange of OSS and NKVD missions in Washington and Moscow. But note how she told the tale. This is her testimony:

> I believe it was in the spring of 1944 that I met him [Duncan Lee] one evening outside his house, I believe, in one of the drug stores. He was very much upset because he had found out that General Donovan was interested in making an exchange of NKVD agents with OSS men. He said this had been brought up in a meeting of, I should say, the top command of the country—the top man from the Navy—Admiral Leahy was there, J. Edgar Hoover, of the Federal Bureau, was there, I think a representative of Roosevelt, and all the top people. He described that meeting in detail to me. He even went into such details as the fact that Admiral Leahy was definitely against such an exchange.[16]

We now know, thanks to Hoover's own correspondence, that it did not happen that way at all. Instead of a roundtable of "the top command of the country" meeting to discuss and approve or disapprove of such an arrangement, the negotiations had been quietly conducted between OSS and NKVD on an agency-to-agency level; that Hoover, far from being personally present at a major conference on the proposal, learned of it from confidential sources; and that, instead of the general high-level debate Miss Bentley pictured, Hoover personally scotched the plan by dispatching a confidential letter to Harry L. Hopkins.[17]

The implausibility of the Bentley account, in the light of Hoover's own letter, is heightened when one considers an additional bit of Bentley embellishment. The House committee, pounding hard on the trail of Duncan Lee, asked whether Lee had known that she was a Communist espionage agent. To this question she replied:

"I imagine so, because that was apropos of that proposed transfer between NKVD and the OSS, and I remember he was quite frightened because he said, 'If they come over here, they will come up to my house, knock on the door, shake my hand, and say, 'Comrade, well done.'

"I remember that distinctly." [18]

Duncan Lee, throughout a difficult time on the witness stand, with the partisan House committee hounding him, was unwavering in his testimony. He gave the impression of a highly intelligent, self-possessed man, one not given to such outbursts of emotional frenzy. Furthermore, can anyone imagine a secret service as skilled as NKVD (whose superhuman wiliness gave our right-wing extremists the jitters) committing the folly of making an open display of its affection for a trusted agent, one whom it would presumably still intend to use?

There were other grave flaws in Miss Bentley's testimony. The 107-page William Henry Taylor brief filed in 1955 enumerated a total of thirty-seven discrepancies, some minor but several, like the story of D-day, of striking significance. Undeniably, Miss Bentley had some facts. A few of the persons whom she accused admitted past Communist affiliations; others, called before Congressional committees, claimed the privilege of the Fifth Amendment. Some of these were undoubtedly Communists, but others may not have been. Victor Perlo, for example, began with an emphatic denial of all Miss Bentley's charges. Then, under relentless committee pressure, he conferred with his lawyer and claimed the privilege of the Fifth Amendment. Karl Mundt commented that such a man must be "guilty as sin" or "an unmitigated ass"; but this was not necessarily so. Informers testifying before this committee were asked no critical questions. Instead, the committee reserved all its skepticism for the grilling of the accused. Under such circumstances, a man who risked denial stared perjury charges straight in the face. It was potentially the easiest legal frameup in the world. All that was needed was the accusation of the informer, the denial of the accused under oath, and some flimsy corroboration of the informer's tale, either through the testimony of another informer or the establishment of a chain of circumstantial evidence. With scales so weighted, the significant fact is not that so many claimed the Fifth but that so many risked denial —Lee, Taylor, Harry Dexter White, and William Remington among them.

Only one conclusion seems possible: no definitive verdict can ever be given on the overall validity of the Bentley testimony, but it is infinitely suspect, especially if it is assessed against the basic implausibility of an efficient FBI permitting a marked Golos and his mistress to run at large in the Washington playpen. The testimony was a melange of some fact and much rumor, the whole clouded by partisan purposes. And in the end, by drawing from Hoover the unequivocal endorsement of Miss Bentley, it served to expose the infallible policeman and his tendency to accept uncritically the tales of informers.

■ 4 ■

The partisan House committee had a second bow in its arsenal: a second informer who could spin a harrowing tale of subversion. He was a portly, moon-faced, perpetually rumpled and disheveled man, brilliant, erratic, and unstable—Whittaker Chambers, a senior editor of *Time* Magazine. Chambers had been a Communist and, by his own account, a member of a Communist cell in Washington. Later he had broken with Communism and had adopted the thesis dear to the hearts of the House committee that there was precious little difference between Roosevelt's New Deal and Communism.

On August 3, 1948, Chambers took the witness stand before the House committee. On this day of days, Mundt was presiding. Chambers testified that he had joined the Communist Party in 1924, that he had stayed in it "until 1937," and that he had served "for a number of years . . . in the underground, chiefly in Washington, D.C." This underground, according to Chambers, had been developed by

Harold Ware, son of a Communist leader known as "Mother Bloor." Chambers testified:

> I knew it at its top level, a group of seven or so men, from among whom in later years certain members of Miss Bentley's organization were apparently recruited. The head of the underground group at the time I knew it was Nathan Witt, an attorney for the National Labor Relations Board. Later, John Abt became the leader. Lee Pressman was also a member of this group, as was Alger Hiss, who, as a member of the State Department, later organized the conferences at Dumbarton Oaks, San Francisco, and the United States side of the Yalta Conference.
>
> The purpose of this group at the time was not primarily espionage. Its original purpose was the Communist infiltration of the American Government. But espionage was certainly one of its eventual objectives.

This ambivalent testimony both denied and held out the prospect of more tales of espionage. The purpose of the group was not "primarily espionage," it was "infiltration"; but espionage would be "one of its eventual objectives." It was and it wasn't—a paradox that characterized much of Chamber's constantly altering testimony.

The confusion in his testimony was compounded in this passage: "I should perhaps make the point that these people were *specifically not wanted to act as sources of information*. These people were an elite group, an outstanding group, which it was believed would rise to positions—as, indeed, some of them did—notably Mr. White and Mr. Hiss—in the Government, and their position in the Government would be of *very much more service to the Communist Party*." [Italics added.]

The language says clearly that this elite group was considered so valuable that it was not to jeopardize itself with espionage. It was to worm its way into the high councils of government, where influence could be exerted to mold American policy toward Communistic aims. This was, if anything, an even more devious and diabolical purpose, though of course not so susceptible to proof as outright espionage; and so it is relevant to note that, in the sequel, absolutely nothing to which Chambers testified in this passage would hold true in his final version.

The elite group to which Chambers referred consisted, in addition to the men he had already named, of Donald Hiss, Victor Perlo, Charles Kramer, and Henry Collins. According to Chambers, they were all leaders of individual cells and met regularly in the apartment of Henry Collins. There Chambers made contact with them, functioning in the capacity of courier or liaison man, bringing instructions and literature from Communist headquarters in New York. All the eight men he had named, Chambers vowed, were Communists, and he collected from them Communist Party dues that "were handed over to me by Collins, who was the treasurer of that group."

From the first, Chambers' testimony focused a strong spotlight on Alger Hiss, who had had a long and distinguished career in the State Department and had left government service to become the president of the Carnegie Endowment for International Peace. Chambers said that when he decided to break with the Communist Party "in 1937," he had tried to persuade Hiss to break with him. This was his testimony:

> I went to the Hiss home one evening at what I considered was considerable risk to myself and found Mrs. Hiss at home. Mrs. Hiss is also a member of the Communist Party."
>
> Mundt: Mrs. Alger Hiss?
>
> Chambers: Mrs. Alger Hiss. Mrs. Donald Hiss, I believe, is not.
>
> Mrs. Hiss attempted while I was there to make a call, which I can only presume was to other Communists, but I quickly went to the telephone and she hung up, and Mr. Hiss came in shortly afterward, and we talked and I tried to break him away from the party.
>
> As a matter of fact, he cried when we separated, when I left him; but he absolutely refused to break.
>
> Representative John McDowell: He cried?
>
> Chambers: Yes, he did. I was very fond of Mr. Hiss.
>
> Mundt: He must have given you some reason why he did not want to sever the relationship.
>
> Chambers: His reasons were simply the party line.

Two days after the signing of the Nazi-Stalin Pact in 1939, Chambers testified, he had gone to Washington to place his information at the disposal of the American government. Isaac Don Levine, the future editor of *Plain Talk,* had made a contact at the White House and had been told that Chambers should see Assistant Secretary of

State Adolf Berle, who was the Administration's expert on security matters. Chambers saw Berle, told him the full story of the Communist underground, named the same names he had named to the House committee. Berle had been shocked and had said, in Chambers' paraphrase, that "we absolutely have to have a clean Government service because we are faced with the prospect of war." But, to Chambers' surprise and disappointment, nothing had happened. Alger Hiss, for one, had continued to rise in the hierarchy of government.[19]

Subsequently, FBI agents had come to see Chambers. They had questioned him many times (he was later to estimate some fourteen or fifteen times in all), but once more nothing had happened. The picture presented was that of two now reformed Communists, now patriotic Americans (Miss Bentley and Chambers) who had tried their best to help the FBI—and somewhere, on some mysterious higher echelon of the Democratic administrations—they had been blocked; their efforts had come to naught. The conflict made the headlines so ardently desired to fan political passions.

So was born the era of suspicion, a miasma of distrust for all things progressive or liberal; so was America, traditionally a free-wheeling democracy, turned into a scared caricature of itself and emasculated into a society in which the only safety was to be found in conformity.

And so it is perhaps wise at this point to inject a footnote of reason.

In December, 1953, after the Eisenhower Administration had been in office nearly a year, Senate and House committees summarized the achievements of their five-year witch-hunt. Their summaries showed that "at least" seventy-five federal employees—out of the literally millions in government service—had been accused of Communist activities. Of the seventy-five, two, Harold Ware and Harry Dexter White, had died. Of the remainder, just two, Alger Hiss and William Remington, had been brought to trial, and they had been convicted. Once all the headline hoopla had died away, only two cases had been left that could stand scrutiny and the test of trial in a court of law.[20]

When one-sided inquisitions can ferret out only two cases, the spuriousness of the spy propaganda campaign that was brainwashing the American people is patent. And it becomes important to determine just how legitimate were even those two cases.

■ Notes ■

[1] Associated Press dispatch from Washington, Aug. 8, 1945, as published in the *New York Times.*

[2] See J. Montgomery Hyde, *Room 3603* (Farrar, Straus & Cudahy, 1963), pp. 166–167; and Don Whitehead, *The FBI Story* (Random House, 1956), pp. 277–278 of Pocket Books edition.

[3] *New York World-Telegram,* Mar. 5, 1948.

[4] For the details of this day-by-day investigation, obviously obtained directly from FBI files, see a series of articles by Frederick Woltman, the *New York World-Telegram,* beginning May 15, 1950.

[5] For example, Frederick Woltman hopped on the Larsen charges, and on Sept. 18, 1946, in an article that began on page 1 of the *New York World-Telegram,* devoted nearly two columns to the theme.

[6] *New York Times,* Feb. 8, 1954.

[7] H. R. Hearings before the Committee on Un-American Activities, 80th Congress, Second Session, p. 548.

[8] *Ibid.,* pp. 534–535.

[9] *Ibid.,* p. 561.

[10] *Ibid.,* pp. 506–508.

[11] *Ibid.,* pp. 510–511.

[12] Rebecca West, "As a Briton Looks at McCarthyism," in *U.S. News and World Report,* May 22, 1953.

[13] H. R. Hearings, *op. cit.,* p. 528.

[14] H. R. Hearings, *op. cit.,* pp. 529–530.

[15] H. R. Hearings, *op. cit.,* 723. See Lee's entire testimony, pp. 715–725 and 733–759.

[16] H. R. Hearings, *op. cit.,* 727.

[17] Don Whitehead, *The FBI Story* (Random House, 1956), p. 277 of Pocket Books edition.

[18] H. R. Hearings, *op. cit.,* p. 729.

[19] Testimony by Chambers in H. R. Hearings, *op. cit.,* pp. 563–584.

[20] This compilation of the five-year probe by Senate and House committees was made from the committees' records by the Associated Press with the cooperation of committee experts on Nov. 30, 1953. (See the *Los Angeles Times,* Dec. 1, 1953.)

10 The Trials— and Harry White

The watershed case of the early postwar years almost certainly was the trial of Alger Hiss. It was one of those symbolic trials that stand for an era. The statistics on the relatively few suspects even partisan Congressional committees could ferret out among federal employees might not register with any great impact on the public consciousness, but what happened to Alger Hiss certainly would. This was personalized drama, Alger Hiss vs. Whittaker Chambers, the high government official vs. the informer. It was much like two knights jousting to the death in tournaments of old, and the public verdict on the truth or falsity of outcries of subversion, treason, and appeasement would depend in great degree on its outcome. It was a trial that had to be won. It was a trial in which, by its very nature, the FBI must stand or fall—because, in the Hiss case, a miscarriage of justice could not be ascribed to inadvertent error or to the unsuspected perjury of witnesses. The basis of this trial lay not in the conflict between the testimony of two men, though that was important. It lay in the validity of factual evidence—the espionage documents that Whittaker Chambers, despite his repeated denials that such things had ever existed, ultimately produced. These documents were either valid and Hiss was guilty as charged—or they were forgeries. There is no other alternative. And since the FBI vouched for the validity of the documents, its prestige is at stake in this case as in no other. Certainly, no man who appreciates the FBI's technical skills—and they are great— can believe that forged documents could have escaped its detection. If Hiss were not guilty, if he were truly innocent as he has always maintained, then the FBI must have been either an accomplice or a silent partner in a frameup that made a travesty of justice.

303

■ 1 ■

Alger Hiss, tall and slender, possessed of quick intelligence and facile charm, was one of those who risked the perjury charge. He lost no time. As soon as Chambers had testified, he dispatched a telegram to the House committee.

"I do not know Mr. Chambers and insofar as I am aware have never laid eyes on him," he wired. "There is no basis for the statements made about me to your committee. . . . I would . . . appreciate the opportunity to appear before your committee to make these statements formally and under oath."

This was the telegram that led to Hiss's appearance before the committee on Thursday, August 5, 1948. His testimony was unequivocal. Under oath he declared:

> I am not and never have been a member of the Communist Party. I do not and never have adhered to the tenets of the Communist Party. I am not and never have been a member of any Communist-front organization. I have never followed the Communist Party line, directly or indirectly. To the best of my knowledge, none of my friends is a Communist. . . .
> To the best of my knowledge, I never heard of Whittaker Chambers until in 1947, when two representatives of the Federal Bureau of Investigation asked me if I knew him and various other people, some of whom I knew and some of whom I did not know. I said I did not know Chambers. So far as I know, I have never laid eyes upon him, and I should like to have the opportunity to do so.

Hiss added that he had known Henry Collins since they were boys in camp together; he had known him subsequently when they were classmates at Harvard, and again after he came to Washington. Lee Pressman had been in Hiss's class at Harvard Law School, and they had served together on the *Harvard Law Review* and later as legal assistants to Jerome Frank on the staff of the Agricultural Adjustment Administration. Since leaving AAA in 1935, he had seen Pressman infrequently. Nathan Witt and John Abt had both been on the legal staff of AAA, as had Kramer; he had met them in that capacity, had seen little of them since. "I don't believe I ever knew Victor Perlo," he added, and he concluded:

"Except as I have indicated, the statements made about me by Mr. Chambers are complete fabrications. I think my record in the Government service speaks for itself."

After Hiss had finished his statement, Karl Mundt reeled off the names of the others whom Chambers had accused.

"There seems to be no question about the subversive connections of the six other than the Hiss brothers," he said, "and I wonder what possible motive a man who edits *Time* Magazine would have for mentioning Donald Hiss and Alger Hiss in connection with those other six."

"So do I, Mr. Chairman," Hiss replied. "I have no possible understanding of what could have motivated him."

Questioning established just how closely Hiss had been associated with the prominent men of his day. He had served as clerk to one of the most famous of modern Supreme Court Justices, Oliver Wendell Holmes. Justice Felix Frankfurter was one of those who had urged him to enter government service. He had served in the Solicitor General's office under Stanley Reed, later a Supreme Court Justice. John Foster Dulles had been largely instrumental in getting him his post as president of the Carnegie Endowment for International Peace. Though Chambers in his original testimony had exaggerated Hiss's importance, Hiss had been one of the State Department technicians at the Yalta conference. He had participated in setting up the United Nations at San Francisco. And he had gone to London in 1946 for the first meeting of the General Assembly of the United Nations, a trip during which he and Dulles first had discussed the Carnegie Endowment job.

It was on his return from London, he testified, that he first became aware of rumors about his loyalty. James F. Byrnes, then Secretary of State, had called him into his office and "He said that several Members of Congress were preparing to make statements on the floor of Congress that I was a Communist. He asked me if I were, and I said I was not. He said, 'This is a very serious matter. I think all the stories center from the FBI. I think they are the people who have obtained whatever information has been obtained. I think you would be well advised to go directly to the FBI and offer yourself for a very full inquiry and investigation.' "

Hiss had done this. The FBI questioning had seemed vague. They had asked him about his associations with a number of persons, mainly Lee Pressman. They hadn't mentioned the name of Chambers. Hiss had never heard that Adolf Berle had been given a report by Chambers, in 1939, questioning his loyalty. In 1947, after he had left government service, two FBI agents had asked him about a man named Chambers, but until Chambers had testified before the committee, the issue had not seemed serious to him.[1]

The clash of testimony was head-on, irreconcilable. The House committee, meeting in secret session in New York's Foley Square courthouse on August 7, 1948, heard Chambers detail his knowledge of Hiss. True, Chambers said, Hiss had never known him as Whittaker Chambers, but simply as "Carl," the only name by which he was known in the Party. He had known Hiss only from 1935 to 1937.

Remember these dates, for in this many-times-told story of Chambers they were to become all-important. He had collected Communist Party dues from Hiss directly. Just four days previous to the Foley Square hearing he had testified that he had collected dues from Henry Collins for the entire group because Collins was the "treasurer" of the group, but now he testified that, about once every month for a period of two years, Hiss had given him an envelope containing his and his wife's dues. He said: "All dues were collected individually." Here was a witness contradicting himself, but did anyone grill him on this discrepancy? No one did. Hiss, Chambers said "was rather pious about paying his dues promptly"—and this was the kind of testimony this committee wanted.

Bolstering his story with certain checkpoints, Chambers declared he had stayed in Hiss's home for as much as a week at a time, making it a kind of unofficial headquarters in Washington. He knew that Mrs. Hiss had a son, Timothy Hobson, by her first marriage to Thayer Hobson, New York publisher. He recalled that the Hisses sometimes vacationed on the Eastern Shore of Maryland; that Hiss was a bird watcher and at one time became very excited because he had seen a prothonotary warbler, a rare species; that Hiss had had an old car which he had donated "to the Party" instead of trading it in when he got a new Plymouth in 1937. He knew that Mrs. Hiss's maiden name was Priscilla Fansler and that she came from a Quaker family whose home had been near Paoli, Pennsylvania.[2]

Now the committee began to draw the noose tight about Alger Hiss. Hiss was called back before it in private session on August 16. He denied that he had ever known anyone just by the name of "Carl," and any impartial person reading the record must conclude that he seemed genuinely puzzled, for he began by trying to recall acquaintances who might have had this first name. But he did confirm one striking detail that Chambers had supplied. He acknowledged he had seen a prothonotary warbler "right here on the Potomac . . . beautiful yellow head, a gorgeous bird." This confirmation seems to have convinced the committee, if any convincing was needed, that Chambers had been telling the truth.

From this point, the going was downhill for Hiss. He recalled that during the 1930's he had met a freelance writer named George Crosley, who had needed a place to stay in Washington. At the moment, Hiss was changing apartments. Since his old lease still had several weeks to run, he let Crosley have his apartment. The issues now were narrowing. On August 17, in another secret session, the committee brought Chambers and Hiss face to face. Hiss professed at first that he couldn't be sure. He asked to see Chambers' teeth because one of his clearest recollections of "Crosley" was that he had very bad teeth. Finally he conceded that Chambers, much more portly now, was the man he had known more than a decade earlier as Crosley. The admission, the about-face from Hiss's first emphatic disclaimer, did incalculable headline damage. The impression was fostered that, in Hiss, the House committee had an evasive witness who was being driven into acknowledgments of basic facts only when they could no longer be denied.

The impression deepened when Hiss was called back to the witness stand in Washington in a public hearing on August 25. He still did not know the details of Chambers' accusing testimony of August 7. So he had no knowledge of the charges he had to meet, no opportunity to point out the flaws in Chambers' account. In addition, Nixon, smelling the political capital that was to catapult him into the Vice Presidency, took over the grilling in the hectoring manner of the public prosecutor. Nixon had handled Chambers with velvet gloves, not batting an eye when Chambers blatantly contradicted himself on the method of collecting Communist dues. But with Hiss, Nixon turned tiger, pillorying the witness on the slightest discrepancies in his story.

And there were discrepancies. Hiss pictured his contact with Crosley as a brief acquaintanceship with a man he hardly knew. Yet he had let this man have his apartment for several weeks; the man hadn't paid him the rent for the apartment as he had promised; Hiss had decided he was a welsher—and yet Hiss had given this man whom he barely knew, this welsher, his old 1929 Ford car because the car was worth only some $25 and he would rather see someone have the use of it.

Chambers' version was that he had never been expected to pay rent, that Hiss had been glad to do a comrade a favor. As for the car, he had never had it. Hiss had been such a dedicated Communist he had insisted on donating it to the Party. Because Hiss's version of these transactions seemed confused and implausible, the palm went to Chambers, and with it went much else—the suspicion that, if he was right on such details, he might very well be right on everything.

It was a human, if not entirely logical, reaction. Much more was at stake here than the possible mystery surrounding the relationship of two men. The issue was the loyalty, the possible treason, of a highly placed and highly regarded one-time government official, Alger Hiss. This would have to be proved by other and more specific details than the loaning of an apartment or the giving of a car. The partisan House committee evidently realized this, and so on this same day of August 25, 1948, the day of the implacable hounding of Hiss on the witness stand, it recalled Chambers for an appearance that can only be described as designed to patch up the loopholes in the tale of its favored witness—and perhaps to lay the groundwork for events that were still in incubation.

There are two extremely curious and suspect facets about this August 25 appearance of Whittaker Chambers. First, with Nixon handling the questioning, a deliberate effort was made to reconcile the irreconcilable—to clear Chambers of self-contradiction on the matter of paying Communist dues. Originally Chambers had said all dues were paid by Henry Collins for the group; next, he had said he collected dues from Hiss regularly because all dues were paid individually; now, with Nixon's considerate help, he tried to reconcile these incompatible versions by testifying that Collins sometimes paid for the group, but that Hiss, on occasion, had paid him individually. Like the monkey who could see, hear, and speak no evil, the members of the House committee accepted the new version, as they had the others, without adventuring a single skeptical, probing question.

The second feature of Chambers' August 25 testimony seems even more suggestive of hidden and powerful forces at work behind the scenes. In all his previous recitals—and Chambers told his story so often during the years that, by the time he first took the stand before the House committee, it should have been well and infallibly rehearsed—he had said specifically that he broke with Communism in 1937. This was the date he had fixed in his talk with Adolf Berle in 1939, two years after the event, when the details must have been still fresh in memory; this was the date he had told Malcolm Cowley, a writer, in a discussion in December, 1940. And in two FBI reports, later introduced in evidence at the Hiss trials—one report dated 1942, the other 1946—he had said he had been a Communist from 1924 "until the spring of 1937." He had testified to this date so positively and so repeatedly in his earlier performances before the House committee that at one point Nixon had told Hiss to limit his testimony "to the years 1934 to 1937 . . . because there is nothing else at issue." Now came the first indication that something else might ultimately be at issue. Now, tentatively, gingerly, this apparently solid bedrock of fact began to change. It was bedrock no longer.

This slight but significant alteration in the time element on which so much was to depend first evidenced itself in this August 25 appearance of Chambers. He was asked by Stripling: "How long were you a member of the Communist Party?" He answered: "I was a member of the Communist Party from 1924 until about 1937 or 1938, early '38." Somebody evidently attached great importance to this date, for five days later Chambers was back before the committee again and, with Nixon's help, he shoved the date of his break with Communism still further ahead into 1938, settling on a time in late February. This was still not to meet the requirements of the ultimate case, but it did at least have the effect of approaching them. The hard, fixed date that had stood unchanged in Chambers' recitals throughout the years— the date that would have made the ultimate case impossible—had now been changed from a positive to a fluid fact. If there was a plot to frame Alger Hiss—and in view of all the later evidence this seems probable—this insidious shift in the basic time element must be accepted as one of the first indications that it was brewing.[3]

Evidently, however, an additional stimulus was needed, and it was to be one of the crowning ironies of a case filled with irony that this stimulus was to be supplied by Alger Hiss himself. In his final appearance before the House committee, badgered by Nixon on the tangled apartment-and-car involvements, he had been nevertheless sure enough of himself to issue a challenge to Chambers. He had defied Chambers to repeat his charges outside the privileged forum of the House, in a situation in which he could be sued for libel. On August 27 Chambers picked up the challenge. He appeared on the "Meet the Press" program and repeated his charge that Hiss had been a Communist. Once more, however, consistent with all his testimony in the past, he denied any knowledge of any overt acts on Hiss's part. In response to a question, he said: "That was a group, not, as I think is in the back of your mind, for the purpose of espionage, but for the purpose of infiltrating government policy by getting Communists in key places."

Q. It was not, then, by definition, conspiracy?

A. No, it was not.

Hiss responded on September 27, 1948, by filing a libel suit seeking $50,000 from Chambers for defamation of character. Less than three weeks later, on October 14, Chambers appeared before a federal grand jury in New York. The jury, probing his accusations against Hiss, wanted to know, as everyone wanted to know, whether Hiss had committed any overt, treasonable acts. The grand jury record, as later revealed at the Hiss trials, shows this question-and-answer sequence:

> Juror: Could you give me one name of anybody who, in your opinion, was positively guilty of espionage against the United States?
>
> Chambers: Let me think for a moment and I will try to answer

that. I don't think so, but would like to have the opportunity to answer you tomorrow more definitely. Let me think it over, overnight.

This answer must strike one as most peculiar, coming from a man who had testified he had been for years an undercover agent. One would think that he must have known, that he must have been able to give a direct answer. But not Chambers. He wanted a night's meditation. He got it. The next day, back on the witness stand—

> Chambers: I assume that espionage means in this case the turning over of secret confidential documents.
> Juror: Or information—oral information.
> Chambers: Or oral information. I do not believe I do know such a name.

It seemed like explicit language. It was certainly a complete denial, given under oath. But with Chambers no language was ever explicit; no word given under oath could ever be trusted. Chambers now was about to demonstrate this himself. Facts that, according to Chambers, had never existed became now the only facts that, all the time, had had any validity.

The about-face occurred at Baltimore on November 17, 1948. In the interim, an astounding political event had occurred: Truman had defeated Dewey. This meant that the Democrats retained at least technical control of the Department of Justice. It could mean, conceivably, that Chambers might face punitive action for his testimony against Hiss. Furthermore, Hiss's attorneys, in pretrial depositions in the libel case, were pressing Chambers hard. It became apparent to Chambers that he might very well lose the action and his attorney advised him that, if he had any incriminating material against Hiss, he had better, for Heaven's sake, produce it. The result was that Chambers suddenly brought forth a batch of sixty-five sheets of documents, plus four small slips of paper, memos in Hiss's handwriting. The larger sheets were typewritten digests of information taken from State Department documents ranging from confidential to secret. The dates, in view of Chambers' prior sinuosity in fundamentally altering his many-times-told tale that he had broken with Communism in 1937 and gone into hiding, were intriguing: Most of the

documents bore dates of February and March, 1938, and the last
was dated April 1.

Hiss promptly instructed his attorneys to turn the documents over
to federal prosecutors. It took two weeks for rumors of something
important having happened in Baltimore to filter out to the press.
Nixon and Stripling heard the rumors and went to Chambers' Maryland farm. Chambers acknowledged he had been holding out information, and, in response to a committee subpoena, at 10:30 on the
night of December 2, he led investigators to a pumpkin patch, reached
inside a hollowed-out pumpkin, and pulled out five rolls of microfilm,
only two of which had been developed. These contained reproductions of more State Department documents.

The "Pumpkin Papers," as all of Chambers' productions were indiscriminately labeled by the press, catapulted the Hiss-Chambers
case into a new spate of page-one publicity. Americans have an
almost worshipful respect for documents, and the instant Chambers
produced *documents* most persons turned from Hiss in disgust and
closed their minds. Anyone sensitive to the mood of the times could
feel the over-night crystallization of public sentiment, and there
seems little reason to doubt that Truman would have been defeated
if Chambers had hurled his bombshell a month earlier. By so narrow
a margin had Dewey missed.

In the climate of the times, a climate that had been germinated in
the daily spy hunts of Congressional committees throughout the
summer and fall, the utter inconsistency of Chambers' actions—an
inconsistency that, from the outset, should have made them infinitely
suspect—never registered with a public mesmerized by the physical
presence of the proof he had seemingly produced. Yet this "proof,"
which at least established Chambers' past perjuries beyond cavil,
should have been most critically examined before it was accepted as
bona fide.

What was Chambers' explanation?

Denying every word he had uttered on the subject for years, he
now contended that the underground group, far from being a high-
level elite not supposed to concern itself with espionage, had been
concerned all the time with espionage. Hiss, Chambers now contended, had regularly passed him documents, beginning back in the

days when he was counsel for the Nye committee, which had probed the munitions profiteers of World War I. When Chambers got ready to break with Communism, according to his new version, he had squirreled away some of the last of the documents he had acquired for use "as a life preserver" in case the Communists tried to kill him. The documents, he contended, had been hidden all these years in the dumbwaiter shaft of the home of his wife's nephew, Nathan Levine, of Brooklyn. Why hadn't Chambers revealed all this earlier? Because, said Chambers, he was filled with such pity for all mankind that he could not bring himself to destroy another individual until Hiss positively drove him into a corner. Not even though, if his story were true, Hiss represented the demoniac evil of Communism, a force inimical to the God and country Chambers now professed to hold so dear.

This explanation was uncritically accepted. After all, it *must* be true, mustn't it, since Chambers had produced the *documents?* Hysteria swept the nation and swept the Truman Administration along with it. On December 1, two weeks after Chambers produced his first batch of documents in Baltimore, the Justice Department had told the press the case was virtually closed. On December 15, less than two weeks after Chambers produced his pumpkin microfilm and a new swatch of sensational headlines, the New York grand jury indicted Hiss on two counts of perjury—one for denying he had ever passed State Department documents to Chambers, the other for denying he had seen Chambers after January 1, 1937. There evidently was considerable sentiment within the grand jury for the indictment of Chambers, about whose perjury there could be no question, but the government itself was now in this particular perjurer's corner and fought off such action on the grounds that, were Chambers indicted, the vital witness against Hiss would be discredited.

Before the case came to trial, there was another key development. Chambers contended that the documents he had produced in Baltimore had been copied by the Hisses, especially Mrs. Hiss, on an old Woodstock typewriter. The Hisses long since had discarded the decrepit machine, which now became vital to the case. If it could be found, it was believed, a matching of the typing with the type face could demonstrate conclusively whether the old Hiss Woodstock had produced Chambers' Baltimore documents. And so a nationwide hunt was launched. On one side two amateurs in the detective business, Alger and Donald Hiss, sought possession of the machine for the defense, convinced it would establish Hiss's innocence. On the other hand, the FBI, with its vast resources, sought to obtain the machine for the government.

It was a most uneven contest and it had a most amazing outcome. Some thirty-five FBI agents in Washington and other FBI forces throughout the nation sought the old Hiss Woodstock. Apparently, they were completely frustrated, for in mid-April, 1949, the Hisses tracked down in Washington a Woodstock, Serial No. 230,099, that seemed to be the one the Hisses had possessed long years before. To their amazement, tests performed on the Woodstock seemed to match the typing of the Baltimore documents. The Hisses, dumfounded, in a state of shock from which their defense never really recovered, notified the government they had found the Woodstock.

Two lengthy trials followed. The first, ending May 31, 1949, found the jury hopelessly divided, eight for conviction, four for acquittal. The second, ending January 20, 1950, found the jury, originally split eight-to-four, resolving its doubts after twenty-four hours of debate by convicting Hiss on both counts.

It is impossible here to do justice to all the trial evidence, but certain points should be noted. Chambers, who consulted daily with agents of the FBI, finally settled on a date for his break with Communism—a date that would not swear at the dates on the documents he had produced. The new date was April 15, 1938. Lloyd Paul Stryker, Hiss's counsel in the first trial, demanded to know when Chambers had fixed upon *that* date. "When I began going over the whole story with the FBI in relation to the documents," Chambers said.

The Court: What date was that?

Chambers: That was from December until about a month ago, I believe.

The FBI's assistance in perfecting Chambers' final court testimony showed in at least one other instance. Chambers had been questioned repeatedly by the House committee; he had been implored to remember every last, least detail of his association with Hiss; he had come up with the account of the prothonotary warbler, the Hiss apartment loan, the old Hiss Ford. He had been questioned again in the Baltimore pretrial deposition, and in all this exhaustive questioning and searching of his memory, there had been no hint of a detail he suddenly supplied after he began his daily conferences with the FBI. In late January, 1949, FBI agents had obtained the full record of Hiss's bank transactions, which showed that on November 19, 1937, just four days before Chambers purchased a new car, the Hisses had withdrawn $400 from their bank account. Chambers promptly declared that he now remembered—the Hisses had given him that $400 to help him purchase his new auto. After Chambers sprang this new detail at the first trial, Stryker demanded to know when he had first recalled this munificent donation, and Chambers: answered: "When I was going over this whole history with the FBI, which was sometime in the spring of this year."

The Hisses' explanation was that they had been moving to a much larger home, and they had withdrawn the money to purchase furniture and new draperies. The explanation seems hardly necessary, for Chambers' belated account challenges credulity. Can anyone conceive of a man's forgetting a $400 windfall that made possible the purchase of a new car? This detail, one would think, would have remained in memory much more vividly than the incident of the prothonotary warbler. Can one believe that the beneficiary of such a gift would have to have his memory refreshed by having the FBI procure for him the donor's bank account? Or does it seem more likely that this was a concocted bit of evidence?

If one hesitates about the answer, the quality of some of the other evidence Chambers gave under oath may help to make up one's mind. For example, Chambers' most stubbornly maintained assertion that he had been known to Hiss only by the conspiratorial name of "Carl" collapsed of its own weight. Chambers told of dining in a Georgetown restaurant with Hiss, of being introduced by Hiss to a woman acquaintance. How was he introduced—as just plain "Carl"? Obviously not. Chambers himself had to admit to Claude Cross, Hiss's second trial counsel, that a full name must have been used, but what name it was he professed himself unable to recall. Was it George Crosley, the name by which Hiss said he had known him, the name which Chambers always had contended he had never used? Chambers was sure it wasn't, but finally, unable to offer any other explanation, he conceded: "It may have been."

Equally significant was the collapse of the first spy charge leveled against Hiss by Chambers. Chambers had insisted that Hiss passed him secret documents at the time of the Nye committee inquiry. This sounded conspiratorial, but it was established at the trials that the Nye committee had never had secret documents. All had been cleared before the committee used them, and all had been subsequently published in the committee's voluminous records and were available to everybody. The implications of this exposure of a prime Chambers' contention are truly devastating. As Earl Jowitt, late Lord Chancellor of Great Britain, later wrote: "If it is established that Chambers was lying in this particular matter, his evidence of the turning over of the other documents can only be accepted with great caution." Even more fundamental, what becomes of Chambers' rationalization of his conduct in repeatedly committing perjury by denying espionage? What becomes of his pose of saintlike compassion? "There would be nothing godlike in fabricating a case against an erstwhile friend by representing him as being guilty of treachery in handing over secret documents, if the truth turned out to be that the friend had done no more than supply copies of documents which were intended to be available to every journalist," Earl Jowitt wrote. "Is this the true view? If it is, the consequences are indeed far-reaching. The reference to the 'god of mercy' stands revealed as the most rank and revolting hypocrisy." [4]

Such exposures cast grave suspicion on the validity of the case against Alger Hiss. Harrowing doubts are raised, not by the strength of the defense but by the patent incredibilities in the case of the prosecution. The prosecution collapsed in almost every instance in which Chambers' word was subject to independent check and verification; it held fast only when there was no possibility of such checks, when one had to accept Chambers' word for what had happened. Yet Hiss was convicted. Why? Very simply, because it seems the jury found it impossible to disbelieve the evidence of the documents and the typewriter.

The defense had been unable to explain them away. The best it had been able to do was to offer alternatives. One of these was the testimony of Julian Wadleigh, another ex-Communist, who had been employed in the Trade Agreements section of the State Department. Wadleigh testified that he had passed government documents to Chambers and to another Communist courier named Carpenter. He had passed so many he couldn't possibly recall them individually, but he identified some half dozen of Chambers' documents as items that may well have come from him. Wadleigh, however, could not have been the complete explanation, for he had been sent to Turkey on March 8, 1938. The documents passed after that date, up to and including April 1, obviously must have come from someone else. Chambers, who was now contending he had remained a Communist and a courier until April 15, insisted that all the documents, the earlier as well as the later, had come from Hiss.

Again the Hiss defense, in its analysis of the documents, scored points in logic if not in emotional impact. Obtaining originals from the State Department, it demonstrated that quite a number of the documents had never been routed to the section where Hiss worked. According to State Department records, he could never have had possession of them, and so he could never have passed them. But all, according to Chambers—and this was crucial—had been copied by Mrs. Hiss on the Woodstock. This was a contention to which the FBI gave full support.

An FBI typewriting expert compared the typing of the documents with the typing of letters known to have been written by Mrs. Hiss on the old Woodstock. With enlargements, he illustrated for the jury how defects in certain type faces used in typing the Baltimore documents matched defects in the typed correspondence. Just one of Chambers' documents, the FBI expert conceded, did not fit this pattern. This had been typed on a different machine, a Royal, and how this stray had gotten into the batch of documents Chambers insisted had *all* come from the Hisses and their Woodstock, neither Chambers nor anyone else could explain. It was a disturbing flaw, but minor. After all, the FBI testimony did tie the documents to the Hisses, and there in court sat the machine that presumably had done the deed, Woodstock No. 230,099. The Woodstock itself was not examined, since Hiss's defense had accepted it uncritically as the

Hisses' old machine. (The anomaly of the defendant, if he were truly guilty, producing in court this key evidence against himself seems never to have registered with the jury or the public.) It is quite obvious that the Hiss defense, having accepted some of the basic premises of the prosecution, was at a loss for explanation. All it could suggest was that Chambers, somehow, must have sneaked in during the dark of night and played a tune on the old Hiss Woodstock, a rationalization so patently ridiculous that it did more harm than good. United States Attorney Thomas F. Murphy, the government prosecutor, had a field day with this contention. He thundered that the documents and the typewriter sat there in court, the "immutable witnesses" against Alger Hiss. And so the jury found.

Not until the second trial was over did Hiss get himself a new lawyer, Chester T. Lane. Lane had had broad experience in government service during the Roosevelt and Truman Administrations. He had served as a special assistant to the Attorney General; he had been during the war associate chief of the special war policies unit of the Department of Justice; and he had been lend-lease administrator under Truman. Lane had had the kind of experience that made him less ready than other attorneys had been to accept the basic premises of the prosecution's case. Convinced of Hiss's innocence, he questioned the validity of the typewriter and the documents.

Lane had hardly entered the case when the FBI's all-consuming interest made itself apparent. Hiss had telephoned him at his office on lower Broadway to arrange for their first meeting and discussion. They had lunched at the Harvard Club, had talked for two or three hours. Lane agreed to represent Hiss in the appeal of his conviction and returned to his law office. When he walked in, he was astounded, as he told this author years later, to discover that "telephone repairmen" were busily at work "fixing" his wires. There had been nothing wrong with the phone lines; he hadn't asked the telephone company to "repair" them as the workmen had said. But he and his associates quickly discovered that, from that moment on, they dared not call a potential witness over their office phones. If they did, somehow, mysteriously, the FBI always seemd to get there first and exert its pressures. Lane and his aides had to adopt the inconvenient policy, when they were making phone calls connected with the Hiss case, of leaving the office and using an outside pay station.

Lane's discoveries were monumental. The courts were to refuse to consider them on the purely technical grounds that, had the defense exercised "due diligence," the evidence should have been produced at the trials. But from the standpoint of logic, Lane wrecked the fundamental bases of the prosecution's case. A pillar of the case that he definitely destroyed was that so carefully altered date on which the FBI and Chambers had agreed for Chambers' break with Communism. At the second trial, Chambers had testified that, after he broke with the Party on April 15, 1938, he hid out for a month before he obtained a book-translation job from the Oxford University Press.

In their posttrial researches, Lane's investigators went to the Oxford University Press, seeking documentary records that might show just when Chambers had been hired for the book translation. According to an affidavit subsequently filed by Paul Willert, the editor who hired Chambers, another translator had first failed at the job, and he had seen Chambers several times, had taken him to lunch a couple of times, wanting to become acquainted with Chambers and make certain he was capable before he engaged him. Chambers at the time had expressed "violent anti-Communist views," had told Willert he was in hiding from the OGPU, and had impressed Willert as "being hysterical and suffering from a persecution mania." Willert, however, had been impressed by Chambers' intellectual capacities, had felt sorry for him, and so had hired him. When had this taken place? Willert could not say, but he felt certain that his first conversations with Chambers had taken place at the end of 1937 or very early in 1938.

Correspondence that Lane's investigators discovered in the Oxford Press files established virtually beyond question that Willert's recollection was correct. A letter written from the London office of Oxford University Press, *dated significantly March 4, 1938,* inquired about *the progress* the new translator was making—a clear indication that he must already have been employed for some time. A shipping tag in the New York office showed that what apparently was the last batch of manuscript—some "extra chapters," to which Chambers himself referred in one letter—had been mailed to Chambers on March 18, 1938. And on April 12 Willert mailed Chambers an additional check for $250, apologizing because it was sent "rather belatedly."

The implications are devastating. The Oxford Press documentary evidence showed conclusively that Chambers had broken with Communism and was engaged on the translation task for some time *before* March 4, 1938. Even the government was compelled to admit that he must have "erred by a few weeks in fixing the time of his obtaining the translation," but it argued that this was a separate and inconsequential matter—it made no difference. On the contrary, it makes every difference. It means that Chambers could not have been a spy ring courier as late as April 15. It means he could not have obtained the March and April 1 documents he swore he obtained from Hiss. It means that someone else, subsequently, must have supplied him with those documents—a feat that, as the *Amerasia* case demonstrated, would not have been too difficult. And it means that, if Chambers did not obtain the documents as he swore he did, then the case to which he testified was a fabricated case, the documents were manufactured documents, and the date of Chambers' break with Communism had been deliberately altered for one explicit purpose: to frame Alger Hiss.

The conclusion, shocking as it is, was reinforced by Lane's other researches. Lane advanced the proposition that Hiss had been the victim of forgery by typewriter. He sought to prove his point by two tactics: by scientific analysis of Woodstock No. 230,099 and a tracing of its history; and by having a typewriter expert build a machine that would duplicate perfectly the typewriting of the Baltimore documents. When Lane turned his attention in this direction, he touched off a flurry of FBI activity.

The Woodstock that the Hisses had once possessed had originally belonged to Priscilla Hiss's father and had been in use in his Philadelphia insurance office, as office records showed, by at least July 8, 1929. But Lane discovered that a Woodstock with the serial number 230,099 would not have been coming off the factory assembly line in Illinois, at the very earliest, until about that time. Joseph Schmitt, Woodstock plant manager, told a Hiss investigator that a machine with this serial number probably would not have been manufactured before August or September. Furthermore, he said, the type faces on No. 230,099, as produced in court, didn't correspond with the type faces it should have been equipped with, because this kind of type had been discontinued at the end of 1928. Schmitt also commented without elaboration that his company "had helped the FBI find the typewriter in the Hiss case"—an act that the FBI disclaimed ever having performed. When Lane tried to get Schmitt to sign an affidavit to these startling facts, something happened. Schmitt protested he'd have to see his lawyer—and he never did sign. Wherever Lane turned in his typewriter researches, he ran into the same roadblocks. In some instances, FBI agents had been before him and seized all the available records; in others, potential witnesses, forewarned by FBI interviewers, refused to talk. Lane, in his court argument for a new trial, came as close as any attorney has dared to accusing the FBI of Gestapolike methods in intimidating witnesses and creating the atmosphere of a police state that is the very antithesis of democracy. He said:

> We ask questions—the FBI will not let people talk to us. We request access to ordinary documents in corporate files—corporate officials fear the wrath of their stockholders. We ask people to certify information in files they have shown us—they must consult counsel, and we hear no more from them. We pay experts to give us opinions—and they decline to back them up in court because they "cannot subscribe" to anything which might support the conclusion we believe the facts point to.
>
> And, even worse, honorable and patriotic citizens who have wanted to help have been deterred by the appearance—whether or not it is reality—of official surveillance and wiretapping, and others who have labored to gather information for us in the interests of justice are afraid to come forward for fear of personal consequences which might result to them from public association with the defense of Alger Hiss.

Despite such harassments, Lane drove ahead. Martin Tytell, a New York typewriter expert, fabricated a machine to duplicate the typing of Woodstock No. 230,099. Lane submitted comparison examples of the typing to Mrs. Evelyn S. Erlich, an expert in the detection of forgeries on the staff of the Fogg Museum of Art at

Harvard. She subjected the samples to intense magnification and startled Lane by reporting that the typing from No. 230,099 was from a forged machine. "When I corrected her," Lane subsequently told the court, "she assured me that the only possible explanation was that No. 230,099, as well as the machine Tytell had made for me, must be a forgery—and not as carefully constructed a forgery as Tytell's."

Lane then had Dr. Daniel P. Norman, a Boston document expert frequently employed by the armed services and other federal agencies, make a scientific examination of Woodstock No. 230,099. Dr. Norman's findings were unequivocal. He declared that type faces had been crudely soldered to the type bars; that some of the faces showed "abnormal tool marks"; that, on such an ancient machine, type faces should have been corroded and eroded more or less evenly, but these showed "a non-uniform finish or polish on various surfaces, indicating mechanical work which laid bare fresh metal." On the basis of these findings, Lane bluntly told the court that Woodstock No. 230,099 was "a fake machine" and that he was prepared to prove it.

What was the government reaction? Ridicule. Not the meeting of fact with fact.

One of the most suspect performances of the FBI in the entire Hiss case may be found in the gingerly manner in which it combated Lane's flat assertion that Woodstock No. 230,099 was a fake. It garnered affidavits from employees in the Woodstock plant in Illinois to the effect that work on the type bars in the 1928–1929 period was sometimes uneven, and that, in examining pictures Norman had produced in his experiments, they could see nothing suspicious in the appearance of the type faces.

This was seeking remote evidence to combat an issue that should have been met by direct evidence: an analysis of the machine itself. One of the most startling aspects of the case lies in the fact that, so far as anyone knows, the FBI never analyzed Woodstock No. 230,099. If it had, if its expert findings had proved the machine genuine, this would certainly have been prime evidence to submit in court. But the FBI did not submit it. Its tactic was to gather remote affidavits, to shun all connection with the machine itself. Not that the machine was unavailable. Except for the period between trials, when it was in the custody of the court, it has remained in the possession of Hiss's attorneys, and they would have permitted an FBI examination at any time. But no such request was ever made. So far as the attorneys know, so far as the records show, FBI experts never examined Woodstock No. 230,099.

One of the hallmarks of a valid case is the forthright manner in which the prosecution meets a challenge on vital evidence with direct and solid rebuttal, and, conversely, one of the hallmarks of a bad case is the failure to meet such issues directly and to hunt peripheral evidence in exculpation. Judged by this common-sense standard alone, the Hiss case is infinitely suspect.

It has become more suspect with the passage of years, as a succession of events has served to spotlight the persistence of the impression that the FBI, despite what it has always maintained, did have possession of a typewriter in the Hiss case.

The chain of reports, all emanating from responsible sources, began even before Hiss was indicted. On December 13, 1948, Tony Smith, of the Scripps-Howard Press Association, reported: "House investigators have found the typewriter they believe was used to copy the stolen documents in the Hiss-Chambers case. Samples of the typing done on the machine are being compared by technical experts with State Department documents produced by ex-Communist Whittaker Chambers. The machine is said by Un-American Activities Committee aids to be the one formerly owned by Mrs. Alger Hiss."

The article recited the background of the libel suit and added: "Ever since the House committee learned of the deposition, its investigators have been searching for the typewriter. *They found it with the assistance of the FBI,* it was reported." [Italics added.]

Tony Smith was a responsible journalist. He was quoting responsible sources. But there was not another mention in the press of the time of this mysterious typewriter. It faded so completely into the mists that even the mention of it was forgotten when, the following April, the Hisses discovered Woodstock No. 230,099. Where did Tony Smith get his information? Having abandoned the newspaper profession for employment in the office of the arch-conservative Senator Barry Goldwater (Republican of Arizona), he has professed himself incapable of the faintest recall.[5]

The next source to reveal the same understanding of events was Representative McDowell. He had been a member of the House committee that questioned Hiss and Chambers. He should have been thoroughly familiar with the details of the case, yet in July, 1956, in a letter to a Hiss partisan, he wrote: "Mr. Nixon helped mightily in the questioning of Hiss, but a generous amount of credit for solving the fact that Hiss was a traitor should go to the Chief Investigator, Robert E. Stripling and his staff, *and to the FBI for finding the typewriter that typed the letters.*" [Italics added.]

The sequence shows that Woodstock Manager Schmitt, Tony Smith, and Representative McDowell had the impression that the FBI found the typewriter. In the spring of 1962, this impressive list became more impressive when Nixon added his voice to the chorus. The first crisis in his autobiographical *Six Crises* dealt with the Hiss case. Describing the efforts made by the House committee, to secure the indictment of Hiss, he wrote:

> Only six days remained before the term of the Grand Jury would expire. But now the FBI finally was given the go-ahead signal to dig out the facts of the case. A massive search was initiated for the key "witness" in the case—the old Woodstock typewriter on which Chambers said Mrs. Hiss had typed the incriminating documents. On December 13, FBI agents found the typewriter. . . .
>
> It was still touch and go. Hiss and his lawyers fought down to the last hour of the life of the Grand Jury. On December 15, the critical last day, an expert from the FBI typed exact copies of the incriminating documents on the old Woodstock machine and had them flown up to New York as exhibits for members of the Grand Jury to see. A typewriter has one characteristic in common with a fingerprint: every one is different, and it is impossible to make an exact duplicate unless the same machine is used. The evidence was unanswerable.[6]

Exposure of this *faux pas* brought a frantic scurrying-around in the Nixon camp. Nixon himself wasn't available for direct comment, but his public relations man explained that it was that dratted old Tony Smith story that had caused all the trouble. A researcher for Nixon's book had come upon the old clip and had been misled by it; and unfortunately an impression the very opposite from the truth had been conveyed. It was an explanation that didn't explain. It left unanswered the delicate question whether Nixon had read his own book before it was published, for, if he had, with his intimate knowledge of the case that had made him a national figure, he would certainly have spotted such a glaring error (if it was an error), wouldn't he? Furthermore, in the second paragraph, Nixon specifically deals with the events of December 15, which happened two days *after* the offending Tony Smith article had been published.[7]

The mystery that had been so compounded by the man who had been Hiss's principal accuser refused to die. Nixon's hoof-in-mouth performance inspired Hiss's attorneys, headed by Mrs. Helen Buttenwieser after the death of Chester Lane, to make a re-examination of all official reports on the case. And so they discovered an obscure paragraph, overlooked before, in an official report of the House Un-American Activities Committee, published December 31, 1951. This read:

"The committee wishes to commend the Federal Bureau of Investigation for its work in bringing this case [the Hiss case] to a successful conclusion. *The location of the typewriter* and certain other pieces of evidence needed during the trial of the case was amazing." [Italics added.][8]

"Amazing," truly, seems the only word to describe it.

It is obvious that, if the FBI or the House committee ever possessed a Hiss typewriter in December, 1948, the machine recovered by the Hisses in April must have been one planted for them to find—a spurious and fraudulent machine whose typing would pass the inspection normally given by the average document examiner; a machine that, once accepted by the Hisses, could be used (without the government itself being in any way responsible for its acceptance) as the vital missing link in the chain of evidence. If this is what happened—and the indications point to that conclusion—it was a truly Machiavellian plot.

One cardinal question remains: Is forgery by typewriter possible? The government, with its reputation at stake in the Hiss case, has always insisted that it is not. Note how strongly Nixon emphasized this point in *Six Crises*. During the argument for a new trial, the FBI and the United States Attorney's Office ridiculed the possibility. United States Attorney Myles Lane (no relation to Chester) heaped scorn on the Tytell typewriter experiment and the forgery charge. He called it "a combination of Grimm's fairy tale with a bit of a Rube Goldberg twist." Yet the truth was the reverse of government contentions. Forgery by typewriter *is* possible. What is more, the FBI, if it is half as skillful as it is believed to be, must have known it.

A graphic example of a typewriter forgery that was carried out so successfully that it deceived everyone is described by H. Montgomery Hyde in *Room 3603,* his book on the activities of William Stephenson's secret service in America during World War II. Prior to American entrance into the war, the British became concerned about the activities of the Italian L.A.T.I. airline flying into Brazil. It represented a major Axis contact with the Western Hemisphere, and the British wanted to eliminate this contact. They managed to purloin a letter written by General Aurelio Liotta, head of the airline, and they decided to duplicate the type characteristics of the letter in composing a concoction ostensibly addressed by Liotta to the line's Brazilian commandante. The letter was to contain insulting references to Brazilian President Getulio Vargas and mysterious references to revolutionary Axis plots to depose him.

Stephenson, Hoover's close collaborator and a man who imparted his secret processes to the FBI, as Hyde makes clear, had established a laboratory in Canada for the express purpose of forging documents. It was called Station M and was headed by Eric Maschwitz, the lyric composer, who later wrote that he had been associated in the endeavor with "an industrial chemist, and two ruffians who could *reproduce faultlessly the imprint of any typewriter on earth.*" When the British decided to frame the Italian airline in Brazil, Stephenson called on the services of these experts at Station M.

They acquired the right kind of paper. "The embossing was copied with microscopic accuracy," Hyde writes, "and a typewriter was rebuilt to conform to the exact mechanical imperfections of the machine upon which the General's secretary had typed the original letter."

When the forgery had been completed, a microfilm was flown to Brazil. A complicated plot was hatched, featuring a robbery of the local Italian agent's home. This got considerable publicity. Then a British agent sidled up to an American reporter, pretended he had taken part in the robbery, and passed along the microfilmed letter. The American reporter took it to the American Embassy. There it was enlarged, studied, determined to be genuine—and passed on to Vargas. The Brazilian President also accepted it as genuine. He closed down the L.A.T.I. airline and in a few weeks broke off diplomatic relations with the Axis—all on the basis of a bit of typewriter forgery. In the light of this example, does it seem possible to maintain the pretense that forgery by typewriter in the Hiss case would have been impossible? [9]

■ 2 ■

If the Hiss case raises hideous doubts about the role of the FBI and the processes of American justice, the case that followed it leaves no room for doubt at all. It produces only deep, shuddering revulsion —and conviction.

The case was that against William W. Remington, a high-ranking government economist. It was the case in which the credibility of Hoover's infallible informer, Miss Elizabeth Bentley, was to be sorely tested. It was to demonstrate, as has no other case of our time quite so clearly, how all the power and machinery of justice can be used to pervert and distort justice—and so obtain the conviction of a man whom it has been determined to convict.

William Remington was the brilliant son of well-educated and conservative parents. His father was an insurance company executive, his mother an art teacher. Remington was born and brought up in Ridgewood, New Jersey, a residential town in the heartland of New Jersey Republicanism. He attended St. Elizabeth's Protestant Episcopal Church, where he became a choir boy. His early bent seems to have been quite religious, quite idealistic. Through his mother he became a follower of the Oxford Group, a moral-rearmament movement. He later testified: "I tried to place all my thoughts and acts in God's service. As a result, I became more than usually concerned with helping the underdog as a part of my religious philosophy."

Over-earnest, over-dedicated, mentally brilliant—this seems to describe the youthful Remington. The 1934 Yearbook of Ridgewood

High School pictured him as a future "Union Square soapboxer" and called him an active orator whose aspiration was "to die a genius of the first water—unrecognized." He was only sixteen when he entered Dartmouth College at Hanover, New Hamphire.

Remington later testified that as a freshman his political philosophy "moved left quite rapidly." He came to believe, he said, in extensive government ownership and control of industry but had "no well-defined concept of what that meant." He was anti-Fascist. He was devoted to concepts of racial equality. He believed in the split-up of big business and in "highly progressive income taxes." In labor unions he saw the answer to what was "unchristian" in society. But, he always insisted, he "emphatically did not agree" with the Marxist theories of dictatorship of the proletariat, revolution, and the suppression of religion.

This was Remington's picture of himself. Those who knew him agreed that it was a true picture. One of my own personal friends, one of the best and most responsible New York newspapermen, was a classmate of Remington's and a co-worker with him on *The Daily Dartmouth.* His intimate, independent assessment of Remington was this:

> He was exceptionally young, exceptionally brilliant. Some of the letters that he and his mother used to write to each other were marvels of English composition; they read like something out of Bertrand Russell. Remington, though he was so young, was tall and strong and handsome. He had the build of a marvelous athlete, but he wasn't interested in trying to make the football team. He was completely wrapped up in intellectual causes. He felt that the mentally brilliant had a moral obligation to devote themselves to the cause of the underdog, the underprivileged.
>
> My roommate, who was a Catholic and very conservative, looked askance at Remington and the intellectual crowd with whom he ran. To him, they all seemed like a bunch of radicals and lefties, if not Communists. To me, Remington seemed more like an intellectual snob.

My friend recalls one incident that convinced him Remington wasn't a Communist. In the late thirties, the Communists were trying to woo the more intellectually brilliant college students, and they had organizers on most of the college campuses, including Dartmouth.

Once, in a group discussion, my friend recalls, Remington tangled with a couple of them and tore their philosophy to shreds. "He really chewed them out."

These college years have been stressed because it was the events of these years that were ultimately to send Remington to prison. His intellectual life on the Dartmouth campus was one phase; his love life, another. When he was a senior, he had what was to become for him the tragic misfortune of meeting and falling in love with a slender, pretty brunette, Ann Moos, of Bennington College in Vermont.

Ann was the daughter of Mrs. Elizabeth Moos, a teacher and school principal, with a large home at Croton-on-Hudson in Westchester County. The mother was about to become an avowed Communist. Her home for years was to be the rendezvous for kindred spirits. And her daughter was already an ideological spitfire, by all the evidence considerably more radical than Remington himself. Remington recognized this—but he was a man in love.

After their marriage in 1938, Remington studied economics for a year at Columbia University. Receiving his master's degree in 1940, he went into government service and rose steadily. During the war he served for two years as an ensign in Navy Intelligence; later he worked on the European Recovery Program; and he became a member of the President's Council of Economic Advisers. In 1948, he was transferred to the Commerce Department and became director of the export programs staff of the Office of International Trade, a sensitive post in determining the allocation of shipments to Russia. He had reached this stage in his career when, in the witch-hunts of 1948, the figure of Elizabeth Bentley crossed his path.

She injected Remington's name into eight-column headlines when she took the witness stand before a Senate investigating committee headed by Senator Homer Ferguson, Michigan Republican. She testified that Remington, for years, had been a Communist. She had been introduced to him first in New York, had met him subsequently many times in Washington, and had collected Communist Party dues from him for himself and his wife. According to Miss Bentley—and this is a point that cannot be too strongly stressed in assessing the validity of her testimony, for it was a key point, positively testified to, that was not to remain positive—she and Remington had met alone. These were "furtive" meetings on street corners, park benches, and at lunches in secluded restaurants. There were about a dozen rendez-vous of this kind during 1942 and 1943 while Remington was with the War Production Board, and Remington gave her, Miss Bentley testified, confidential details he had written out on slips of paper. Never did she see confidential government documents. And she was vague, as always, on specifics. Some of the confidential details, she said, related to American airplane production, and once Remington gave her a secret formula for making synthetic rubber out of garbage.

Remington appeared before the committee the next day. In his testimony then, in subsequent newspaper interviews, and later in his testimony at two trials, he was to tell the same unvarying story. It was a story that confirmed Miss Bentley on surface details but con-tradicted her emphatically on the specifics of what had happened.

One of Remington's crosses in life had been his mother-in-law. An inseparable friend of Mrs. Moos had been Joseph North, editor of the Communist publication *New Masses*. Remington testified that he had encountered North in his mother-in-law's home and that he had argued heatedly with him because North had doubts about the sincerity of big business in the war effort. The argument led to a fateful invitation: North suggested Remington have lunch with him in New York to continue the discussion.

Remington agreed. At the luncheon, he said, North introduced him to "John" Golos (Miss Bentley's Jacob Golos), and this Golos, "acid in his remarks and outlook on life," said he was preparing a book on war mobilization and would like to talk to Remington about it the next time the young man was in New York. Remington, young and perhaps a bit naïve, testified that he was flattered by the idea a writer might need his help.

On his next visit to New York, in March, 1942, he and his wife dined with Golos in Schrafft's. Golos had a woman with him whom he introduced as Helen Johnson, a researcher who was helping him gather facts about his book. Golos explained that she was also doing research for other writers, including a couple of columnists on Marshall Field's experimental newspaper, *PM*. It was not until years later, Remington always insisted, that he was startled to learn that spy queen Elizabeth Bentley was the woman he had known as Helen Johnson, researcher.

In an experience that seems to parallel that of Duncan Lee, Remington described the manner in which this "Helen Johnson" quickly attached herself to him. At the end of their luncheon engagement in New York, Remington testified, Golos had remarked casually that "Miss Johnson" might give him a call sometime when she was in Washington, and Remington had said, "Oh, sure"—and promptly forgot all about it, never expecting to see her again. He figured without Miss Bentley.

He was surprised when, shortly afterward, she phoned him. She said she was in Washington and in a terrible hurry, but she would like to have lunch with him, could he meet her? Remington agreed. It was the first of some six such meetings that took place in 1942 and five or six other meetings in 1943. "Miss Johnson," Remington said, would never come up to his office; she was always either too far away in the city or so busy she didn't have time. Sometimes, he said, she would bring him copies of the Communist newspaper, *The Daily Worker,* or of *PM* and other periodicals. And she would ask him to check certain details in their articles for her because she wanted to know "if the facts are straight." Remington insisted he had never given her any information except what was publicly available to any correspondent and that he had never paid her Communist dues. On one occasion, he said, he had given her $30 as a donation to the Joint Anti-Fascist Refugee Committee, later exposed as a Communist front, but he insisted he didn't know of its Communist connections at the time. He was simply, as he had always been, anti-Fascist.

This was the story—and the whole story—Remington testified. He said that he had become "a little suspicious" of "Helen Johnson" in 1943, when he learned that she did not represent writers on *PM,* as she had pretended, and that he then broke off all contact with her.

Remington's confirmation of Miss Bentley's testimony regarding the surface pattern of their relationship did him incalculable harm with the members of a committee oriented toward a spy hunt. His insistence that it all had a far different meaning was received with skepticism, but there seemed at the time little chance of proving the issue one way or the other. According to the uncontroverted and dovetailing testimony of both Remington and Miss Bentley herself, no third party had ever been present at their Washington meetings, at which, she testified, information had been passed. It was his word against hers.

But there were more ominous clouds on the horizon. Remington revealed in his testimony that he and his wife were in the process of getting a divorce. His offhand remarks, sprinkled through the record of the hearing, reveal an especially bitter, deep-seated animus toward his Communist mother-in-law. At one point he noted that after Mrs. Moos became a Communist, "She became, God forbid, even more arbitrary." At another point, in an almost prophetic vein, Remington commented on the temper of the times in an exchange with Senator Ferguson: "When we are threatened by an external enemy and one from within, I realize we cannot stand by our democratic processes in full relation to the individual."

Senator Ferguson, like a good politician, took umbrage at this. "We can stand by them," he assured Remington.

"Not in the same way," Remington demurred.

The issue was to prove, in a tragic manner, how correct he was.

Miss Bentley's accusations against Remington precipitated a hearing before the Loyalty Board to determine whether he was fit to hold his government job. For anyone hunting the kernel of truth in the conflicting testimony, these proceedings were to prove the clearest guide. There can be no question that Remington was handicapped. Friends in government service, fearful of wiretaps, refused to talk to him except in the most circumspect way, from pay telephone booths. Many on whose support he had counted faded away at the first whisper of the accusations against him. But many others stood firm and, by so standing, registered two telling points that speak loudly in Remington's favor.

The first point: He could never have been a secret Communist. It was for him completely out of character. If he had been a Communist, he would have climbed on a soapbox and shouted it from the housetops.

The second point, more conclusive, deals with his well-established pattern of action as a government official over the years, which showed that, in his conduct of official affairs, he had been almost too strongly anti-Communist.

Remington's high school English teacher, the former president of Dartmouth, and Dean Lloyd K. Neidlinger, of Dartmouth, all underscored the first point. Dean Neidlinger perhaps put it best when he wrote: "If he believed in Communism, he might go out and preach it from a soapbox and risk being stoned by an unfriendly audience." Mrs. George W. Martin, his high school teacher, who had known him since he was five, wrote in an affidavit that she questioned Miss Bentley's testimony the instant she applied the word "furtive" to Remington. "I am positive he couldn't even be coached to *be,* or even to *appear,* furtive," she wrote.

As to actions, by which, after all, a man should be judged, there appeared even less doubt. David K. Bruce, former Assistant Secretary of Commerce and Ambassador to France, declared in an affidavit that Remington was sometimes so anti-Russian in the policies he advocated that he had to be restrained. Richard M. Bissell, Jr., who had been Remington's boss on the Harriman European Recovery Committee, testified that Remington had been so enthusiastic about extending aid to Western Europe to counter Communist aggression that some of his suggestions had to be toned down. A State Department official deposed that Remington had been much tougher-minded about Russia than State. A high military spokesman said that from the military's standpoint his thinking had been right on the beam. The picture so developed was the very antithesis of that of a Communist conniver. Yet the Loyalty Board, reacting to the new era in which suspicion, once cast, outweighed facts, however positive, ordered Remington dismissed from government service.

Remington had an impulse, as he later said, "to throw in the towel." It was the only way, indeed, by which he could have saved himself.

Instead, he elected to fight for vindication. He obtained for the first time an attorney, a redoubtable one, Joseph L. Rauh, Jr., then chairman of the executive committee of Americans for Democratic Action. Rauh, a fighting liberal whom rightists as a consequence have always been eager to try to smear with a Communist tar brush, was extremely wary of the Remington case at the outset. At his first meeting with Remington, he grilled the economist in his toughest courtroom style from 6 o'clock in the evening until two the next morning. Then he took another week probing every angle of Remington's life, questioning everyone he could find who had ever known him. Finally, convinced, he took the case.

His first move was to ask the Loyalty Review Board to summon Miss Bentley for examination. The board had no power of subpoena, but it asked her to appear, first on Nov. 22, then on Dec. 15, 1948. Miss Bentley was always too busy to show up. First she was lecturing in Buffalo, then in New Orleans. The review board's patience began to wear thin; and on January 10, 1949, when the *New York Post* quoted Miss Bentley in an interview as contending she had never been asked to testify, the board publicly contradicted her. On February 10, 1948, the board ordered Remington reinstated.[10]

It was, it appeared, complete vindication, and it was followed by another triumph. Remington had sued Miss Bentley, the National Broadcasting Company, and General Foods, the sponsor, for $100,-000 worth of libel because Miss Bentley had repeated her charges against him on "Meet the Press." Over Miss Bentley's protests, the corporate defendants, though denying the libel, decided it was better to settle out of court for $10,000.

Remington had scored a triumph that threatened the very structure of the witch-hunt. It was a triumph that could not be allowed to stand.

As Joseph Rauh later wrote in his petition to the United States Supreme Court: "His case received so much public notice that it was natural for the issue of Bentley's credibility to focus on whether she was right about Remington." Rauh pointed out that Miss Bentley's livelihood had come to depend on writing and lectures in which she related her experiences as the Communist spy queen. He asked a pregnant question: "How could she continue lecturing or publish a book about experiences that had been successfully challenged by Remington, and about which the Government had done nothing, unless something were done to prove Remington a liar?"

There began now what can only be described as a determined campaign to "get" Remington. In April and May, 1950, the House Un-American Activities Committee took up the cudgels, producing evidence designed to show that Remington had been a Communist in Knoxville, Tennessee, in 1936–1937 when he worked there for a year with the Tennessee Valley Authority between his sophomore and junior years in college. Remington was called before the House committee. He was called before a grand jury in Washington. This grand jury, like another grand jury that previously had studied the evidence, refused to indict.

Now a third grand jury was impaneled, in New York. The setup, as it was later exposed over the bleats and protests of the government, was enough to make one shudder. The foreman was John Brunini, who had a contract with Miss Bentley to help her prepare a book on her spy-ring appearances for the Devin-Adair Company—a book that would name Remington as a Communist and a spy, a book that could not possibly be published unless Remington were indicted and convicted. The prosecutor presenting the evidence to the jury was Thomas F. Donegan, one of Hoover's former FBI agents, a lawyer who, prior to returning to government service, had represented Miss Bentley as her attorney and had been successful in obtaining some $7,500 for her in one legal action.

One other vital element of the case had now been changed: the Remington divorce had been completed. Under our laws, a wife cannot be compelled to testify against her husband, but, ironically enough, a divorced wife, whose testimony it would seem might run far more risk of bias, can be required to testify to events that were not strictly private during her marriage—in other words, to occurrences at which outsiders were present.

The New York grand jury, taking advantage of this opportunity, subpoenaed Ann Remington to testify before it. Brunini and Donegan hounded her (no gentler word will serve) through a long day of third-degree style questioning. Subsequently, Remington himself was called before the jury, and for five successive days Brunini and Donegan battered at him. The purpose, Rauh maintained in his Supreme Court brief, obviously was to protect Bentley at the expense of Remington, for the questioning covered a wide spread of extraneous matters with which the jury properly had no concern. "Examples," Rauh wrote, ". . . were what Remington's investigators during the libel suit uncovered about Bentley. Who was financing Remington's defense? Whether he knew certain reporters who had written favorable stories about petitioner and unfavorable stories about Bentley? Why hadn't he resigned from the government? What had these subjects to do with espionage—the only matter which the special grand jury was impanelled to investigate? Obviously, their only purpose was to aid the campaign to rehabilitate Bentley."

Finally, Remington "was asked the crucial question upon the answer to which the rehabilitation of Bentley's credibility depended." The question was: "At any time have you ever been a member of the Communist Party?" Remington answered: "I never have been." On June 8, 1950, for giving this answer, he was indicted for perjury. The day the indictment was voted Remington resigned his government post.

He now sought a reputable New York attorney to represent him at the trial. His choice fell on William C. Chanler, an independent Democrat who had served as city Corporation Counsel in the Fusion administration of Fiorello H. La Guardia. A corporation lawyer, Chanler was a member of the Wall Street law firm in which the distinguished Henry L. Stimson had been a partner. He was certainly no radical, and he was disturbed at the outset by the implications of his possible involvement in the Remington case. He wanted to make certain, as he himself frankly says, just what he was getting into, and so, in Washington on business, he went to see the attorneys who had represented Mrs. Remington in the divorce action.

Mrs. Remington's attorneys made it clear that they did not feel very kindly towards Remington. They had had a difficult time with him in the divorce action, and they felt he was a penny pincher because he hadn't wanted to give his wife a dime of alimony for the support of herself and their two children. Nevertheless, they said, it was perfectly clear to them that Remington had never been a Communist. Chanler asked how they could possibly be so certain, and they told him that, when Ann Remington was subpoenaed to testify before the New York grand jury, she came to them seeking advice. They asked her: "Well, what's your story?"

Her story, as she related it to her own lawyers, Chanler says, "was a perfectly innocent" one. In essence, it was this: Ann and Remington had never been actual members of the Communist Party. They had been, of course, through her mother, quite close to many members of the Party; they had been well-acquainted with Joseph North, with whom Remington often argued violently. Remington, indeed, had never been as far left in his political philosophy as Ann herself had desired. As the years passed, they had had less and less to do with her mother's Communist friends. And as for Helen Johnson, they had known her only as a magazine researcher. Hearing this story, Ann's Washington attorneys could see no danger in it, and they advised her to go ahead and testify to it. She went to New York, had the day-long session before the grand jury, and when she came back wouldn't say much about what had happened. But the upshot had been that Remington had been indicted.

Chanler was convinced that the grand jury performance must have been a real star-chamber, third-degree session, and he strove desperately at Remington's first trial to gain access to the minutes that would have proved this. A hostile court denied him this elementary right, but later (too late to do Remington any good) the appeals court reversed this ruling and permitted Remington's attorneys to inspect the minutes. Even then, however, even in their final appeal to the Supreme Court, they were not permitted to quote directly from the minutes, but only to indicate the pages of the grand jury testimony. With an understanding of these restrictions, it is illuminating to read Rauh's summary in his final brief. He wrote:

> The minutes of Ann Remington's testimony show that she told the first grand jury substantially the same story concerning her own and her husband's activities and beliefs that petitioner [Remington] has consistently maintained through six years of questioning. She testified that she and petitioner started off as persons interested in the American Student Union, Loyalist Spain, and labor unions, who were sympathetic to Communism. She steadfastly maintained that they had never been members of the Communist Party (GJ 7747, 7748, 7754, 7761, 7766, 7767, 7783, 7793) and even related that they had had the usual disillusioning experience of persons sympathetic with Communism in the 1930's when the Nazi-Soviet Pact and the Russo-Finnish war came along (GJ 7764)—two years, incidentally, before they met Bentley. Foreman Brunini's efforts to get Mrs. Remington to change her testimony by poisoning her mind with alleged lies Remington had told about her and her mother (GJ 7766, 7806) and by implications that he was spending his money on a libel suit against Bentley instead of supporting her (GJ 7775–7776) were unsuccessful and Mrs. Remington stuck to her earlier answers through the continuous grilling (GJ 7741–7826), flattery (GJ 7795) and threats of perjury (GJ 7761,

7803). After hours of grilling—it was now about three o'clock in the afternoon—Mrs. Remington stated that she was getting fuzzy and incoherent because she hadn't eaten for such a long time, apparently having flown up from Washington in an airplane early that morning. She repeatedly referred to her hunger and need for something to eat (GJ 7825, 7826). At this stage, fuzzy and denied food, she asked whether hunger was being used on her as a third-degree weapon (GJ 7825). Foreman Brunini's response to this and to Mrs. Remington's repeated request for something to eat was that the grand jury hadn't shown its teeth yet (GJ 7827). At this point, the foreman stated categorically that Ann Remington had no privilege to refuse to answer any question and threatened her with jail if she did refuse to answer (GJ 7827). Ann Remington thereupon reversed her testimony and gave Brunini and Donegan the answer they had been seeking for hours and the corroboration necessary for the purpose of rehabilitating Bentley and indicting the petitioner. A minute later, at 3:16 p.m. (GJ 7830), she was allowed to eat (GJ 7830). Foreman Brunini's guilty conscience became evident later in the day when he asked the witness if she felt they had tried to starve her out (GJ 7845). Despite the fact that Mrs. Remington at this time was "cooperating" fully with Brunini and Donegan, she indicated clearly that the answer she had given at their urging had been the result of hunger (GJ 7845).

If the facts already related could leave any possible doubt that Brunini was representing Bentley in the grand jury room, the Court's attention is respectfully invited to pages 7806 through 7809 of the grand jury minutes. There Brunini says that it is not Remington himself who is important; that he is a very minor figure in Bentley's story of her espionage activities, but he had become extraordinarily important because he has chosen to talk and fight back at Bentley. There, too, Brunini lectures Mrs. Remington (and the other grand jurors) that it is extremely important for the American people to be awakened to the dangers that have been related by the ex-Communists, such as Bentley, who have come forward and told their stories, but who have been smeared by persons such as Remington.[11]

Obviously, no such quotes-banned, restricted summary can do full justice to the horror of that scene in the grand jury room. Judge Learned Hand, whom the lower courts could not muzzle as they could Remington's attorneys, later wrote a Brandeis-like dissent in the Remington case in which he lifted the veil on some of the dialogue used in bludgeoning Mrs. Remington. Declaring that this had gone beyond the bounds of what he deemed permissible, Judge Hand wrote:

> Pages on pages of lecturing repeatedly preceded a question; statements of what the prosecution already knew, and of how idle it was for the witness to hold back what she could contribute; occasional reminders that she could be punished for perjury; all were scattered throughout. Still she withstood the examiners, until, being much tired and worn, she said: "I am getting fuzzy. I haven't eaten since a long time ago and I don't think I'm going to be very coherent from now on. I would like to postpone the hearings. . . . I want to consult my lawyers and see how deep I am getting in." This was denied, and the questioning kept on until she finally refused to answer, excusing herself because she was "tired," and "would like to get something to eat. . . . Is this the third degree, waiting until I get hungry, now?" Still the examiners persisted, disregarding this further protest: "I would like to get something to eat. But couldn't we continue another day? Or do I have to come back?"

At this point, Brunini, Miss Bentley's collaborator, took over with a long, threatening question that finally "broke" Mrs. Remington and made her testify as Brunini and Donegan wanted her to testify.

"Mrs. Remington, I think that we have been very kind and considerate," he said, though the record is certainly such as to make any man shun Brunini's kindness and consideration. "We haven't raised our voices and shown our teeth, have we? Maybe you don't know about our teeth. A witness before a Grand Jury hasn't the privilege of refusing to answer a question [here he painted for her a picture of the manner in which a judge could send a witness to jail for refusing to answer a grand jury question]. . . . You have no privilege to refuse to answer the question. I don't want at this time . . . I said 'showing teeth.' I don't want them to bite you. But I do want you to know that——"

Actually, as Judge Hand pointed out, Mrs. Remington did have a privilege. It extended to all confidential communications between herself and Remington while she was his wife, and her testimony dealt largely with just such confidences. Again, as Judge Hand pointed out, this must have been clear to Donegan, a lawyer, but he stood idly by and did nothing to correct the impression the blustering Brunini had implanted in the mind of the witness. In this situation, unaware of her rights, obviously accepting Brunini's word that she had no privilege, threatened with jail, threatened with perjury, hungry and worn out by the unremitting ordeal of the day-long questioning, Mrs. Remington began to give the testimony that would doom her former husband and the father of her two children.[22]

Against this background, Chanler walked into New York Federal Court, facing the almost impossible task of trying to establish the innocence of his client. He was confronted by a formidable array of federal prosecutors. The government team was headed by United States Attorney Irving S. Saypol, who was assisted by Roy M. Cohn (later Senator McCarthy's legal brain) and Donegan. On the bench was Judge Gregory F. Noonan.

Chanler's first move was to argue that the indictment should be dismissed because it did not spell out the crime of which Remington stood accused. Just what constituted Communist Party membership? What would be considered proof? What did his client have to meet? Chanler had asked the government to define its concept, and it had refused. He argued (an argument that was to be upheld on appeal) that the government was accusing his client of lying in denying a certain status—and at the same time was either unable or unwilling to define "what constitutes that status."

Judge Noonan set the tone for much that was to follow when he snapped back, "Your argument is ingenious but without merit." He added that it was "not incumbent on the Government in a perjury trial to define terms relating to Communism." Let the defendant do it. The defendant could say whether he was a Communist or not "and what that means," Judge Noonan ruled, adding that "the double-talk that goes on in Communism defies definition."

Chanler fired back that the judge's statement that Remington knew best what Communist Party membership meant carried with it the inevitable implication of a presumption of guilt—and "I must remind Your Honor that this defendant is presumed to be innocent." Noonan responded that he "personally resented" the insinuation that he would presume the defendant to be guilty, though it is difficult to see what other interpretation could be placed on his words and his conduct.

Now came the first witness for the prosecution—not Elizabeth

Bentley but the former wife of Remington. Now, just as in the Hiss case, the entire basis of the prosecution suddenly changed. What had been solid fact, what had been testified to repeatedly under oath and had evidently been accepted even by the government itself as solid fact, was fact no longer. From the start, everyone had agreed— Elizabeth Bentley had so testified, Remington had so testified—that when they met in Washington, they met alone. No third party had been present. Now, suddenly, on the witness stand, needing corroboration for Miss Bentley, the prosecution presented the invisible woman—Mrs. Ann Moos Remington. She had been there all the time.

She had been present, she testified, at that very first rendezvous for two at Pennsylvania Avenue and 14th Street in Washington, to which both Miss Bentley and Remington had previously testified. Only it hadn't happened at all the way everybody previously had testified it had happened. The meeting had taken place in the Remington family car, with Mrs. Remington herself an interested spectator. Remington, his former wife testified, had given Miss Bentley "some pieces of paper." And she herself had been "disappointed" because the spy courier had failed to bring along any interesting Communist tracts to elevate the spirit.

At a second meeting, she testified, her former husband gave Miss Bentley a "top secret" formula for making "explosives" out of garbage. Miss Bentley had always testified that the formula was for making synthetic rubber out of garbage, but why haggle over such little details? The important thing was, wasn't it, that Remington had been a Communist and a spy?

Miss Bentley, having been corroborated by Mrs. Remington in advance of her own appearance, now testified that Mrs. Remington had been, indeed, present at "three or four" of the meetings between herself and Remington. Chanler, on cross-examination, hammered hard at the conflicts in Miss Bentley's testimony, but she always had an explanation. She had been a poor, awed, confused little woman when she testified before Senate and House committees. "It was the first time I had ever testified in public, and I can assure you it was nerve-wracking," she explained. Chanler shot back: "More nerve-wracking than stealing government documents?"

Two striking events that occurred during the course of the trial

were indicative of the massed, overwhelming pressures a lone defendant had to combat if he dared, in this atmosphere, to try to establish
his innocence. The first dealt with a determined government effort to
try to prove that Remington had been a Communist in 1936–1937
while he was working for the TVA—and that he had attended Communist meetings in Knoxville. The meetings were supposed to have
been held in the apartment of one Betty Malcolm. A key witness for
the prosecution in this phase, Howard A. Bridgman, a Tufts economics professor, had testified that he saw Remington in these sessions
in the winter or early spring of 1937. This new testimony against
Remington had been widely publicized before the trial, and Joseph
Rauh had spotted a rather important discrepancy. Employment records showed that Betty Malcolm had not even arrived in Knoxville
until June 17, 1937. Rauh had called this vital contradiction to
Donegan's attention when he was presenting the evidence to the grand
jury, but did this make the government the less reluctant to advance
the contention? It did not.

Bridgman under cross-examination by Chanler admitted that he
was absolutely "floored" when confronted with proof that Betty
Malcolm had not arrived in Knoxville until June 17. He admitted
that he couldn't reconcile this vital discrepancy in his story, though
the FBI had done its best to help him. FBI agents had called on him
once a week or at least once every two weeks between June, 1950,
and the time of the trial, January, 1951. They had even taken him
down to Knoxville and driven him around there in an attempt to
refresh his memory, Bridgman testified; but the best he could say
now was that the meetings at which he had seen Remington must
have taken place not in the winter but in June.

This June date was not much more propitious for the prosecution than Bridgman's earlier winter time-table had been. As it happened, Remington's father, Frederick C. Remington, had cultivated
the years-long practice of keeping a diary in a little black notebook.
A notation in it showed that Remington had arrived home from his
TVA job on either July 1 or 2, 1937, after hitchhiking all the way
back from Tennessee, making it clear that it would have been virtually impossible for him to have participated in a series of Communist
meetings in the apartment of a woman who was not even in Knoxville
until June 17.

The eagerness of the prosecution to use any testimony that could be scraped up, however dubious, was not half so shocking as another tactic of crass intimidation used by the government to keep Remington from adequately defending himself. This was the practice of keeping a federal grand jury in session while the trial was in progress and of calling potential Remington witnesses before the grand jury prior to their appearance in court. This unconscionable action, upheld by Judge Noonan over Chanler's protests as perfectly proper, succeeded in blocking for all time testimony that might well have been pivotal to Remington's defense.

Great suspicion was cast on Remington's denial that he had ever been a Communist by the accounts of his conduct during his student days at Dartmouth. His former wife had now testified that he had been a Communist at that time, and the government bore down hard on the angle. Chanler was convinced the point was phony. He had located in New Hampshire ex-Communists who could testify that Remington had never been one of them. Furthermore, Communist Party records in New Hampshire had been carefully kept, and Chanler had located an official of the party, a woman, who had them in her possession and who could testify that Remington's name had never appeared on the rolls.

"We told our witnesses to wait, we would call them when we needed them," Chanler says. In an account that reminds one of the experiences of Chester Lane and his staff in the Hiss case, he continues:

Then, I suppose, I made a mistake. I telephoned them from my office, using my regular phone, and told them to come to New York. The next morning when they arrived, two FBI agents were waiting on the station platform with subpoenas for them to appear before the grand jury. They were so frightened that they notified us they would claim their constitutional privilege and refuse to testify. And so we had to let them go back to New Hampshire, unheard.

The result was hardly surprising. On February 7, 1951, after deliberating 4 hours and 25 minutes, the trial jury convicted Remington.

On appeal, the Federal Court of Appeals, in a unanimous decision, threw out the conviction, sharply criticizing both Saypol and Judge Noonan. Upholding Chanler's contention, it ruled that Judge Noonan had erred in not spelling out to the jury what constituted proof of Communist Party membership. Even at the conclusion of the trial, the appeals court held, Remington could not have known "what he had to meet" properly to defend himself. The court, however, did not quash the indictment. It left the door open to the government, if it wished, to do battle on the same grounds again.

The government did not wish. In an action that can only be construed as tantamount to a confession of past sin, it had Remington indicted for a second time on October 25, 1951, charging that he had committed perjury during his testimony in his own defense at his first trial. Having produced this new charge, the government then blandly moved to dismiss and so get rid of the original Brunini-Donegan indictment.

The second trial was brief, almost perfunctory. John McKim Minton, one of New York's foremost criminal-trial attorneys, represented Remington, who had virtually exhausted the means to defend himself. The jury eliminated three counts of the five-count indictment, but it convicted Remington on two charges—lying when he denied passing secret documents to Miss Bentley and lying in response to a question that Saypol had slipped inobtrusively into his cross-examination in the first trial, that he had *knowledge* about the existence of the Young Communist League on the Dartmouth campus when he was there.

The defense argued on appeal that Remington had been made the victim of a clear case of entrapment. The faulty first indictment, obtained by methods so indefensible that the government had been compelled to abandon it, had been used to place the defendant, if not technically, certainly actually, in double jeopardy. This was the view that Judge Learned Hand upheld in a stinging dissent in which he referred to star-chamber practices of the past and the Spanish Inquisition. He held, not just that the conviction of Remington should be reversed, but that the indictment should be quashed and the entire case against him abandoned. The other two members of the appeals court, however, sustained the conviction.

Rauh carried the appeal to the Supreme Court, but the court refused, just as it had refused in the Hiss case, even to consider the argument. According to Chanler, Judge Hand afterward confided that he felt the Supreme Court had made a great mistake. The Remington case, he said, had caused him greater concern than any case that had come before him in a long career on the bench.

Remington, who had married his secretary after his divorce from his first wife, was sentenced to three years in prison, and on April 15, 1953, was sent to the Lewisburg, Pennsylvania, federal penitentiary. There, on the morning of November 22, 1954, the final act in his tragedy took place. Three convicts, who apparently had been looting prison cells, entered his cell. When he tried to resist, he was beaten savagely over the head with a cloth-wrapped brick. His skull fractured in several places, Remington was rushed to the prison hospital, where he died on the operating table without regaining consciousness. He was only 37.

Less than two months later, a little-reported footnote cropped up in New Hampshire. Attorney General Louis G. Wyman, on January 5, 1955, filed with the legislature a 289-page report detailing the results of his 18-months investigation of Communist activities at Dartmouth. He cited testimony that Remington, in his college days, had never been a Communist. One witness especially, the Attorney General said, had testified that the Communists in the Dartmouth undergraduate circles at the time had wanted no part of Remington "because he was considered too erratic as to timing and sense of responsibility." This was the very testimony that Chanler had hoped to introduce in the first trial—but had been prevented from introducing by that obvious wiretap on his telephone line and the government's tactic in subpoenaing and intimidating his witnesses.

Such was the manner in which the government obtained, out of all the sensational charges of Whittaker Chambers and Elizabeth Bentley, two convictions. Such were the developments that enabled J. Edgar Hoover to boast before a Senate committee, with evident satisfaction, that the testimony of Elizabeth Bentley had been upheld by trial and appeal and had been found on all counts to be reliable.

■ 3 ■

Alger Hiss had been convicted. William Remington had been convicted—and murdered. There remained now only to try the dead. In one of the most ghoulish exhibitions of the witch-hunt, staged by men insensitive to all but political advantage, this feat was now to be attempted.

The victim was Harry Dexter White. The charge was that he had been a Russian spy.

Both Whittaker Chambers and Elizabeth Bentley had implicated White in their original testimony, but their testimony against him had been far less positive than it had been about many of the others, notably Hiss and Remington. Neither had been able to testify positively that White had ever been a Communist. The best they could say was that he was widely known in Communist circles as a sympathizer—and, if he hadn't been a Communist, he should have been.

Here is the way Miss Bentley put it in her testimony before the House committee on July 30, 1948:

> Miss Bentley: I don't know whether Mr. White was a card-carrying Communist or not.
> Mr. Stripling: What was the extent of his cooperation with your group?
> Miss Bentley: He gave information to Mr. Silvermaster which was relayed to me.

Here is Whittaker Chambers on the subject three days later:

> Mr. Stripling: Is Harry Dexter White a Communist?
> Mr. Chambers: I can't say positively that he was a registered member of the Communist Party, but he certainly was a fellow traveler so far within the fold that his not being a Communist would be a mistake on both sides.

Harry Dexter White was a brilliant man. Of Russian-Jewish extraction, as later propaganda was heavily to emphasize, he was born in Boston in 1892, served overseas as a First Lieutenant in the Army in World War I, later attended Massachusetts Agricultural College, and did postgraduate work at Columbia, Stanford, and Harvard. He was an economics instructor at Harvard for six years and received his Ph.D. from Harvard in 1930. In 1934 he went to Washington as an assistant to Secretary of the Treasury Henry M. Morgenthau and became one of Morgenthau's right-hand men. He headed the Division of Research, became Assistant Secretary of the Treasury, and finally, in the Truman Administration, was appointed to the International Monetary Fund. His brilliance and ability impressed the top-grade British economists with whom he was thrown into close contact in the international monetary conferences that preceded the close of World War II.

When White's name was catapulted into the rash of spy-scare headlines by Miss Bentley and Whittaker Chambers in August, 1948, he had already been out of government service for a year. He had suffered a severe heart attack the previous year, and from Labor Day into December he had been confined to his bed, recovering from the ravages of his illness. The Klieg-light atmosphere of the House hearings could hardly be recommended therapy for such a man, but White asked to take the witness stand and appeared before the committee on August 13, 1948. He denied every tittle of the tales of Bentley and Chambers in testimony whose candor subsequently impressed Earl Jowitt, the former British Lord Chancellor. At one point, much to the discomfiture of the committee, White drew a spontaneous outburst of applause from the audience when he stated his creed. He testified:

"My creed is the American creed. I believe in freedom of religion, freedom of speech, freedom of thought, freedom of the press, freedom of criticism, and freedom of movement. I believe in the goal of equality of opportunity, and the right of each individual to follow the calling of his or her own choice, and the right of every individual to an opportunity to develop his or her capacity to the fullest.

"I believe in the right and duty of every citizen to work for, to expect, and to obtain an increasing measure of political, economic, and emotional security for all. I am opposed to discrimination in any form, whether on grounds of race, color, religions, political belief, or economic status.

"I believe in the freedom of choice of one's representatives in Government, untrammeled by machine guns, secret police, or a police state.

"I am opposed to arbitrary and unwarranted use of power authority from whatever source or against any individual or group.

"I believe in a government of law, not of men, where law is above any man, and not any man above law.

"I consider these principles sacred. I regard them as the basic fabric of our American way of life, and I believe in them as living realities, and not as mere words on paper.

"That is my creed. Those are the principles I have worked for. Together those are the principles that I have been prepared in the past to fight for, and am prepared to defend at any time with my life, if need be."

White denied ever knowing either Miss Bentley or Chambers, bringing himself into direct conflict with Chambers, who had described an emotional scene in which, after his own break with Communism, he had gone to White and pleaded with him to break too—that is, he explained, since he did know whether White had ever actually been a Communist, to "break" with the philosophy. On the other hand, White acknowledged knowing nearly all the suspects on Miss Bentley's list. Some, he said, he knew only vaguely, having been thrown into brief contact with them in his official capacity; some he knew better; and others he knew well and admired—and would be very surprised if they turned out to be Communists.

One significant bit of byplay indicated the miasma of official suspicion that clouded every inconsequential word of White. He had remarked that he fancied himself as a Ping-Pong player, and Chairman Thomas pounced like a cat on a mouse.

Thomas: Just a minute, right there. Let me see that note. One thing I cannot reconcile, Mr. White. You send me a note and you say that: "I am recovering from a severe heart attack. I would appreciate it if the chairman would give me 5 or 10 minutes' rest after each hour." For a person who had a severe heart condition, you certainly can play a lot of sports.

White: I did not intend that this note should be read aloud. I do not know any reason why it should be public that I am ill, but I think probably one of the reasons why I suffered a heart attack was because I played so many sports, and so well. The heart attack which I suffered was last year. I am speaking of playing Ping-Pong, and I was a fair tennis player, and a pretty good ball player, many years prior to that. I hope that clears that up, Mr. Chairman.

Thomas: Yes, sir. (Applause.)

Throughout White's testimony, there runs a subtle thread that has been generally ignored but should be noted. Asked if he had "investigated all these people" who served under him in Treasury, he responded that he had not personally, "but we have a very excellent Secret Service in the Treasury, and all cases were turned over to them for investigation." He plainly implied that, if Secret Service approved the employees, as it had, he would be content to take the word of Secret Service above all others. White, who had known Silvermaster well, had been shocked at the first intimations of Communist ties in Silvermaster's case. He had read Silvermaster's detailed reply to the charges and then had asked a friend on the Loyalty Board to make certain the facts were carefully investigated. Silvermaster had been cleared for continued government employment. Parenthetically, it should be noted that, following an earlier and more secret rumor, he had been thoroughly investigated by Army G-2 and had been cleared personally by Undersecretary of War Robert P. Patterson, a Republican, after a personal conference with Major General G. V. Strong, head of G-2. It is clear that the FBI and the House committee, with which, as Thomas's earlier statement showed, it was in close partnership, were relying heavily on the trustworthiness of informers. It is also clear, from reading White's frank testimony, that he was not prepared to accept any such criterion, that he would not brand a man unless informer testimony had been subjected to test in a court of law, with the defense having proper opportunity to cross-examine.

His testimony was that of a polite, urbane, self-possessed witness, and he traded good-natured barbs with the committee with such devastating effect that, at one point, the committee virtually begged for mercy, one of its members asking Chairman Thomas to instruct White that he was obviously "a great wit . . . a great entertainer," but please would he just stick to the questions.

The late Thomas L. Stokes, one of the best Washington correspondents of his day, later wrote that White's performance was "reminiscent of a wise college professor . . . a salty philosopher. . . . A less urbane person would have exploded in such a situation, denounced his persecutors, and perhaps waved his arms, shouted and thrown chairs and tables about the room—and with perfectly good reason." Stokes added:

> Watching this finale of the species of persecution which Harry White had endured stirred up a hot lump of indignation within you so that you wanted to rise up and do some of those things yourself and

you wondered, as you watched, why some of our leading figures who believe in fair play do not speak out boldly and bluntly about the tyranny over the mind and the intellect that is practiced in this room. It is frightening, and more so because it is to go on and on.[13]

Those were prophetic words.

Self-possessed though he had been on the witness stand, the ordeal before the House committee proved too much for Harry White's weakened heart. The following day, feeling ill, he visited his doctor in New York and was advised to go to his home in Fitzwilliam, New Hampshire, and stay in bed. On the train ride home, he suffered severe chest pains, and as soon as he arrived, his local doctor was called. In the next two days, two doctors treated him. A cardiogram showed a heart attack in progress. On the afternoon of August 16 he died.

The possible inference that he might have been hounded to a premature death by the witch-hunters naturally was one that could not be permitted to endure. So some of the largest newspapers in the nation—and some prominent right-wing writers—began a campaign to intimate that he had committed suicide. But the truth, according to the physicians who attended him before his death, seems to have negated the propaganda.[14]

Once Harry White was dead, he became free game. One right-wing writer of the period, preparing a magazine spy-ring exposé based on nothing more solid than a vivid imagination, exclaimed joyfully: "Dead men don't sue."

Whittaker Chambers, who had denied that any such thing as espionage had ever been involved in his Communist underground activities, produced after White's death four yellow-pad pages of handwritten notations that White supposedly had passed to him. The handling of this alleged documentary evidence was one of the most peculiar aspects of the entire witch-hunt.

Chambers evidently first exhibited the White memoranda at the November 17, 1948, Baltimore libel hearing at which he produced the alleged Hiss typewritten documents, for on the reverse side of the last sheet occurs the notation "65 big sheets, 4 little slips," evidently referring to the Hiss documents, which totaled exactly that number. Hiss's attorneys, with an obtuseness that seems to have characterized the early stages of his case, retained and turned over to federal prosecutors only the material that directly concerned them, and neither then nor in the later trials did they exhibit any curiosity about the White memoranda. From one obvious standpoint, documents allegedly passed by White were no concern of the Hiss defense and might be expected only to broaden the basis of the case and do Hiss harm. But from another standpoint, they could have been of vital concern, for the White documents came from the same self-proclaimed courier, from that courier's same cache, and any evidence about the validity of one segment of that cache certainly affects the validity of all.

The trail of the White memoranda after the Baltimore libel hearing becomes obscure. They were not part of the so-called "Pumpkin Papers" so dramatically turned over to the House committee by Chambers, for these were all reproductions of State Department documents on rolls of microfilm. Nixon in a speech in the House on January 26, 1950, referred publicly for the first time to the White memoranda but shed no light on how they came into the possession of House investigators. A later published version, written evidently with the collaboration of committee sources, would seem to indicate that Chambers gave the White memoranda to Mundt and Nixon at a call they made on him at his Westminster farm on December 28, 1948. At this meeting, according to this report, Chambers told Mundt and Nixon that White, like Hiss, had been a member of "my special group," feeding him information for transmission to Russia. "The report of this meeting with Chambers—still stamped 'restricted' by the committee—also discloses that Chambers said White gave him original government documents as well as penciled notations of what was afoot." [15]

The gingerly handling of these documents, once the House committee had possession of them, is sufficient in itself to raise goose bumps of suspicion. One might have thought that the FBI's huge technical laboratory, the last word in scientific analysis, would be put instantly to work checking these precious memoranda for proof of their validity. But the FBI's reputation was not to be put on the line in this instance. Instead, Harold J. E. Gessell, a handwriting expert in the Veterans Administration, of all places, was asked to pass on the validity of the documents. In a still more curious move, he was not entrusted with the originals, from which document examiners prefer to work. He was asked to base his opinion on photostats. Gessell did so. He stated that the handwriting was that of Harry Dexter White but he qualified his conclusion by saying that this was subject to verification on examination of the original documents.

The contents of the White memoranda seem hardly earth-shaking: notations like "The Van Zeeland report was not taken seriously here," or "Sec. reading *Red Star over China* and is quite interested." This is information a spy would trouble to transmit in his own handwriting? Earl Jowitt concluded it seemed more likely that these memoranda, marked by crossed-out words and occasional interlinear corrections, were rough notes that White had kept, perhaps for reference in compiling a later diary, and that they never had been intended to serve an espionage purpose.[16]

This conclusion is reinforced by the illogic of one of the notations —a notation so incomplete that it makes no sense. It seems inconceivable that any intelligent man would have written it the way it appears, and it exhibits some evidences of tampering. It reads: "Purchases of Japanese goods by _____ _____ _____ are decreasing sharply while our exports to these countries are increasing."

Evidently Harry White, in this item, used blanks to represent the space required to write the names of certain countries. It is ridiculous to assume that the writer of rough memoranda, as these were, would measure blank spaces so meticulously; it would seem that something must have been written on those lines. Furthermore, why would the writer, if writing a memorandum to himself for future reference, omit the names which represented the only really important information in the memorandum he was writing? Or why would a spy omit the names that represented the only information he had to transmit?

Nathan I. White, Harry White's brother, in an analysis of export-import figures, subsequently showed that the names of three countries—and these alone—evidently fitted the requirements of this memorandum. The three countries were the United Kingdom, India, and the U.S.S.R.! But would a Soviet spy be sending the Soviets information about *their own* export-import figures? To ask the question is to pose the ridiculous. But the evidence, according to Nathan White, does not rest upon such logic alone. He wrote:

> In the enlarged photostat copy made by the writer there is a faint evidence of the capital letter "S" near the end of the blank space in the first line. None of the other countries . . . have the capital letter "S" in the spelling which would place it where the evidence shows it originally was written.
>
> Furthermore, the fact that *all* the names were erased is additional evidence that the U.S.S.R. was one of the countries originally written in this sentence. There is no other possible reason for the erasure of all the names to have been made. For it is obvious that the inclusion of the U.S.S.R. among the countries named would have provided the best proof that the entire memorandum was not intended as information to the Soviets. . . . However, since the erasure of the U.S.S.R. alone would have left a tell-tale blank space, it becomes necessary to erase all the names. It does not matter who made the erasure. The fact that the names were erased is clear proof that the erasure was made to prevent the discovery of indisputable evidence that the memorandum was not written as a report to Russia.[17]

Was this erasure (if Nathan White was correct) the reason the FBI was not asked to examine the White memoranda? Was it the reason that Gessell was asked to work, not from the originals, but from photostats that would be less likely to show the tampering?

The implications are, of course, enormous. For if the White memoranda were really altered—faked to appear to be espionage notes— then we have here the evidence, not of espionage but of a political plot by unscrupulous men to climb to power by framing and smearing high officeholders of the New Deal era. Clearly, if the White memoranda were altered to serve a fraudulent purpose, then all of the suspicions about the Hiss documents are reinforced thousandfold, for both sets of documents came from the same source, and if one is spurious, so almost certainly is the other.

The Bentley-Chambers revelations served political purposes. They led directly to the era of Senator Joseph McCarthy, who filled the land with outcries of subversion and treason in high places. His fantasies were grist for the Republican mill.

The 1953 election, following so closely on the heady Eisenhower triumph of 1952, inflicted a deep shock on Republicans. In key contests, the nation went Democratic. The reflex action of orthodox Republicanism was to whip up a new spy-treason scare. The groundwork had already been laid in a report by the Senate Judiciary Committee titled "Interlocking Subversion in Government Departments." Some 50,000 copies of the report had been distributed to Republican Party workers prior to the fall campaign, and committee sources acknowledged, in the aftermath of the November debacle, that they were getting "help" in distributing another 150,000 copies through private groups and individuals.[18]

Attorney General Herbert Brownell, Jr., supplied a spark to this tinder. In a speech to the Executive Club of Chicago on November 6, 1953, he virtually accused former President Harry Truman of treason by leveling the sensational charge that Truman had promoted Harry White to the International Monetary Fund, though knowing him to be a spy. Brownell declared:

> . . . Harry Dexter White was a Russian spy. He smuggled secret documents to Russian agents for transmission to Moscow. Harry Dexter White was known to be a Communist spy by the very people who appointed him to the most sensitive and important position he ever held in Government service.
>
> The FBI became aware of White's espionage activities *at an early point in his Government career* and from the beginning made reports on these activities to the appropriate officials in authority. But these reports did not impede White's advancement in the Administration. . . .
>
> I can now announce officially, for the first time in public, that *the records in my department show* that White's spying activities for the Soviet Government were reported in detail by the FBI to the White House . . . in December of 1945.
>
> In the face of this information, and incredible though it may seem, President Truman subsequently on Jan. 23, 1946, nominated White, who was then Assistant Secretary of the Treasury, for the even more important position of executive director for the United States in the International Monetary Fund.[19] [Italics added.]

This was the charge that touched off one of the most sensational controversies of the witch-hunt era. Truman responded with a bellow of outrage. He accused the Republicans of the rankest demagoguery.

They had had their pants paddled in the recent election, he said, and they had such a paucity of ideas and issues they could think of nothing but the smear. On the specifics of Brownell's charge, however, Truman exhibited great confusion. First, with the unfortunate tendency he had always shown to join his critics by trying to prove he was tougher on accused Communists than anybody, he declared that, as soon as doubts were cast on White's loyalty, "we fired" him. This plainly wasn't so. White had been promoted and eventually had retired because of ill health, with Truman's glowingly expressed regret. In the face of this clear record, Truman amended his stand to contend that he had let White's nomination to the International Monetary Fund go through, after he became aware of the FBI charges, so that the FBI could keep a better eye on him.

In the uproar that followed, most responsible commentators agreed (see James Reston, for example, in *The New York Times* of November 13, 1953), that everyone involved was being tarred and damaged in one way or another. Damaged most of all was the prestige of the United States and the image of the Presidency. Foreign newspapers reacted with scorn and shock. Eisenhower, who had approved Brownell's attack before it was made, apparently without knowing just what it was going to be, hastily dissociated himself from the whole business, proclaiming he had no doubts about Truman's loyalty and agreeing that his Attorney General, having made so sensational a charge, ought to back it up with evidence. Brownell refused to submit to a press conference and showed no sign of producing the evidence.

This was the situation when, on November 17, 1953, Brownell and Hoover testified before the Senate Internal Security Committee. Brownell's testimony made it clear that the White case traced back to the information supplied by Elizabeth Bentley. He put into the record Hoover's first warning (December, 1945) to the White House, based on Bentley's information; a 71-page report on the Bentley tales of espionage; and a report on White that had gone to the White House in February, 1946, after his appointment to the monetary fund became known. Brownell stressed that there was other corroborative information. Much of this, he said, could not be divulged "without jeopardizing confidential sources of information and techniques of intelligence operations. . . . We will never impair the most impor-

tant work of the FBI by making public FBI reports." What this meant
was that Brownell was proclaiming the right to use FBI reports for
political purposes, as he had done—and at the same time was taking
advantage of the fetish of FBI secrecy to avoid proving his case. The
American public was going to have to take his word—and Hoover's
word—on faith; judgment was going to have to depend, not on trial,
not on proof, but on what officials said those secret files showed.
Such a technique represented, in essence, the enthronement of the
policies of the police state.[20]

Hoover, following Brownell to the stand, backed up the partisan
Attorney General in his partisan charges. He made it clear that he
was the same Hoover of the days of GID, hipped on the theory of a
great internal Red Menace, oblivious of the fact that most Americans
couldn't name a Communist if their lives depended on it. He said:

> There is more involved here than the charges against one man. This
> situation has a background of some thirty-five years of infiltration of
> an alien way of life into what we have been proud to call our consti-
> tutional republic. Our American way of life . . . has been brought
> into conflict with the godless forces of Communism. These Red Fascists
> distort, conceal, misrepresent, and lie to gain their ends. Deceit is their
> very essence.

Having painted the picture, Hoover left no doubt that White had
been a spy and a traitor. He said that, from November 8, 1945 (the
first Bentley flash) to July 24, 1946, seven communications went to
the White House on espionage activities, all specifically naming White
among others. The information, he declared, came "from a total of
thirty sources, the reliability of which had previously been established."

Just how reliable were these sources? One may gather an idea of
their reliability from the only two whom he mentioned—Elizabeth
Bentley and Whittaker Chambers. "I would like to mention one in
particular," he said, in discussing his sources. He then launched into
the blanket endorsement of Miss Bentley, citing the manner in which
her testimony had stood up in court and on appeal. He backed up
Miss Bentley with Whittaker Chambers "and the documents in White's
handwriting, concerning which there can be no dispute"—a highly

unusual accolade for documents that had been handled so circum-
spectly by the House committee. In one cryptic reference, apparently
alluding to the documents, he declared that since White's death
"events transpired which produced facts of an uncontradictable nature
which clearly established the reliability of the information furnished
in 1945 and 1946"—that is, that White had been a spy and a traitor.

This performance staked Hoover's personal reputation and that of
the FBI on the credibility of Elizabeth Bentley and Whittaker Chambers. There can be no boggling of the fact that Hoover was playing
a partisan role, infinitely helpful to the Republicans, infinitely damaging to the Democrats.

Most destructive to Truman's amended contention in the White
case was Hoover's statement that he had never agreed to let White
retain his International Monetary Fund post because this would aid
the FBI in its surveillance. On the contrary. He asserted that White's
appointment actually hampered the FBI, actually reduced its opportunities for surveillance. Furthermore, though Hoover had for years
maintained the fiction that the FBI only reports its findings—it does
not evaluate them, it does not recommend, it does not try to influence
decisions—he now testified he had assured the Attorney General that
his information on White was completely reliable. He added: "I told
the Attorney General I felt it was unwise for White to serve." This,
as Arthur Krock later wrote, "was evaluating plenty." [21]

The unseemly brawl produced one winner: J. Edgar Hoover. James
Reston wrote that Hoover had emerged as "probably the most powerful figure on Capitol Hill," and a digest of editorial opinion throughout the nation supported this view. The overwhelmingly conservative
American press, though not endorsing Brownell's treason charge
against Truman, agreed that the former President had been incredibly naïve or incredibly stupid in retaining White in government after
the FBI first raised a warning flag about him. Nowhere was there
a disposition to question the judgment, so positively stated, that
White had been a spy and a traitor.

Yet there were ample grounds for doubt. Hoover in his testimony
made it clear that the FBI had kept White under close surveillance.
From the time of Elizabeth Bentley's 1945 disclosure (and perhaps
much earlier, as Brownell indicated in his reference to the FBI's

awareness "at an early point" in White's career) Harry Dexter White
had been subjected to every known investigative technique. Arthur
Krock wrote that some 500 FBI agents had been assigned to track
down leads supplied by Elizabeth Bentley and Chambers and to keep
tabs on White.[22] Other reports said that White's mail had been
opened, his telephones tapped. What did all this feverish activity
produce? We will never know, for it is in the sacred files of the FBI.

Wiretap evidence could not have been used, of course, in the
prosecution of White; but it could have been used by Brownell to
justify his charges against a dead man and a past administration.
Washington reporters made every effort to get Brownell to release
such information, if he had it, but he never did. Ernest K. Lindley,
a veteran writer with solid contacts in Washington, noted that the
case against White in 1946 apparently had been inconclusive. He
wrote that he had inquired two years later, in 1948, whether wiretaps
and other evidence not usable in court had nailed down the charge.
"I was told no," he wrote. "My informant was in a position to
know." [23]

The full case against White (except for the suspect memoranda
produced only after his death) was submitted to a federal grand jury
in New York in 1948. This was the grand jury that indicted the top
leaders of the Communist Party. It heard, one must presume, every
iota of evidence the FBI had amassed against White—and it refused
to indict. Hiss and Remington were to be indicted and tried in infinitely suspect procedures, but the case against White, apparently,
was not even that good.

■ 4 ■

Such was the record of the FBI in its collaboration with witch-
hunting Congressional committees. The actions of the FBI in this
area have to be judged infinitely suspect. The admissions of prosecution witnesses in both the Hiss and Remington cases revealed a pattern of intensive, weeks-long, pretrial collaboration with the FBI to
perfect the testimony. Chambers practically lived with the FBI five
days a week for months. The trial records show oppressive FBI

activity—wiretapping and surveillance. Yet the most precious heritage of America is its guarantee of individual freedom, founded on the premise of innocence until proved guilty, on the promise to each and every man of a fair trial. When defense attorneys' telephones are tapped, when witnesses are intimidated before they can testify, there can be no fair trial—and no justice.

■ Notes ■

¹ H. R. Hearings before the Committee on Un-American Activities, 80th Congress, Second Session, pp. 642–659.

² Chambers' private testimony of August 7, 1948, is on pages 661–672 of the H. R. Hearings. Though committee sources, in leaking details to the press, insisted that Chambers had proved his knowledge of Hiss and had sat there "for hours" rattling off facts, the entire transcript of his testimony takes just eleven pages. It is probably the most valuable single checkpoint on Chambers' credibility in the entire case, for while he had some facts, his testimony before this favorable forum, whose members were practically pleading with him to tell more, reveals great gaps of specific knowledge—and little of it was to agree, in its vital details, with the perfected case that ultimately was presented in court.

³ See H. R. Hearings, pp. 1076–1206, for the August 25 testimony of Hiss and Chambers; see pp. 1278–1290 for the August 30 testimony of Chambers.

⁴ For this account of the evidence in the Hiss-Chambers case, I have relied on my own earlier research for *The Unfinished Story of Alger Hiss* (William Morrow & Co., 1958). That book, in turn, was based on the House Hearings, the transcript of the second Hiss trial, newspaper accounts of the time, and such supplementary sources as Chambers' *Witness* (Random House, 1952); Earl Jowitt's *The Strange Case of Alger Hiss* (Doubleday, 1953); and Hiss's *In the Court of Public Opinion* (Alfred A. Knopf, 1957).

⁵ See my article, "Haunting the Hiss Case, Ghost of a Typewriter," in *The Nation*, May 12, 1962.

⁶ Richard M. Nixon, *Six Crises* (Doubleday, 1962, first edition), pp. 59–60.

⁷ The tendency of high, responsible officials quickly to brush under the rug any controversy that might bring them into conflict with the FBI was illustrated by the conduct of Attorney General Robert Kennedy in this instance. I first exposed the Nixon *faux pas* in a short article, "Nixon Kicks a Hole in the Hiss Case," *The Nation*, April 7, 1962. The issue was on the stands on Monday, April 2, and the *New York Times,* wire services, and other newspapers across the nation headlined it. The furor impelled Attorney General Kennedy to take a quick look at the FBI files; just two days later, on April 4, he announced that those files showed nothing to substantiate the new charges. "All the pertinent files and records in the case have been reviewed carefully," he said. "This review confirmed that the FBI never had possession of the disputed typewriter. The FBI investigation and scientific examination of both typed and

handwritten documents were conducted in a thorough, impartial manner, and the facts in this regard were considered carefully by both the trial and appellate courts. Accordingly no further action in this case is contemplated." The most vital facts in the Hiss case, of course, never were considered by the trial courts, because they were unearthed only after Chester Lane became Hiss's attorney, and they were never truly considered by the appellate courts either, because the courts avoided this painful necessity by adopting the technically correct legal position that such proof should have been produced earlier. Furthermore, just what constitutes a thorough review? Hardly Attorney General Kennedy's swift brushoff. Helen Buttenwieser, who became Hiss's attorney after the death of Chester Lane, asked: "I wonder if in its investigation the Department of Justice interrogated Mr. Smith of the Scripps-Howard newspapers or Mr. Schmitt of the Woodstock Company; consulted Mr. McDowell's files, or talked to Mr. Nixon and asked him how he made his investigation." (See the *New York Times,* Apr. 5, 1962.)

[8] "The Shameful Years, Thirty Years of Soviet Espionage in the United States," Report of the House Un-American Activities Committee (Government Printing Office, 1951), p. 58.

[9] J. Montgomery Hyde, *Room 3603* (Farrar, Straus & Cudahy, 1963), p. 135 and pp. 145–146.

[10] The extremely conservative makeup of this board, the highest loyalty authority in the nation, initially had caused Remington to despair of a favorable decision. The chairman was Seth W. Richardson, who had served as counsel for the Senate committee investigating the Pearl Harbor disaster, and another prominent member was Harry W. Colmery, former national commander of the American Legion.

[11] In this account of the Remington case, I have relied primarily on my own earlier research for the article "An Overdose of Curiosity," *Saga* Magazine, April, 1957, later reprinted in *The Nation,* Dec. 28, 1957. This, in turn, was based on the accounts of the Senate Hearing, trial testimony, the newspaper accounts of the time, and the extremely detailed Reporter-at-Large feature "The Days of Suspicion," in *The New Yorker,* May 21, 1949. It was also based on personal research that included talks with William C. Chanler and John McKim Minton, Remington's attorney in the second trial. New material quoted here on the third-degree type of treatment of Mrs. Remington may be found in Rauh's brief filed with the October term of the U.S. Supreme Court in 1953 (Brief No. 506, pp. 23–26).

[12] Judge Hand's dissent, from which these quotes are taken, was appended to Rauh's Supreme Court appeal brief, pp. 50–59.

[13] These quotes are taken from T. L. Stokes's daily Washington column of August 18, 1948, written after White's death. White's testimony is in the H. R. Hearings, *op. cit.,* pp. 877–906.

[14] See the account printed in the *Boston Globe* of Nov. 15, 1953, as quoted in a book dedicated to White's defense, *Harry D. White—Loyal American,* by White's brother, Nathan I. White, and privately published by Bessie (White) Bloom, of Waban, Massachusetts.

[15] *New York Daily News,* Nov. 11, 1953.

[16] Photostats of the documents were reproduced in Nathan I. White, *op. cit.,* pp. 81–97.

[17] Nathan White, *op. cit.,* pp. 106–110.

[18] *New York Times,* Nov. 11, 1953.

[19] From the text of Brownell's address, *New York Times,* Nov. 7, 1953.

[20] The Brownell and Hoover quotes are taken from the texts of their statements in the *New York Herald Tribune,* Nov. 18, 1953.

[21] See Arthur Krock's column in *The New York Times,* Nov. 19, 1953.

[22] *New York Times,* Nov. 14, 1953.

[23] *Newsweek,* Nov. 30, 1953.

11 The Postwar Scene

The postwar scene, aside from Congressional witch-hunts in which the FBI so greatly aided, has been filled with the typically furious clamor of FBI activity. It is a strangely ambivalent activity; fierce as a tiger is the FBI on the trail of suspected Communists, righteous and patriotic in warring with the United States Supreme Court, yet strangely reticent in tackling syndicated crime and civil rights in the South.

Hoover's major fetish remains the Communist menace. His books in recent years have been devoted to trumpeting the reality of the menace in an age when Communism inside America has become so negligible it is hardly a puny kitten. Even Hoover can maintain the illusion of the menace only by espousing a couple of transparent tactics: He accepts Communism on its own terms when its leaders contend it has ten "sympathizers" for every actual Party member. And since no one can define just what constitutes a "sympathizer"— or, to use other favorite Hoover terms, a "pseudo liberal" or a "fellow traveler"—everyone except the members of the John Birch Society becomes suspect. In the miasma of suspicion thus created, Hoover attacks his menace with a fanatic religiosity, propping up the illusion of reality by a discreet refusal (as in his best-selling *Masters of Deceit*) to quote the latest figures on Party membership.

The indiscriminate nature of Hoover's private war on Communism has been one of its worst features. No longer does the FBI confine itself to the overt act. That sensible dictum of Stone's went out of the window the instant Roosevelt put the Bureau back into the field of general and undefined subversive investigations. Boundaries ceased to exist; anyone might be suspect, anyone might be investigated.

The extent to which suspicion may stretch has been demonstrated by the activities of FBI agents on college campuses. From the days of GID to the present, Hoover has been convinced that college youths do not have the mental capacity and maturity to understand Communism—and that it's his job to protect them from it. So FBI agents have shadowed students. Such police surveillance is a restraint on intellectual freedom. It is no accident that an age of conformity, the symbol of the police state, has been spawned in America. Security has come to depend on the beliefs and actions of the infallible policeman.

The extreme fervor of Hoover and the FBI for crusades against the left contrasts sharply with their lack of enthusiasm for the most sensitive domestic issue of our time, civil rights. Hoover has never exhibited any passion to crusade in this area. Indeed, he has done his best to argue that the FBI should not be saddled with civil rights duties at all. Though various Attorneys General have decreed that the FBI has definite civil rights tasks, the record shows quite conclusively that the Bureau has dragged its feet. Negro homes and churches in the South have been bombed with impunity. Always the FBI rushes in to investigate—but then nothing seems to result except that more bombings occur and, as happened in the late summer of 1963, four little children get blown to bits in a church in Birmingham. The years-long record of the FBI in the civil rights field shows, at this writing, a strange lack of success in infiltrating the White Citizens Councils and other racist organizations, a feat that should have been no more difficult than the infiltration of Communism. It is perhaps no coincidence that this lack of FBI fervor for the civil rights crusade has done nothing to lessen the idolatry with which Hoover is regarded by Southern politicians and the ultra-conservative element in Congress.

■ 1 ■

The years 1949 and 1950 brought the FBI two fresh headline sensations—the Rosenberg case and the Coplon case.

The first, allegedly, involved the theft of the atom-bomb "secret" and has been called variously the "crime of the century" and "a crime worse than murder." The much-publicized enormity of the crime is predicated on the belief that information channeled through the Rosenbergs enabled Russia to copy our A-bomb and menace the future of the world. Curiously enough, no responsibility for the leak ever attaches in the popular mind to the FBI. Whitehead, indeed, conveys the impression that the FBI had nothing to do with security on the Manhattan Project. "The Army had exclusive responsibility for guarding atomic security and for clearing personnel assigned to the Manhattan Engineer District, which directed the atomic energy program," he wrote. He cited the terms of a delineation agreement under which the Army took full responsibility for the investigation of personnel and security. It is a version that leaves the FBI completely out of the picture.

Actually, the Army, though it had responsibility for final decisions, did not work alone and did not work in the dark. It had active and important and constant help from the FBI. The FBI's statement that it had checked 269,303 fingerprints of Manhattan Project applicants, that it had checked every person employed on "the atomic-bomb development," is evidence that it must share responsibility for the screening.

The most serious flaw in the protective setup involved a member of the British mission sent here to work on the bomb. Klaus Fuchs, a German refugee who had become a prominent British atomic scientist, had been cleared by British security, and the evidence indicates that this clearance was accepted without question, logically enough, by American authorities who could not be expected to know as much about Fuchs as did the British.

In December, 1949, however, Fuchs confessed to British authorities that he had been a Communist spy. During the time he had worked on the atomic bomb, he said, he had passed information to a spy courier whom he knew only by the name of "Raymond." The FBI, after exhaustive search, identified "Raymond" as Harry Gold, a chemist employed at Philadelphia General Hospital's heart station. Gold had been among those named by Elizabeth Bentley as an active Communist; he actually had been questioned in 1947 and released. Questioned again after Fuchs's confession, Gold finally told his story, acknowledging that he had funneled the information he obtained from

Fuchs to Anatoli A. Yakovlev, Russian Vice Consul in New York.

Gold's far-ranging confession implicated others. He recalled that he had been sent to Santa Fe, New Mexico, to pick up data from David Greenglass, an Army technician employed on the atomic-bomb project. Greenglass, questioned by the FBI, also confessed. He said that he had been recruited for the Soviet spy-ring by his brother-in-law, Julius Rosenberg. Greenglass described how he had passed details of the lens mold, the triggering device for the atomic bomb, both to Gold for delivery to the Russians and to Rosenberg personally.

This espionage had gone undetected by the FBI and Army security, yet there had been some obvious clues that might have given cause for suspicion. Greenglass in his youth had been a member of a Communist organization for young people, a circumstance that seems to have escaped notice when he was employed on the atomic-bomb project. While it is understandable that this old and not too definite tie might not have been picked up (though FBI security checks are usually so thorough that even a parking ticket is noted), a more positive link was supplied in February, 1945, when the FBI identified Rosenberg as a Communist, questioned him, and had him fired from his Signal Corps job. The family tie between Rosenberg and Greenglass evidently excited no curiosity at the time—a pity, because it was after the exposure of Rosenberg that the alleged A-bomb theft took place. Gold left for Santa Fe and his first meeting with Greenglass in late May, 1945, some three months after the unmasking of Rosenberg; and Greenglass, by his own subsequent testimony, at least, gave Rosenberg drawings of the triggering device of the Nagasaki A-bomb much later, in September, 1945.

This missed opportunity to catch Rosenberg in time and so to preserve our most vital secret, if indeed it could have been preserved, seems to have been lost to public view in the dramatics of the Rosenberg case. In the hysteria of the times, in the headline propaganda about the spy crime of the century, much else was also lost to view —most elementary of all, the simple fact that in the A-bomb we really possessed no secret.

Though high and responsible levels of government recognized this basic fact in the nuclear age, the American people had been brainwashed to believe the opposite, and there had been no effort of leadership to make them aware of the truth. The brainwashing that was to lay the popular foundation for acceptance of the Rosenberg "crime of the century" myth had taken place in the same hectic pre-election days of 1948 that had been devoted to the Bentley-Chambers revelations. The same House Un-American Activities Committee that had developed the Hiss case pressed on to explode a new swatch of sensational headlines. In September, 1948, with the Dewey-Truman election less than two months away, the committee began to harp on the thesis that the Russians had stolen our A-bomb "secret." Major General Leslie R. Groves, head of the Manhattan Project, testified that the Communists had been persistent termites and that "there well might have been leaks." Headlines screamed: "Army Man Says Russians Stole Atomic Secrets" and "Indictment of Five Is Urged in Report on Atomic Spying." The House committee made headline capital for days, and, by constant charge and reiteration, it insinuated into American minds the idea that Communist spies had stolen A-bomb "secrets." [1]

Yet scientists had recognized from the outset that, in the A-bomb, we had no really retainable secret. The development of the bomb had been predicated on Einstein theories advanced years before, theories known to scientists of all nations. The "secret" lay not in any mysterious bomb mechanism, not in any single device, but in a complicated process of manufacture that had required the development of entire scientific cities to process uranium and plutonium and develop the ingredients for the bomb. Even these technical developments were not beyond the capacities of the scientists of other nations; they would certainly be achieved by them as soon as it was known that we had made a workable bomb. The only real "secret," then, was the fact that basic theory could be brought to life, that the bomb could actually be made to work. And that "secret" we unveiled in 1945 for all the world to see at Hiroshima.

In one effort to clear up the "confusion" that surrounded the nature of atomic secrets, the Joint Congressional Committee on Atomic Energy reported in 1949:

> . . . There existed, for instance, an unfortunate notion that one marvelous "formula" explains how to make bombs and that it belonged

exclusively to the United States. Actually, the basic knowledge underlying the explosive release of atomic energy—and it would fill a library
—never has been the property of one nation. . . . The Soviet Union,
for its part, possesses some of the world's most gifted scientists . . .
men whose abilities and whose understanding of the fundamental
physics behind the bomb only the unrealistic were prone to under-
estimate.

This unrealism was to shadow the entire Rosenberg case. It was
to be nearly ten years before top American publications would begin
to acknowledge the truth in the kind of reappraisals of Russian science
that were virtually forced on them by the spectacle of the first Sputniks. Typical of the slow emergence of truth was a reassessment made
by Henry Luce's *Time,* hardly a left-wing publication, in its issue of
June 2, 1958. *Time* reported that Russian "physicist Igor Kurchatov
possibly knew the basic principles of the A-Bomb before the U.S."
It noted too—a fact now generally, if not prominently, conceded—
that the Russians developed a workable hydrogen bomb before we
did; that they put their first pure-jet airliner into operation more than
two years before we did; that their protective radar screen, in the
words of one of our own scientists, "appears to be better than our
own"; and that, in a word, "Soviet science is universally acknowledged to belong in the world's top drawer."

When the Rosenberg case is approached in the light of these realities, rather than in the atmosphere of "secret" and "theft" that per-
vaded the trial, it becomes apparent that one must proceed with
caution. The background performances of Hoover and the FBI, if at
all realistically evaluated, serve only to emphasize this need. The
plain fact is that Hoover and the FBI have always had a tendency to
magnify the importance and conclusiveness of their spy-subversion
cases. The great Christian Front fiasco and the overblown *Amerasia*
case bear witness to this dangerous tendency. Such precedents clearly
warn that "crime of the century" and "crime worse than murder"
hyperbole must be regarded with reservation. Another element, perhaps the most disturbing of all, is the well-established habit of the
FBI, as shown in the Hiss and Remington cases, to embark on long
periods of pretrial collaboration with important witnesses. Since these
witnesses were informers, since they were persons who themselves had

been engaged in shady conduct and might need consideration, such "perfected" testimony always runs the risk of embellishment, and it becomes extremely difficult, if not impossible, to determine just where truth ends and fantasy begins.

Such were the little-perceived elements of doubt and suspicion that hovered over the Rosenberg case at its beginning. In the light of post-trial discoveries, the doubts are magnified.

The trial opened in New York Federal Court before Judge Irving R. Kaufman on March 6, 1951. Technically there were four defendants—Julius and Ethel Rosenberg, David Greenglass, and Morton Sobell, a young scientist who had been implicated in the activities of the alleged Rosenberg ring. Actually, the fate of only the Rosenbergs and Sobell would depend on the trial outcome, for David Greenglass had already made his choice. He had decided to plead guilty and to testify against his sister and her husband, with their lives at stake. The prosecution team was led by the same Saypol-Cohn tandem that had tried Remington. The battery of defense attorneys was headed by Emanuel H. Bloch, who represented the Rosenbergs. In the prosecution's trial strategy, two witnesses loomed large above all others—David Greenglass, who had been a machinist at Los Alamos and who would testify that he had passed drawings and details of the triggering device of the Nagasaki bomb, and Harry Gold, the self-confessed spy courier, who would testify that he had obtained the material from Greenglass.

David Greenglass was the first of these major witnesses to testify. He spoke in an almost inaudible voice and had to be constantly urged to talk louder so that the jury could hear. The press noted that, as he testified, giving the details that ultimately would send his sister and her husband to the electric chair, he never once met the eyes of Ethel, who was staring fixedly at him. The tableau makes one wonder: What kind of man was David Greenglass? What stresses and strains and motivations underlay his testimony?

Posttrial discoveries—documentary evidence mysteriously but admittedly stolen from the files of Greenglass's attorney, O. John Rogge—were to reveal a picture of a highly unstable man. His wife, Ruth, who had known him since she was ten and they were children together on the streets of New York's poverty-stricken Lower East Side, told Rogge's aides that he had a "tendency to hysteria." According to the Rogge assistant who interviewed her, she stated that Greenglass "would say things were so even when they were not" and that he often talked of suicide "as if he were a character in the movies, but she didn't think he would do it." [2]

Though this intimate portrait of Greenglass was not to become available until later, enough was known about his background at the time to have made any astute defense attorney intensely suspicious. David had been the looked-down-on member of the Greenglass family. His sister Ethel had been exceptionally bright, and, in Rosenberg, had married a college graduate, an engineer of promise. David, on the other hand, had been a failure in school. He had enrolled in Brooklyn Polytechnic High School, had taken eight technical courses in his first semester, and had flunked all eight. He had resigned himself to the poorly paid life of a hack machinist, and then, during the war, in the service, the Army had sent him to Los Alamos. There he had engaged, apparently quite extensively, in black market activities in Albuquerque, selling precision tools and other stolen Army equipment. On one occasion, though this was not to be known until later, he had even stolen a piece of uranium, and shortly after the arrest of Klaus Fuchs in England, FBI agents had come calling at his door and had questioned him about this theft. He had told them he had thrown it in the river, but David and Ruth Greenglass continued to be under FBI surveillance, and they had been aware of it as Mrs. Greenglass's talks with Rogge's aides later revealed. Greenglass, clearly, was a man in need of a deal, and the memoranda later lifted from his lawyer's files clearly show that, almost from the start, he was considering collaboration with the FBI as the best way out. Though this collaboration was not to win him the full leniency he doubtless expected, it is perhaps significant that his wife, who incriminated herself in supporting his story, never was prosecuted, never was indicted.

Such were the facts in the background of the Greenglasses' family life. When Greenglass took the stand, he drew a portrait of Rosenberg as the master of a spy ring devoted to stealing atomic secrets for transmission to Russia. On one occasion, he said, Rosenberg had driven him in his car for a conference with "a Russian." He said that after he had gone to work in Los Alamos, Rosenberg had explained to Ruth (in New York) how important it was for David to commit espionage for Russia. Greenglass said that when Ruth told him this (in Albuquerque), he was scared and refused to do it, but later, thinking it over, he agreed and sent back with Ruth some general details about the physical layout of Los Alamos and the identities of the physicists working there. Home in New York on furlough about January 1, 1945, he had a discussion with Julius Rosenberg, drew sketches of the lens mold on which he had been working, and wrote out pages of descriptive material. Ethel Rosenberg, according to Ruth Greenglass, retyped all this material for transmission to the Russians. A few nights later, at a dinner at Rosenberg's home, Rosenberg took the top of a Jello box and tore it in half in a jagged pattern; the Greenglasses were to keep one half, and the other half would be presented to them by the spy courier (Harry Gold) who would call on them to pick up still further information. On Sunday, June 3, 1945, Gold showed up at the Greenglasses' apartment in New Mexico. When Greenglass opened the door, Gold said, "Julius sent me." He presented the Jello box top; it fitted the Greenglasses' piece, convincing them that this was the courier.

Greenglass was unprepared for the call, which occurred at 8:30 in the morning and told Gold he would have to have time to write up his material. Gold gave him an envelope containing $500, which, he said, he had obtained from Anatoli A. Yakovlev, the Russian Consul in New York, and left Greenglass to compile his information. Greenglass testified he prepared "some sketches of a lens mold and how they are set up in an experiment" and "some descriptive material that gives a description of this experiment." In September, 1945, back in New York on furlough again, he had another conference with Julius Rosenberg and prepared a sketch that he described as a cross section of the atomic bomb. On the witness stand, he identified sketches he had recently drawn—sketches that, he testified, duplicated those he had originally given to Gold and Rosenberg. Now there occurred, at the very outset, an incident that irretrievably doomed the Rosenbergs.

An alert defense, it would seem, would have challenged Greenglass all the way. Here was a witness who had flunked every technical course he had taken in high school. Was he competent, was he capable, without coaching, of reproducing vital details of a device so new and complicated as the A-bomb? Here was a witness whose motives for testifying against his sister practically cried aloud for investigation, an admittedly guilty conspirator in the plot who was now seeking exculpation by his testimony. How valid, in these circumstances, was that testimony? These were questions even a fledgling law student might have been expected to ask; but what Emanuel Bloch did was to make a patriotic grandstand play that, in effect, acknowledged the validity of the government's case.

The move came as the prosecution started to develop testimony about the meaning of Greenglass's last sketch. The Russians, at the time of the trial, already had the bomb; they had demonstrated this by exploding it in September, 1949. Furthermore, the details that were about to be put into the trial record had all been examined by high authority; they had all been cleared for trial use as data that no longer would give aid and comfort to the enemy. Yet Bloch suddenly asked the court to "impound" Greenglass' last cross-section bomb sketch "so that it remains secret to the Court, the jury and counsel."

Saypol seems to have been completely taken aback. He could hardly have expected this virtually complete concession by the defense—a concession that went to the very heart of the case, acknowledging that the information Greenglass had transmitted could have been so valuable it needed *even now* to be impounded for the security of the nation.

"That is a rather strange request coming from the defendants," Saypol remarked. "If I had said it or my colleague, Mr. Cohn, had said it, there might have been some criticism."

> The Court: As a matter of fact, there might have been some question on appeal. I welcome the suggestion coming from the defense because it removes the question completely.
> Saypol: And I am happy to say that we join him.
> The Court: All right. It shall be impounded.[3]

This move was followed by another equally amazing. With Bloch agreeing with the prosecution every step of the way, it was decided that Greenglass' testimony now verged on such sensitive areas that the entire courtroom should be cleared. Bloch flourished his sympathy with the move "as an American citizen and as a person who owes his allegiance to this country." Even the press was kicked out. This, of course, gave the trial the atmosphere of a star-chamber proceeding, and when the press protested, it was readmitted and read a lecture by Judge Kaufman on the necessity for it to use its patriotic discretion about what it reported. The press obliged, and the result was that few details about Greenglass' impounded sketch ever saw the light of day. *Time* Magazine, however, rendered the judgment that "some of his testimony made little scientific sense." And the *Scientific American* reported: "What the newspapers failed to note was that without quantitative data and other necessary accompanying information the Greenglass bomb was not much of a secret."

Bloch's action in not attacking this seemingly vulnerable testimony made an impact on press and jury that is virtually impossible to overestimate. I can recall asking one of the reporters who sat through this scene and subsequent scenes what she thought. Were the Rosenbergs really guilty? She no longer had any doubt. "They must be," she said. "They've practically admitted it." Such was the inevitable result of Bloch's grandstand play.

Even worse was his handling of Harry Gold. There was no reason why Bloch should not have known all about Gold, for, as long ago as the previous November, Gold had testified at the conspiracy trial of his former employer, Abraham Brothman. In this trial, an able defense had torn into the past of Gold and had exposed him in his own words, by his own admissions, as a pathological liar.

A bachelor who had been tied all his life to his mother's apron strings, lonely, frustrated, twisted, Harry Gold had developed such a vivid imagination about the life he would have liked to live that, for six years, he had kept his employer and co-workers enthralled by his accounts of his mythical family—a nonexistent wife and nonexistent twins, a boy and a girl, capped eventually by the emergence on the scene of a nonexistent wealthy lover who had destroyed Harry Gold's nonexistent domestic bliss. Gold had embellished the tale with realistic details about the house he had purchased in a Philadelphia suburb, about a brother who had been killed in the war, about the problems of the twins in school, about the manner in which on one occasion "the girl" broke her leg and "the boy" contracted polio. None of it had ever happened, but Gold kept embroidering the fantasy until, as he himself admitted in the Brothman trial, "It is a wonder that steam didn't come out of my ears at times." Such was the witness who was vital to the prosecution's case as corroboration for the Greenglasses. Yet, when Gold took the stand and told of his visit to New Mexico, of getting the lens mold sketches from David Greenglass, Emanuel Bloch let him escape *without a single question in cross-examination*. The picture of a man who for six years had lied habitually and purposelessly was one that the Rosenberg jury never got.

Why? Bloch's reason, given in summation, was that Gold hadn't uttered a word of direct testimony against Rosenberg; he'd never met Rosenberg; so he did not matter. This, of course, was idiotic. If Gold's testimony about his trip to the Greenglasses with Rosenberg's Jello box top in his pocket stood unchallenged, if his account of getting the lens mold data from Greenglass stood unchallenged, if his corroboration of the Greenglasses at every point stood unchallenged, then the Rosenbergs were guilty as sin, and there were no two ways about it. Bloch should have appreciated this elementary legal fact. Yet, in his summation, we find Bloch saying of Gold: "He got his 30-year bit and he told the truth. That is why I didn't cross-examine him. I didn't ask him one question because there is no doubt in my mind that he impressed you as well as impressed everybody that he was telling the truth, the absolute truth." [4]

Bloch was not done yet. In one final, inconceivable demonstration of legal maladroitness, he placed Rosenberg on the witness stand, had him deny in its entirety the story of the Greenglasses—and then had him claim the privilege of the Fifth Amendment when he was questioned about his past Communist affiliations. It was ridiculous for a man on trial for his life to resort to such a legal subterfuge. Where only outright denial, if denial were possible, or frank confession of past error, if it were not, could possibly have served Rosenberg, the defendant was placed in the untenable position of falling back on his Constitutional rights—in these circumstances, a Constitutional quibble—which could only serve to incriminate him in the eyes of the jury. The result was inevitable. The Rosenbergs were convicted, and so was Sobell, who had been linked to them only by the most tenuous strands of evidence. The sentence: death for the Rosenbergs; 30 years for Sobell; and for David Greenglass, as a reward for his cooperation, 15 years in prison.

Now came one of the most infinitely suspect maneuvers in this infinitely suspect affair. It is not generally realized, but the Rosenbergs, up to the moment their doom was sealed, had been ignored by the Communist press. During the entire 23-day trial, not a line had appeared in the *Daily Worker* or other Communist organs. Yet, almost the instant the Rosenbergs were convicted, Communist policy did a 180-degree about-face, and a propaganda campaign began to picture them as martyrs. On the night of their execution, mass meetings were held, placards were waved, the American system of justice was denounced. This performance suggests that the Communist organization, grim and ruthless, not caring a fig about two human lives, may actually have wanted a conviction and were happy with the extreme verdict that they could twist for their own propaganda purposes.[5]

The execution of the Rosenbergs failed to still the doubts and the controversy. In the continued agitation, there was much Communist conniving, but it is not true that all who have doubts, who are deeply disturbed, are Communists. For anyone not blindly committed the instant a Communist spy charge is flung, the posttrial discoveries in the Rogge memoranda are enough to raise again the specter of the coached witness, of the manufactured case. For example, on Saturday, June 17, 1950, David Greenglass in a handwritten memo for the Rogge office told his lawyers this:

"These are my approximate statements to the FBI:

"1. I stated that I met Gold in N.M. at 209 N. High St. my place. *They told me that I had told him to come back later because I didn't have it ready. I didn't remember this but I allowed it in the statement. . . .*" [Italics added.]

This was a suggestible witness.

Greenglass told of getting $500 from Gold, but in the rest of the account there were many discrepancies. At the trial he had testified positively about Rosenberg's driving him to meet "a Russian." In the handwritten memo to Rogge, the same incident becomes virtually meaningless. Greenglass wrote:

"I then mentioned a meeting with a man who I didn't know arranged by Julius. . . . I talked to the man but I could recall very little about which we spoke. I *thought it might be* that he wanted me to think about finding out about H.E. lens's used in experimental tests to determine data on the a-bomb." [Italics added.] How remote can you get?

The Jello box top, such a graphic detail in the trial, didn't appear at all in this Greenglass recital, nor did the identifying phrase, "Julius sent me." The way Greenglass said he told it the first time to the FBI was:

"One more thing, I identified Gold by a torn or cut piece of card, but I didn't tell them where or how I got it. Also I definitely placed my wife out of the room at the time of Gold's visit. [In the trial testimony, she was there.]

"Also I didn't know who sent Gold to me.

"I also made a pencil sketch of an H.E. mold set up for an experiment. *But this I'll tell you I can honestly say the information I gave Gold maybe not at all what I said in the statement."* [Italics added.]

Greenglass, as his wife had told Rogge's office, obviously was a man who would tell any tale, regardless of truth.

If more be needed, it almost certainly was supplied by Gold and Greenglass themselves in the shocked aftermath of Russia's first Sputniks in 1957. Robert Morris, counsel for the Senate Internal Security Committee, rushed to the federal penitentiary in which Gold and Greenglass were serving out their time. There the pair obligingly told him (as he triumphantly announced) that the Russians had stolen the "secret" of Sputnik from *us.* Even the *New York Herald Tribune* gagged on this one, commenting in a tart editorial that, if this were true, we had better dust off the carbon copies of our old "secret," because we could sure enough use it.

Each one who examines the evidence in the Rosenberg case must arrive at his own conclusion, which will vary according to the predilections of the observer. There seems little doubt that the Rosenbergs were Communists. How successful they were in gathering and forwarding information is another matter. It seems likely that theirs was a fumbling, amateurish type of endeavor that did not accomplish much.

The government case was pieced together with the collaboration of unstable and malleable witnesses. The ultimate tragedy of the Rosenberg case is that here were two inconspicuous people, not admirable in themselves but still human beings, who came fatally to be crushed by two monolithic opposing forces. The upper millstone that crushed them was represented by the FBI and the government, wanting to refurbish their image (stained by Fuchs) by producing and convicting the spies of the century. The nether millstone was represented by a Communist Party wanting martyrs and ruthlessly willing to sacrifice the Rosenbergs for its propaganda ends. Between the two, the Rosenbergs never had a chance.

■ 2 ■

The spy case of Judith Coplon was entirely different from the Rosenberg case—and just as significant in its own way.

Miss Coplon had been a top student at Barnard College in New York. After her graduation, she had obtained employment in the Department of Justice in Washington. She was twenty-seven, an analyst in the department, when on the night of March 6, 1949, trailing FBI agents nabbed her on a New York street in the company of Valentin A. Gubitchev, an attaché of the Soviet delegation to the United Nations. In Miss Coplon's handbag, at the time of her arrest, were a number of documents, including one memorandum in her own handwriting. This, probably the most damaging evidence against her, read:

I have not been able (and don't think I will) to get the top-secret FBI report which I described to Michael on Soviet and Communist intelligence activities in the U.S. When the moment was favorable I asked Foley [William E. Foley, a security officer in the department] where the report was (he'd previously remarked that he had such a report). He said that some department official had it and he didn't expect to get it back. Foley remarked there was nothing "new" in it. When I saw the report, for a minute, I breezed through it rapidly, remembered very little. It was about 115 pages in length and sum-marized, first, Soviet "intelligence" activities. . . . It had heading on Soviet U.N. delegation but that was all I remember. The rest of the report, I think, was on Polish, Yurgo, etc., activities and possibly some information on the C.P., USA.

Miss Coplon was indicted on espionage charges both in Washing-ton and New York, one case being based on the theft of information, the other on the attempt to pass it along. In the first trial, held in Washington in April, 1949, Miss Coplon's attorney tried to explain away the remarkable handwritten memo by arguing that it was "allegorical" and referred merely to "prototypes" in a novel she was planning to write. In view of the specific contents of the memoran-dum, a more far-fetched rationalization could hardly be imagined. Understandably, the jury found some difficulty in swallowing it.

The defense's explanation of Miss Coplon's constant association with Gubitchev was that they were just a couple "crazy, crazy" in love. This, again, seemed a too obviously easy way to explain a dubious association, but the government had some difficulty combat-ing it because it could not show that Miss Coplon had ever passed Gubitchev anything. When arrested in New York, she had the mem-orandum, as well as Justice Department papers the government called "restricted," in her handbag. A long parade of FBI agents took the witness stand at the Washington trial, detailing the thoroughness of the surveillance that had been set up over Miss Coplon. They had watched her every movement for weeks. Sometimes as many as five FBI men at a time had tailed her and watched her meetings with Gubitchev. The Russian and the girl had been seen together numer-ous times, but, as the Associated Press reported on May 16, 1949, when the trial entered its fourth week, "the government has not yet established 'contact' between Miss Coplon and the Russian." [6]

Two other disturbing elements peeped out from the mass of evi-dence submitted by the government at the Washington trial. Robert R. Granville, the supervising agent in New York, acknowledged that, when Miss Coplon was arrested, the FBI did not have a warrant as required by law. He was also questioned closely concerning defense charges that the FBI had indulged in wiretapping. Asked if he had ever given orders to tap Miss Coplon's phone or the phones of any member of her family, he answered: "No." When the defense, skeptical, pressed the issue, government prosecutors, on their word of honor as lawyers and gentlemen, assured the court that the FBI had indulged in no wiretapping in the case. FBI agents sat there in court and heard them—and said nothing. With such assurances that the investigation, with the exception of that little matter of the warrant, had been handled in the most legitimate of fashions, the case against Miss Coplon went to the Washington jury. And the jury promptly convicted her.

With the defense appealing this conviction, the government decided to proceed with a second trial of Miss Coplon in New York, based on the second indictment accusing her of passing information to Gubitchev. This trial opened in late December, 1949, and Miss Coplon's defense now pressed more vigorously the wiretapping issue that the government had so emphatically denied in the Washington trial. Federal Judge Sylvester Ryan ordered the FBI to produce its records. It suddenly developed that, despite the flat assurances given to the federal judge in Washington, the FBI had been tapping Miss Coplon's telephone all the time.

There had been, the federal prosecutors assured Judge Ryan, absolutely no intention on anyone's part deliberately to deceive a federal judge in Washington. They themselves as a matter of fact, they said, had had no idea of such a thing until the previous week, when they consulted with FBI agents to get affidavits that there had been no wiretapping—and discovered that, unfortunately, after all, there had been. The prosecutors protested that they still did not know which agents had done the wiretapping.[7]

When Judge Ryan pressed for a fuller explanation, he was assured that the great bulk of the wiretaps had been destroyed. It was FBI routine, he was told, to destroy wiretap records within a short time after they had been made. Judge Ryan, determined to find out just what went on here, called FBI agents to the witness stand. One acknowledged, a bit reluctantly, that he had "reason to believe" the defendant's phones had been tapped, because he had seen the disk recordings and had been responsible, as a matter of fact, for destroying the tap reports and burning the records.[8]

The disclosures were getting murkier and murkier, and Judge Ryan called on the FBI to supply the court with all the information available anywhere, in New York or Washington, about the conduct of this wiretapping that, originally, had been so vigorously denied. So was turned up a most curious document, whose discovery was reported by the *New York Herald Tribune* in these words:

> This was a Washington memorandum, dated Nov. 9, 1949, from Howard B. Fletcher, FBI inspector, to D. M. Ladd, assistant FBI director:
>
> "The above named informant (Tiger, the code name of the tap) has been furnishing information concerning the activities of [Miss Coplon]. In view of the imminency of her trial, it is recommended that this informant (tap) be discontinued immediately, and that all administrative records in the New York office covering the operations of this informant be destroyed.
>
> "Pertinent data furnished by the informant has already been furnished in letter form, and having in mind security, now and in the future, it is believed desirable that the indicated records be destroyed."

The scope of the wiretapping in the Coplon case was now reluctantly admitted by the FBI. Though the original disks had been destroyed, the wiretap-gathered "evidence" had been preserved, as the Fletcher memorandum indicated, in letter form. From this it developed that the government had wiretapped Miss Coplon's home phone, her phone in the Justice Department in Washington, the phone in her parents' home in Brooklyn, the phone that she used to confer with her lawyer while the first trial was in progress. Some thirty FBI agents, the FBI conceded, had taken part in the electronic eavesdropping—an operation of such scope that it could hardly have been innocently overlooked when the government, with the FBI in attendance, informed the judge in the first trial that it had never happened.

Though the New York jury, like the Washington jury, convicted Miss Coplon on the basis of the evidence found in her handbag and her admitted association with Gubitchev, the wiretap and no-warrant revelations wrecked both convictions on appeal. In the Washington case, Leonard B. Boudin, Miss Coplon's appeal attorney, accused the FBI of "rankest perjury" in denying to the court that wiretaps had been used. He said it was "incredible" that the prosecution could have been ignorant of the fact that Miss Coplon's phone was being tapped even while her trial was in progress. Fred E. Strine, special assistant to the Attorney General, was hard-pressed to justify the government's actions. In his argument before the District of Columbia Court of Appeals, he contended that the wiretapping really hadn't made any difference to the case because the evidence so obtained hadn't been used against Miss Coplon. Chief Judge E. Barrett Prettyman broke in with the tart comment that this was "an extremely optimistic view," and he added: "I'd like it explained to me how any appellant can have a fair trial if conversation between him and his counsel is intercepted."

In arguments on the New York appeal, Judge Learned Hand clashed sharply with Strine. The federal prosecutor had argued that the government had not been guilty of "deliberate or wanton destruction of wire-tap records." Judge Hand took him up sharply, asking: "Could there have been anything more wanton and deliberate than was shown by the evidence?" He cited the FBI's specific order to destroy. Strine argued that this had been issued merely for "security reasons," but Judge Hand disagreed emphatically. In words that, it seems, should be remembered, he snapped: "You can point a finger at any person and say for security reasons."

Judge Hand later wrote the decision by which the New York Court, by a unanimous vote, threw out the guilty verdict. He softened his stand a bit on the wiretapping, saying that the destruction of the recordings wasn't too vital, since copies had been kept in Washington, but he stressed that the government had failed to show that the taps had not helped its case. He wrote that Miss Coplon's "guilt is plain," but held that the FBI had in effect ruined its own case. He argued that on the validity of Miss Coplon's arrest "concededly depends the validity of the seizure of the incriminating packet [of documents] and its competence as evidence at the trial." Only if Miss Coplon had been a fugitive trying to escape would arrest without a warrant have been justified, he said, and in this case, patently, this was not so. "No sudden emergency forced the hand of the agents," Judge Hand wrote. "They made everything ready except for the one condition which would have made the arrest lawful: a warrant."

Congress, as it usually does when the FBI has been inconvenienced by the necessity of adhering to the niceties of the law, subsequently decided that in the future the Bureau should not be bothered by having to observe such a legal technicality as the obtaining of a warrant in espionage cases. It passed legislation specifically exempting the Bureau from such normal statutory procedures when it was pursuing spies, but nothing could be done to resurrect the Coplon case which the FBI had wrecked beyond redemption. Nothing much could be done either to eradicate the impression that deliberate deceit had been practiced on the trial court in Washington.

The Coplon case is not the only case in which such deceit has been practiced. In February, 1958, an almost identical situation developed in an appeals hearing on an action brought by the Justice Department to make the Communist Party register as a subversive organization. Throughout the entire earlier course of the action, Justice Department lawyers had repeatedly told the courts that no recordings had been made in 1945 of talks between the FBI and Louis Budenz, the Communist leader who had broken with the Party. The Communist Party, not satisfied, petitioned for a re-hearing and asked for more explicit assurance on this point. As a result, James T. Devine, a Justice Department lawyer, asked FBI agents to furnish affidavits. Instead of supplying the affidavits, the FBI acknowledged the truth— that, unknown to Budenz, it had taken recordings of the talks; it had had them all the time. Devine assured the court that this sudden admission came as a complete surprise to him and, he believed, to all other government attorneys working on the case.[9]

Clearly, the FBI had become a law unto itself, making its own rules, practicing a degree of deception on even the assistant attorneys general of the Justice Department who, originally, had been supposed to supervise its actions. However, more than the Bureau's blithe disregard for its titular superiors is involved. Basic principles of justice are vitally at stake. Not only does it become impossible for a defendant, whose attorney's phone is tapped, adequately to defend himself, but deceit on the part of the FBI and the Justice Department, both of whom flaunt the prestige of the flag, makes truth the cat's-paw of a desire to convict. In a nation brainwashed into believing that the FBI is always 97 percent right, the word of the FBI and the Justice Department should be above reproach in our own courts of law. No rationalization can justify the solemn insistence of law enforcement authorities on an assertion that is the reverse of truth—when they know it to be the reverse of truth. It will take a very great rationalization indeed to reconcile the wiretap coverups in the Coplon and Budenz cases with the image of the FBI as an organization whose principles are so lofty and whose dedication to ideals is so steadfast that its word on anything and everything must under no circumstances ever be questioned.

■ 3 ■

The unique power and prestige of J. Edgar Hoover and the FBI have placed them on a pedestal above the law they are supposed to serve. This power and prestige is such that no Attorney General can contain it or supervise it, and Congress cowers before it. Even the decisions of the highest court in the land, if they draw the Hoover scowl, have to be amended in accordance with Hoover's wishes. If that seems like an overstrong statement, consider the events of 1957.

Clinton Jencks was a New Mexico labor leader, an official of the Mine, Mill, and Smelter Workers Union. He had been tried and convicted on charges that he had committed perjury when he signed a non-Communist affidavit. The principal witness against Jencks had been Harvey Matusow, a professional informer, first for the FBI, next for Senator McCarthy's witch-hunters. However, after Jencks had been convicted, Matusow demonstrated that he possessed those traits of instability and unreliability for which informers are often noted. He joined a church, professed to have discovered conscience, proclaimed that he had lied in his testimony involving Jencks and others—and promptly was jailed as a perjurer by an indignant government.

Matusow's startling about-face served only to underscore the legal issue that had already been joined. During the trial of Jencks, Matusow had testified that he had made several reports about Jencks's supposedly communistic ties and activities to the FBI. Jencks's attorneys, perhaps sensing that Matusow might be a witness who would tell one story today, another tomorrow, fought a losing battle to obtain these earlier reports. It should be stressed that the attorneys did not seek the privilege of conducting a fishing expedition through the FBI files. They asked only to be permitted to inspect original reports Matusow had mentioned from the witness stand. Their purpose was a time-honored and legally respected one: the right of the defense to examine such original statements as a means of checking the veracity of the witness.

In an age in which the original statements of informers have been distinguished for their notable lack of resemblance to the court-produced case, this would seem to have been an elementary request, except that, of course, once such cases *have* been court-produced, once the prestige of the government *has* been staked on them, the sanctity of the informer becomes a cause that transcends all other causes. And so the privilege of inspecting Matusow's first accusations against Jencks was denied to the Jencks defense. The case was fought to the United States Supreme Court, and the court on June 3, 1957, in an overwhelming 7-to-1 decision, threw out the conviction of Jencks. Justice William Brennan, a Catholic and an Eisenhower appointee, wrote the decision that was soon to be smeared from coast to coast as a prime document of subversion.

Actually, all that Brennan and the high court had done was to uphold a basic principle of American justice—that the accused is entitled to a full and adequate defense. The decision did *not* do precisely what the American public was soon to be brainwashed into believing that it *did* do. It did not open the door to indiscriminate rummaging in the FBI files; it did not threaten with exposure a single secret informant. It merely held that, once the government had produced a witness and put him on the stand, the defense had a right to examine his prior statements on the subject about which he was then testifying. Brennan called attention to a prior court decision upholding the right of the defense to "specific documents," but not "any broad or blind fishing expedition among documents possessed by the government."

"We reaffirm and re-emphasize these essentials," Brennan wrote. ". . . Every experienced trial judge and trial lawyer knows the value for impeachment purposes of statements of the witness regarding events before time dulls treacherous memory." [10]

In another memorable paragraph, one that should be enshrined in American law, Brennan wrote: "It is unconscionable to allow it [the government] to undertake prosecution and then invoke its governmental privileges to deprive the accused of anything which might be material to the defense."

This, of course, was the point, and Matusow's subsequent renunciation of the story to which he had testified for the government should have emphasized, for all to see, the necessity of subjecting informers to the closest scrutiny and protecting the rights of persons who might be recklessly accused by them. But this was not the point that registered; this was not at all what happened. If Brennan in his opinion had traduced motherhood, the screams from the FBI could not have been more anguished.

Justice Tom Clark, always a strong FBI partisan and the lone dissenter from the Jencks decision, had contended that the ruling would open the door to fishing expeditions in the FBI's secret investigative files. This was all that was needed. Hoover, with strong support in Congress and in the ultraconservative press, took up the cry, and almost overnight the impression was created that the Court had given the Communists carte blanche to force revelation of the FBI's most closely guarded secrets.

A brief chronology of events shows how vigorously the campaign against the Court was pressed, how the anti-Court image in the press was cultivated. On June 28, 1957, *The New York Times* reported that Hoover was "understood to have passed the word that his agency will drop out of some espionage and other criminal cases if this becomes necessary to protect its confidential informants." On July 28, in a report to Attorney General Herbert Brownell, Jr., Hoover stressed for the record that confidential informants had been responsible for the arrest of 2,700 persons in the nation in the past year, and he furnished ammunition to the anti-Court faction in Congress by this declaration: "The very basis of our success is the FBI's assurance to this country's citizens that information they give will be maintained in the strictest confidence in our files." Hoover followed this on August 14 by writing a "Dear Joe" letter to Representative Joseph W. Martin, Jr. (Republican of Massachusetts), minority leader in the House, demanding legislation to protect the FBI files from disclosure.

He said that some informants already had clammed up as the result of the Court decision and that he had had to drop some cases in preference to opening the files. In the light of this assertion by the Man himself, a subtle rumor that the FBI publicity bureau industriously purveyed was picked up and flaunted by the press. This was the suggestion that the upcoming espionage case against NKVD Colonel Rudolph Ivanovich Abel would have to be dropped if the Jencks decision were not nullified by Congress. The action of vast sections of the press in uncritically echoing every assertion of Hoover and the FBI about the Jencks decision conveyed such a false impression that even many knowledgeable newspapermen, deluded by the propaganda in their own product, accepted as an article of faith that the Jencks ruling would open the FBI files.

While the public hysteria against the Court was being created by such alarmist statements, Hoover's lobby on the Hill was industriously at work. Lou Nichols, his fast-talking, likable public relations man and lobbyist, was buttonholing Congressmen and urging them to introduce legislation that would "protect" the FBI files from the capricious Court. Congress, having long ago decided that it paid better to worship Hoover than to fight him, was happy to oblige. Representative Kenneth Keating, the New York Republican who was to grow into a Senator and acquire wide fame as the prophet of Soviet missile activity in Cuba, sponsored the FBI-desired bill in the House, and Senator Joseph C. O'Mahoney, a Wyoming Democrat, made it a bipartisan endeavor by taking up the cudgels for it in the Senate. The language of the bill was cleverly worded so that, without quite giving the appearance of doing so, it would in effect nullify the Court's Jencks decision. The key language limited inspections of FBI records in court cases to such "reports or statements of the witness in the possession of the United States as *are signed by the witness, or otherwise adopted or approved by him as correct* relating to the subject matter as to which he has testified." Under this provision, all the FBI would have to do to keep its files closed would be to have its agents summarize what a witness told them or to take a statement that had not been signed or specifically reaffirmed by the witness to be true.

Senator Wayne Morse (Democrat of Oregon) sought to amend

this language to narrow the loophole. But the propaganda campaign in the press was now in full gear. The *Daily News* in New York, the nation's largest-circulation daily, was running a stream of editorials devoted to the theme that the Bureau's files must be protected from "the secret-pickin' hands of Commie spies." Its Washington columnist, John O'Donnell, was frothing on the subject. So was Westbrook Pegler. So was Walter Winchell, with his immense reading audience. And finally, in a story timed to appear on the Hill on the very day the FBI-inspired legislation was being ironed out in a Senate-House conference, *Newsweek* Magazine contributed a flattering cover story about Hoover and the Bureau. Beneath an angry portrait of Hoover mounted on a huge blue fingerprint, it asked this pregnant question: "Handcuffing the FBI?" [11]

Men of high repute and great legal learning insisted that no action by Congress was needed, that all the Supreme Court had done was to reaffirm a basic principle of American justice. Dean Erwin N. Griswold, of Harvard Law School, put it this way: "There is absolutely nothing in the [Jencks] opinion giving the public access to the secret files of the FBI. It simply blueprints procedures used right here in Boston and in every criminal court." [12] No such sober and responsible appraisal could be expected to cope with the nationwide and irresponsible outcry Hoover had stimulated. Only slightly modified, the legislation he wanted was passed.

Full of his triumph, Hoover paraded before the thirty-ninth annual convention of the American Legion in Atlantic City on September 19, 1957, and capped with a crow his war against the Supreme Court. He charged that the campaign to "open" the FBI files was the work of "a hard core of propagandists" (there is always, it seems, some monstrous secret conspiracy whenever anyone opposes Hoover), and he put everything in correct perspective with this statement: "The bland refusal to recognize the right of the public welfare and the proper use of common sense result too often in the prostitution of the law in favor of evil." The American Legion, enthralled at having before it the one man on whom our survival depended, passed a resolution praising Hoover and criticizing recent Supreme Court decisions, especially the Jencks ruling that would have "opened" FBI files.

Why did Hoover stir up such a nationwide frenzy on such a distorted issue? An educated guess is that his prestige and the prestige of the FBI had been linked unqualifiedly to the veracity of informers whom they have sponsored—and that the contents of the FBI files with respect to this breed will not bear examination in the full light of day.

The pattern of drastically altered testimony—testimony that veers from and conflicts with its original version—has been exposed sufficiently in the Hiss, the Remington, and the Rosenberg cases to justify speculation about what might happen in such informer-type prosecutions if the lid were ever fully lifted on their origins. In addition, enough information has seeped out from under the Justice Department rug in a number of other cases to indicate that the cult of the informer is one of the most pernicious a great democracy ever was deluded into sanctifying.

A major explosion, quickly hushed up and rapidly forgotten, occurred in 1954 when Joseph and Stewart Alsop called Attorney General Brownell's attention to some sharp discrepancies in the testimony of one of the department's favorite testifiers, Paul Crouch. Crouch had been the leading government witness in the Smith Act trial of a number of second-grade Communist leaders accused of teaching and advocating the overthrow of the government. He had testified in explicit detail about the activities of David Davis, a member of the National Committee of the Communist Party. Crouch testified that he and Davis had worked together in the Communist cause from 1928 through the mid-1930's. He described numerous contacts with Davis, recalled specific incidents that had occurred while they were together. His testimony sounded impressive, conclusive, but the Philadelphia bar in this case had decided the defense should be ably represented, and the court had named Thomas D. McBride, Philadelphia's leading expert in criminal law, to represent the accused. McBride and his staff studied Crouch's past informer testimony for the government—and popped the cork. They discovered that, in 1949, in the second trial of Harry Bridges, the West Coast maritime leader, Crouch had been questioned about his knowledge of all members of the Communist National Committee. He had been asked particularly about David Davis. He had testified that he "did not know or remember" David Davis. He had denied this knowledge of Davis "no less than four times, and in the most specific manner," the Alsops wrote. "He stated at one point: 'I had no knowledge of David Davis.' " [13]

Discovery of these vital discrepancies in the witness-stand performance of Crouch led the Alsops to investigate, as well as mere reporters could, the informer setup within the Department of Justice. They found that the department was keeping "a special stable" of witnesses "under the guise of 'consultants to the Immigration and Naturalization Service.' " Since July 1, 1952, "approximately fifty persons have received payment for serving as political informers or witnesses." Twelve of these formed a hierarchy of real specialists, regular witness-stand performers who had received more than $1,500 apiece from a grateful government. Crouch was a high priest among the high priests. He had been paid $9,675 by the Justice Department in the previous two years, not bad for a man who, before he took to informing, had been earning 85 cents an hour working for an airline in Texas.

Close behind Crouch in eminence and reward came Manning Johnson. He had been paid $9,096 in two years, an average of almost $407 a month. He had made himself conspicuous by testifying in the loyalty case of Dr. Ralph Bunche, eminent Negro leader and United Nations official. His testimony in this case was backed up by that of a third testifier in the "special stable," Leonard Patterson, who had been paid some $3,775, or about $160 a month, for two years. The quality of Manning's and Patterson's testimony against Bunche may be gauged by the fact that, even in the atmosphere of the times, the Loyalty Board cleared Dr. Bunche by a unanimous six-to-nothing vote and referred the testimony of his accusers to the Department of Justice for examination. The Alsops noted that "Manning Johnson has testified under oath that he would lie under oath, if directed to do so by his present employers." The Alsops wrote:

> The practice of putting political informers on the Government payroll, which has been regularly denounced as pernicious and dangerous since the time of the Roman historian Tacitus, is a part of the "Truman mess" inherited by the Eisenhower Administration. It is one part of the mess that has quite markedly not been cleaned up as yet. It raises

certain obvious questions of great long-range importance in any free society.

First, those of the informers and witnesses who mainly live by this new trade, or importantly supplement their incomes by it, have a clear financial interest in being used as much as possible. As former Communists, their characters are clearly suspect. What happens when they have told all they genuinely know, but still want to maintain their incomes from the Justice Department? [14]

A government that had sanctioned this system was a government that was not answering such questions. As long ago as the trial of Senator Wheeler, the government had thrown its protective arms around a perjurer who had perjured in a favored cause. And it could not now, with the Lord only knew how many suspect witch-hunts on its books, afford the decency to be squeamish about the quality of some of the evidence its pay-for-telling policy inevitably had produced. Though a few crazy idealists demanded that the Justice Department examine its records and its conscience, and give some accounting of the number of informers whose testimony had proved unreliable, such requests were met by a grave and lofty and protracted silence. The critics finally became hoarse and lost their voices from crying so long unheard in the wilderness—and the whole issue eventually died and was quietly interred.

Such was the background against which Hoover fought and won his furious Jencks case battle on the spurious grounds that the Supreme Court's decision would have wrecked FBI security and left us wide open to Communist connivance. The completeness of Hoover's triumph was underscored on June 22, 1959, when the Court, in effect, reversed itself by upholding the defense-crippling law that Congress had passed at Hoover's behest. In this decision, the Court imposed further limitations on the defense in examining pretrial statements by government witnesses. It even gave federal agents, as Justice Brennan noted in a sharp dissent, the right to keep pretrial statements out of court entirely if agents took them orally and not "substantially verbatim."

The entire controversy, as the *New York Post* subsequently commented, had been "most notable as a case-history of FBI propaganda technique. Few men in politics or the press chose to explore the large constitutional issues involved. Steadily the controversy deteriorated into a sort of national loyalty test: Are you for or against the FBI, the corollary being: Are you for or against subversion? When a serious issue is reduced to those crude terms, Hoover can't lose, and he didn't." [15]

■ 4 ■

An FBI so powerful that it can roll back a Supreme Court decision is an FBI that increasingly penetrates every facet of our lives. Millions depend for their livelihood, for their bread and butter, on its smile or its scowl. Radio and television licenses, most franchises granted by federal agencies, come to depend on its approval. Millions of government workers and even more countless millions employed in private industries having contact with government projects must not risk its disapproval—or they may not work. So hypersensitive are the FBI and its Director to the possibilities of internal subversion that even college students are followed and checked up on and made the subjects of special dossiers.

This is a free society? In outward form, certainly, it still is. But, in inner vitality, in matters of the mind and the spirit, it has become steadily less so.

If a date were selected for the great changeover from an intellectually fearless and free society to a sheeplike and conformist one, it might well be March 21, 1947, the day that President Truman signed the executive order creating the federal loyalty program. The purpose was one that appeared necessary in the atmosphere of the times, in the panic among the high echelons of government that still-secret advices like the first hot flash on the Bentley disclosures evidently had caused. The feeling was that Communist spies might be everywhere, and the government had to protect itself from their wiles. Checks were therefore to be run on every federal employee. The Civil Service Commission or the employing agency would be the final arbiter of their fate, but every name would be checked against the background files of rumor, report, and gossip amassed by the FBI, by Congressional committees, and by other security agencies. If any suspicious item turned up, the FBI would investigate and put the case in evidentiary form for presentation to the Loyalty Review Board. It would seek to establish "reasonable grounds," later changed significantly to "reasonable doubt," for determining whether an employee was disloyal.

The purpose of the program, on its surface, was laudable—to guarantee the security of the nation. But the trouble was that, once such a system is started, it is almost impossible to limit it, to keep it from becoming a restricting and stultifying influence on the national life. Men's political beliefs and actions inevitably would be subject to scrutiny—and to scrutiny by an agency with a built-in fixation, as its Director demonstrated in almost every speech, that led it to equate "fellow travelers" and "pseudo liberals" with the Menace.

There were some at the time who saw the inevitable road ahead. One was Clifford J. Durr, a Montgomery, Alabama, lawyer and a member of the Federal Communications Commission. Less than a month after Truman issued his executive order, Durr in a New York speech entitled "Freedom and Fear" quite accurately posed the ultimate issue. He referred to the post-World War I hysteria, described pressures more subtle and more massive in the making, and foresaw a time of even greater danger and menace to the American spirit.[16] He said:

> If our freedoms are, in fact, endangered, do we endanger them even more by the methods employed to defend them? . . . Can we safely vest in our secret police jurisdiction over the "association" and "sympathetic affiliation," and thoughts of men, and be sure that we are safe? Can men be fairly tried when their right to face their accusers, and to be fully advised of the nature and cause of the charge against them, depends upon the "discretion" of those who accuse them?
> . . . The Executive Order mentioned applies only to government employees and officials. But will the example of government stop with government itself? Once it has been established and accepted, can its influence be kept from spreading to business and industry, to the press, to our schools and universities, and even to our churches?

When he made this speech, Durr had in mind a specific example of the insidious process he was describing. The previous year, a group of California businessmen had formed a corporation and had made application to the FCC for a license for a radio station. Unsolicited by the FCC had come a memorandum from Hoover listing the sponsors and some information on their backgrounds. "I thought you would be interested in knowing," Hoover wrote, "that an examination of this list reflects that the majority of these individuals are members of the Communist Party *or have affiliated themselves with the activities of the Communist movement.*" [Italics added.]

On November 27, 1946, the chairman of the FCC wrote Hoover asking for more specific information. He pointed out that the FCC had no right to deny an application without a hearing and asked if the FBI could furnish any information in evidentiary form. Hoover replied that to do so would disclose confidential sources, but he sent along an apparently complete summary of all the rumors and reports the FBI had accumulated about the individual stockholders. The sequel is best told in Durr's own words. In a letter to *The Nation* he wrote:

> Not being able to get anything specific from Hoover, we sent staff members to California to see what they could find out. They reported back that it was impossible to guarantee who was or who was not a Communist, but the people referred to were on the whole well regarded and that their main political activity had been in the direction of re-electing Roosevelt.
>
> There being no basis for an unfavorable action on the application, the Commission failed to act at all, haunted by the fear of what might happen at the next appropriations hearing, if the application should be granted. The Applicant, of course, did not know what it was charged with or even that any charge had been brought. All it ever knew was that other applications filed much later had been acted on. The result was to deny the application by not acting on it.[17]

Durr was so disturbed by this action-through-inaction that he finally made reference to the incident in a speech before a group of educational broadcasters in Chicago. Marquis W. Childs picked up his remarks and devoted a column to the topic in the *Washington Post* on November 19, 1947, emphasizing that, if Hoover was offering "unsolicited" opinions in such sensitive areas, there was nothing to prevent similar critiques "on the attitudes of those who deal with opinion and news. The mere suggestion of such a step would be enough to frighten the timid into curbing any stray thoughts that could be judged to fall outside the narrowest traditional mold." Childs's column put the fat in the fire.

Hoover responded angrily. He demanded that the FCC "repudiate" Durr, and in a statement to the press he declared that the FBI was only doing its job, was only being helpful. It always passed along, he explained, whatever information it gathered that might assist other federal agencies; it did not "evaluate this information" nor did it "make recommendations or decisions as to action, if any, to be taken thereon." It was a contention that, like the identical contention in the Harry Dexter White case, demonstrated the ambivalence of Hoover. His contention that he was not evaluating seems strange in the face of the one emphatic sentence he had written condemning the radio sponsors as Communists or badly tainted individuals. If this was not evaluation on the only point that mattered, what was it?

Facing the fury of the powerful boss of the FBI, the members of the Federal Communications Commission held a meeting on December 1, 1947, to decide what they should do. Durr, in defending himself, gave a summary of what he considered the FBI intelligence-gathering had produced, and so lifted a lid on the kind of rumor and innuendo that finds its way into FBI dossiers and, as indicated by Hoover's evaluating action in this case, is taken seriously. Durr said:

> It . . . seems to me that it is of little help to the Commission to be informed that an applicant was, in 1944, at the height of the war, reported by an unidentified source as being in contact with another unidentified individual "who was *suspected* of *possible* pro-Russian activity"; or that the applicant was reported by an unidentified informant to have been a visitor in the residence of another individual who was reported by another unidentified source to have been identified by still another unidentified source with Communistic activities . . . or that "according to an unknown outside source" the name of the applicant "appears" as a member of a committee of an organization of artists and professional people which was active in support of the Democratic presidential nominee in the 1944 presidential elections; or that another unidentified source has described such organization "as a Communist infiltrated and/or influenced organization". . . or that a local Democratic Committee has been reported by an unidentified

informant "to be under the influence of the Communist element"; or that according to a newspaper account of a speech delivered by Vice-Presidential candidate Bricker in the 1944 campaign, the speaker charged that the Democratic Party had become the "Hillman-Browder Communistic Party" and that the applicant had left his job with the government to support the campaign of President Roosevelt, the founder of this "Communistic Party"; or that the applicant has been reported by an unidentified source to have been a member of the committee to greet the late president of a large labor union. . . .[18]

This had been the kind of "evidence," backed by the prestige of Hoover and the FBI, that had resulted in the FCC's denial, by inaction, of the application for a radio license. In the light of this courageous stand, the Commission's attitude in the Durr-Hoover imbroglio was entirely predictable. It wrote Hoover a conciliatory letter that, in effect, repudiated Durr. Durr, the FCC pointed out, had been speaking as an individual, not on behalf of the Commission; the Commission wanted to continue to receive advices from the FBI; and it wanted to express "its confidence" in Hoover and his organization.

In Congress, as usual, Hoover partisans came roaring to the defense of their hero. The loudest bellow was emitted by Senator Homer Capehart, a right-wing Republican. Capehart threatened an investigation that never materialized; accused Durr of dereliction in not exploring adequately the tips the FBI had furnished; and charged that "evidence unfolds daily that in our own Government household Communists and their New Deal fellow travelers are being harbored in key positions where they can sabotage our Nation's policies." Capehart, as can be seen, was right in line with the kind of evaluation that is threaded through the FBI gossip-mill report to the FCC: the New Deal and Communism were one.

Hoover always flies into a rage whenever anyone accuses the FBI of being a "thought police." But the activities of the FBI verge closely, at least, on this opprobrious status when, in league with the rabid right in Congress, it helps to equate New Deal liberalism with Communism.

Let's now take a look at the persistent Hoover-FBI surveillance of college activities.

With characteristic duality, Hoover has always upheld the ideal of academic freedom but——. College students, he feels, are not mature enough to evaluate Communism sensibly; they must be protected from its insidious virus. The FBI must be ever watchful, must ever guard the campuses of the nation against subtle Red infiltration.

Hoover's attitude was expressed in a typical Hoover-type speech before one of his favorite sounding boards, the American Legion, in October, 1962. Communists had managed to infiltrate all facets of our society, he declared. Though he condemned extremists of both right and left, he concluded his speech with a strong denunciation of the misled youth of America, especially college students. He declared that the students who had staged the 1960 San Francisco protest against the House Un-American Activities Committee had unwittingly aided and abetted the Communist cause. Such demonstrations by students, he said, were a danger to American democracy, and the misled students who engaged in them were, unwittingly perhaps, the fellow travelers of Communist conspiracy. Safety obviously can lie only in shunning all demonstrations, all expressions of opinion, for how can one ever tell when one's sincere convictions may mislead one into the heinous crime of fellow-traveling? [19]

Strange things happen in this world of academic freedom that Hoover so much admires. Perhaps one of the strangest happened in 1960 to Howard Higman, a sociology professor at the University of Colorado. Professor Higman was teaching an extremely popular course titled "Contemporary Social Issues." In it, students were encouraged to suggest public issues for debate. If nobody in the class had a vital matter exercising him at the moment, Higman would take over and deliver his lecture. During debates in the previous semester, he had expressed some critical opinions of the FBI, but on the day in late February, 1960, when all the trouble broke about his head, the FBI hadn't even been on the agenda. The topic for the day was the changes wrought by atomic energy. But the topic was suddenly switched by one of Professor Higman's students, none other than Miss Marilyn Van Derbur, the former Miss America.

"She stood up and started reading passages from a book," Professor Higman said. The book was Hoover's *Masters of Deceit*. As reported in the *Rocky Mountain News,* Higman gave this further account:

"Then she asked me to comment on my position regarding the FBI. I smelled a plot, but it is not my habit to duck questions. So I answered her.

"In brief, I said I belonged to that group which disapproved of the rise in America of a political police; that I doubted whether the FBI had contributed significantly to the security of the United States.

"When she said that the Rosenbergs had given the secrets of the atomic bomb to Russia, I said I doubted that any scientist believed that Russia developed the bomb principally because of the contributions of the Rosenbergs.

"I gave the FBI credit for developing one important and useful thing in America—a system of fingerprinting." [20]

What happened next was a development so curious it seemed to justify Professor Higman's suspicion of a plot. By some mysterious system of telepathy, news of the earthshaking colloquy in the classroom at Boulder, Colorado, traveled all the way to Washington, D.C. Miss Van Derbur always insisted that she had nothing to do with the word getting out. But somehow, in far-off Washington, the FBI evidently heard, for the Scripps-Howard press was tipped; its Denver affiliate, the *Rocky Mountain News,* got after Professor Higman, and there was the very devil to pay.

Once the story broke in the press, Hoover wrote a personal letter to the *News* denouncing the professor for "numerous inaccuracies and distortions." He said he always welcomed "constructive criticism" (a paradoxical phrase that seems to accord to the critic the license to praise), but added that Professor Higman's remarks were "at such great variance with the facts" that he had to "set the record straight." The charge that the FBI was a "political police" was, Hoover declared, "a blatant falsehood." He read the roll of government officials and Congressional committees supposedly having authority over the FBI, implying, of course, that they all performed their tasks in most rigorous fashion. The FBI, he stressed, "did not pass" on the guilt of the Rosenbergs; the courts had done that and had settled the issue in the most fair and impartial manner. The FBI simply devoted itself to its assigned tasks under federal law and, of course, on occasion, Hoover remarked puckishly, it did make news. Then, in a line that, one might think, would have made even Hoover gag, he added: "We do not seek publicity but have always conducted our operations on the premise that efficiency will bring its own notice to the public." [21]

The debate thus touched off raged for days, with Hoover and Miss Van Derbur exchanging letters of mutual praise and admiration; with the *Colorado Daily,* the university newspaper, defending the embattled professor; with Hoover writing the *Daily* a chiding letter. Summing it all up, Ron Krieger wrote in a signed editorial in the *Daily:*

"The only effect the situation can have on the academic mind— whether intended or not—is the effect of intimidation. The huge amount of public abuse heaped on the professor for attacking the FBI serves notice to even the most bold of scholars that it is dangerous business to speak one's mind about the federal police." [22]

Professor Higman's experience was not unique. Anyone who reads the college press across the nation must be aware of the grim reality of the process known as "the security check." It is justified on the ground that prospective employers of graduating students want to know their background. Depending on the job the prospective employee may fill, the check is made by agents of the FBI, or the Department of Defense, or the Civil Service Commission. If any suspicious tidbit of information turns up in the preliminary check, then the FBI would be asked to make "a full field investigation." Just what kind of activity by the student while he was in college might lead to a "full field investigation"? This is difficult to say. Such actions as reports of theft, dishonesty, drug addiction, drunkenness, or financial irresponsibility would obviously lead to searching inquiry. But actions are not the whole score; there are beliefs, too.

A hint of the kind of student activity that might later cause a student trouble may be found in an incident brought to light a few years ago by the *New Mexico Lobo,* of the University of New Mexico. Tau Kappa Alpha, a national college debating society, had selected a challenging topic for the annual collegiate debates. Should the United States grant diplomatic recognition to Red China? According to the *Lobo,* a debater on the Duke University team received a warning letter from Representative Edward J. Robeson (Democrat of Virginia). Representative Robeson wanted the names of those on the National Debating Committee and the name of the member of the Duke faculty responsible for the debating team. He warned: "I hope you will not undertake to debate the positive position of this subject, as quotations from your statements may embarrass you for the rest of your life."

Hoover promptly denied that the FBI had any interest in this particular debate. "I can assure you that the FBI has no interest whatsoever in college debates as such," he wrote the *Lobo*. Notice that "as such." It makes Hoover's denial a little less flat than would at first appear. The suspicion remains that a student taking the affirmative of the question might win for himself a demerit if the time ever came for "a full field investigation" into his beliefs. Is this the hallmark of a free society? A society in which any and all issues can be debated on their merits?

The prying into student beliefs and associations is done on a large scale. The *Golden Gator* of San Francisco State University reported in one survey that some twenty-five security agents visited the university each semester, checking on the background and affiliations of fifty or more students. The *Gator* tried to find out just how the FBI checks on beliefs. A special agent answered:

"We do not ask direct questions about the beliefs and associations of students unless unfavorable information of this kind comes to our attention during the routine investigation." Then: "We have to depend on what people think of an individual."

Sometimes the activities of security police go far beyond the bounds of checking up on graduates seeking employment and extend into on-the-spot dossier-compiling and surveillance. In December, 1962, the Yale University campus was rocked by the disclosure that the university's top policeman had been compiling a set of security files on both faculty and undergraduates. The Yale top cop was a former FBI agent, who had been made the university's Security Director and Associate Dean of Students after a number of Yale students had been involved in a sex scandal. He immediately instituted an FBI file-gathering system, going to such lengths that his own cop force was driven to revolt and funneled news of his activities to the student newspaper. Frederick Bissinger, Jr., on the *Yale News*, said:

We learned the file contained such items as press clippings from campus publications referring to groups that "might go that way," any group he considered suspicious or liable to be engaged in subversion. The men protested that [the director] insisted on their putting on the record every minor infraction, including a student who might be playing his hi-fi too loud.

But the most serious charge against [the director] by his men involves his allowing security officers from government agencies and private business firms to examine some of the ultra-complete records he keeps on students.

The director in typical FBI fashion, had "no comment" when the *Yale News* exposed the situation, but indications that the college publication hadn't overstated the case may be found in the swift action university officials took. Provost Kingman Brewster, Jr., sent the director a curt memorandum, advising, "You are not authorized to engage in the investigation of student or faculty political activities or views. It is understood that you are not authorized to respond to any outside inquiry with regard to student or faculty political activities or views." [23]

Other campuses, other students, have encountered the specter of FBI surveillance. In 1957, an FBI agent rushed to the Amherst campus after evidently intercepting in the mail a communication addressed to an Amherst alumnus who happened to be undergoing a loyalty check. The letter had been sent by the ominously sounding "Committee of 14." The Amherst Dean and Registrar finally succeeded in allaying federal fears. The "Committee of 14," it developed, wasn't a subversive organization plotting the revolution. It was just a committee investigating the college's chapel system. [24]

In the Midwest, a left-wing firebrand named Danny Rubin has become such a menace to the Republic that FBI agents descend on college campuses, hot on his trail wherever he may appear. In November, 1961, Rubin, then editor of the left-wing newspaper, *New Horizons for Youth,* addressed the University of Chicago Students for Civil Liberties. He had told the staff of the university newspaper, the *Chicago Maroon,* that the FBI tailed him wherever he went, and so the college journalists decided to have some fun and see for themselves. A member of the staff of the *Maroon* undertook to drive

Rubin to an El station to get a train home. He put the lecturer in the back seat of his car and then began to drive slowly through the college campus. Sure enough, another car began to follow. It followed so closely that industrious photographers from the *Maroon* even managed to take pictures of the *Maroon* member's car and its shadow.

Cruising around the campus, doubling back at times on his own trail, the staff man finally identified four cars, each with two men in them, that obviously had been assigned to follow every move he made. If one car lost him, another would pick him up. Testing his belief that he was really being followed, he timed lights so that he crashed through them just as they were going red (so did his pursuers); he turned down narrow alleys (so did his pursuers); and once he even wound up in a dead-end street (so did his pursuers). Just for the devil of it, he stopped on one occasion and told a local cop that he thought he was being followed. The cop looked at the pursuing car and reassured him: "It's all right, he's a policeman." [25]

For the staff man, it had all been pretty ridiculous and great fun. But in February, 1963, the matter became far more serious for John McAuliff, a junior at Carleton College, Northfield, Minnesota. Rubin, now editor of *Communist Viewpoint,* had made a speech on the Carleton campus under the auspices of "Challenge," the student youth organization that sponsors controversial speakers. McAuliff, on behalf of the sponsoring organization, sent Rubin a check for his appearance. That, according to McAuliff, was the only contact he ever had with Rubin. The FBI must have been keeping a close watch on Rubin's mail, for almost instantly it began a checkup on McAuliff.

McAuliff might never have known of the FBI shadow that had fallen across his life except that a close friend of his at the University of Indiana didn't feel that it was quite cricket that he should remain in ignorance. The friend was N. Paul Harmon. Right after a Special Agent came knocking at his door, Harmon wrote a letter to McAuliff, describing what had occurred. The FBI wanted to know whether McAuliff would have an "academic or serious interest in Communism." Harmon explained that McAuliff was on the board of "Challenge," a student group that had had George Lincoln Rockwell, the

American Nazi leader, as well as others of all shades of opinion, make addresses at the college.

Harmon explained that he and McAuliff had made a trip to the South during their last Christmas vacation and that they had discussed racial and desegregation issues with people in Jackson, Mississippi, and Atlanta, Georgia, trying to gain some firsthand knowledge of the situation. "Further, I said John was a liberal so far as I knew," Harmon wrote. ". . . When pressed, I said he was a little to the left of the average Democrat. [The agent] asked me to name others with such a position. I named Sen. H. Humphrey and Rep. J. Roosevelt. 'Was John a good American, loyal to his country?' Yes, I replied. . . .

"[The agent] thanked me for my help and assured me that it was nothing, in view of our conversation, to worry about. Nevertheless, I was asked not to mention our conversation to anyone lest they be disturbed."

McAuliff was indeed disturbed. He dispatched a sizzling letter to Hoover himself. His only contact with the editor of the Communist periodical, he explained, was to write him a brief letter and send him a check from "Challenge." He added:

> But, really, I find my reason for writing to the Communist Party irrelevant. . . . Whatever the content of my letter, I have a belief, which your office may consider quaint, that it was a private communication. I also have a quaint belief that to be a free man means to be able to write to whomever one pleases without having the government investigating you. . . .
>
> I am not arguing that counterintelligence activity is unnecessary. Your office bears the grave responsibility of keeping track of potentially treasonous people without serving as a brake on the free and fearless expression of all ideas. From this experience of mine, I would say you are seriously failing that responsibility.[26]

The degree of Hoover's failure was demonstrated by his conduct with respect to the San Francisco riot of 1960. The House Un-American Activities Committee, long a favorite partner of Hoover in the witch-hunt, had brought its road show into California for the fourth time within a relatively brief span of years. In 1953, 1956, and 1957 it had tackled the specter of Communism in the Bay Area. In 1957, especially, it had scored a notable triumph: It had driven a well-regarded scientist, William Sherwood, to commit suicide because he could not face the ordeal of a televised hearing. The committee followed up the suicide of Sherwood by subpoenaing 110 public-school teachers for a hearing in 1959, an action that caused such an outburst of resentment and protest that the projected sideshow had to be abandoned. The postponement was only temporary, however. The month of May, 1960, found the HUAC back in San Francisco.

This time the committee took no chances. It made certain that the hearing would be stacked in its favor even more than is usually the case. William A. Wheeler, a committee investigator, handed out white cards to "friendly" organizations before the hearings opened. Admission to the small hearing room in City Hall was to be by white card only. Students in the Bay Area gathered to protest. They demanded that admission be on a first-come, first-served basis. The agitation came to a head on the second day of the hearings, Friday, May 13, 1960. When demonstrating students, trying to get into the hearings, pressed against the barriers set up by police, the cops forced them back. The students surged forward again, and the police turned fire-hoses on the students. When the students withstood the drenching, refusing to leave the premises, the police went to work with their nightsticks.

Veteran San Francisco newsmen and television cameramen were on the scene. All seem in general agreement on what happened. "Never in 20 years as a reporter have I seen such brutality," wrote Mel Wax the next day. George Draper, of the conservative *San Francisco Chronicle,* reported: "I saw one slightly built lad being carried by two husky officers. One held the boy's shirt, the other held him by the feet. He was struggling, but he was no match for the two bigger men. Then, from nowhere, appeared a third officer; he went to the slender boy firmly held by the other two officers, and clubbed him three times in the head. You could hear the hollow smack of the club striking. The boy went limp and was carried out. . . . Police were now clubbing the demonstrators at will."

Mel Wax added: "I saw teenage college girls pushed down the marble stairs by big, hulking motorcycle policemen who answered the riot call. The girls bounced down, step by step, their skirts flaring above their hips. They screamed and cried, but no one heard." [27]

Sixty-four students were arrested, charged with inciting a riot, resisting arrest, and disturbing the peace. The charges against sixty-three were quickly dismissed. This did not look too good for the forces of the law that had been so sorely set upon by the youthful revolutionists, and so a desperate effort was made to drum up charges that would stick against at least one of the demonstrators. The selected victim was Robert Meisenbach, 22, a student at the University of California at Berkeley. The official charge was that Meisenbach had precipitated the riot by leaping the barrier, seizing a policeman's nightstick, and whacking him over the head with it. This was the act, said officialdom, that had caused the hoses to be turned on. Unfortunately for this contention, Robert Campbell, a photographer for the *San Francisco Chronicle,* had snapped a picture of the scene just *after* the hoses went into action—and there, clearly visible in the picture, standing some feet away from the melee and calmly smoking a pipe, was Meisenbach. When Meisenbach was brought to trial in the spring of 1961, he was promptly acquitted.

In the light of this well-established record, what was the attitude of J. Edgar Hoover? It was what anyone, knowing the man, might expect. The San Francisco riot, he said, was the result of a deep-dyed Communist plot.

Hoover was contradicted by fifty-eight of the sixty-four arrested students, who signed a statement declaring that no one had incited them to act. This disclaimer cut no ice with Hoover. On July 17, 1960, in an 18-page report to his favorite Congressional committee, the HUAC, he called the riot "the most successful Communist coup to occur in the San Francisco area in 25 years." The riot had demonstrated, he said, that American youth was no more immune to Communist manipulation than the students of Japan and Uruguay. He charged that California Communist leaders, naming no names, had engineered and financed the San Francisco riot; that the Communists were planning more youth demonstrations of a similar nature (strikingly, in the years since, there have been none); and that the American Communist Party was elated and believed the riot was the best thing that had happened to it in years.[28]

Twenty-one of the arrested students challenged Hoover, declaring his statements "either are based on lack of information or are made in bad faith." Assemblyman John A. O'Connel, who professed that always previously he had been an admirer of Hoover, declared in a public speech that he believed Hoover "had lied," and in a letter to Hoover, he repeated the statement and made this comment on Hoover's pamphlet, "Communist Target—Youth":

"The pamphlet, published and distributed by the HUAC, clearly implies that there was no legitimate reason for any non-Communist to oppose the Committee hearing. Many San Franciscans considered that a political judgment which was unfounded in fact and also outside the rightful scope of the supposedly non-political function of your office." [29]

Such protests had no effect. The House committee, with Hoover in its corner, proceeded to produce the distorted film "Operation Abolition," giving its and Hoover's "Communist plot" version of the San Francisco riot. This film, which Mel Wax, who was there, has called "distorted and false," which has been branded a distortion by such a non-Communist organization as the National Council of Churches, nevertheless has become a major hit in the propaganda arsenal of the rabid right and has been viewed, under the sponsorship of business and civic organizations, by literally millions of Americans.

The sequence tells its own story. It raises some disturbing questions. What becomes of true academic freedom when the FBI rides herd on the college campuses, when its director distorts, as he certainly did distort, the meaning of an event like the San Francisco riot? What happens to truth and understanding? Is it possible, under the intimidation (for it is nothing else) of FBI surveillance and security checks, to maintain free discussion, so vital in informing the people of the truth and thrashing out issues in a democracy? And can this democracy, any democracy, long tolerate this police intrusion into its intellectual life, into its freedoms?

■ 5 ■

There is one field in which the vaunted FBI has been a complete and abject failure—the field of civil rights.

Hoover can successfully defy the Supreme Court. By his merest frown, he can block the issuance of a radio franchise. He can watch the college campuses and make certain that the Communist virus does not take root in the young. But when it comes to doing battle with the racist South, to infiltrating White Citizens Councils the way the Communist Party has been infiltrated, to coping with sadistic police forces that beat and kill Negro citizens with impunity, to avenging Negroes slain because they tried to exercise their right to vote, to solving the bombings of the homes of Negro civil rights leaders and the bombings of Negro churches, Hoover and his FBI have been little more than disinterested spectators, unmoved by scenes of national shame and disgrace.

In one sense, their sideline role in this moral crisis of our times might have been anticipated. Hoover's passion has always been that of the archconservative intent on preserving the established order without change. A martinet to the bone, he seems instinctively antipathetic to social changes of any sort. His world of order, of Spartan severity and Prussian-like efficiency, is a world innately oblivious to the surging tides of idealism that periodically disrupt existing systems and sweep mankind on to new frontiers. Confronted with epochal change, Hoover, with his astigmatism, is apt to see only a new manifestation of the Communist menace.

The great moral upheaval of 1963—a nation's outrage at the spectacle of police dogs in the hands of sadistic police attacking Negro demonstrators in Birmingham, a nation's shock at the church bombing that cost four little girls their lives—stirred no wrath and indignation in the soul of the all-powerful master of the FBI. Hoover has thundered from the rooftops about the menace of gun-toting desperados, of bank robbers, of espionage, of subversion, of juvenile delinquency, but one listens in vain for his alarmist shouts on civil rights.

On the contrary, during the summer of 1963, with the civil rights crisis at its height, there were intimations that the civil rights movement in the South might be a part of the devious Communist conspiracy. Southern political leaders, with whom Hoover has maintained a long and loving rapport, persisted in trying to smear the Negro movement for equality and justice in the twentieth century with the Communist label. They intimated that the FBI endorsed this view.

State Senator John C. McLaurin, of Mississippi, in a hearing on the civil rights bill proposed by the Kennedy Administration, challenged the Senators to call Hoover. The boss of the FBI, he said, could expose the "brazen coverup" by his own titular chief, Attorney General Robert Kennedy. Hoover, he asserted, "could present ample evidence that the Communists were and are now using the self-styled Negro leaders as part of the Communist conspiracy."

Did such statements truly represent the attitude of Hoover and the FBI? The *New York Post* challenged the Senate to call Hoover, challenged Hoover to speak out and set the record straight. But there was only silence. Hoover, who had felt compelled to appear before a Senate committee in the cause of truth in the Harry Dexter White case, felt no similar compulsion to clear the air and the issue now.[30]

This lack of disclaimer gives the charge by Southern racists an appearance of validity that it might otherwise not have had. This same attitude on civil rights had shown up in Hoover's past. In 1920, in the memorandum on "The Revolution in Action," prepared by Hoover's GID for submission to Congress by Attorney General Palmer, the race riots of 1919 were discussed in terms that plainly implied they were the result of Communist intrigue.

"The Reds have done a vast amount of evil damage by carrying doctrines of race revolt and the poison of bolshevism to the Negroes . . . ," the report said. "This business has been perhaps the most contemptible and wicked performance of our American revolutionary fanatics." [31]

In the intervening years, Hoover's indifference to civil rights activities has become clearly evident. He has even made attempts to have his bureau relieved of all necessity for dealing with the issue.

The United States Commission on Civil Rights, in a 1961 report, described Hoover's lukewarm attitude in words that parallel the criticism ex-Agent Jack Levine leveled at the Bureau. The Commission wrote:

It has been reported from time to time that the Bureau has little enthusiasm for its task of investigating complaints of police brutality. If the contention is accurate, that fact is, to some degree, understandable. The Director has used the strongest possible language to stress the need for cooperation between the Bureau and law enforcement officials at all levels. Apparently, without this cooperation the FBI could not maintain the excellent record it now enjoys in the enforcement of a long list of Federal criminal statutes. Although the Bureau states that it "has not experienced any particular difficulty or embarrassment in connection with investigation of alleged police brutality," there is evidence that the investigations of such offenses may jeopardize that working relationship. . . .

Still another difficulty may arise from the cooperative relationship between the FBI and local policemen. Although the Bureau has declared that it knows "of no instances of any individuals being fearful to bring complaints to the attention of the FBI," there is evidence that some victims and witnesses, especially among Negroes in the Deep South, are afraid to bring information to the Bureau's field offices. . . . Some of their fears appear to be based upon the fact that agents and policemen often work closely together, and that officials somehow soon learn the name of complainants.[32]

In footnotes to this report, the Civil Rights Commission spelled out in considerable detail the background of the FBI's lackadaisical performance. It quoted in full a letter Hoover wrote to the Attorney General on September 24, 1946, in which he made it clear that he would prefer to withdraw from the civil rights field. He argued that the Bureau was "expending a considerable amount of manpower" investigating crimes in the South "in which there cannot conceivably be any violation of a Federal statute." When the Bureau investigated such cases, he pointed out, it became saddled "in the public mind and in the press with the responsibility" for their solution. This was not good for the prestige of the Bureau. And, while Hoover did not at all "condone the type of activities" involved in such cases, he felt that jurisdiction resided "in the State Courts." He concluded that he felt "it is a mistake of policy for the Department to accept for investigation so many of these cases in which, as I have indicated, there is no probability of federal prosecutive action and in which the Bureau and the Department are merely assessed in the public mind with a responsibility which is neither discharged nor executed."

In his reply to Hoover, the Attorney General agreed that many cases might not constitute a violation of federal law, but, he pointed out, "in each case the complaint made is indicative of a violation, and if we do not investigate we are placed in the position of having received the complaint of a violation and of having failed to satisfy ourselves that it is or is not such a violation. I know of no way to avoid at least a preliminary inquiry into the facts of a complaint which alleges a civil rights offense. I am sure you agree that we should not be in the position of avoiding such action." [33]

According to the Civil Rights Commission, the Bureau sometimes felt civil rights cases were "burdensome." The policy adopted, in the words of Hoover in his annual reports, was for the FBI to conduct "a preliminary investigation immediately upon the receipt of a complaint alleging a federal civil rights violation." References to "preliminary investigations" began to disappear after 1958, and by 1959 Hoover was noting merely that "1,292 alleged civil rights violations were received." In 1960, his report noted merely that "1,398 alleged civil rights violations were reported to the FBI during the 1960 fiscal year." [34]

The attitude of Hoover and the FBI, implicit in such actions, was plainly stated by a former FBI agent who was interviewed by a staff member of the Civil Rights Commission. The Commission reported:

In 1961 a Commission staff member interviewed a former FBI agent who had served with that agency for many years, but who, in his capacity at the time of the interview, handled certain complaints of civil rights violations, including police brutality. The Commission staff member's field notes state:

"I asked him why he did not refer complaints to the FBI, especially since he was formerly a special agent. Mr. (name withheld) stated that he does not turn civil rights cases over to the Bureau, because they don't like them. He explained that it is very embarrassing to agents to have to investigate police department officials in the morning and then attempt to enlist their cooperation on other cases in the afternoon. He stated that the Bureau distributed a monthly bulletin to police departments all over the country and makes no secret therein of the sort of information in which the FBI is interested, i.e., kidnaping, bank robberies, but never civil rights. He stated that the Bureau feels that 'civil rights cases shouldn't even be in there.' "

The ex-agent made it clear that he was in accord with this position which, however, has never been stated by any official FBI source. [35]

Such is the hidden face of the FBI in the civil rights battle, which poses the great domestic moral issue of our time. You won't find it flaunted prominently, even in the reports of the Civil Rights Commission. J. Edgar Hoover is too powerful for that. But you will find it among the footnotes to the Commission's report.

Take a good, close look at that half-seen, unlovely face. And take a good close look at the sadism it supports by its acquiescence. Take the case of James Brazier, Negro, done to death by the police of Dawson, Georgia, in 1958 because he had had the effrontery to buy a new car.

Mrs. Hattie Bell Brazier, his widow, told the Civil Rights Commission that they had purchased a new Chevrolet in 1956, another in 1958. In November, 1957, "Officer Y," of the Dawson police, arrested James Brazier on a speeding charge and took him to jail. According to Brazier's story to his wife, this happened:

"When I first entered the door of the jail, 'Y' hit me on the back of the head and knocked me down and said, 'You smart son-of-a-bitch, I been waiting to get my hands on you for a long time.' I said, 'Why you want me for?' 'Y' said, 'You is a nigger who is buying new cars and we can't hardly live. I'll get you yet.' "

"Officer Y," according to Brazier's story, then hit him several more times, put his foot in the small of the prostrate Negro's back and stamped with such force Mrs. Brazier saw the footprints in the skin afterward. He warned: "You better not say a damn thing about it or I'll stomp your damn brains out."

After his release from jail, James Brazier was bleeding from the ear and vomiting blood. From this time in the fall of 1957 until his second and fatal encounter with the law in April, 1958, Brazier was under the care of a local white physician for his injuries.

On Sunday evening April 20, 1958, police arrested James Brazier's father on a charge of drunken driving. According to the police, James protested, tried to interfere, and "threatened" them. Again, according to the police, they got a warrant for his arrest; he resisted violently; and they had to subdue him with a blackjack. He was taken to the county jail, where a doctor examined him and found no serious injury.

According to the Brazier family and a flock of Negro eyewitnesses, it didn't happen this way at all. No warrant was produced. The officers simply jumped out of their patrol car, ran to Brazier, grabbed him, and started beating him with their blackjacks. Mrs. Brazier's affidavit was quoted in the Civil Rights Commission's report:

" 'Y' then said, 'You smart son-of-a-bitch, I told you I would get you.' James said, 'What do you want to hurt me for? I ain't done nothing. I got a heap of little chillun.' 'Y' said, 'I don't give a goddam how many children you got, you're going away from here.' . . . 'Y' pulled out his pistol and stuck it against James' stomach and said, 'I oughta blow your goddam brains out.' "

Brazier's 10-year-old son pleaded with the officers to stop beating his father—and was knocked flat by "Officer Y." Brazier was thrown to the floor in the back of the police car, his legs dangling outside. "Y" kicked him twice in the groin, slammed the car door on his legs, threw a hat full of sand on his bloody face, and drove off.

When Brazier arrived at the jail and was examined by the doctor, he was bloody but in one piece. The next morning, when he appeared in court, he was incoherent and could hardly stand. Taken to a hospital in Columbus, Georgia, he died five days later of brain damage and a fractured skull.

Obviously something fatal must have happened to James Brazier during that night when he supposedly was locked safely in his cell in the jail—and in the custody of police. Marvin Goshay, 23, another Negro who was in the jail at the time, signed an affidavit for the Civil Rights Commission in which he said that, around midnight, Officers "X" and "Y" took Brazier from his cell, and when Goshay saw him again the next morning, Brazier was a wreck. "We had to carry him to the car because he couldn't walk."

When a federal grand jury investigated Brazier's death, Goshay, though subpoenaed, never did get to testify. Officer "Y" picked him up on the street and held him in prison for a week, not releasing him until the grand jury had dismissed the case. Goshay was slated to be a witness in a federal court civil suit brought by Mrs. Brazier against Officer "Y," but again he never got to testify. On March 14, 1961, he was found mysteriously dead in a Dawson undertaking parlor, apparently of asphyxiation.

For his services in upholding law and order in Dawson, Officer "Y" was promoted.[36]

The case of James Brazier is not unique. It has been repeated, with variations according to individual circumstances, innumerable times throughout the South. A Lamar Smith, too active in trying to register Mississippi Negro voters, is gunned down in the broad light of day, in the presence of a full fifty witnesses, virtually on the steps of a Mississippi courthouse—and nobody is even brought to trial. Since 1947 forty bombing have wrecked Birmingham homes and churches. Until the blast that killed four little girls on September 15, 1963, a case in which arrests finally were made, not one of those bombings had been solved.[37] Between January 1, 1958, and June 30, 1960, the FBI investigated 461 cases of police brutality against Negroes in the South—and not one of those cases resulted in a conviction.

The repeated beatings, mutilations, slaying of Negroes by police officers in the South, and the shootings and bombings in the campaign of terrorism by the shining knights of the Klan and the White Citizens Councils, have not provoked a single word of protest from Hoover. He does not "condone" such actions, of course, but he feels that such minor incidents should be left to the states to handle, which means, in effect, that he does indeed condone them. Is there any wonder that Negroes in the South, from the Reverend Dr. Martin Luther King down, fear and distrust the FBI almost as much as they do the local police? They fear and distrust with good reason, for the record indicates that Hoover and the FBI have not blushed to stand four-square in the corner of the white supremacists, the racists who have made sadism a part of the culture of the South.[38]

■ Notes ■

[1] See *The New York Times* and *New York Herald Tribune* for repeated articles during the month of September, especially the issues of Sept. 12 and 27, 1948.

[2] For a reproduction of the Greenglass memoranda found in Rogge's file, see the appendixes in John Wexley, *The Judgment of Julius and Ethel Rosenberg* (Cameron-Kahn, 1955). See also Malcolm P. Sharp (professor of law, University of Chicago), *Was Justice Done, the Rosenberg-Sobell Case* (Monthly Review Press, New York, 1956).

[3] The trial record, p. 705.

[4] See Bloch's summation, pp. 2214 and 2215, of the trial record.

[5] The theory that the Communists wanted the conviction of the Rosenbergs and actually conspired to get it has been forcibly expounded by Irwin Edelman,

a former West Coast Communist. Edelman's presentation of the facts drew the endorsement of Albert Einstein and inspired a group of nonaffiliated lawyers to make a last-minute appeal to Justice William O. Douglas for a review of the case. Douglas was so disturbed that he issued a writ, halting the execution, but he was overruled by a hastily summoned full Supreme Court bench on June 18, 1953. However, as Justice Hugo Black later wrote, the Supreme Court never did examine the evidence in the Rosenberg case. As in the Hiss and Remington cases, the court simply ducked the hot issue—and the Rosenbergs were executed. See Edelman's long summary of his position and the evidence in *The Independent,* November, 1956.

[6] For accounts of the first Coplon trial see the *New York Times* and *New York Herald Tribune* for the months of April, May, and June, 1949. See also Max Lowenthal, *The Federal Bureau of Investigation* (William Sloane Associates, 1950), pp. 434–435.

[7] *New York Times,* Dec. 14 and 15, 1949.

[8] *New York Herald Tribune,* Jan. 13, 1950.

[9] *New York Times,* Feb. 8, 1958.

[10] For a concise summary of these elements of the Jencks decision, see Drew Pearson's column of July 2, 1957.

[11] See the *New York Post,* Oct. 11, 1959.

[12] See editorial in the *Washington Post,* July 8, 1957.

[13] Joseph and Stewart Alsop, "Matter of Fact," in the *New York Herald Tribune,* May 19, 1954.

[14] Joseph and Stewart Alsop, "Brownell Probing His Own Spies," in the *Washington Post,* July 4, 1954.

[15] *New York Post,* Oct. 11, 1959.

[16] The quotes that follow are from the text of Durr's speech delivered at the annual luncheon of the Associated Church Press and the National Religious Publicity Council, Hotel Commodore, New York, April 17, 1947.

[17] Letter from Durr to Carey McWilliams, editor of *The Nation,* Nov. 21, 1953.

[18] From the minutes of the FCC meeting debating what reply should be made to Hoover.

[19] *New Mexico Lobo,* of the University of New Mexico, Oct. 11, 1962.

[20] *Rocky Mountain News,* Denver, Colo., Feb. 18, 1960.

[21] *Ibid.,* Feb. 25, 1960.

[22] *The Colorado Daily,* Mar. 4, 1960.

[23] See the *New York Herald Tribune* and the *New York Post,* Dec. 4, 1962.

[24] *Columbia Spectator,* Sept. 30, 1957.

[25] *Chicago Maroon,* Nov. 30, 1961.

[26] See *The Carletonian,* Feb. 20, 1963; and the *Minneapolis Morning Tribune,* Feb. 28, 1963.

[27] *New York Post,* Mar. 3, 1961.

[28] Associated Press dispatch from Washington, July 17, 1960.

[29] *San Francisco Chronicle,* May 3, 1961; and text of letter from O'Connell to Hoover, Apr. 28, 1961.

[30] *New York Post,* Aug. 1, 1963.

[31] House Rules Committee, 1920, Part 2 of Palmer vs. Post, p. 239. A further indication that Hoover's attitude has not changed and that his FBI files would

indeed have backed the contentions of the Southern racists had he been called upon to testify may be found in an entirely separate New York court case in October, 1963. Though the case in question had nothing to do with the Southern crisis, an FBI informer-witness, Mrs. Elizabeth L. Williams, testified at a hearing before the Subversive Activities Control Board that she had attended Communist meetings for the FBI and that then, at the FBI's behest, she had attended meetings of the National Association for the Advancement of Colored People. She testified that, as a result of this double espionage, she had recognized Communists at NAACP meetings. (See the *New York Daily News,* Oct. 2, 1963.)

[32] *Justice,* Book 5 of 1961 report of Commission on Civil Rights (Government Printing Office), pp. 61–62.

[33] *Ibid.,* pp. 213–215.

[34] *Ibid.,* pp. 217–218.

[35] *Ibid.,* p. 219.

[36] *Ibid.,* pp. 9–12; also footnote, p. 174.

[37] See James Wechsler, the *New York Post,* Sept. 18, 1963.

[38] For example, see interview with Dr. King in the *New York Times* of Nov. 19, 1962. Dr. King charged bluntly that the FBI sides with segregationists in the South. He said: "One of the great problems we face with the FBI in the South is that the agents are white Southerners who have been influenced by the mores of the community. To maintain their status, they have to be friendly with the local police and people who are promoting segregation. Every time I saw FBI men in Albany, they were with the local police force."

12 The Final Judgment

The greatest sin of Hoover and the FBI is that, by a monumental propaganda effort, they have made themselves sacrosanct. Once a man, an institution, is enshrined on a pedestal above the law, impervious to criticism, democracy loses the fine edge of its freedom and takes a long stride toward authoritarianism. The police state looms on the horizon.

Few Americans have any realization of the potential harm they do by their uncritical idolatry of Hoover and the FBI. They remember only the good—and there is undeniable good—that Hoover and his FBI publicity bureau have propagandized.

The FBI agent has become to the public the clean-cut, square-jawed, pure-as-snow American lad, flawless as a comic-strip hero, and the nemesis of crime. The Bureau's huge fingerprint collection, its scientific methods of crime detection, its successes in gunning down desperados and jailing bank robbers and kidnapers—these are the achievements that have fostered a national faith in the perfection of the FBI.

Hoover has been accorded a reverence, an immunity from criticism, such as has not been the lot of the greatest Presidents in our history. Washington, perhaps the greatest of all Americans, was savagely attacked in his time; so was Jefferson; so was Lincoln; so were Theodore and Franklin Roosevelt—and so, after the honeymoon of his first Administration, was that most popular of recent Presidents, Eisenhower. Some of the criticism was just, much was unjust, but that is not the point. The point is that it existed—and that, as long as criticism exists, the checkreins that are essential to the preservation of democracy exist. Remove those checkreins; enshrine the figure of the infallible policeman above the law, above the Supreme Court, and

414

you create a police-state atmosphere of intimidation that brings on the perversion of the democratic processes.

This treacherous undermining of a free society has already gone far. Hoover's enormous and unchecked power—the clandestine wire-tapping, mail checking, and surveillance; the gossip, the rumor, the damaging truth and half-truth that repose in the secret dossiers of the FBI—has served to intimidate the highest officials in government and to repress debate. As Jack Levine and William Turner reported, there isn't a legislator on the Hill who dares to risk a conflict with Hoover, however good the cause. A similar faintness of heart pervades the mass media of information. For anyone curious to know the reasons, a case study is provided in the experience of the *New York Post* when it set out to do an uninhibited study of Hoover and the FBI.

■ 1 ■

Hoover's campaign to protect himself and the FBI began almost a full year before the *Post* series was published. In October, 1958, my own first, critical assessment of the FBI had appeared in *The Nation*. About the same time, the *Post* assigned reporters to a similar project. The instant it did, a publicity campaign began to discredit its disclosures before they could be disclosed. The hypocrisy of Hoover's contention that he always welcomes "constructive criticism" was probably never better exposed than in the extent to which he went to kill off this criticism before it could be born.

The tactics were predictable; indeed, I had outlined them in advance in my article in *The Nation*. Hoover kept in the shadows of the background, maintaining his characteristically saintlike pose above the battle, while, out on the front lines, his ideological helpers went to work to protect him from the great, new, devious communistic "plot" that might "destroy" the FBI. The first blast was fired by Preston J. Moore, national commander of the American Legion. My already committed offense, and the *Post*'s contemplated offense, were denounced by Moore as "similar to the Communist Party's unsuccessful efforts in 1940" to wreck the FBI. Moore accused the *Post* of attempting to do a "character-assassination job" on Hoover; its reporters in Washington and other cities, he said, were going to "skulk around the restaurants and other public places in the hope of digging up information that could be used against Hoover and the FBI." [1]

The cry that poor, helpless Hoover was being made the victim of some colossal Red conspiracy now resounded on all sides. In Boston, Archbishop Richard James Cushing (later Cardinal Cushing, the principal spiritual presence at the inauguration of President Kennedy) denounced the "smear campaign" that, he said, had been started. "If we are to survive in this country," he told 1,500 Massachusetts state employees at a Communion breakfast, "we must continue to use the services of this great FBI protective force against violence, crime, and sedition. . . . We cannot allow those who are enemies of the nation or who are dupes of these enemies to befuddle or to control us." [2]

In Washington, Senator John Marshall Butler (Republican of Maryland) said he would ask the Senate Internal Security Committee to investigate "a deliberate smear campaign" against Hoover and the Bureau.[3] And in New York the ultrarightist news sheet *Counterattack* attacked *The Nation* and the *Post* and urged: "All Americans should join in supporting the FBI. Write your Congressmen and Senators that you back the FBI against *The Nation* and this attack." [4]

Of course, this alarmist outcry about a subversive plot to undermine the FBI was as phony as some of the statistics Hoover uses to build up his favorite menace of the moment. Hoover's own actions in his arrogant attack on the Supreme Court in the Jencks case had convinced *The Nation* that the time had come for a full and fresh appraisal of his power and its nature, and I had been asked to do the assessment. As for the *Post,* neither anyone at *The Nation* nor I had any idea that the paper contemplated doing a series on Hoover until the FBI-sparked campaign disclosed it.

Hoover's distaste for running the risk of the "constructive criticism" he so favors became evident when the *Post* pressed its investigative work in preparation for its series. Mrs. Dorothy Schiff, the paper's publisher, subsequently revealed the cloak-and-dagger atmosphere that quickly enveloped her and her staff. She wrote that Robert Spivack, the *Post*'s Washington correspondent, was "approached" and the news was "leaked" to him that "the FBI had begun an inves-

tigation of me and a young female member of my family." Next, Mrs.
Schiff happened to dine in a New York restaurant with a major New
York advertiser, who was a close personal friend. Some indication
that she was, perhaps, the object of surveillance swiftly developed.
A few days later, the advertiser, again dining out, was approached
by two men who asked him if he would like to meet J. Edgar Hoover.
Hoover had always been one of the big advertiser's heroes, and he was
greatly flattered when Hoover and his shadow, Clyde Tolson, came to
his table. During the course of the conversation, Hoover expressed
grave concern about the series the *Post* was contemplating; it would
be, he felt, "a smear" that would harm him and the FBI in the eyes
of the American people. What made Hoover so sure? The big advertiser said Hoover had confided that James Wechsler, the *Post*'s editor,
"had had it in for him ever since the FBI had Wechsler's wife fired
when she was secretary of some government committee. . . .
Hoover, according to the advertiser, asserted that she had been dismissed as a Communist." [5]

This, as Mrs. Schiff later wrote, was "as slanderous a piece of
McCarthyism as has ever been perpetrated." She had documentary
proof of these facts: Nancy Wechsler, a lawyer, had been a member
of President Truman's Civil Rights Commission in the 1940's. In this
capacity, she had criticized the FBI for the handling of some civil
rights cases in the South. Though she had been, in her teens, a member of the Young Communist League, she had quickly become dis-
enchanted with the Party. She had never been a Communist—and
she had never been fired because she was. Indeed, when she left the
Civil Rights Commission, she left it with high praise for her work by
all the Commission members. The Hoover maneuver, Mrs. Schiff
wrote, had been an attempt "to intimidate a publisher through an
advertiser."

This is the kind of muscle that Hoover musters at the first whiff
of criticism. It discourages all but the most dauntless. Especially does
it discourage politicians, who dare not risk being linked to the Communist conspiracy, however unjustly. The result is that they keep
their mouths shut about Hoover even when they are themselves ob-
jects of FBI investigation.

Mrs. Schiff and the *Post* discovered that some of the most distinguished political figures on the Hill simply would not risk being quoted on the subject of Hoover. At a public dinner one evening, Mrs. Schiff wrote, she happened to be seated beside "a veteran liberal Senator." She remarked to him that apparently members of Congress were reluctant to discuss Hoover for fear of retaliation, and that Hoover apparently had a dossier on every congressman. What did the Senator think about Hoover? At first he evaded the question, but when Mrs. Schiff described some of the experiences she was having, he confided that he "didn't like a police state."

"The Senator then told me," Mrs. Schiff wrote, "that during his last reelection campaign he had been warned by someone stationed at the White House that his office and home were 'bugged.' When the Senator expressed disbelief, the man passed on certain trivial information, known only to the Senator, his trusted administrative assistant, and his wife. These details convinced the Senator that he indeed was being watched." [6]

Hoover has always denied that he makes investigations of congressmen or prominent citizens "as such." Note again that qualifying "as such." He investigates, he says, only when there is a complaint charging a federal law violation. But in this age of unrestrained suspicion about subversion, when any man may be suspect, it could hardly be difficult to obtain "a complaint" warranting "an investigation." There is little question among journalists in Washington or among legislators on the Hill that the FBI does maintain dossiers on virtually everybody of any prominence. One "important member of Congress who has intimate dealings with the FBI in the course of his official duties" told the *Post*: "It is true that the FBI has detailed dossiers on everyone in Washington."

He added: "I think it can be viewed with a good deal of misgivings. The *Times* said it could give the holder of dossiers 'possessive power' over Congress. Only criminals or potential criminals should be included in those dossiers." [7]

Why don't the elected representatives of the people rebel against the "bugging" of their homes and offices, the compiling of dossiers on their private lives and beliefs? A liberal Senator, promised anonymity by the *Post,* put it this way: "I'd say more than 90 percent of the Senate is behind him [Hoover] politically. Hoover is not *vul-*

nerable. In politics you do not attack Santa Claus and you do not attack God. If it got back to my district that I attacked J. Edgar Hoover, I would be pilloried. Those who were concerned with the growth of the federal police—men like Senator Norris and others— are dead now, or back home. Those that are here cannot afford to speak up." [8]

Power? The American system has never seen its equal.

■ 2 ■

It is this power and Hoover's unbridled use of it that represents today one of the greatest dangers to American democracy.

The FBI is needed; it is, at its best, highly efficient. And Hoover, had he been content to fulfill his duties as the nation's No. 1 police-man in the pursuit of crime, could have won for himself an untar-nished place in history. That he was not content, that he had to domi-nate ever more and more of the national scene is his tragedy—and the nation's danger. No policeman, however infallible, should be allowed to become in effect prosecutor, judge, and jury.

There can be no denying Hoover's great ability. Among his out-standing accomplishments are his building up of a sound and gener-ally incorruptible organization, his bringing into the FBI men of high caliber, his creation of a fine esprit de corps in the FBI. However, similar achievements distinguish some other federal agencies, notably the Secret Service and the Federal Bureau of Narcotics. And though Hoover deserves credit for molding a highly efficient FBI, he is not the only administrator who has achieved an efficient organization. And the others have done it without such overwhelming and danger-ous fanfare.

Given his pivotal position in the federal crime-fighting structure, it was inevitable that Hoover's role would be more important than that of any other chief of detective forces. It is to his credit that he has used his opportunity to elevate the nature of police work across the nation. His establishment of the central fingerprint file was a boon to crime-fighting on every level. The FBI scientific laboratory stimulated the use of science in crime detection. The National Police Academy has given advanced training in the most modern methods to police departments throughout the nation. These are solid, valid, praise-worthy accomplishments.

If Hoover could have been content with such important contributions, all would have been well; but Hoover is a man who can never be content. As soon as he embarked on the publicity campaign to create in the public mind the image of the infallible FBI, he began to become an overblown figure, dangerous to himself and to others. The phenomenon of universal praise can hardly be good for Hoover, for the bureau he heads, or for the American people.

That Hoover has become the greatest untouchable in American history is not entirely his own doing. He has been helped by many hands. One of the most important initially was Franklin Roosevelt, who took pride in Hoover's accomplishments and felt that they redounded to the credit of his Administration. It was Roosevelt, too, who made the cardinal mistake of violating Stone's wise dictum that the FBI should concern itself only with crime; it was Roosevelt who, in his concern with the problems of World War II, put the FBI back into the field of undercover work, back into the business of ferreting out potential dangers in men's ideas. Once this step had been taken, there was no chance of confining or limiting the activities and the influence of the FBI, for the possibility of subversion, the need for security, could always be advanced as justification for the investigation of any and every man. Roosevelt doubtless felt that, with his own masterful hand at the helm, there was little danger of the FBI's running amok, and perhaps, for the time and the moment, this was true. But FDR was not immortal; once he was gone, there was no figure of comparable magnitude to cope with, to contain and restrain, the activities of Hoover.

And there were powerful forces egging Hoover on, puffing up his image. One of the most powerful has been the American press. Perhaps it would be more accurate to say American publishers, for the working press on many levels recognizes the dangers implicit in the overglorification of Hoover and the FBI. Hoover, of course, has always had his shouting partisans in the press corps; but there are many Washington correspondents, of all shades of political opinion, conservative as well as liberal, who would be glad to set the record straight. That they have accomplished so little in this regard can be attributed to the pressures that influence many publishers and to the fact that Hoover's hard right-wing ideology makes him a shining knight in many echelons of the publishing business.

About Hoover's political bias, there can be little question. He has, of course, sedulously cultivated the myth that he is nonpolitical. His pose is that of the impartial civil servant, enthroned above the political battlefield. His success in maintaining this pose, even while he is joining lustily in the battle, exemplifies his political ambidexterity. But if you cast aside the correct words, which Hoover always utters, and examine the Hoover actions, you will see on which side he throws his influence.

The Congressional witch-hunts of 1948 were clearly sparked by material funneled from FBI files. The Chambers and Bentley revelations, even with the help of 500 FBI agents using all the techniques of wire-tapping, mail-opening, and surveillance, had not been enough to produce indictments under the normal processes of the law—and so they had been funneled to committees before whom witnesses, if they sought to establish their innocence, could be entrapped on perjury charges. In the Brownell-White affair, Hoover dropped the pretense that he does not "evaluate" and showed his bias by supporting Brownell's partisan charge to the hilt, doing his utmost to tear down the reputation of Truman. Even more revealing was Hoover's buddylike relation with Joe McCarthy.

The McCarthy love affair stigmatizes the man who could indulge in it. No more irresponsible man than Joseph R. McCarthy ever lived. After the hysteria that he generated began to die away, there was a growing agreement that probably no man of recent times has done more damage to the American image here and abroad. In the 1952 Presidential campaign, McCarthy had committed a blatant and unforgivable affront to democratic traditions. On the day Eisenhower tripped on his halo by publicly embracing McCarthy in Wisconsin and proclaiming he was for good old Joe, for good Republicans everywhere, the Senator put on one of his typical this-leads-to-this-and-that performances, seeking to link Adlai Stevenson to the dark devices of Moscow. He wound up by declaring that if someone would only smuggle him aboard the Democratic campaign special with a baseball bat in his hand, "I would teach patriotism to little Ad-lie."

This was the technique of Mussolini and Hitler. All you have to do to demolish your opponent is to shout treason; you don't have to discuss issues. Yet Hoover could publicly bestow his blessing on Joe McCarthy.

This occurred while the two men were staying at the same seaside hotel in La Jolla, California, Hoover's favorite vacation spa. In an interview with the *San Diego Evening Tribune,* Hoover lavished praise on the modestly bowed McCarthy head. He said:

> "McCarthy is a former Marine. He was an amateur boxer. He's Irish. Combine those, and you're going to have a vigorous individual, who is not going to be pushed around.
>
> "I am not passing on the technique of McCarthy's committee or other Senate committees. That's the Senators' responsibility. But the investigative committees do a valuable job. They have subpoena rights [so, of course, do grand juries] without which some vital investigations could not be accomplished. . . .
>
> "I never knew Senator McCarthy until he came to the Senate. I've come to know him well, officially and personally. I view him as a friend and believe he so views me."

The closeness of the tie between the two men was demonstrated by deed as well as by word. When McCarthy's chief investigator, J. B. Matthews, injected an anti-Protestant theme into the witch-hunt by charging that the clergy were tinged with treason—a charge not too unlike the one Hoover himself had made in the frenzy of 1940—the resulting outcry was such that it became politically inexpedient for even McCarthy to retain Matthews. So McCarthy fired him, then let it be known that he was conferring with Hoover on the selection of a successor. When the choice was made, it turned out to be one of Hoover's top aides.

The pattern makes it clear that, behind the scenes, loftily above the battle and unsmudged by the battle smoke, Hoover has been the heart and soul of the witch-hunt era. His persistent overestimation of the threat of domestic Communism has been a major factor in creating a national mood of hysteria and unreason. His predilection for the use of such imprecise terms as "fellow traveler" and "pseudo liberal" has fostered the technique, so beloved by the right, of spattering with the treason label all liberal ideas and liberal opponents.

In such an atmosphere, only he is safe who keeps his mouth shut or, if he opens it, opens it but to agree. An age of conformity has resulted—an age in which the voice of debate is muted and stilled. Issues like Quemoy and Matsu, or the admission of Red China to the United Nations, cannot be intelligently discussed in the American forum, for even to raise them is to make one suspect as a "dupe" or a "comsymp" who is disloyal to the Republic.

Yet free discussion is essential in a democracy. The public's ability to make a right choice rather than a wrong choice depends upon it. The nation's ability to test the new, the unexplored—to expand the horizons of mankind—depends upon it. Dictartors may make the railroads run more efficiently, but democracy nourishes the freedom of the mind, the interplay of ideas that underlie the great advances. Repress that freedom, and you dilute the nation's most precious heritage. It is precisely here, in the final analysis, that the influence of the FBI has been most baneful.

The almost slavish adulation that has been lavished upon the Bureau and its all-powerful director has acted as an inhibiting force. No man wishes to court the scowl of the FBI. No man dares to suggest that it would be healthful for the country if the FBI should be curbed a bit, restricted from investigating the thoughts and associations of men, and confined to its proper task of fighting crime. The fears of the Sixtieth Congress—fears that we might create a federal "secret police" force like the French ministry of police under Fouché —seem to have been justified.

■ Notes ■

[1] See Associated Press article carried in many newspapers, Oct. 28, 1958.
[2] See the *New York Journal-American*, Nov. 19, 1958.
[3] See Associated Press article, *New York World-Telegram*, Nov. 19, 1958.
[4] See *Counterattack*, Oct. 31, 1958.
[5] See Dorothy Schiff, "My Secret Life with J. Edgar Hoover," in the *New York Post*, Oct. 5, 1959.
[6] *New York Post*, Oct. 6, 1959.
[7] *Ibid.*, Oct. 20, 1959.
[8] *Loc. cit.*

Index